The Gays of Our Lives

The unvarnished memoirs of an aging fruit

Denial Leonardo Murphy

Table of Contents

Yeh, it's sad, believe me Missy,
when you're born to be a sissy
without the vim and verve.

But I could show my pro-wess,
be a lion, and not a mou-ess
if I only had the nerve.

I'm afraid there's no denyin'
I'm just a dandelion,
a fate I don't deserve.

Lyrics of the Cowardly Lion's song, "If I Only Had The Nerve," from
The Wizard of Oz,
written by Harold Arlen & Yip Harburg

Disclaimer

I was a resident of Flint, Michigan, while writing this book, and drank its water. Therefore I was under the influence of Flint River water, and all that follows should be read with that understanding.

And by the way, if you are Christian, Republican, or at all conservative, you should probably put this book down right now, because it will most likely offend you. You have been forewarned.

Dedication

This book is dedicated to Chiquita, whose tumultuous life inspired me to write. God bless him, and all my other fruity friends.

Acknowledgement

I would like to acknowledge and thank my dear friends Linda Molto, David Warda, Bette Chapel, and Tommy Taylor, for their support and guidance; Jorgen Vonsegebaden for his technical assistance, and Mike Turner for editing.

Preface: Writing Wrongs

The word GAY is defined as:
1. a. homosexual
   b. of or for homosexuals: a gay club
2. a. carefree and merry: a gay temperament
   b. brightly colored; brilliant, showy: a gay hat
   c. given to pleasure, esp. in social entertainment:
      a gay life; having or showing a merry lively mood

Please allow me to quote the author Mark Twain: "This book is not a revenge record. When I build a fire under a person in it, I do not do it merely because of the enjoyment I get out of seeing him fry, but because he is worth the trouble. It is then a compliment, a distinction: let him give thanks and keep quiet. I do not fry the small, the commonplace, the unworthy."

And I agree with Samuel Clemens. Who wants to read about boring people—wouldn't you much rather read about characters who are showy, colorful, and gay? He also had the good sense to wait one hundred years before publishing the dirt he'd written about his contemporaries so they wouldn't sue the shit out of him. Well, I am not waiting one hundred years to share my queer stories. I'm blabbing now, because my white-haired mother had a little quotation, too: "Don't say anything about a person *unless it's good*...and *boy* is this *good!*"

I have some stories to share that I believe are both *good*, and *gay*. So prepare yourself, because you are about to be given a glimpse inside the "Gay World." A few of these fractured fairy tales have been gathered during my years of living a gay old life, and are loosely based upon my experiences; while others chronicle the gay escapades of some special sissy friends I've known throughout the years.

Hopefully they will also find these fabulous fables humorous and harmless and be flattered by my immortalizing them through my colorful storytelling; either that, or they'll be mortified that I've blabbed all their business and want to sue the shit out of me.

So...I suppose... this would probably be a really good time to state that any connection found between the *completely fictitious characters* portrayed in these harmless confections and any real person is completely coincidental, not intentional, and I swear I made all this shit up.

Okay, truthfully, you can't make this kind of stuff up; you just have to live long enough, listen well, and take *good* notes. But I would also like to remind you that these stories were not meant to be a recorded history because the truth has nothing to do with telling a good story. So let's just say these annals are at least somewhat based in truth, and perhaps a bit of "yeast" may have been added in a place or two for dramatic effect. And not one of the characters names have been changed, because no one included within...is *innocent*...of *anything*.

Hopefully, while reading you will also find these odd-fellow characters as touching and endearing as I have, and learn that being gay is not always fun, games, and gaiety.

And lastly, I will ask you to remember what my fruity friend Phil from Florida says: "You can say anything you want about somebody—*no matter how bad it is*—but you've got-ta say, 'Bless your heart' afterward."

So, "Bless each and every one of your twisted hearts," 'cause here it comes.

Yabba dabba do, let's have a *gay* old time.

Chiquita

long line of Spanish-speaking women preceded Chiquita in the role of domestic slave, with most of the little brown-skinned women coming from countries such as Chile, Mexico, Guatemala, and other places south of the border. You see, Nikki, the homeowner, never bothered to learn any of their names because that would be *much* too personal. They were, after all, just the help, and he chose to refer to each of them as Chiquita.

Just how many maids came before *this* Chiquita was forgotten. Was he currently on number eight, or ten? He lost interest in knowing how many were employed, or any of their names, and went through domestics like a box of Kleenex, just use 'em and lose 'em. "Don't give me any shit, Chiquita, just get the job done." That was his directive.

I happen to know about this long line of Latina laborers because I worked in the household, too, retained as the *interior* painter. And yes, there was also a crew of colorful men who painted the *exterior* as well, applying the eight delicious colors that adorned the "Overly Painted Lady." When Nikki asked me to choose the colors for his historic home, I selected sumptuous shades such as fresh-churned butter (light yellow), spicy Dijon (mustard yellow), periwinkle and French bleu, too, and lipstick red—or as the homeowner liked to refer to it—cocksucker red.

While working there I would often see the curt notes he'd left on his counter for the countless maids. "Chiquita, make sure that you clean-up the stinking mess that's stuck in the kitty-litter machine, rendering it useless." *Why*, I found that most peculiar, because on several occasions I'd observed him telling houseguests, "You know, that brand-new automatic self-cleaning kitty-litter machine is simply a magical marvel, I tell you. I will never have to deal with that shitty kitty-litter ever again." But only the Chiquitas truly knew what that meant: more shit would be coming their way. And yet another note said: "Chiquita, something is stinking dead and oozing inside the vegetable crisper. Clean it up!" That toxic green ooze would be a rotten head of broccoli he'd sent to meet its maker many months ago.

Believe you me, it took an awful lot of spit and polish to keep his impressive dog and pony show on the road. There were countless other communiqués left on the cultured carrera counters that detailed other dreadfully disgusting duties for the domestics to perform that he would not do himself. But when his last Spanish-speaking maid was dismissed, or quit, depending on who was telling the story, for breaking a priceless Lalique vas (that's a vase he paid way too much for) and then having the unmitigated gall to blame it on his precious Persian pussy, Consuela went into a shelter for abused women, and he was left to dwell in his own filth.

Word quickly spread through the Latina community: "Don't *ever* work there—you will regret it." *Mucho travajo, poquito denero* ("too much work, too little money"). Indeed, his house was overly stuffed with exquisite and expensive artistic artifacts and priceless pretty pieces he'd purchased during a lifetime of world traveling and pillaging of third world countries. Justifiably, the maids were afraid to touch anything, because they were repeatedly reminded, "Careful there, Chiquita! That vas you are now cleaning is worth more than that rusted-out old Pinto you drive," and in reality it *was* the equivalent of a year's wages, since he paid them a hefty eight dollars an hour in undocumented coldhearted cash.

You see, it was only a year ago that Nick had moved from his small one-bedroom ghetto apartment into this grand new place, and several months had passed before he finally attempted the decoration, which was most unusual, because he was gay and that was always the first thing *they* do. But for some peculiar reason he couldn't decide on a theme this time, and as my hairdresser friend Lee says, "You *always* need a theme to decorate, Den. *Jeez*, even *you* should know that."

Feeling the need for a theme, and divine inspiration; he decided to revisit Europe, the origin of classical opulence, and absorb some culture. While there he would scout for hot new decorating ideas, do some serious pillaging, and pick up a few artsy tchotchkes. What the hell, he'd make it one of his "I need to get the hell out of stinking Flint, do some serious shopping, and see some fabulous Broadway shows," only this time in London's West End. He had those entertaining urges several times a year.

"London is so very civilized, don't cha think?" he chirped.

He rather reluctantly booked a room at the Ritz because it wasn't his usual haunt, or up to his exacting standards, but it was the only thing available for this hastily arranged weekend jaunt. And it was there, while in the midst of a scanty continental breakfast, that he happened to gaze up to view the lovely and intricately painted ceiling. Well, let me tell you, he was spiritually moved, emotionally inspired, and had his light bulb moment. He'd found his inspiration.

"Oh my *Gawd!*" he exclaimed, dropping his fork and jaw at the exact same time. "That is *exactly* what I've been looking for!" he said, talking with a mouthful of crumpets and jam. What he wanted was to have the ceiling from the London Ritziest dining room replicated on the ceiling of his Flint, Michigan, ghetto apartment. Yes, that would suit his new position in life, tuna with good taste.

You see, Nick had moved from a puny apartment into his much larger—and yet rather modest —Greek revival rental less than a year ago, but he was still wrestling with the décor. His wish was to transform it into the petite palace he envisioned; chic, elegant, artistic, dramatic, and substantial—quite like him. He would impose his mighty will upon the tiny house and turn it into a McMansion, a residence that would be an outward reflection of the man within.

Now, the gene for decorating is prevalently displayed within most gay males, and God knows he had it in spades; believe you me. But something was amiss this time, and for the first time he was having trouble bringing his decorative vision into focus. Oh, he'd made several halfhearted attempts already, but nothing seemed grand enough, rich enough, substantial, or just plain right. So, for the first time in his life he decided to consult a professional, a decorator. After all, almost every one of his rich-bitch clients had a deck-o-ray-tor to assist them—that, and the bucket of money to pay for them.

Joany, a dear *old* friend, informed Nick of a world-class painter she knew, and just raved about the magic he could accomplish with plain old paint. According to her, I was "nothing short of a genius, a miracle worker with a paintbrush, and no one else could possibly do. He worked on the Library of Congress, he did, the state Capitol rotunda, he did, and for lots of rich and famous people, he had, and movie stars such as George Hamilton, Ingrid Bergman, and Imelda Marcos. Worked all over the world, he had. Famous he was. Simply performed miracles on my little country place, you know, transformed my brand-new condo into a hundred-year-old shack, he did. You simply *have* to have *him* translate your apartment, because he's brilliant, and no one else could possibly do."

"Well, if he's that God-damn good what the hell is he doing in Flint?"

"He's a native," Joan said, most assuredly. "From the Buick Tribe."

Being the dear friend she was, Joany took it upon herself to make the introductions.

"Dear sweet Denny," she purred on the phone. "This is your dearest friend, Joany."

"Who is this?" I asked, teasing her a teensy bit.

"*Joan!* Joan Meddler, you *have* to remember me. How could you possibly forget me?"

"You're so right, no matter how hard I try to forget you, you just won't let me."

"I'm so glad you agree. Well, now, the reason I am calling you is this: you see, I have this aging and decorating-challenged friend with just bucket loads of money, and he desperately needs your help. He's simply clueless, and tasteless, you understand? So would you please consider helping the poor, old, artistically challenged guy out? And if not for him, would you do it for me, your dear friend?"

"Who is this?" I asked again.

So Auntie Joany made the introductions, but we quickly discovered that they were unnecessary because we recognized each other from living in the same neighborhood many years ago. I definitely remembered; you couldn't forget him—he made sure it. He definitely stood out in a crowd.

To the outside world, Nick Clark was flashy, larger than life, theatrical, and self-aggrandizing. But this outward persona was a glossy self-defense mechanism, because when you really got to know him you discovered that he had a marshmallow core, nonetheless, there were several significant layers of padding wrapped around that mushy middle. And in spite of his many extravagances and eccentricities, he was really quite kind and generous.

Now, Nick was gay—there was simply no hiding it. He didn't even try. So it came as no big surprise when I saw him in the Pink Poodle, Flint's one and only gay bar. That perverted place held everything from soup to nuts: blacks, whites, Latinos, Asians, women and men, old and young, drag queens, and a few who were yet undecided; and they all swam in the same polluted cesspool. Before the invention of the Internet this was where we all met, and it was an amazing time.

In his day Nick was a fierce thing who stood five foot ten with a twenty-eight-inch waist. He was also absolute hell on the dance floor. After popping one of his "Black Beauties," those divine diet pills his doctor prescribed, he could stay up all day doing hairdos and up all night doing shouldn't-dos.

Discoed out from head to toe, he always wore the finest of polyester ensembles: hip-hugger bell-bottomed slacks paired with a matching bolero jacket, a coordinating silky polyester print shirt adorned with a hubcap-size medallion hanging from a chunky gold chain, and platform shoes custom dyed to match each ensemble. But his crowing glory was his perfectly blown-back Farrah Fawcett hair. Tragically, his beautiful blond hair was a short-lived glory, because by his early twenties it was aleady thinning so quickly that you could read the newspaper through it. And what a shame it was, because he was so gifted at doing hair, but prematurely balding—most prematurely.

During the '70s he lived in a rambling two-story barn of a house with moss green asbestos-shingled that sat on Thompson Street, kitty-corner from John's Mini Mart, the local stop-and-rob. His little brother, Kenny, lived with him too, and he was what you'd call developmentally challenged today. The Clark brothers shared their big old apartment with a long-haired, big-bellied, Buddha-like, bearded beatnik buddy named Ronnie, or Aunt Rita as we all knew and loved him. Cider, an elegant blonde Afghan bitch, was their family pet, and together they'd all go for long leisurely strolls, while smoking those skinny silly "millimeter longer" Virginia Slim cigarettes.

Nick was the only one in the house who worked, and Slims were what he bought, so that's what they all smoked, by the carton. Hot Cider's lustrous coat was Nick's responsibility because he was a stylist, and he kept her coat clean, conditioned, and tangle-free. That hot dog was hot shit and she knew it as she pranced around the shady neighborhood, lapping up all the heavy petting she could.

Even a blind man could see the four of them out walking, because Aunt Ronnie wore a noisy jingle bell necklace around his neck that rode on his bulbous belly and jingled as he jiggled, and reeked of patchouli. Sporting a long and wispy Heidi's grandfathers' beard with a daisy shoved in it, his well-rounded face always beamed with a Buddha-like smile because he was constantly stoned.

Aunt Ronnie had a peculiar hobby of collecting pretty shiny things, particularly rhinestones, which he proudly displayed under a glass-topped coffee table in the living room for all to admire, next to the flowery cloisonné box containing his finger and toenail trimmings. Often he'd have an outlandish broach or a gaudy pin on the bib of his faded denim overalls, and if it was a particularly festive day, he might even feel like wearing one of his shiny tiaras as well. Sometimes he wore a mammoth ring in the shape of a grand piano, or the enormous ring of Rootin' Tootin' that looked like a pyramid. Some days he had a different ring adorning every finger, because in his eyes each one was lovely and he couldn't make up his mind which was the prettiest.

Always smiling, he had an amiable Friar Tuck quality, making him easily approachable. Being so big, the only things that fit his huge frame were dashikis and denim overalls, so that's all he wore. Birkenstock sandals adorned his big Flint-stoner feet, and his exposed chubby toes had the nails painted cocksucker red. To keep his fat flat feet dry during the winter, he placed them inside plastic Wonder Bread bags, and then in the sandals. Lovely.

Often his best friend, Teddy, an antique Steiff teddy bear, would accompany him on his walks, riding in the chest pocket of his faded overalls. Quite like Aunt Ronnie, Teddy liked to smoke reefer, eat chocolate, and go on long leisurely investigative strolls; he was a very gregarious bear.

During the sixties and early seventies, hairy hippies abounded in this colorful low-rent neighborhood, commonly referred to as the East Village, which was conveniently located around the corner from the University of Michigan-Flint's campus. Many students resided there while attending college, including myself.

◦ ◦

So let's fast-forward some twenty years to the 1990s, when once again I find myself in the bohemian East Village, at the home of Nick Clark. Today he's much older, much larger, and much blonder. What was left of his beautiful blond bouffant pretty much up and vanished many years ago, and was replaced by hairpieces that grew larger, and blonder, over the years—just as he did. Nick had been a hugely successful hair designer for decades, and it showed. He'd done very well for himself.

A few years back Nick's sweet baby brother, Kenny, went to live with their mother, Lois, when she returned to Flint after losing her third husband in Florida; she claimed he went out for cigarettes and just never came back. Then Auntie Ronnie took a vacation to San Francisco, noticed that his mood ring had turned the loveliest shade of pink, discovered the quirky queer-embracing city suited his many idiosyncrasies, and moved there. Within a year he'd become a guru, the Bhagwan Ronnie Rita Gonga. That sexy bitch Cider ran off with a big black Doberman pinscher and was never seen again. And for the first time in his life Nick was completely alone.

So Nick used this solitary time to cocoon and reassess himself, figure out who he was, and decide what he wanted from the next stage of life. Ultimately he chose to reinvent himself and super-size his entire life. His improvement began by moving into the larger apartment. Then he traded in his domestic automobile, a forest green Lincoln Continental land-barge with a buckskin landau roof, and upgraded to something more upwardly mobile, sleek, sophisticated, and European: a brand-new Jaguar in complete black. And lastly, he changed from plain old Nick to *Nikki*, because it sounded much more artsy, European, and exotic. Don't cha think?

"Henceforth and forever more, you are *all* to address me as Nikki. *Got it*?"

"Got it."

To our circle I jokingly referred to Nick's—sorry, Nikki's—new digs as the "Château Ghetto" because it sat in the middle of the East Village, which was now a run-down, low-rent neighborhood, with the accent on *hood*. Why, right next door to his place sat a derelict abandoned house with all the windows broken out, but Nikki paid no attention to that, and went about making his *place* into a *palace* suitable for a queen—and ooh-la-la grand.

Before occupying the new place he'd only been concerned with overdecorating an interior, because he'd never owned a home with a yard, but now he had an inside *and* an outside to decorate, too. Goody, goody, goody, more shopping! Well…his first attempts at yard decorating, or as some people call it, gardening, were like his first attempts at interior decorating: to put it bluntly, laughable.

His previous place had a pathetic puny patch of parched and trash-strewn dirt, right next to the back door, in total shade, and that's where he started his garden. Visiting the most exclusive gardening shops in town, he purchased the most magnificent specimens available, in spectacularly full bloom, and took them home. Digging a hole with a tablespoon just large enough to hold the pot, he'd stuff it in the hole—plant, pot, and all. And when the plant died, usually from lack of watering, he just went out and charged another to replace it; out with the old, in with the new. But then he placed planters on the front porch, where they accidentally received sun and occasionally rainwater and he started to see results.

This only encouraged him.

He discovered there really *was* a knack to this gardening thing, a science if you will, and he decided to read up on the subject. Knowing that many of his rich old ladies were expert gardeners, he would often chat them up on the topic while working his magic, and making them younger, blonder, and beauty-fuller. Oh, he'd listened to all their aged advice, but decided to solicit his advice from the attractive young man living across the street instead. He'd much rather ask him than some dried-up old biddy, because he admired the way he made his yard look proper and casual at the same time, as if it was a proper New England farmhouse nestled into the city. And it also didn't hurt that he was tall, tanned, handsome, and of the masculine persuasion.

Spying the lanky neighbor dragging his hefty hose around the front yard one summer's eve, Nikki decided to just take a stroll over and introduce himself. "Yoo-hoo, yoooo-hooooooo. Howdy, neighbor!" he bellowed, while waving his flapping fleshy arms about and casually sauntering across the street as if he owned it.

"Hello there, I'm your nay-bore from across the street, over there," Nikki said, pointing toward his apartment. "The name is Nikki," he purred. "And by the way, your yard is...well, three words, just fab-you-luscious. I must say, you certainly have a flair for gardening."

"Well, hello Nick, and thank you for saying so," the suntanned young man said, blushing while suppressing a chuckle. "You know, I do try, ha-ha, ha-ha. The name is Jim," he replied, laughing easily and accepting the lackluster handshake.

"It's Nikki. Well, it certainly shows, because your yard is lovely—just lovely. As you may have noticed, I moved in across the street last winter, and I've been wanting to do a little something to my yard, too; but as you can see, I haven't gotten around to it yet."

"Well, thank God you're gettin' 'round to it, because that place has looked like shit for years. Ha-ha, ha-ha, ha."

Nikki suspected he was slightly under the influence, just a wee bit. But what the hell, there's nothing wrong with feeling good on a summer's eve, now, is there?

"Have you lived here long?"

"Guess you could say that. Goin' on twenty years now."

"Shut the front door! Really? You don't look old enough to have lived anywhere that long. Was this your parents' house?"

"No, Nick! I'm thirty-eight years old, ha-ha, ha-ha. And this here is my house, yes sir, mine."

"It's Nikki. You look just like a kid. You're so slim, tanned, and athletic—just look at you! And you did all this yourself you say? So tell me, what's your little secret, hon?"

"Well, Nick, the secret is in the preparation. You need to have the soil nice and loose, and rich."

"Ooooohhhh, I like that in people too—nice, and rich, and loose."

"As I was sayin', you'll need lots of organic matter, sand, bonemeal, iron pellets, twiple twelve fertilizer...it requires a whittle bit of work but it wheely pays off in the end." Jim had slurred his speech again; perhaps he had a couple of cocktails this evening.

"Well, jeez, I didn't realize all that was involved with raising a few petunias, ha-ha, ha," Nikki said, while laughing too much at his remark.

"Oh yes, oh yes, years of practice, years. Ha-ha, ha-ha." Jim echoed in reply.

"Well," Nikki said, pursing his lips and purring, "If you wouldn't mind, I'd like to hire you to prepare my bed for planting." There was something a wee bit off-putting in the way he exhaled those words. It was definitely wordplay meant to be sexually suggestive and pro-vocative, as he was outright flirting. He'd noted what good shape the neighbor was in, young, slim, athletic, toned and tanned, blond with a nice smile, because Nikki appreciated the male form in all its flavors, and he had no shame about it.

Jim contemplated running back into his house and locking the door, but he also realized taxes were due shortly, thought about it, re-lented, and consented to help landscape the neighbor's yard. But what poor Jim didn't realize was that Nikki had visited Versailles just the summer before, and he had no idea what he was in for. Bless his hill-billy heart.

Now, Nikki was no fool. He was smart, ambitious, and wouldn't have gotten this far in life without being clever. So he began to read books about gardening and before long started to understand the basic principles: genus, phylum, species, perennials and annuals, shrubs, bulbs and seeds, compost and soil amendments, sun-loving variet-ies, shade-loving trees, and taxonomies. Suddenly he was throwing around terms such as *trowel*, *dibble*, and *mulch*, and plunging headlong into the dirt.

When Jim was conscripted, Nikki stepped aside. Jim, wielding the mighty chain saw, removed the encroaching trashy trees and invad-ing underbrush that sprang up around the neglected house during the years it was a rental for commoners. Once the tangle of under-brush and invading trees were cleared away, much-needed sunlight came streaming into the yard, revealing a home with lovely bones and a simple symmetry. They agreed that the gardens should be laid out to follow those pleasing lines.

Nikki's proud little Greek revival was comfortably nestled into a shady grove of mature sugar maples, resting upon a grassy knoll, and elevated above the others on the block. Three rustic fieldstone steps rose from the street and connected with a sidewalk leading to a gracious portico-covered porch. A classically white wooden pergola, supported by a pair of squat wooden columns, dominated the entire front side of the residence, practically covering it. It just made sense that two flowerbeds should be located in front of the portico and veranda, on either side of the walk.

To create those new flower-beds, Jim began jumping on the spade and overturning the hard trampled, deceased and depleted dirt, and removing the copious glass, trash, car parts, and debris. Nikki followed him. Plopping his plump rump down by the dewy edge of the beds, he wiggled it around and got comfortable, and grabbed a clump of weedy sod and began beating it on the sidewalk to release the anemic soil from the tangled roots. He was pounding, pounding; pounding, and dirt and debris were flying. His perfectly manicured nails were caked with mud and completely ruined. His Martha Stewart unbleached linen gardening ensemble was stippled with soil, his bigwig dotted with dirt and debris, and bits of leaves were clinging to his cherubic cheeks.

Happier than a pig in shit, he was.

This simple act of salvaging soil from sod seemed somehow satisfying. The smell of freshly tilled earth triggered fond memories from his childhood of gardening with his grandmother so many, many, many, many, many years ago. This gardening thing pleased him.

On the south side of the house sat another narrow strip of debris-riddled gravel that was driven over for decades, making a deeply rutted two-track driveway. Once used for overflow parking, it was now completely root-bound, shaded by big old maple trees, and useless for gardening.

"This is where I shall locate my woodland shade garden," Nikki proclaimed, completely ignoring those obvious facts. Apparently he'd read up on shade gardens as well. "The greatest room and dining niche shall gaze out upon the woodland shade garden," he proclaimed, as if he'd be gazing at a pastoral country estate, instead of a crumbling ghetto shithole.

The once-proud house did have good bones and spacious rooms, with plastered walls, twelve-foot-high ceilings, massive cast plaster crown moldings, and hard-maple floors. For years it was a two-unit rental, so he just left it that way and chose to occupy the larger space—on the sunny south side. Above the backyard's potting shed was an enclosed sun porch that Nick annexed as his bedroom, and both apartments shared the nasty Michigan basement.

Even though it was only an apartment, Nikki started making improvements to the ratty rental as if he owned it, simply because he wanted it to be "nice." Those updates included completely renovating both baths with all new fixtures, ceramic tile, and *lots* of mirrors; he *loved* his mirrors. The kitchen was also reworked with marble countertops, stainless steel appliances, garbage disposal, trash compactor, and a dishwasher. And then the rest of the place was renovated to reflect his new position in life: rich.

"Who can live without double-stack ovens? Certainly not me!"

When it was time to have his new apartment painted I was one of the people interviewed. During our initial consultation he described his "decorative vision" for the home's transformation. After listening to his lengthy decorative dissertation, I showed him the portfolio of photographs and articles that chronicled the many impressive homes, churches, museums, and public places I'd work on around the country during my years as a decorative painter.

"Perhaps," he said, "with a great deal of supervision, you might just be able to fulfill my grand design. But first I will have to see if you're up to my exacting standards."

Putting on a pair of white cotton gloves he took out a hefty coffe-table book and carefully opened it. "This precious book was a special gift given to me by the concierge of the London Ritz Hotel, because he loves me. It contains a photograph of the lovely ceiling I wish to have recreated."

That grandiose gilded-era ornately painted ceiling he showed me was big as a football field, complicated as hell; and that colossal classical ceiling is was what he wanted painted—in exact replica—in his tiny Flint, Michigan, ghetto apartment.

"Yes, I can do that," I said. I had taxes due, too.

"Agreed."

The project was estimated to take two weeks to complete and cost in the neighborhood of $2,000 for labor, plus the cost of scaffold rental, paint, gold leaf, and other materials. Pffftt, mere chicken feed to him, just a couple weeks' of tip money.

Our first "artistic difference" arose when I attempted to explain proportion, scale, and content. My suggestion that we take the "essence" of the Ritzy ceiling went over like a fart in a popcorn factory. No acknowledgment. "This painting will have to look correct in this room. That Ritzy ceiling has to be simplified considerably; otherwise it will look way too diminutive, like living in a Barbie Playhouse." This displeased him immensely because he wanted everything, not just part of it—all of it! And now.

"Don't give me any shit, just make this happen!"

In an attempt to explain the problem more fully, I created a scale-model sketch for his approval, and it was only after several heated discussions that we finally reached a compromise; when I agreed to do every thing he wanted. The greatest-rooms ceiling was twelve feet tall, and with three sets of eight-foot-tall, double-hung windows it a grand and light-filled room. And just to increase the rooms' bling factor he had the big bay window clad in mirrors, making it kaleidoscopic and even more sparkling.

With the room measuring twenty-five feet long by fifteen wide, it took two eight-foot sections of rolling scaffold to deck it out for painting. Most of the first day was spent getting that set up, tools laid out, and the paint colors selected and purchased.

Over the next two days Nikki scrutinized my every move and watched me closely while I measured and sketched the elaborate architectural illusion, and interrupted continuously. Thankfully, for the next two days he went to work, so I didn't have him constantly pestering me. Instead he'd leave me these little pink post-it notes that I would arrive to find stuck to the scaffold. Usually the love-notes explained what he *didn't* love, and his suspicion that he wasn't getting enough of whatever I was doing at that particular moment. His motto was, "'Anything worth doing is worth overdoing.' So overdo it a little more, would ya? Because I'm paying a whole lotta money for this good-taste bullshit."

Mondays and Thursdays were particularly grueling for me, because those were his days off from Salon Riché-Chienné. On those difficult days I'd arrive to find him already lounging in his old, snagged-up, once-white, thigh-high terry cloth bathrobe that barely concealed his ample girlish girth. Noisily slurping coffee, while comfortably plopped into a pile of overstuffed pillows in the corner of the parlor, he was reading the newspaper and watching the morning show on the largest television I'd ever seen. That monstrous TV looked like the monolith from 2001, and it weighed *waaaay* too much to move. I would simply have to work around it.

"Hey, Murf, what are you doing in that big blank spot, over there? You don't have anything up there!" he said, while emphatically pointing repeatedly to the only section of the ceiling not sketched. "I haven't gotten that far yet," I said defensively.

"Well I have a fabulous idea for you; try picturing this, Michelangelo's Sissy Chapel—you know, the famous ceiling at the Pope's place in Italy? Imagine me up there in the heavens, naked, glorious, and floating on a fluffy white cloud. Maybe God is touching my finger, and handing me a hairbrush, or hairdryer. Whaddya think?"

"Sure, Nikki," I said, rubbing my aching neck. "But I'm tired and sore now, because it's taken the better part of two days just to sketch this ceiling, and it required math."

"Well, I'm glad you brought that up, because I've been meaning to ask what's taking you so long to get this painting started. It's been two whole days now and you've hardly done a thing."Stymied, I stared at him not knowing what to say. Was he kidding? That ornate ceiling had extremely complicated architecture, diminishing perspective, and several decorative borders. It would take a great deal of time to complete; it was elaborate as hell.

"Do you actually think this ceiling has drawn itself? Please go to work and leave me alone."

"*Well...that* doesn't sound very professional!"

— ⁓

Trompe l'oeil is a French phrase that means trick of the eye, and this tricky technique is often used to create the illusion of depth in artwork by juxtaposing light and shadow. The Ritzy ceiling he selected was extremely complicated, and it would take lots of exacting measurement to transform that flat horizontal surface into virtual three-dimensional architecture. As in so many things, it was all illusion.

By the third day I could finally begin to paint the ceiling. His castle in the sky was constructed from a warm buff-colored stone that turned shades of ocher, brassy yellow, sienna, rust, and umber in the deepest shadows. A large oval opening was cut from the center of the stone ceiling, revealing a soft blue sky dotted with wispy white clouds. A massive carved stone balustrade surrounded this celestial opening, and it appeared to magically move away from the viewer and recede into that cerulean sky. Magenta and shockingly pink climbing rose's grew up, over, and through this architectural illusion, and weaved through the balustrades. At the ceilings four corners porthole windows were carved from the stone, revealing the brilliant blue sky, and the rambling roses.

Two lion skins were used as cartouche enclosures. Their massive mouths were opened wide, fiercely roaring, and revealing giant man-eating teeth. Heavy paws with sharp threatening claws were extended and crossed, meaning X marks the spot. It was ornate as hell, and a real challenge to paint. Think, what would Liberace do to his boring old ceiling? Now go even further, much further.

— ⁓

Thursday was his day off, again, and he was still quite concerned that he wasn't getting enough *up there*. By the time I'd arrived he was already stoked on truck-driver coffee and ready for another one of his "artistic discussions." In fact, he'd started making demands even before I could close the door.

"Murf, that's not all you're putting *up there*, is it? You're not done *up there*, right? 'Cause there's certainly not enough *up there* for me"

"Well, no. I only started painting yesterday."

"Don't I know," he quipped sarcastically. "And I've been meaning to talk to you about that."

"Why yes, Nikki, I'd love a cup of coffee, and thanks for asking," I said, trying to lighten the mood. But he was not in the mood for levity.

Picking up the Ritzy book, he started pointing at the photograph so emphatically that I was afraid he'd break a French manicured nail. "Look here. There's all kindsa stuff in this picture that you have not put up there. Look, look," he said, his baby blues bulging for added emphasis.

"Nikki, you are looking at a ceiling that is two hundred feet long by a hundred, and I'm working with a ceiling that is twenty-five feet long by fifteen. The painting has to be scaled for *this room*. If I were to include everything you see in the photo, it'd be completely out of scale and look like a cartoon. It has to be proportioned for this room and viewed from this distance. And another thing, I've just started, so give me a chance. This isn't my first rodeo, you know."

"Well, well, well, maybe not, buckaroo, but this displeases me. I thought I was getting more."

"Believe me; you're getting plenty," I said, definitely not in the mood for more "discussion."

After the last shot was fired he retreated to his pillow pile to loudly slurp coffee, angrily scowl at me over his half-empty glasses, and impatiently wait for me to resume painting the masterpiece that he desired, deserved, and damn well expected—and right now, damn it. It really was unnerving having him scrutinizing my every move, every moment, but eventually his fat ass faded away as I concentrated on

the tasks at hand. Except for an occasional grunt or fart as he reposi-
tioned himself on his feathery nest, I hardly knew he was there, until
he shouted.

"Hey, hey, hey! What are you doing?" he demanded, once again
interrupting my concentration.

"I'm using three different brushes with three different colors to
blend a shadow, and it's difficult to do with you continually interrupting. You try holding your arms above your head for ten minutes,
or an hour. Then try doing it for eight hours a day, with the painting
Gestapo watching your every move."

"Oh, don't I feel your pain, honey. Why, my poor arm just aches
somethin' terrible after a hard day-a doin' hair," he said, while lounging on his pillow pile. But he finally shut-up, became transfixed, while
watching me methodically painting the stone balustrade on the shaded
side of the ceiling as if it was a television show. I narrated. "You see,
half of the ceiling has to appear to be in the light, and the other side
in shadow. This is a technique called *trompe l'oeil*, that's a French phrase
meaning 'trick of the eye,' and it's used to create the illusion of depth
by contrasting light and shadow."

"Yada, yada, yada, you just keep painting. But ya know what, Murf?
I am startin' to get hungry from watching you do all this work. How'd
you like to go to Angelo's for lunch? My treat."

"I was hoping for some time alone, but yes; I will accept your greasy
offer."

Angelo's Coney Island was a Flint institution. They have been operating from the same location for over fifty years, busy 24/7, and
running three shifts just like the factory workers they served.

"You know," Nikki proclaimed, "I've discovered that they're really
much better when you have them wrapped in tissue, like when they're
made to-go. It must trap in the steam, or something, because they taste
so much better; so, waitress, please wrap me two Coneys, for here. Oh,
oh, and give me a big order of chili cheese fries... And...oh, oh, oh, a
large double chocolate milk shake topped with extra whipped cream.
And oh, oh, oh, oh, and put a cherry on top."

"Uh-huh. An' ju?" the beehived leathery waitress inquired, bending a bony hip in my direction.

"One Coney to-go — for here, an order of French fries—well done—and a Coke."

"Comin' right up."

When I was young, restaurants were an extravagance we couldn't afford. But once while I was shopping with Mother, she told me we were going to "Pony Island," and I couldn't wait to go there. To a young and impressionable boy with a vivid imagination, that was an incredible vision—an island filled with ponies. When we entered the greasy restaurant, I demanded, "Where are the ponies?"

"What are you talking about?" Mother responded, quite annoyed with me.

"You said we were going to Pony Island, so where are the damn ponies?" Lied to again.

There is a hierarchy of Coney's. Angelo's Coney dog was distinctly different from Detroit's, or even Nathan's Coney Island from the Atlantic shore, because they had a secret sauce. Their sauces secret included finely ground beef heart—which kept it firmer. Hamburger was used too, and some of yesterday's hot dogs were also ground-up and added, along with garlic, salt, pepper and other spices, and tomato paste was used instead of sauce—keeping it drier. The hot dog was always a grilddle-cooked, Flint-made Koegel's wiener, placed inside a steamed doughy white bread bun, topped with finely minced sharp white onions, and finished off with a generous squirting of hot yellow mustard.

The waitresses who tabled there were kinda tough-looking gals with dyed and ratted, lacquered hair helmets, up-do's, French twists, and beehives sprayed stiff enough to hold up to blizzard winds. They were big on costume jewelry, too, and artificially tanned to a nice leathery brown. Running their shapely legs off, while popping gum, they shouted out short-orders and smoked in-between customers. Hell, just about everybody smoked back then—it was a God-given right—and the greasy air hung with a moist cloud of blue smoke.

"Nikki, you're right. Wrapping them does make 'em taste better. Thanks for the tip."

"Anytime, honey. Believe you me, I know about good food," he said, while shoveling the grease-drenched chili cheese fries into his mouth with his bare hands. "Num, num, num."

His lunch was gone in no time flat, with nothing left but the sounds of ten greasy fingers being sucked clean, one after the other. This restaurant was a well-greased machine that operated like all the other factories in town, and we were in and out in only a few minutes. Nikki paid the modest bill, leaving a hefty tip for the wiry waitress, and we drove back to the Château completely satiated, especially him. Num, num, num.

After dropping me at his house, he continued with his weekly errands. First he visited the dry cleaners to drop off the dirty clothes and pick up the clean ones. Next came his spray-painted suntan, because, "Fat always looks better when it's browned." Next was the hoof-and-nail treatment, because, "There is nothing more intimidating than ten perfect nails." Usually he and his brother Kenny had their mani-pedi together, and afterward they'd have another lunch. Lastly, he'd fetch his two fat cats, Caesar and Cleopatra, from Groomingdale's Pampered Pussy Parlor. And while he was off and tending to his weekly chores, I was left in blissful peace and quiet for the rest of the afternoon to paint uninterrupted.

But then... his phone rang, making the answering machine kick on and play its flatly delivered prerecorded message. "Hello, this is Nikki, tell me what I need to know and I'll get back to you—when I feel like it...depending on how important you are." And then it recorded a message: "I just called to let you know what a fabulous person I think you are! You're so kind, smart yet sweet, talented, and so good-looking, too. I just love you and think you're a wonderful person, and thought you should know. *Love ya*, bub-bye." Click.

It was Nikki; he'd called his own phone and recorded that gushy message. But I was confused. Was it intended for me? As I was preparing to leave, I saw his Jag pulling into the driveway, and when he entered I inquired, "Nikki, what was that phone message about?"

Pushing the replay button, he listened to the entire message, and then smiled broadly. "That? Well... sometimes I just need to hear that sort of thing. I just love getting those kinds of messages, and I don't get them nearly enough."

"Good night, Stella."

"Good night, Leonardo."

— ⁓

Day five, and the end of the first week, I arrived to find another love note taped to my scaffold from the lady of the house. "Denial, if you'd look in the London Ritz book, on page fifty-nine, there are several borders in that photograph that you have *not* included *up there*. I am not pleased. Not pleased at all. Can't I get even one teensy-weensy border *up there*, or two? It just looks so barren *up there*. By the way, there are these adorable little green glass bottles of Coke in the fridge, so help yourself. I'm off to make the world a more beautiful place, one ugly old rich bitch at a time. Love, Nikki."

If you saw his handwriting you'd notice it was as flashy as the rest of him, having a Liberace-like flair. I immediately took the damn Ritzy book and shoved it behind the seat of my pickup, hiding it for the duration of the job.

On Monday morning I arrived to find Nikki all ready lounging in his snagged-up old bathrobe, sprawled out on his pillow pile, reading the newspaper, and noisily slurping coffee. "Morning, honey, can I get ya a cuppa coffee? Cream, no sugar, and paper-bag brown, right?"

"Right." He was being so nice I thought I better check the basement for the pod.

"By the way, have you seen my London Ritz book? I can't find it anywhere, strangest thing."

"Yes, paper-bag brown, and thank you."

Oh, joy of joys, his day off, *again*. He returned with one of his expensive, hand-painted, fancy-schmancy, ceramic MacKenzie-Childs coffee mugs. I would prefer a paper cup, because there was less chance of breaking that on a rolling scaffold.

"I swear that book was here just a minute ago. So tell me, Leonardo, what are you painting *up there* today? Are you going to paint me in the heavens?"

"Yes, it's nearly time to paint the sky. One step leads to the next."

"One thing leads to another, huh? I've gotten myself into a lotta trouble that way," Nikki said.

While he was impatiently waiting for the Murfart Show to begin, I did some prep work, mixed a few colors, fetched clean water, and climbed the scaffold. After a few minutes I was painting the cool blue of the sky next to the warm yellow stone, and that contrast of color made them visually separate, and suddenly the architecture popped! Sometimes you can work on a painting for days and not see much movement, and by adding one color it changes everything.

"Oh, honey, that's looking just wonderful," Nikki said, and genuinely meaning it.

"Thank you. So do you think I might know what I'm doing now?"

"Well, let's just put it this way: if you keep at this, you might just get good at it."

We both laughed, and I climbed down to take a look from farther away. After a mini-break, I finished the sky by adding some wispy white clouds, and by the end of the day I was painting the pink rambling roses with their thorny stems, and weaving them throughout the architecture, and into the sky. Nikki appeared to be quite happy, entertained with the show, and pleased with the progress.

"Oh...that looks absolutely lovely, honey."

꘎ ꘎

Nikki was always such the avant-garde, and soon he began to invite people over to view his most recent acquisition. Mostly these were people he wanted to impress, or royally piss off, and Joany, his dearest frienemy—who unselfishly arranged our reintroduction—was the first one to get it. He just loved to piss her off, because they had this crazy little Sybil-rivalry thing going, to see who could outdo whom, and now he was getting something she'd never have: good taste. She was duly impressed with the ceiling's classic decor, and called the local media insisting that they send a reporter to see what was going on. They assured her that they would get back to her. I'm sure she heard that a lot.

By Thursday, his next day off, the entire ceiling was nearly completed, except the porthole windows in the four corners and the rambling climbing roses that grew through them. By the end of the day the ceiling *was* completed, and the only thing left to do on Friday was adhere the gold leaf to the borders and crown molding; which acted as a picture frame finishing the ceiling.

No more snippy notes were left, because he was finally pleased. I was paid, and I was pleased. And I do have to admit that it looked beautiful, if you like that sort of grandiose Liberace stuff.

— ~

I digress so. This chapter is about Jim, the leggy neighbor...and not Nikki. So... this Jim was proving to be most useful outside, tending to the gardens, washing all the windows—inside and out—mowing lawn, snow blowing, removing leaves, and performing overall maintenance; all of which Nikki knew nothing about and had no interest in doing. He'd also changed furnace filters, fixed faulty toilet valves, replaced broken vacuum belts, repaired broken electric sockets, and jumped the battery of an expensive foreign car often; so he was admitted to the staff, and became the Chateau's hired husband.

When Nikki's curiosity overwhelmed him he forced an invitation inside Jim's house, and he was immediately impressed with its spic-and-span spotlessness. He wanted him to clean his house, too. For some peculiar reason, he hadn't been able to find another maid since the last one quit, and was living in his own filth. "How do you keep your house so spotless?" he asked in all seriousness.

Jim explained it this way: "I don't live like a pig, Stella, and I clean up after myself. But in all seriously, my white-haired old German grandmother taught me how to clean. She'd give that dirt the stink-eye and literally chase it right on outta the house. And I won't work for taco money, neither."

So Nikki, rather reluctantly, and on a test basis, mind you, hired him to do the housecleaning. After all, he was already there doing chores—albeit most of them man's stuff and out-of-doors. Why, this Jim guy was a cleaning and organizing genius. Nikki never had such a clean and well-organized home. The place looked clean, smelled clean, and actually sparkled; so Jim was hired, at twice the price—still undocumented and under the table you understand—to become "*Chiquita*, the thirteenth."

Before long he became a fixture in the household, doing absolutely everything Nikki would not do or could not do, and became so indispensable that he wondered how he had ever lived without his assistance. But when Nikki's cushy cash-heavy clients heard him bragging about his fabulous new cleaning lady, his "man-maid" domestica Chiquita, they were mortified.

"Why, Nikki, you can't call him that. It's demeaning, demoralizing; you simply can't do that!"

"Well, why not?" he retorted. "He calls *himself* Chiquita. Denny calls him that all the time; in fact, he was the first one to call him that. 'So you're the new Chiquita,' he says to Jim. So it's okay for him to call him that and not me?"

So it was said, and so it was done, from that day forward Jim would be known as Chiquita; house-husband, handyman, and gardener extraordinaire.

— ~

Now, Jim/Chiquita had the slim golden-boy good looks of a Ralph Lauren model to begin with, but then Nikki insisted on highlighting his already blond hair so it would look "sun kissed, as if the sun was dancing upon his golden hair." And truthfully, it looked so natural that you'd assume he'd spent all summer sunning on the shore. Always well dressed, youthful, and casual appearing, you think he'd just thrown himself together, but in reality he was meticulous about appearance. And just in case you'd missed the brand-name attire, he drove a Lincoln to reinforce his position in life.

And after proving *I* was worthy of painting a room in the palace, I was expected to continue on, becoming the Château Ghetto's artist in residence, like Eldon on *Murphy Brown*. While I was painting Chiquita was often there cleaning, or caring for the estate's grounds, so we crossed paths freequently. After many months of sharing coffee and cigarette breaks we eventually became buddies, trading tips on gardening and cleaning, gossiping, and joking about Nikki and his extravagances and eccentricities.

I found that Chiquita was fueled by strong black coffee and hand-rolled no-filter cigarettes. Caffeine and nicotine kept him running at full steam, but Ritalin kept him focused. To my surprise he was only seven years younger than me, even though he looked much younger; mostly because of the hair. He also shared that he had a younger brother who was also gay and an extremely religious sister who was on her knees a lot, too, praying— and mostly for her two misguided brothers.

But Chiquita's clean-cut and conservative all-American-boy-next-door good looks were a cleverly crafted disguise that masked a checkered childhood. You'd never know he'd had a dirt-poor, white trash upbringing, because his current life was far removed from the realities of his childhood.

Their old farm was way out in the boondocks, in redneck country, Klan land, Terry Nichols's neck of the woods. Both his parents were uneducated seasonal agricultural workers, pickle pickers who were barely scraping the bottom of the barrel, and theirs was a real hard-scrabble existence. The rickety old farmhouse they inhabited was never finished or insulated and drafty as the windswept plains. Their only heat came from a portly potbellied woodstove sat right in the middle of the shabby living room. A hand pump mounted on a tin-lined trough was the only water in the house, and when primed it would haltingly spew out rotten egg–smelling rusty water. Their powder room was a nice and social two-holed outhouse complete with pinup girls, behind the leaning garage, surrounded by towering blossom-laden hollyhocks.

Little Jimmy was an anomaly. His folk's didn't know what to think of this blond-haired, blue-eyed bright light because he wasn't like them. He was smart, started reading early, and even liked books. He always wanted to be clean and willingly looked after his younger brother and sister.

His folks did a lot of drinking, and when they were he was smart enough to stay out of the way. She wasn't much of a role model, but Jimmy dearly loved his mother, and he tolerated his dad because he had to. Secretly he despised him, vowed he'd never drink, or ever be anything like him.

Grandma Johanna, his daddy's mamma, had spent all her life on the farm or down the road from it just a spit, and all ready raised thirteen kids of her own. But when she knew her grandkids were being neglected, she stepped up to help raise them, cared for them best she could and taught them right from wrong, and tough-loved 'em till she died of old age at sixty-two.

They loved staying at Grand-mutter's because she had had food, heat, and a television; TV mesmerized them, became their babysitter, companion, best friend, and role model. But all Grand-mutter ever wanted to do was sit in front of her TV in *peace* and *quiet*, so from a very early age they learned to be invisible and mute. Silently sitting in the flickering blue-gray darkness, they watched their favorite black-and-white shows: *Petticoat Junction*, *Mister Ed*, *The Dick Van Dyke Show*, *Lassie*, *The Beverly Hillbillies*, and their extra favorite, *Green Acres*. Jimmy just loved Lisa Douglas, because quite like him, she certainly didn't belong on a farm. Even though she lived in a broken-down, half-finished farmhouse, quite like his, she had great taste, furs, jewelry, and beautiful clothes—as he wanted. And through all the show's ridiculousness, she always managed to come out on top, as he did.

Jimmy didn't belong on this farm either, but he was born and trapped there. When he was nine, Bobby eight, and Debbie six, Grandma died. That meant they had to move back in with their folks. But they thanked God they'd inherited her television, and everyone was happier when the power was paid so they could watch it. They'd chop wood and burn it to keep warm, use the hand pump for water, and frequent the outhouse without complaint, but they needed power to watch TV. That magic box brought another world into their lives: hope.

By tender age of seven Jimmy was aware of the deep depression that dwelled within his mama. She was always sad, seemed old way before her time, and her pretty face careworn and tired. He knew how hard she worked, first on the farm and later at the Dykhouse pickle plant just down the road. She met big Jim there. Oh, he was a handsome dog alright, but the trouble was, the lights were on but no one was home. Betty fled her folks' and moved in with big Jim *anyway*, because she'd figured that startin' out with nuthin' was far better than what she was leavin' behind.

Betty Redfeather became Betty Fagan right before Little Jimmy was born, exactly nine months from when she'd met Big Jim. She was only nineteen when the last of her three kids were born, and she made sure to have it fixed, so there wouldn't be any more; she was uneducated, not stupid. Painfully sullen and shy, she was a silent shadow retreating in the background, and afraid to voice any opinion. Most likely she'd been abused, most probably was severely depressed, and at most times just existed. But when she was drinking it was an entirely different story, because she changed, lit up, and was much more vivacious.

Dr. Jekyll and Mr. Hyde drank from the same bottle.

Dark-haired, dark-eyed, and half American Indian, she didn't have the ability to resist alcohol's seductive effects, and was enslaved and addicted at an early age. Drinking liberated her and made her feel alive, and when she wasn't drinkin' she was sad—really sad.

The kids knew when she was drinkin' because she'd put on her pretty makeup, sweet-smelling perfume, and colorful costume jewelry. Little Jimmy was glad when his momma was "happy" because she would sing and dance with him on the blue-and-tan-checkered linoleum kitchen floor. "El Paso," by Marty Robbins, was his favorite song, and as the song played his mother would pretend to be the beautiful and wicked Felina, the evil temptress. Singing, dancing, and twirling, her colorful shirt-dress flared way out as her petite feet stomped out the rhythm like a flashy flamenco dancer. Enthusiastically strumming the air guitar, Jimmy accompanied her while pretending to be the lovesick cowboy who forsakes everything to be with his true love. Those were such happy memories.

"Out in the West Texas town of El Paso, I fell in love with a Mexican girl...I, I, I."

But when Big Jim was drinking it was an entirely different story. He was dark, unpredictable, volatile; happy one minute joking around with the kids and wrestling, watching television, and it was all good. But then something would happen, storm clouds would gather, and a black mood would come over him; he'd grow mean and angry. Like a spark igniting gasoline he'd suddenly explode, curse and rant, accuse his faithful wife of committing unspeakable sins, and want to fight. The kids knew this was when you made yourself scarce, hide in the closet and curl up in a ball, close your eyes, shut your ears, and pray for it to end. But they prayed even harder that the door would never be opened.

"Ah hell, that Betty's so damn clumsy. She's always walkin' inta doors," he'd laughingly say, while snorting his demented laugh, "ha-ha-ha, snort, snort, ha-ha-ha."

The next day Betty would be trying to explain away the black eyes and bruises. "Well, ya see, I got up in the middle-a the night needin' to tinkle an' didn't wanna turn on the lights and wake Big Jim. Well...I ran smack inta...the..." It was a real love-hate relationship they had. She loved him, and he hated himself. But they both loved their drinkin'.

The kids learned to like the stuff, too, because whenever her bawling brood was teething, or Betty was simply at her wit's end, she'd put a little of her precious whiskey into the baby's bottles, along with a little sugar, a couple of drops of peppermint extract, and some warm water, and that'd usually shut those screaming babies right up.

Those poor kids were shell-shocked, PTSD-affected, because they never knew when their daddy would go off, or if he'd be lovin' or hatin'. Would they get dragged outta bed at two in the morning, in their footy pajamas, to ride around the backwoods during a blizzard and look at the Christmas lights? Or would it be another fight waking them? They never knew which way the wind would blow, hot or cold, but they were certain if he'd been drinkin' things would heat up. And he was always drinking.

But there were things worse than drinkin'. Once, at the tender age of seven, Little Jim walked in on his dad and Uncle Dick while they were "wrestlin'" on top of the pool table in his uncle's basement. They had been drinkin'. Jimmy wasn't sure what he'd walked in on, his dad called it wrestlin', but he didn't understand why they were doing it practically neck-ed. Oh, they hurried up and got dressed, but he knew it wasn't wrestlin'. Or playing Tarzan either—that's what his mom called it when his dad went running through the house stark naked and screamin' like a wild banshee. Drinking unleashed demons.

Jimmy was just a little boy when he learned about sex. At a very early age he grasped the mechanics. There was abuse in the family—yes, he was a child. That's all you're going to hear about it, but you need to know it happened because it affected the rest of his life.

―   ―

TV was the only *real* entertainment the kids had, and if lucky they'd pick up two channels on the rabbit-ears atop the Zenith, early American, pecan-finish console; that was grandma's pride and joy. Both channels featured *Big Time Wrestling* on Saturday afternoons, with players having names like Bobo Brazil, The Sheik, Skull Murphy, Killer Kowalski, and The Shadow. They'd pound and pummel each other in badly choreographed bouts, and this became their entertainment, circus, and teacher. Wrestling put fun some into their dys-fun-ction, and it quickly became a favored pastime with the numerous cousins and distant neighbors who littered this gnarly patch of backwoods. They came up with menacing names and had regular bouts, where they'd wrestle, thump, pounce and pound on each other. Light-weight Jimmy was "The Destroyer," and he went on to capture the championship and coveted silver pie tin belt.

But after Grandma up and died he was pretty much through with wrestling and other kids stuff, because he'd gained a whole lot more responsibility. Now he had to take care of himself, the house, and both siblings. He got real old, real quick.

"When I was still livin' on the farm, there was a widow, named Geneva, who lived down the road from us, and I really liked her. We'd often have coffee and cigarettes, and visit like grown-up's do. I was 'bout fourteen then, and havin' a bad time of it, and it seemed I had the weight of the world on my young shoulders. So then, outta nowheres she turns to me and says, 'Jimmy, darlin''—she's from Arkansas—'I got somethin' to tell ya, son. If you hain't figured it out yet, you're queer. Oh, it's fine by me, don't bother me none 'tall. But what I want ya to know is this: while yur young and purdy you just get all you can get, 'cause when you get to be my age, what you want you can't get, and what you get you won't want. So you just get all you can while you're young and purdy. Okay?'

"Well, I was stunned at her frankness, but I took her advice. Heck, I'm only thirty-eight and already buried three husbands. Rob and I are just kinda playin' house and our arrangement is more of a business transaction than love affair. Ya know, I honestly loved my first husband, but he died of AIDS, and left me a truck. My second husband was a real good man, too, and he died of AIDS, at forty-two; a real shame. I used his life assurance to pay off the house. And thankfully my third husband just died of a plain old heart attack and didn't leave me with any bills."

We prayed for poor Rob. He was a good man, but not a joiner, preferring to stay inside while keeping company with the remote control, computer, and having the air-conditioning cranked so low that it felt like a meat locker. Chiquita, on the other hand, was an extrovert, outdoorsman, collector and antiques dealer, buyer, seller, and horse trader. And he knew his business.

Jim had read just about everything available on collecting, buying, and selling, and he had a clear idea of the worth of most things. He'd make an incredible contestant on the *Price Is Right*. He was a faithful watcher of *Antiques Road Show*, *America's Longest Yard Sale*, and any other programs dealing with the buying or selling of "stuff." Primarily he was interested in buying and selling *stuff*, because since leaving home at fourteen, he made his living by buying and reselling *stuff*.

His closest friends had a name for *him* and his *stuff*: Mr. Haney. That was a character from the sixties sitcom *Green Acres*, and this shifty corn-fed huckster was a smooth-talking salesman who had a real knack for showing up with exactly what you needed, right when you needed it. He just happened to have one of those in his truck. Jim bought and sold just about everything, at estate sales, thrift stores, yard sales, and at flea markets while selling the stuff he'd bought there earlier. He purchased stuff he knew he could resell for more than he paid for the stuff, and that's how he made his living. And to tell you the truth, he managed to make a pretty good livelihood from reselling the stuff.

Chiquita's home, being quite like the homes of many other queers at that time, was decorated in high Victoriana. His antiquated vision of homeliness was based upon a refined color scheme of dusty rose, burgundy wine, and oyster shell. His was a handsome home complete with massive mahogany cabinets crammed with colossal cut crystal pieces, perfectly polished platters, hand-painted ceramic doodads, lotsa tchotchkes, and collectibles too numerous to mention. The parlor, or as Jim liked to call it, the "courtin' room," held two colossal, claret-colored, curved couches covered in cut chenille sitting face-to-face. Next to them was a pair of hall trees, two umbrella stands, two spittoons, and old baskets galore; he loved symmetry. Big, poufy, dusty-rose water-silk moiré window treatments, with long silky oyster-colored bouillon fringe dressed the double-hung windows, making the house look authentic to the Victorian era; that, or a fucking French whorehouse.

The common rooms had a gilded picture-rail molding running along the upper wall that held his collections of ornately framed De Longpré fruit-and-flower cornucopia lithographs, the elegant Icart art deco prints of willowy women with whippets, and a few fluidly flowing Mucha prints of sweet-faced Gibson Girls. Hanging alongside them were several original oil paintings by Rob's mother, which were quite lovely. His home was a particular vision of Victorian perfection, and yet it felt homey, clean, relaxed, like a place that had been happily lived in for the past hundred years.

Chiquita and Rob's queer little family consisted of an elderly wrinkled shar-pei named Miss Anne, two aging skittish and eternally shedding cats named Fido and Butch, and a pair of extremely horny gray cockatiels named Lusty and Busty, who screeched, squawked, and screwed constantly.

Each year at Christmastime, Chiquita would go whole hog decorating. He loved playing house, and the holidays were his hap-happiest season of all. He'd put up six different trees because, "How can I possibly narrow it down to just one theme when there's all the different eras and schemes for holiday decorating?" Victorian themes and fifties schemes, big trees and small, bottlebrush and flocked; but his favorite tree was made of silver al-you-min-e-um and came with a rotating light that changed the color from red to blue, then to purple, green, yellow, and back to red again. It was too wonderful.

He'd collected thousands of antique ornaments and wanted to see each and every one of them prominently displayed. Making the season extremely gay, he delighted in decking the halls, turning his house into a glittering showcase, and carrying on traditions that his dysfunctional family never had.

Word of Chiquita's domestic expertise was spread via that blabbermouth Nikki, because he'd just go on and on, while holding patrons at sharpened scissor point, and rave about how marvelous this Chiquita guy was; an absolute marvel at cleaning, a organizing whiz, and handy with tools and repairs, he was. And *my*, how good he was in the garden, too, with two green thumbs. He simply sounded too good to be true and those greedy girls wanted in on the action, too. Secretly they loved calling him Chiquita; too— it was so naughty. "And as you well know, hard help is *so* good to find."

One of Nikki's favorite clients, and a longtime friend, too, was raising three big-bruiser sons and desperately needed household help. Why, she was overwhelmed with just the laundry alone. "You have no idea how many clothes three growing teenage boys, who all play sports, can dirty up," she'd complain. "All they do all day is make messes and leave them for me to clean up." Well, Saint Nick's oversize heart went out to poor Katie and her perilous plight, and he suggested she seek professional assistance. When no one was looking, he hooked her up with Chiquita's number, discretely slipping it into her hand, written on the back side of her hairdo receipt.

"Don't you dare give his number to another living soul, *ever*. This is his private line. Destroy it when you're through."

"I will guard it with my life," Katie said, taking her solemn oath and discreetly shoving the secret slip into her slime-green Kate Spade bag while making sure no one was watching. Running straight home, she made the call.

911 Chiquita!

Well, wouldn't you know it, Chiquita and Katie hit it right off— and he had his second job, cleaning a lovely rambling, four-bedroom lakefront home, complete with two golden retrievers and minivan. Most unfortunately they were Republicans, and living in a gated community on a golf course, but he would overlook those shortcomings and help a poor woman in desperate need. His days were really becoming quite busy now, what with working at Nikki's three days and Katie's the other two. Plus he was still selling stuff at flea markets on weekends, because selling shit was his real business.

These mindless little cleaning jobs just brought in a little extra chump change.

Each week Chiquita cleaned and organized, washed mounds of dirty clothes, and fixed the broken vacuum cleaner belt, box fan switch, blinking desk lamp's socket, and the rocking, ass-pinching toilet seat. He took out the mounds of trash that were forever accumulating, shampooed the carpets and the dogs, too, and was there when she really needed assistance. Why...not one of those three big-galoot sons of hers would ever think of loading a dish in the dishwasher, running the vacuum, or doing a load of laundry. And the truth was he was fun, funny, and just plain enjoyable to be around.

Chiquita quickly became a fixture in the household, another one of the boys, and their older gay brother. That lucky dog also came into quite a windfall as the recipient of Katie's over-grown sons' cast -off, classy clothes, and he began to style in a more youthful upper-crust way when wearing labels such as Ralph Lauren, Lacoste, and Aeropostale. When wearing their clothes he even started to look like one of her kids, and deliverymen would often ask him, "Is your mother home?" That would really piss her off, because he was only three years younger than her. And with his new preppy youthful attire and conservative gold wire-rimmed glasses he began to look Republican, too.

Before long Katie's dear friend Lucy wanted in on the action, too, because she simply had no time for housecleaning with the grueling schedule she had to keep. "Busy, busy, busy, busy, busy—you have no idea how the time flies when you have social obligations. There were art classes on Mondays at the Institute in town, and bridge Tuesdays and Thursdays in Birmingham, always at a different home – mind you, and you are expected to come up with something new and clever to take every single time. Then there's my standing appointment with Nikki Wednesdays and Saturdays, and someone has to do the weekly shopping." (Because wealthy people do a lot of consuming.)

Somewhere in her busy week she still had to fit in a round of golf with the girls, an evening of dance club with the hubby, and keep that enormous house clean and running. *Plus*, she had two other complete households to maintain, one "Up North" and another in West Palm. She desperately needed help, and Katie's big heart just went out to the poor exhausted thing, because after all, it was her Christian duty to help those in need.

Chiquita, being the understanding kind, took pity on poor over-loaded Lucy and consented to give her one day a week—another one of Nikki's days. That went over like a fart in church. Everybody smelled the stinker and yet nobody acknowledged letting it go. Nikki secretly stewed. Now, he was willing to help one of his dear friends in need, but not at *his* expense. This *displeased* him *immensely*.

Wouldn't you know it—Chiquita and Aunt Lucy quickly became great friends, too, bonding over a mutual love for fine antiques, Christmas shit, and booze. She would truly look forward to his visits, because to-gether they'd clean closets, organize cupboards, and plant bushels of daf-fodil bulbs in the pastoral woodlands surrounding her stately lakefront estate. And after work was finished they'd lift a glass—for medicinal rea-sons, you understand; because you have to keep your fluids up. Chiquita was the daughter she never had, a faithful companion working alongside her, telling her funny stories and actually listening to her litany of com-plaints. Granted, he was getting paid for doing it, but it was a mutually satisfying tryst, and not so bad in a scrunch-or-be-scrunched world.

Chiquita enjoyed hanging out in these more stylish, lavish, up-scale surroundings. These homes were much nicer than anything Nikki had to offer. These people had real money. *Hell*, they didn't even *have* to work; their money worked and made money *for* them. He had never been privy to the lives of wealthy, comfortable, educated people of means, and never knew anyone who belonged to a country club, had a second or third home, or owned a luxury car or watercraft. Growing up in poverty, he'd only read about such things, or saw them on *The Beverly Hillbillies*. Now he was on the inside, albeit only the help, but he was privy to a world he'd never experienced except on television, and it enamored him. He liked being among them, one of them, and passing.

Lucy's summer shack was a hulking log lodge that sat on the shore of pristine Walloon Lake, the very same lake where Hemingway once lived and wrote. Each spring, Chiquita would accompany her to the woodsy retreat for a couple of days of cleaning, organizing, and intoxicating. They'd reopen the place each summer, clean it well, and put everything out, and in the fall they'd clean again, pack the shit back up and close it. Her husband would never help with these mundane chores because he was too busy tending to their holdings and the kids weren't interested in working. So she and Chiquita cleaned and organized while sharing vitamin waters: cocktails—vodka and tonic, and the good stuff, too. While nursing on cocktails they gabbed away the hours, shared silly stories, and laughed their fool asses off. He was just plain fun to be around.

But Chiquita's greatest thrill came at Christmastime when he helped decorate the spectacular, fifteen-foot-tall live Fraser fir that stood in the grand two-story bay window overlooking Aunt Lucy's frozen lake. Her magnificent bush was drooping from the weight of the heavy, ornate, expensive hand-blown and hand-painted glass ornaments; it was beyond his wildest dreams. He had never seen such a magnificent bush. He knew exactly what those Christopher Radko ornaments cost, so he calculated the cost per ornament, estimated the amount hanging on the tree, multiplied that number in his mind, and the grand total made his hillbilly head hurt. Cha-ching, cha-ching. He definitely knew he was a peon when he finally saw how the 1 percent spent.

But he was never resentful of this discrepancy of currency; it was quite the opposite, ya see. He adored these people, felt welcomed and accepted, and benefited in many ways by his associations with them—and vice versa. Wealthy people were excellent consumers, always sloughing off surplus stuff, so it was in his interest to help them declutter the closets, clean the cupboards, and organize the garage. Then he'd offer to further assist them by hauling their unwanted excesses away, and take the trash/ booty/inventory straight to the flea market and sell it. It was whatcha'd call a win-win situation.

But we all know that closeness can sometimes have its downside. What's the old saying? "Familiarity breeds contempt." Well, contemptuous Chiquita could sometimes tell these teensy little stories about his cleaning clients. Fairy tales.

"Say, Murf, are you gettin' any wind over ta yer place? No, ya say? Well, a big ol' gust just blew through this here kitchen a bit ago and some-a these papers and invoices fell onta the floor, and it's my job to pick them up, ya understand. Well, I sorta glanced at 'em while doin' just that, and you wouldn't believe what she's shellin' out for some-a this here stuff. Just guess what she's paid to have those rocks shoved around in her backyard? Forty-two thousand dollars! My God, forty-two thousand dollars for rocks. My whole house isn't worth that much."

"Chiquita, that little story you're sharing is exactly why I will never have you clean for me."

"Well, I'm just sayin'. There's that, and I damn near got myself a hernia from carryin' all their empty gin bottles to the curb this week."

"Chiquita!"

Chiquita was always a very private person. Oh, he was always more than happy to tell you about Lucy's gin bottle collection, but he was very tight-lipped about his own household dirt. He never shared much about his personal life and claimed he didn't have a social life to speak of or many family associations either. So the idea of company "dropping in" would put him over the edge, and that's what happened. His darling cleaning clients/friends/employers, Katie and Lucy, decided to drop in one night. You see, the naturally bleached-blonde beauties were taking an evening painting class at the Art Institute, just a teensy block away, and they were more than a little bit curious about this Chiquita fella.

"Don't you just love the arts, Kay-tee? They adds so much to our dreary lives!" Aunt Lucy said, while slathering paint straight from the tube onto a canvas using a palette knife. What the hell, they were having fun painting, laughing their asses off, and quite well toasted after consuming a thermos of smuggled cocktails. When class ended they were not in the mood for the frivolity to end, and that's when Aunt Lucy had a magnificent brain fart.

"Let's go see Nikki and Chicky," Aunt Lucy declared. "They're just 'round the corner."

So off they flew in Lucy's brand new Mercedes runabout. Careening around the corner on two wheels, then pulling onto the curb, screeching on the brakes, and throwing it into Park, she slid out the door and went marching across the street. Then she started banging on Nikki's door, and damn hard.

"Open up, damn it! Come on, open up—we know you're in there! Hey, you in there, it's your favorite clients."

They were loud as hell, laughing their asses off and getting the notice of the nosy neighbors. But Nikki was already in bed for the night, with his face uselessly slathered with an anti-aging cream, because he'd have to be up early tomorrow to face another grueling day in the beauty trenches. So he peeked out the window, saw who it was, rolled over and shut his eyes, and said, "Drunken bitches. Fuck off and leave me alone."

Somehow sensing this un-Christian-like rejection, they stopped banging. "Let's go see Chicky. I'll bet cha he's up," Katie said.

"Hey, let's take him some-a these pretty flowers of Nikki's—that'll teach him. Hep me steal some-a these two-lips—aren't they be-you-tea-full? Hurry before he catches us." Leaving a trail of plucked plant parts behind them, they stumbled across the street and resumed their boisterous banging on Chiquita's back door.

"Open up, damn it; it's your favorite clients. And hurry—'cause I gotta tinkle real bad." *Bang, bang, bang* was heard resounding through the big old house as Lucy kicked the door with her elfin foot.

"Keep your shirt on, Lucille, Jesus," Chiquita said, while trying to unhinge three security locks and pry the squeaky swollen door open.

"What the hell took you so long to open this damn door? We needs mo-rice. *Well*...aren't you happy to see us? Are you gonna lettuce sin? *Well?* We just finish tart class, and was outta ice, so we went to Nikki's. He defused to open the door. Bitch. *Any-ways!* We knee mo-rice, our smelted."

"Look, we bought you sum petty flowers. Aren't they be-you-tea-full?" Katie added.

Chiquita, who never had company, quickly let them in because they were creating such a spectacle on his porch that the rubbernecking neighbors were wondering what the hell was happening at the fruitcakes on the corner. Taking the mangled flowers from her tiny clenched fist, he placed them into a cut crystal vase. Then he fetched three of his best cocktail glasses from the vitrine, wiped them clean, and poured cocktails.

"What da hell's goin' on out dare, LeRoy?" the woman across the street asked her boyfriend.

"Uh...I don't know, baby, look like a couple drunk blonde bitches is ova to the peter-eater's. It's all right. He let-um in."

Once inside, Katie and Lucy scanned the house, taking it all in. "Jesus Christ. I am never going to let you bully me around anymore about putting things away. Just look at this place. You've got shit stacked everywhere," Aunt Lucy declared, stamping her tiny foot for added emphasis.

"*Yeah*, that goes for me three. And where-the-hell's that damned ice? My dink swarm," Katie replied, miffed.

"Ya know, Princesses, I hadn't planned on entertaining royalty this evening, or I woulda cleaned up a little. This here stuff you see lyin' around is called merchant-dice, in-vent-ory, because I'm runnin' a business outta here. There's mo-rice is in the freezer—hep your shelf, I'm not the barterer."

"Ohhh, look what he's got in here, Lucy, the good stuff— Gray Goose, my flavorite!"

"Hole-in-out, are ya?" Katie said, eyeing him suspiciously and blinking in slow motion.

"What the hell? Whatever, help yourself to ever-thin' in the house. Clean your shelf a place to sit and pour me a dink, too. 'Member—I'm 'posed ta be cleanin' yer place 'morrow."

"Clean, shmean. I can't be-leaf Nick was so mean, pretendin' he didn't heard us," Katie said.

"Hellll-ooooo...the whole neigh-bor-hood heared you two, sheesh," confirmed Chiquita.

"Chiquita, can ya do your Aunt Lucy a lil flavor? Can you break s-more-a Nikki's MacKenzie dishes? 'Cause Katie and I are makin' s-more them broke pot-terry pieces-es, an' we knee mo'. Can you do that lil thing?"

"Well, no, that snot a good idea. He's already cussin' me out for breakin' all his finery as it is. *No, no, no,* not me!" Chiquita said, defensively.

"Oh, shaddup and pour," Lucy said. "We knee mo-rice."

Well, the party rolled along full-tilt until what was left of the Goose had nearly flown the coop, and with little fuel left in the liquor cabinet, the party was quickly nearing an ugly, untimely end.

"Running out of booze? How could you possibly let that happen?" Lucy asked, most befuddled.

"Unlike some people, Aunt Lucy, I do not have a *machine* in my back room printing up more money each time I need it," Chiquita said.

"Money? Oh *yeah*, that reminds me, I got *money*," she said, with her pretty Doris Day eyes suddenly lighting up and twinkling. "Chiquita, you got a joint?"

"No! Now...you know I don't do that stuff. Denny's the drug-a-dick, not me. I drink, like you."

"*Well*, I'll betcha *someone* in this ghetto does," she said, as she headed for the door. Chiquita wove to the left while trying to intercept her, but it was too late. Lucy dodged to the left, made a quick weave to the right, flew out the door and onto the porch, threw back her bleached-blonde blunt-bobbed Dorothy Hamill do, shaking it from side to side in defiance, and saying, "Don't mess with me, *miss*-er, I'm on a miss-shun." Marching into the street, she started waving a newly minted twenty in the air. Spying the nosy neighbor still sitting on his porch, she yelled to him, "Yoo-hoo, miss-er. Hey, miss-er, 'mere, 'mere. I got money. You got a lil reef-er?"

"Nah, lady, nah. Sorry," he quietly hollered back.

"What the hell is goin' on out dare, LeRoy?" his girlfriend yelled, all pissed.

"It's dem drunk blonde bitches from across da street. She want sum herb, an' she got money."

"Money? Shit. Sell her a blunt. Hell, I'll sell her one a mines. Call her back here."

But it was too late, because she was halfway down the block by then, waving the money in the air, and yelling at the top of her tiny lungs. "Yoo-hoo, yoo-hoo, I got mon-ey. Who's got reef-er?"

Why, it was the strangest thing, just like a science fiction movie where everyone disappeared. Every single soul had vanished from their front porch, and not one person remained. They probably feared it was a police drug sting using Junior League members as decoys, or some drunken sorority hazing ritual from the college; either way, they weren't having any part of it.

"Strange-s-ting," Lucy reported. "Nn-nobody left in the nay-bar-hood. Poof! All dis-peered."

"Hey! Jimmy!" LeRoy shouted, motioning for him to come over. "'Mere, 'mere."

Chiquita crossed the street. Le Roy leaned close saying, "Hay, I got some herb."

"For twin-knee damn doll-ahs," came echoing from inside.

"Hey, Ruby," Jim replied.

"Hey, my ass. You just get that twin-knee an' git yo' black ass back in here."

Transaction completed: one joint for twenty dollars, a windfall for LeRoy and Ruby. They immediately took the newly minted money to the mini-mart for a malt liquor and a bag of salty chips, courtesy of Aunt Lucy. Then they hurried back to the porch, got comfortable, and waited for Act Two.

So much fun was going on across the street that they cranked up the radio, and then turned it up again. Oldies were listening to old-ies, singing along with the radio, and laughter was pouring from all the wide-open windows and doors. As darkness descended streetlights flickered on, making them feel even more emboldened. The next thing you know they're traipsing outside, tripping the light fantastic and teetering atop the porch railing while doing The Pony and The Jerk, just like on *Hullabaloo*. By now the entire nosy neighborhood had crept back onto their porches to see the floorshow at the bum-bandit's on the corner, where two drunken blonde bitches were dancing and singing loudly, badly, way off key, and laughing their fool asses off.

"What you wan', bay-bee I got-tit. What you knee, bay-bee I got-tit. Just a lil-lil-lil little bit."

Chiquita was feeling the groove now, too, singing along with them, and shaking his bony little moneymaker. But their festivities came to a screeching halt when the booze finally ran out. Thank God he had the foresight to call Katie's husband to fetch them, because they were far too gone to drive. By the time Mr. Jones arrived, Lucy was sacked out on the green metal lawn chair on the porch, snoring and drooling, while Katie, sitting next to her, was still singing, loudly, badly, but quite wholeheartedly.

The strangest thing happened that night. They all contracted some exotic flu bug that presented symptoms of nausea, stomach distress, and excessive dizziness that persisted for two days and required complete bed rest. On the third day they rose from the bed, made a pact, and decided to never speak of the incident again. Nikki, however, did not participate in this pact, so he could blab the story to the world. And there you have it.

Katie and Lucy were first clients of Nikki, and then I worked for them, and then Chiquita. It was a fairly small social circle in Flint, and Nikki was the golden orb at the center of the solar system. He serviced the areas affluent people, and made it his business to know who was who. I received many of my business connections through him too, because I also had a valuable service to offer them, being able to make them look rich, tasteful, established, or crusty-old with money.

But this was the 1990s. Things were good, work was easy to find and money was flowing like a just-tapped gusher. Everyone was working overtime.

Around this time Nikki began viewing openings at the Institute of Arts, attending symphony performances at Whiting Audatorium, enduring ballet recitals at MacArthur Hall, and becomming as cultured as buttermilk. Hobnobbing more and more with his wealthy clients, he spent less and less time with us poor gay guys. He knew a select crowd frequented these cultural events, and rightly figured by schmoozing with the area's rich bitches he could make more business connections. Most of his fruitcake friends had no interest in *that* kind of culture anyway or they couldn't afford to attend those events. Nikki did, and by doing so he became a bigwig.

— —

So Nikki continued to futher renovated and feathered his lovely nest and cultivate the ever-expanding gardens surrounding the lovely Chateau' Ghetto. But many, including myself, flat out told him he was just plain stupid to be dumping such huge sums of money into a house and yard that he didn't even own, and Aunt Lucy was the loudest advocate of all.

"You dink, you're just plain stupid to be spending that kind of money on a rental, something you don't even own, you dink! Buy the goddamned house, or I'll buy it and you can fix it up and make money for me." It was good advice. So, after renting for five years he finally approached the landlord and they worked out an agreeable deal to purchase the place.

At age fifty-five he was a first-time homeowner. Now the Château Ghetto was truly his, or it would be in thirty years when it was paid off. And now he could really get serious about fixing up the peaked old place and spend some serious coin.

Cha-ching.

Young Nick

Young Nick grew up on the grimy streets of Flint. His nomadic adolescent parents moved around a lot when he was a child, usually when the rent was due. But their road-roaming life came to an end when they moved into a couple of rooms above a Sinclair gas station on the city's near-east side, downwind of the Buick foundries' smoke stacks, which spewed noxious smoke 24/7, fifty weeks a year, with two weeks off each summer for new model changeover.

Nick was only eight when his dad started operating the run-down two-pump filling station and auto repair shop that sat on the corner of Broadway and Lewis, just past the I-475 freeway viaduct but still within earshot of its constant rumblings. Fifty years ago it was a gritty neighborhood. You should see the place now. It's a goddamn war zone. Growing up in such a constantly threatening environment he quickly learned to be tough. He had to be hard to survive in that miserable concrete jungle.

There were five of those Clark brothers, with just four years between them. Timmy was the oldest, and barely a year old when his brother, Nick, arrived. Bing, bang. Then Ned and Ted the twins came along, less than a year later. Bing, bang, boom-boom. And baby brother, Kenny, arrived the year after. Badda-bing, bang, boom-boom.

Each year they'd celebrate their birthdays together, because they were born within days of each other.

Lois, their mom, had the last of her five boys when she was only twenty-three. By that tender age she was already used up, defeated, broken, shut down, and hardened, because she'd witnessed the worst life had to offer. It was difficult to imagine that the pitiful life she was living above a filthy filling station was better than the one she left, but it was. She'd survived the Great Depression, but she wrestled daily with her own melancholia. Just getting by was an enormous effort for her, and taking care of five boisterous boys was usually more than she could handle.

Lois Askew was born the sixth child of nine, to dirt-poor itinerant farmers during the depths of the depression. When she was a tiny baby her little leg was broken badly and never repaired correctly, and the traumatized limb never grew right. This shortcoming resulted in her left leg being three inches shorter than the right, which made her tiny torso tilt to the left. The mean kids taunted her something terrible, calling her "I-lean."

When the other little girls were wearing pretty patent leather Mary Jane's, Lois had to wear an ugly brown orthopedic shoe with three inches of hard black rubber stacked at the heel. This heavy and unyielding medieval torture device was held in place by two icy-cold metal braces that were strapped to her withered little leg, making it possible for her to walk—if you could call it that. When she walked she dragged the bad leg behind her and then used it as a pivot, step, drag, step, drag, step, drag. It was exhausting just watching her walk.

Over the years she had plenty of problems with her bum leg. It grieved her terribly, constantly, and especially when it was cold—and in Michigan it's constantly cold. Continually carrying a crying kid on her cockeyed bony hip probably didn't help either, but she learned to live with the ever-present pain, thinking it her lot in life.

You could see the pain on her plain face. But Nick's school friends never saw any pain on his face, or knew about his fucked-up home life, and he was happy to keep it that way. He'd be mortified if he knew I was telling about his childhood, so let's keep this between us, shall we? He never referred to his mother as Mom, Momma, or any other term of endearment. It was just Lois. And he wouldn't even speak his dad's name. Phew!

There were few fond memories from his childhood, and he spoke of the past when only absolutely necessary—or when drinking. Thank God that didn't happen often because when drinking he sobbed uncontrollably, and confessed the unspeakable things that happened to him as a child. His friends made sure he never drank, because it was not pretty. Not pretty at all.

As an adult Nick avoided alcohol altogether, but that was probably because his father's greatest lifetime achievement was drinking himself to death. Consequently, Nick never wanted anything to do with either of them: drinking, or his father. His goal was to be nothing like his dad, and I do believe he achieved it. This is his quote about his father: "The best thing I can say about him is this: The chocolate mayonnaise cake at his going-away party was really good." You see, Stan was eternally drunk. He never went a day without getting plastered, so from a very early age the boys learned to run the filling station by themselves. In the beginning they cleaned up around the place, pumped a little gas, ran the till, occasionally changed a car's oil, and repaired a flat tire or two. That was how the family made its living, measly as it was. Hell, it wasn't a living at all—it was just an existence.

They weren't nearly old enough to work, but they were smart enough to realize if they didn't work they wouldn't eat. Stan wasn't a friendly drunk either; he was a mean and miserable abusive drunk who usually started drinking when he woke in the afternoon and kept on saucing until well into the night when he passed out. He was a mean hateful son of a bitch and his only friends were Jimmy Beam, Jackie Daniels, and Johnny Walker.

Mornings were quiet while he slept off the previous day's bender. But once awakened he would resume his drinking and raging, and there was never any peace in the house. Alcoholism is a family disease.

The boys felt fortunate on the evenings when he'd have money to visit Frank's Pub to do his dirty business, because they could relax and sleep a few hours undisturbed. Down at Frank's he'd have someone else to beat down. But when school was out, on evenings and weekends, the boys totally ran the station, with their dad doing the infrequent auto repair. At times they went to bed hungry, because the food money was drunk up, and many nights' supper was a candy bar; bag of chips, soda-pop, and a snowball from the station's vending machines because Lois and Stan were off drinking and forgetting about them.

Along the sun-baked west side of the shitty building stood a rickety old Tinkertoy of a wooden staircase that was completely exposed to the elements. This shaky plank-walk led up to three crummy rooms—without any insulation—that were nothing more than a storage area for spare tires, batteries, fan belts, and hoses. And these three crummy cinderblock rooms above a greasy gas station were the only place they ever knew as home.

The "great room" was a makeshift kitchen and living room combination that ran along the back wall. A varnished yellow pine picnic table—with the words "Property of the Genesee County Parks Department" wood-burned into its top—sat right smack in the middle, and each boy had his name carved in front of his space.

A green rubber garden hose was snaked up from the filling station to deliver cold water to a bulky cement slop sink in the kitchen. Next to the sink sat a greasy bottle-gas cook stove, and after that came a well-rounded International Harvester refrigerator. Practically the whole back wall was a bank of cold-conducting, drafty-as-hell, rusty steel-cased windows that overlooked a parking lot filled with broken-down rusting car carcasses.

The five Clark brothers shared the front room overlooking Broadway Street and the Brass Rail Bar. The BRB served courage to factory workers 24/7, and it never closed except on Christmas Day. Lois tended bar there days, some nights, and most weekends, too. So the boys would pop in and out daily and Stan was usually parked there at night, so the neighbors jokingly called it "The Clark Bar." The boys' room had two sets of bunk beds pushed up against the far walls, with a lumpy, scratchy, olive-drab mohair couch shoved against the other wall facing the street, and that was Nick's bed. There wasn't a closet, dresser, or bathroom.

No bathroom meant they had to take the rickety outdoor staircase to use the toilet in the station. But those boys were resourceful, so for number one they found a length of green garden hose, stuffed it into a tin funnel, snaked the hose through a hole in the second-floor window, and aimed it toward the alley. "Look out below," was their warning call.

A chipped-up rusty enamel washbasin sitting inside a cement slop sink was their bathtub, and after filling it with water warmed on the stove they had their birdbaths. Seven people lived up there that way, for too many years.

That damned dirty place was industrial as hell, and not homey in the least bit. There wasn't a picture hanging on the wall, rug lying upon the cold cement floor, or any comfort in sight. And just to add another element of depression to their dilapidated decor, the ceiling was covered with water-stained beaverboard panels that drooped ever threateningly above them, looking as if they'd cave in at any second.

Cold and drafty steel-case windows were constantly sweating and sending bloody rusty stains trickling down the unpainted, cold gray cement block walls, but their stupid little screen-less slits only opened wide enough to let in mosquitoes, flies, and bees, but never a cool breeze. Without any insulation, and practically no ventilation, it was suffocating all summer and cold as ice all winter. No one wanted to be up there because it was never meant for habitation.

During the worst of the winter, when it got so brutally cold that the snow squealed when you walked on it, the water would freeze inside the dishpan they used for dishes and birdbaths. Down in the garage where it was a couple of degrees warmer, an inch of ice would form on the greasy gas station's toilet bowl, and they'd have to chip it away to even use the filthy thing.

A stinking, hulking, monstrous fuel oil space heater used up a good chunk of their living space. Big as it was, it was no match for what Mother Nature could dish out during a Michigan winter. At times it was so brutally cold all they could do was wrap up in their dirty blankets and huddle together in front of the oven with it cranked up to broil and watch television.

As time passed and the boys grew it became apparent that something wasn't quite right with little brother Kenny. He just wasn't developing as the other boys had. But he was never a bother; in fact, he was sweet as the day was long, smiled and laughed all the time. There never was a happier baby, and he was happiest when with his brothers. He had trouble with speaking, walking, and doing the things most babies' do, so his big brothers stepped in where they could. Mean kids called him retarded, and you'd better believe they fiercely defended him. No one dared pick on Kenny, or they had a serious whooping loosed upon 'em.

Unlike his brothers, Nick had feelings and emotions he didn't deny and couldn't conceal or suppress, and he especially looked out for his little brother. Whatever Nick had, Kenny got some, too. "You da bess butter ever, Nick." At first it was candy, sodas, and treats, and later it was cigarettes. All the Clark brothers smoked. In fact, so much smoke poured from those second-floor windows that the fire department was called a couple of times.

Their grandma Effie was the one bright spot in their otherwise dismal lives. She looked out for those rambunctious boys and kept them for long stretches on her tidy little farm. I wish you could've seen her spread, because it was the sweetest place you ever saw, looking like the scene from a sentimental old greeting card.

Gran and the boys had painted her house a pale shell pink, and used an equally pale mint green for the louvered shutters that sat outside the twelve-paned windows. A white picket fence protected a patchwork garden overflowing with colorful perennials such as foxgloves, poppies, delphiniums, geraniums and peonies, rose trees, lilies, dahlias, daisies, and sweet peas, too. Out back she kept a respectable farm complete with livestock and a big fruit and vegetable garden.

The boys just loved going there, and she loved having them. Between milking Clarissa, the beautiful brown-eyed Guernsey heifer, and feeding the chicks and ducks, she made sure they were kept relatively clean and quite well fed. Gran would send them home with packages large enough to last a couple of weeks, crammed full of her put-ups: chutneys, relishes, chow-chows, spiced apple butters, jams and jellies, sweet pickles and dilly ones, too. And as an extraspecial treat, she'd include a tin of her squishy-soft oatmeal-raisin spiced cookies, a couple of loaves of homemade bread, and a good-size pat of her hand-churned Clarissa butter.

Gran's mini-farm measured just a little over four acres, and was ten minutes out of town, but it was a far-away magical world for those scrappy inner-city boys. Her tiny spread was an enormous outdoor playground, where they could run and jump, climb, throw things, yell, get dirty, and just enjoy being boys. Nick never cared for the getting-dirty part, and neither did his younger brother Ned, the smaller, smart-mouthed twin and, come to find out, his gay brother.

Nick loved working alongside his grandmother in the garden, because they'd chat away the hours while hoeing rows of beets, peppers, onions, and squash, and picking the corn, string beans, and red ripe tomatoes. "Seems they-is a bug for every plant, ain't they, Nikki?" Gran would say, and cackle away, as they plucked stinking potato bugs from the infested plants and plunked them into a red Philip Morris tin with a quarter inch of even stinkier kerosene.

To Nick the garden was the source of all things good, and Gran really had it good. In her garden of eatin' she had two sweet Stanley plum trees; the oblong egg-shaped ones, with a hazy-blue veil over deep purple skin. She also had pairs of golden Bartlett pear, tart red cherry, fuzzy-skinned clinging-pit peach, and two different kinds of apple trees. "Two by two, right Nikki? 'Cause ever' feller needs a friend," Gran would say, while winking at him.

Pale chartreuse transparent apples were the first of the season, and ready to eat by late July. They were pretty, tart and tasty, but didn't keep worth a darn. Those boys would stuff themselves with those little green apples till they got bellyaches and cried. Gran's other apple was a fall-ripening variety, a winter keeper with deep russet skin and flesh as white as snow. In fact, that's what she called it, a snow apple.

She'd turn those tart scabby apples into the most delicious applesauce, apple butter, and deep-dish butter-crusted spiced apple pies you'd ever tasted. Making them with sugar and spice, she baked them to a golden brown in her cast-iron wood-burning cookstove; chopped all of her own wood, too, except—of course—when those big strapping boys were there to do it.

The ancient snow apple stood behind her old bungalow, just outside the lean-to porch, and she claimed it was planted there by Johnny Appleseed himself. In springtime it was truly a spectacular thing when covered with delicate white blossoms having the faintest blush of pink that smelled just like being in love. How could one twisted-up, half-dead old tree possibly have so many beautiful sweet-smelling flowers upon it? Nick held his breath and prayed there wasn't a breeze while it was blooming, because that was all it took to send the pale petals cascading. Even the slightest hint of a breeze would send them drifting down like wintery snow, carpeting the newly greened lawn and turning it into an exotic, magical, pale pink Persian parlor carpet.

Nick's happiest childhood memories were his days spent at the farm canning with Lois and Gran. But most unfortunately, canning always happened during the late August heat waves, and it was Nick's job to keep the wood stove stoked and blazing. While sweating he listened to them gab the hours away and washing things, peeling produce, and packing the aquamarine jars with red ripe tomatoes, green and yellow string beans, salty garlic dill pickles, and spicy brown apple butter. They'd reminisce about how hard it was in the old days. But he couldn't imagine life being tougher than it already was.

And you know he was the only one of the boys who ever volunteered to help, because the other boys never wanted anything to do with the women, cooking, or being inside. But Nick knew how hard his Gran and mother worked at the hot thankless job of canning, and he wanted to help. Besides, while working alongside them washing jars and peeling things, he could listen to their stories, and even got to see Lois laugh a time or two, which was a rare sight.

Queenie was Gran's collie, and she was magnificent. A massive shaggy mane of black, tan, and white fur surrounded her pretty pointed face, and the boys dearly loved her. They were never allowed to have pets of their own, so they considered her to be their dog, too, she just stayed at Gran's. When she and the boys were young they played together in the yard, and she barked at them while keeping them away from the busy road, guarding them as if they were her own. But as the boys grew she grew older quicker, and arthritic, and only wanted to snooze in front of the warming woodstove. She'd light up like a lantern when those boys came pouring into that kitchen, calling her name all at once. "Queenie, Queenie, 'mere girl."

Nick was ten when Gran died, and it was devastating for him. All those big tough boys bawled their eyes out, and life got a whole lot tougher for everyone. Lois even cried, too, and they never saw her cry. Removing Gran's last care package from the fridge, she carefully untied the string, opened the brown paper wrapper, and tenderly held it while gazing at it lovingly for the longest time. Tracing her mother's tiny handprints, still holding in the butter pat, she wept.

Without Gran acting as a buffer and looking out for them, those boys were practically on their own, and they were just little kids. The love/hate war going on between Lois and Stan was ratcheted up another notch or two; drinking escalated, fighting escalated, and the boys' misery escalated in direct proportion. It got so bad that they spent most of their time away from home, when they could, because it was practically unbearable being there.

~ ~

Cue the song "I Am What I Am" from *La Cage aux Folles*. "I am, what I am, and what I am needs no excuses. I am my own special creation..."

It was Baccarat crystal clear, from a very early age, that little Nick was gay; there was really no way of hiding it. That's just the way God made him, and he gave him a good strong dose of it. Being born "that way" made it difficult for him to survive in the ever-threatening world he was thrown into. Nick was born way too tenderhearted and sympathetic for his own good, and in the industrial jungle he lived in, those traits were considered signs of weakness.

Nick was a good natured boy, but he had the ability to be fierce when he had to, especially when it concerned Kenny. He made it his job to look out for his baby brother, by making sure he was kept clean, fed, and far from the fray. And while Nick did his best to protect Kenny, he could not as easily protect himself.

Predators can sense vulnerability in young children and they actively search out the damaged, weak, neglected, and defenseless, and then use those traits to exploit them. It was Nick's funny, friendly, goofy-acting Uncle Freddy who recognized the desperate need to be loved, wanted, and cared for in those clear blue trusting eyes. Lois was often out working, or hitting the honky-tonks with Stan, so the boys were often left alone or farmed out to anyone who'd take them, and by default that was usually Aunt Lucinda and Uncle Freddy.

Fred and Lucy lived a couple of blocks over, on the corner of Mabel and Lewis, above the Thunderbird Lounge. Even though funny Uncle Fred had kids of his own, he took a special shine to Nick, the golden boy. He'd find ways of spending extra time alone with him and give him special attention, bring him sweets, treats, and presents trying to buy his confidence. But there was a terrible price to pay for this attention, because it cost his innocence. Freddy knew that the trust in those innocent blue eyes was the way in, and once inside he used that closeness to exploit his vulnerability every chance he could.

Alcohol was fueling a great many fires back then, as it still does. Alcohol lowered the inhibitions, made blurred edges fuzzier, and cast deep shadows over the truth. Uncle Fred liked his Black Label beers and those fuzzy edges. Unlike his brother-in-law, he was what you'd call a touchy-feely, happy kind of a drunk. Sexual abuse wasn't talked about back then, but that is what it was, plain and simple. Nick was a defenseless child being manipulated by an abusive alcoholic adult. You don't need to hear all the dirty details, but you need to know this happened, quite often, and for years.

You need to know about this, because it changed his young life forever. Sexual abuse ends childhood; period, end of sentence.

It ended Nick's childhood. After the abuse started, everything was seen differently, just as pure light is bent when passing through a prism. From the day it began his life was forever changed, and he looked at the world differently. At an early age Nick knew about sex, felt its powerful lusty lure, and knew the secret shame and terrible guilt that accompanyied it. So when Nick was old enough and felt strong enough to fight the fat disgusting bastard off, threatening him with exposure, he stopped.

And when Freddy was through with Nick, he quietly turned his attentions to his younger brother. Be the circle never broken, by and by, Lord, by and by.

— ~

Quite often their parents' alcohol-fueled frenzies would end in fierce fighting matches, or even worse, in loud, drunken, violent lovemaking sessions in the room right next to theirs. The boys learned to sleep with the television playing, and to this day Nick still does; he still can't go to sleep without one on.

But no one at school ever knew about any of this dysfunction, he made damn sure of it. Nick was never what you would call retreating, in fact he was smart, smart-mouthed, and funny; well liked, well spoken, with perfectly pressed clothes and iron straightened beachboy blond hair that was swept to the side, just so. In school he was the blue-eyed, blond, all-American boy who looked like Timmy from *Lassie*, only much funnier. Because at an early age Nick learned that humor was his ultimate defense. "If you make them laugh they won't kick your ass."

No one knew the deplorable conditions he experienced at home, because great efforts were taken to make sure they'd never find out.

Wearing the same clothes over and over day after day got boring, but he made sure they were spotlessly clean. A short-sleeve baby blue tab-collar seersucker shirt was worn with well-ironed chinos, and polished oxblood wingtips worn with dark thick-and-thin socks. All the boys kept up similar appearances, each in their own ways.

Emancipating himself at fifteen, he moved into his first apartment, a one-bedroom shit-hole he shared with a couple of buddies from work. But his ratty place had a real bathroom with a tub, shower, and toilet, which was more than he ever had living at home. He could easily walk to work from there, too, at the Varsity Drive-In, on the corner of Twelfth and Grand Traverse. So by lying about his age he started washing dishes there, worked every chance he could get, and squirreled away money for the future.

Nick instinctively knew his future was in hair. He styled anyone's hair he could get his delicate hands on, and spent a lot of time practicing on his high school girlfriends. They always had the most stylish and up-to-date hairdos, as well as himself. His lifelong ambition had been to enroll in beauty school, so he focused on that dream to make it through all the ugliness in his life and into the Promised Land. After graduating he enrolled in Mr. David's Beauty Academy, in beautiful downtown Flint, to receive certification in ratting, back combing, bleaching, cutting, coloring, and permanenting. He loved hair, and learned he had a gift for styling it.

After graduating Cosmetology College—at top of his class—he found immediate employment at the Curl-Up- and-Dye Beauty Salon, at their second satellite location over on Flushing Road, next to Flint Memorial Gardens mausoleum and mortuary. The rest, as they say, is hair-story. So move your bony ass over, Vidal Sassoon, 'cause here he comes.

But at an early age he *also* learned that life can be strange and cruel, because he was robbed of the very thing he so dearly loved and so good at doing: his own hair. Most tragically, he began balding at the early age of nineteen, and by thirty he was already wearing complete hairpieces. Brutal, isn't it? Like being a diabetic and owning a candy factory.

— —

Now, it's no secret that *many* hairdressers are queer, ergo they probably went to the queer bar. Nick was just sixteen when he first went to the Pink Poodle, and being young, blond, and vivacious he quickly became a favorite. Soon the gay bar became the the hub of his social life, and quite like many other young people during their mating years, he went to "the bar," because liquor is a mighty powerful aphrodisiac. But because of his father's history with alcohol, Nick was decidedly against drinking.

At the bar, he was more of a "performer" than a drinker. Yes, he did a little amateur drag, as Helen Flames, but that's not what I'm referring to. He was a disco dancing queen. He commanded the disco dance floor with his elegant friend, Doug-gay, whom we lovingly referred to as Madame Scarf, because he was so fucking elegant, a real lady.

Doug-gay was not just another homo hairdresser. He was a professionally trained ballroom dancer. Yes, he ratted hair during the day, at The Hairport on Bristol Road over by the airport, but at night he taught cha-cha classes at Arthur Murray's on Corunna Road, up-above June's Antiques. He was so fucking professional that he even performed each year in the *Nutcracker* at Christmastime, dancing as the Sugar Plum Fairy.

Tall and thin, pasty and incredibly lithe, he had a narrow Ichabod Crane kind of face, was haughty, elegant, and always wore a long flowing scarf around his scrawny neck. He drank pink champagne out of a three-part plastic glass that he carried in his rhinestone clutch. Nikki and Doug-gay would float around the dance floor commanding attention and adulation from adoring fans, awestruck wannabes, and admiring onlookers. "Just throw money!" Nikki would shout to his adoring audience, and he meant it, too. This queer floorshow was the closest thing the local fruits had to real entertainment, except for the amateur drag shows.

* P.S. A drag queen is a man who had enough nerve, or consumed enough alcohol, to put on a dress and wig, get on stage, and move his liquored lipstick-slickened lips to a record.

* P.P.S. There is also a subspecies, called drag kings, and those were womyn who'd dress like men and perform Wayne Newton or Neil Diamond. {*Woman* is spelled *womyn* on purpose, because they wanted *nothing* to do with men.}

Those were the days, when we disco danced till the bar closed, hopefully got laid, and maybe caught a couple of hours sleep before dragging a nasty ashtray-smelling ass back into work, wearing the same clothes as yesterday, and having a *cock*-eyed satisfied smile. We really should have done a whole lot more of it, and taken pictures to prove it.

Now, Nick always had a story to tell, or joke to repeat, and was surrounded with people laughing their asses off, attracted to his gayness like moths succumbing to a brilliant flame. Ned often accompanied him on his fruity forays, but he was more of a wallflower and content to sit at the mahogany bar nursing a beer and watching the backward action in the smoky mirrors.

You see, Ned was balding as quickly as Nick and already had the classic monk's crown hairline, but unlike his brother he learned to live with it. But Nick, on the other hand, decided to fight depilatory progression with all the forces in his beauty school arsenal. When his hair first started disappearing, at nineteen, he did the classic combover technique where he'd pile it up on the right side and rat-it-up, sweep it over the no-hair-left side, secure it behind his ear, and spray it until it was completely immovable. That technique temporarily masked the balding, but he had to avoid stiff winds at all costs. His dearest friends called this technique "tieback curtains."

When there wasn't enough hair left for the window treatment concealment to work, he tried Hairisol. That was an aerosol spray paint formulated to match his hair color, and when sprayed directly onto his ever-expanding scalp it would temporarily mask the quickly departing hair. As his lovely blond hair continued to rapidly depart, things got progressively worse, and soon he was wearing hairpieces, which became bigger, blonder, and bawdier over the years.

There was comfort for balding hairdressers at the local watering hole for deviants. If you were a hairdresser, artist, ballet dancer, window fluffer, florist, or antique dealer, it was likely we'd be seeing you in the queer bar, too. But we also saw plenty of factory workers, accountants, farmers, coaches, priests, policemen, truck drivers, lawyers, doctors, firemen, fathers, mothers, sisters, and even some weird uncles, too; a real cross-section of humanity.

— —

"Well...would ya look who's queer? I thought I might be seeing you in the bar tonight.," Nick said to Randy as we walked into "The Pink Poodle".

"And I just knew I'd be seeing you queer, too. How are you, Nick?"

"Three words, darling: fab-you-luscious. And it's nice to see you again, too. I've got a table over here with my brother and a couple guys from the neighborhood. They just bought that old farmhouse on the corner of Pierson and Second. Come sit with us."

"Well, all right, we will. Nick, this is my friend Denny."

"Hello. Randy and Denny, I'd like you to meet Jim and Bill, they're new to the neighborhood. And this is my older brother Ned."

"Younger brother," Ned said, in his defense. "Nice to meet you both."

"So, where'd you say you lived before moving to Flint, Jim?" Nick said, quizzing the gangly boy with the Coke-bottle glasses, who would unknowingly be his cleaning lady one day.

"I was reared in the Thumb, Bad Axe; took me three days to hitch-hike from Saginaw." He was the May part of the May-December relationship, tall and maybe eighteen. Can't recall what Bill looked like, but he was really old, maybe thirty or better.

"You guys are a real hoot," Jim would say repeatedly during the evening, sounding like a hooty owl; that, or someone from the Upper Peninsula. Christ, he was just a goofy kid.

Turning to Nikki I said,"It was difficult to hear in here when they had that old jukebox blasting, but with the disc jockey constantly cranking up the volume now it's even worse."

"Then shut up and dance," he said. Extending a slender hand he led me to the dance floor as "Disco Inferno" blasted from gigantic, refrigerator-sized speakers, and we were off, Flint's version of *Dancing with the Stars*. As we effortlessly glided along Nick's brother, Ned, twirled by us with his cha-cha partner, Scotty, the unbelievably skinny black dancing queen.

"Sparkle, Zena, sparkle," Nick shouted to his only competition, his retreating, balding brother. Nick truly was an excellent dancer, and all I had to do was follow everything he did—backward, in army boots. He made it seem effortless.

When the bar finally closed, mean old dyke Melva kicked us out, so we rendezvoused down the road, at Wally's Supper Club, for a greasy breakfast of deep-fried beer-battered fish and chips, just the thing to top off a belly full of booze. Those were the days.

❧

Days quickly passed, turning into weeks.
Weeks flew past, turning to months.
Months melted into years.
One day we awoke and found ourselves middle-aged.
It happens.

In queer terms that meant we'd become yester-gay's, "old trolls," undesirables, dried fruit and ready for the wrinkle room. For many the party life was over and it was time for settling down, or just plain settling.

For many the weekend queer bar routine eventually grew tiresome. Some found mates and coupled, and spent more time at home. Nick found he was spending more time playing house, too, and eventually he became domesticated, and that was something we never though we would see. But while he was working on his man catching skills, he took up home-cooking, home-decorating, home-o-sexualizing, and baking decadently delicious deserts. And after eating all this rich and tasty food he blossomed, and grew some serious middle aged curvature.

— —

After living with Nick for many years Kenny was moved into an apartment with Lois that Nick quietly paid for. But since Lois didn't drive, Nick continued to look after his needs—taking him to doctor appointments, getting his prescriptions filled, keeping him well dressed, and supplied with cigarettes. And in spite of his tumultuous young life, Kenny managed to retain his childlike innocence well into middle age.

Each Monday afternoon, like clockwork, Nick would pick-up Kenny and together they would get man-cures and even pet-cures sometimes, too. Kenny loved getting attention from the pretty girls at the salon. But even more, he loved spending time with his big butter, Nick. After having their beautification they'd have a big lunch and he could order anything he wanted, and he even got to eat his dessert first, just like his big brother.

"That way you always have room for it. Right, Kenny?"

"White, Nick! You the besses butter ever."

Sin
Strangers In the Night

*M*y Mother was dyslexic. When I was born I was supposed to be named Danny, as in "Daniel in the Lion's Den," but since she saw things sort of ass-backward, she misspelled the name on my birth certificate, Denial, as in, "Don't look at me—I didn't do it," and not Daniel; and that's the name I've been saddled with ever since. Understandably, I chose to go by Denny, or Den, to my friends.

I'll spare you from having to hear all the boring minutia spanning between my birth and childhood, and skip right to the summer of 1972 when I turned eighteen. It was really quite an intense year for me, because that summer I graduated from high school, bought my first car—a 1962, two-ton, arctic-white Buick Wildcat—got my first real job—selling booze at Baker's Drugs—started college, and went to my first gay bar. It was really quite a summer.

Oh, I'd certainly heard about the "queer bar" for years before I ever imagined going there. Most people in town knew about that wicked place, but polite people didn't talk about that sort of thing. Good God-fearing folks would only whisper the taboo bar's name in disgust, and its lecherous patrons could only whisper its illicit name in the strictest of secrecy.

The Pink Poodle was Flint's one and only queer bar. The den of iniquity was located way out on Dirt Highway, in a narrow cinder-block building that stood all alone at the outskirts of town, and that's exactly where most folks figured it belonged—waaaaaaay outside of town. An insignificant backlit plastic sign reading "Liquor and Lottery" was all that marked the lair of the Sodomites. Probably best if you drive by quickly and try not to look because you just might catch something incurable. I was absolutely certain that inside that shadowy hellhole it was dark, dank and smoky, filled with beady eyes, Russian hands, and Roman fingers.

As children we weren't supposed to know about that wicked forbidden place, but we knew it was out there. Back in those days, when you really wanted to piss someone off, you would call him queer, fag, homo, sissy, or faggot. Those were about the worst things you could possibly be, especially if you were a boy. I certainly didn't want to be called queer, so I tried my damnedest not to be "that way." For years I tried to not be *that way*, but no matter how hard I tried suppressing it, it never seemed to work, and the queer in me just kept coming out.

Now, there was no blame to be assigned for this sexual misalignment, because I was raised in a respectable Irish Catholic working-class family and reared in the Catholic Church. The Holy Church decreed that their parishioners had to send their large broods to parochial schools, and you didn't dare question the church's dictums. That's just the way it was.

Many neighborhoods were nothing more than Catholic ghettos built around the church, and Saint Luke's, our church, was just such a parish. The modern church and school were built during the post-war boom years to minister a Levittown type of neighborhood with nearly indistinguishable cookie-cutter tract homes on Flint's rapidly growing northwest side.

Back then, as in feudal days, the holy church functioned as a patriarchal institution with all life revolving around it. Socialization was structured around church, too, because attending Mass was mandatory every school day, always on Sundays, and all Holy Days as well; which somehow always managed to fall on a Saturday, the only church-free day. On meatless Friday's there was a fish fry in the church's basement, and bingo was played in the rec hall Wednesday's and Saturday's. Our dad belonged to the sainted Knights of Columbus, a private drinking club. Mom was a member of the dutiful ladies of the Altar Guilt, big brother Tim was an altered boy, and I was a soprano in the all-boys choir.

But it wasn't until later in life that I discovered there was a special place inside the church that embraced the more "sensitive" boys, such as me. Sensitive, nonathletic, intellectual and "artistic boys" became priests, while the others had to marry good Catholic girls and raise more loyal and obedient parishioners.

This closed system may have worked for centuries for others, but at a very early age I knew there was trouble looming between me and the church. Now, the Holy Catholic Church decreed that *being* a homosexual was sinful, unacceptable, and an abomination in the eyes of the Lord (and just about everyone else's eyes, too), and secretly I suspected that I just might be abominable. Now, according to the Holy Church, it was all right to *be* a homosexual, just as long as you didn't *practice* your perversion. But I ask you, now, how are you ever going to be *good* at *anything* unless you practice?

Oh, believe me I tried to be a *good* boy having only God-centered thoughts and actions, but it wasn't easy. As I reflect back now, I can remember feeling and being very different from the other boys—way before I figured what that "difference" really was. At first I just naturally assumed I was switched at birth, and someday soon my real parents would arrive in their shiny black limousine to take me to my real life; the life I was meant to have, with classy people who understood me, actually listened to me, appreciated my fashion advice, and liked to listen to Broadway show tunes instead of beer-drinking polkas.

Why wasn't my life more like one of those idyllic televised families, where everyone was white, clean, rich, loving, and so very understanding? I wanted to be listened to as if I was a real person, and not just another miniature nuisance. But instead, I was repeatedly reminded that: "Children are meant to be seen and not heard." Consequently, from an early age I wasn't heard, and once I'd figured out I was a goddamned queer, and an outsider, I tried my best not to be seen. And ultimately it was this unseen difference that made me feel I didn't belong to these people, this neighborhood, or this gritty shitty town.

When beginning to mature I never allowed myself to even entertain the thought that this difference could possibly mean I was homosexual because it went against everything that I was taught by my parents and the Holy Catholic Church, amen. I swore upon the Bible I was not a homosexual, could never be, no, not me. My Catholic upbringing taught me to go to the priest and confess my unspeakable sinful thoughts, and pray for forgiveness. And after I confessed to Father Kidplucker he told me to pray as hard as I could, have no more impure thoughts, say fifty Our Fathers and a hundred Hail Marys, and maybe then I would remain straight.

As if.

So I prayed to God with every fiber of my being to see no evil and do no evil.

— ⁓

As *I* saw *it* there were very few alternatives to being a gay. I could:

1. Remain single forever and be chaste (Saint Got-none).
2. Become a priest and *supposedly* practice celibacy (as if *that* was gonna happen).
3. Be a confirmed bachelor and need a lifetime of therapy.
4. Marry a Catholic girl and have a bunch of screwed-up kids who'd need therapy.
5. Accept who I was and go along with the program as God intended. After all, he made me this way, now didn't he?

Understanding ones sexuality does not happen all at once; it starts at an early age and is revealed and grasped over time. Now, I understood that a tiger couldn't change its stripes or a leopard its spots. And I also knew I was born this way —gay, queer, homo—and realized that I would have to accept myself, even if the church didn't. If there wasn't any acceptance of me or my kind by the church, I felt fine leaving it behind. Fuck 'em. But I also understood that God loved and accepted me the way I was, even if the Catholic Church didn't, and I could have a perfectly good relationship with God without having the Church acting as an intermediary.

"I am in my Father, you in me, and I in you."

During the sixties there were no templates for being a gay. It was considered a sin, a crime, and definitely not acceptable. So if you were gay you had to find your own way. Usually this sexploration was accomplished under the cover of darkness and in total secrecy, because homo-sex was thought to be abhorrent and definitely not an acceptable lifestyle choice. People were still being institutionalized until 1973 just for being homosexual, because it was regarded as an incurable mental defect.

For the troubled souls who needed professional assistance figuring all this confusing sexy stuff out, there were sympathetic therapists ready to listen and give their learned insights, if you could afford their hefty fees. For conflicted and sexually confused Christians, who were the borderline heterosexual/ homosexual types, and trying to figure out which way their door would swing, there was Christian conversion therapy where churchy conservative counselors could help them figure the confusing sexy stuff out.

At that time gay conversion was considered to be a legitimate form of psychotherapy. This straightening out process began with sympathetic Christian counselors who would swear to make you straight by using a combination of therapies, such as talk therapy (get that penis out of your mouth, Johnny), prayer sessions (on your knees, Johnny), and teaching you to do manly stuff such as change your motor oil and play football (but definitely not touch, Johnny).

These religious zealots claimed they could teach perverts how to leave the sinful homo and sexual life behind and thus become a normal, sanctified, heterosexual person again, and still make it into heaven right along with them. But this transfiguration was achieved only through devout faith, abundant prayer, redemption, and severe self-righteousness. As for me, I prefer to remain a little bent, thank you very much. Truth be told, I will probably be having much more interesting friends keeping me company in hell.

According to the 1948 *Kinsey Report*, there was an entire spectrum of male sexuality running the gamut from being a 100 percent John Wayne straight heterosexual to being a five-alarm-fire flaming Liberace faggot, with many stages of bisexuality falling in between. And this data also included the normal adolescent same-sex curiosity, which is a part of growing up.

But honestly now, we all know that horny is horny, and most men— regardless of their sexual orientation—have an amazing ability to compartmentalize the different parts of their lives; consequently a lot of homosexual sex happens to straight amnesiacs who simply don't remember a thing after it has happened.

Nearly every town had a known homo, sexual hangout—be it a bar with a dimly lit back room, dark secluded park, or shady low spot down by the river—knowingly entered with a wink and a nod. Flint's Nancy Boy bar was the Pink Poodle, wink-wink, nudge-nudge; ya know what I mean? It was a queer bar for cocksuckers, dykes, fudge packers, homos, pinkos, perverts, and those who were found to be light in the loafers. It was "queer" before "gay" was even invented. And that dingy hole-in-the-wall was still operating, having earned the dubious distinction of being one of the oldest gay bars in the state, and serving beers to queers for over fifty years.

Back in the sixties and seventies, the Pinko was owned and operated by a tough old dyke named Melva. She was a big-boned gal, a heavy smoker and even heavier drinker who liked her hard stuff. Sporting a platinum blonde, slicked-back duck's ass hairdo with an Elvis waterfall front, she wore big black cat's-eye glasses *without* rhinestones, and was built like a linebacker. Nobody ever messed with Melva, because she could easily kick their ass and wipe the floor with their pathetic remains.

Her alternative watering hole was long, narrow, and shotgun shaped, just like a bowling lane, and measuring maybe twenty feet wide by fifty feet deep. Behind the massive mahogany bar, and lying next to a shiny brass till, sat a nicotine-yellowed photograph of the big old dyke sitting in her bubblegum pink bathtub and soaking in soapy bubbles clear up to her big old tits. Her apricot pink toy poodle, Frenchy, sat on the matching commode watching her bathe, while wearing a chunky rhinestone collar that sparkled like diamonds in the camera's flash.

Surrounding the Pink Poodle, named after her pampered Parisian pooch, on three of its four sides, was an unkempt muddy, pothole-riddled parking lot with a tiny "Enter at your own risk" sign posted at the entrance. Like riding on a roller coaster, your car would uncomfortably tumble in and out of the giant craters lining the crummy lot. During summer those enormous potholes filled with water becoming massive mudholes, and in the miserable winter they iced over and semi-froze into slushy sinkholes that could swallow small foreign cars whole.

On sultry summer evenings the parking lot was often busier than the bar, especially after the two o'clock closing. Plastered patrons who weren't finished partying, and horny perverts out searching for alcoholically impaired male companionship, circled the bar repeatedly, eventually parked, and trysted. A blind eye was turned to the parking lot trade and all the "goings-on" out there. I guess they figured they'd eventually get thirsty or need to use the head.

Many of these needy men were afraid to go inside the seedy bar, probably because they didn't want anybody to see them entering that forbidden place and be forever labeled as queer. Maybe they were just curious, only experimenting, just a little bisexual, and didn't want to get a full-blown case of "the gay." Or, maybe they'd just come from dropping off a nice girl named Jane, because what they really wanted was to play with Dick. Truth was, they were horny and wanted sex, so they chose to remain outside bar, inside their car, where they would remain straight. And there, in the backseat of that car, do just about every unimaginable thing that two men could possibly do with each other.

Cue the song "Secretly," by Jimmy Rodgers: "Wish we didn't have to meet secretly..."

That same memorable summer, the very day I turned eighteen, I started my first *real* job: selling booze at Baker's Drug Store. Before that I had a job scooping ice cream at a joint called the Gay Nineties Ice Cream Parlor (I kid you not) where I made a whopping dollar-an-hour, before withholdings.

Quite thoughtfully, Baker's had conveniently located their liquor department right next to the drugs, for easy one-stop shopping. Fred, Dave, and Tom were the revolving druggists, and an older woman, named Linda, was their administrative assistant, taking care of the many insurance forms and helping customers at the checkout.

At the tender age of twenty-one, Linda seemed to be old already. I believe she was born an old soul. She was also divorced, and a self-proclaimed lesbian and the first one I'd ever met. She was not Catholic, divorced, a lesbian, a Democrat, and sold drugs for a living. My proper Catholic mother didn't want me to have anything to do with her. Period.

But she was pretty, in an unusual way, neat and petite, with blue-green eyes and long blonde hippie-girl hair that cascaded down her slender back all the way to her little dyke butt. Her handsome hair was her crowning glory and she was forever flipping it back and playing with it, and she and her well-maintained mane ran a very tight ship.

Quite often after closing a group of us would rendezvous to have a few drinks, dance, party, and blow off some steam. Inevitably Linda and I would end up being paired together, and eventually we became friends. Even though she partied the same as the rest of us, there was a pervasive sadness about her, that and a Southern, don't-give-me-any-shit attitude, which made it difficult for people to become friendly. It's hard to make friends with a porcupine.

It was on one of these alcohol-fueled after-work outings that she took me into her confidence. "When I was less than a year old I was taken from my mom, ya see, she was only fifteen when she had me and considered underage by the state. So, while she was giving birth to me, my fucker father was out getting some other woman pregnant. She insisted he marry her, so he divorced my Mom. But because his family had money and influence, he had me taken away from Mom - just to punish her. Hell, he didn't want me; he just didn't want *her* to have me.

"When I was about nine one of my stepmoms finally told me she wasn't my real mom, and suddenly it all made sense; why I was treated so differently than the other kids, and why I was passed around from relative to relative so much.

"Well... when I was twelve I found out about my real mom. She was real pretty, ya know. By then she was living up in Flint and married to her third husband, so that summer I went up and spent a few wonderful weeks with her. Then I had to go back to live with my fucking father. But the very day I turned sixteen I got the hell outta there.

"Now, I've been taken advantage of plenty by men. But the worst of it happened when I was eighteen. I'd just finished high school and was livin' in Tallahassee, when...when ... I... when I was beaten and raped. It was terrible. I spent a whole week in the hospital..."

"Oh my God, Linda, I never knew."

"Yeah, it was really bad. But the real problem came after that, when I thought I was pregnant. I didn't know what to do, and this was back before abortion was legal; and to tell ya the truth, I don't know if I coulda done that anyway.

"Well...there was this squirrelly little hippie who hung out with our group, who went by the name Rabbit; he stepped up and offered to marry me. So, we went on and got married. Later, when I found I wasn't pregnant, we separated as friends and eventually divorced. That's when I moved to Michigan, to be near my mom and maybe get to know her better."

"My God, Linda, I never knew."

"Yeah. But there's something else. You see, even though I think of myself as being a lesbian, I guess I'm really not, yet, because I've never been with a woman. Technically that's what it means, right? A lesbian is defined as a woman that has relations with another female, right? Now, even though I despise the idea of ever being with a man, I sure do wonder what it would be like to be with a woman."

"What? How can that be? You're always telling everyone that you're a lesbian."

"Truth is, honey...I'm scared."

"Of *what*, women? I don't blame you."

"Nooo...I'm afraid to go there by myself."

"Go where?"

"To the *gay bar*, honey! *Jeez*, I want to go...but I'm afraid to go by myself. I desperately want to meet somebody...I'm so lonely." Then she began to blubber, and the one thing I cannot abide is seeing a woman cry. "Would you go with me, please, just once, so I can see what it's like, and maybe then I can meet someone?"

Just like Nancy Reagan, every bone in my body told me to "Just say no" and run in the opposite direction; but felt I shouldn't, couldn't, because she seemed desperate and this was so important to her. Feeling pressed into a corner, I reluctantly agreed, hoping she'd forget the whole conversation when sober. And as you may know, no good deed goes unpunished.

"Once, I'll go once," I said, thinking, *Jesus, what the hell am I committing to?*

"Oh, thank you, honey. Thank you so much," she said between slobbery sobs. But she didn't forget. She may have possibly been a lesbian, but she was definitely still a woman, and she did what females do: made plans. "We arrive at the bar at eight o'clock this coming Friday," Linda informed me.

It also happened to be the thirteenth. Wouldn't you know it? To tell you the truth, I was extremely anxious about the whole damn thing, and felt as if I was committing mortal sin just going near the place. The very thought of it made my heart race, pulse speed up, and face flush scarlet red. What if someone saw me going in there? What would they think? What if one of them spoke to me, or touched me?

What was it like inside there? I was absolutely certain it was pitch-dark, with writhing naked bodies just like a scene from *Caligula*.

——— ———

We arrived at "The Bar" on Friday, the thirteenth, at eight o'clock sharp; she was always one to be punctual. Like an old lady, Linda drove her shiny new '72 bittersweet-orange AMC Gremlin hatchback into the nasty pothole-riddled parking lot, stopped on the south side, and parked under a sign reading "Enter from the Rear," which made me even more anxious. I made damn sure we parked facing the road, in case we needed to make a quick getaway.

Two dimes were hidden inside the flaps of my polished Bass Weejuns to make the call for the police or ambulance, because I was absolutely certain that inside there I'd be groped, molested, manhandled, and probably catch something incurable. As an added safety precaution I memorized the number for 911 and repeated it like a mantra, in case something happened, *911, 911, 911.* And like any good Catholic boy, I prayed to Jesus to protect us...just in case.

"I shall fear no evil as I walk through the door of depravity, into the den of debauchery, for thou art with me."

Linda wore her best rebel-blue knit top with a fold-down collar, gray wool dress slacks, and Hush Puppy suede oxfords, and was really quite dressed up for a Flint lesbian wannabe. She was nearly as nervous as me, prattling away about something completely irrelevant, such as billing forms for Blue Cross or some other shit.

From out in the parking lot, with the windows rolled up, we could hear barroom ballads blasting and smell the stinging stench of a Lysol-like disinfecting that was recently tossed onto the parking lot's greasy gravel after giving the sticky floor a lackluster mopping.

I made certain we took our sweet time getting to the door by straightening the collar of my tan seersucker shirt, adjusting my argyle socks, and brushing the ashes off my chinos. When Linda opened up the door to the netherworld, it was dark as midnight inside there, pitch-black, and so much smoke came boiling out that I was certain the fires of hell were burning within.

Temporarily blinded by coming from sunlight into total blackness, it took some time for our eyes to adjust. While acclimating I became acutely aware of the sudden hush that had fallen over the bar, and had the uncomfortable sensation that every eyeball inside that hellhole was staring right at the front door and the two newest victims. Us.

I couldn't see, but I could still smell, and I detected Brut cologne mixed with yeasty beer, stale cigarette smoke, and the disinfectant, making a most memorable bouquet. Scanning the dimly lit den, I could barely make out a burly bartender, who resembled Mr. Clean, standing behind a massive red mahogany bar. Bushy brows were deeply furrowed as he disapprovingly glared at us, with his sturdy arms folded tightly to his steel-wooly chest. Thankfully they were not very busy; just a handful of old men seated at the bar, nursing longneck bottles of beer and sticky cocktails.

The only female was an aging waitress with a very low center of gravity. The bottom-heavy barmaid stood less than five foot tall, but you'd never know she was practically a midget, because she'd borrowed a few tricks from the drag queens: stiletto heels and a hairdo that made her closer to six feet tall. Dyed-black cotton-candy hair was ratted into a tangled rat's nest, piled high atop her empty head, sculptured into overlapping curls, and shellacked until completely immovable. Think Marge Simpson with big, black, hard hair and thick black Bakelite cat's-eye glasses—*with* the rhinestones.

While contentedly chewing and popping a giant wad of Doublemint gum, her cherubic cherry lips were mindlessly mouthing the words to Frank Sinatra's "Strangers in the Night."

"Doobie, doobie, do...La, la, la-la-la."

With Frankie providing protection, we stumbled through the darkness toward a beacon of safety: a plastic stained-glass replica Budweiser pool light hanging over a green felt-covered pool table, at the back of the bar. Groping our way along the sticky wall, we skirted past the big red bar that was mirrored from behind to showcase its many multicolored alcoholic elixirs. The nicotine-tinged mirrors were used to make the bowling alley sized bar seem twice as wide as it really was, and allow those buzzed old bastards to scrutinize our every move.

Opposite the bar were several shabby red vinyl booths with brassy hobnail trim, and right between them sat the dance floor and a hulking Wurlitzer jukebox. Chipped-up asbestos floor tile, laid in a red-and-tan checkerboard, designated the dance floor, and silvery aluminum foil covered the ceiling above it. Strings of multicolored holiday lights outlined its perimeter; dimly glowing against it. Was this an inept attempt at creating a big-city mirrored discotheque look, or lights left over from Christmas? It was August, for Christ's sake.

A pungent yellow dusting of Shinola floor-wax lay undisturbed on the checked floor, awaiting its first tango of the evening. Beyond that was our safety zone, an oblong light hanging over a pool table, in the deepest, darkest part of the bar. At the very-very back were the dingy bathrooms, where I was certain something terrible lurked, so I closely monitored my fluid intake, and prayed. "Please let me hold it till I get out of here. Amen."

We surely must have looked like a couple of terrified deer caught in the headlights, because I could feel my face flushing and turning hot, mortified, as if I was caught naked, masturbating, and being brought before the entire school for humiliation.

The cocktail waitress eventually ambled over, smiled pleasantly, and said, "Yous twos are news here, aren't chas?" Then she stood there popping gum, appearing quite satisfied with her clever deduction.

Shaking heads up and down in unison, like a Katherine Hepburn bobblehead doll on a bumpy stretch of road, was our only response. "New Meat" stamped upon our foreheads.

"My name's Sin-d. Now, don't you kids worry 'tall, 'cause the folks here is real nice. You'll be just fine, so you just relax and have yerselves a good time. Now, if anybody bothers yous guys, yous just let me know. And if there's anybody you'd like to meet, yous just let me know, and I'd be happy ta introduce chas."

Again we nodded in unison. Sin-d did make us feel a bit more comfortable, and as the pretty red-and-orange Tequila Sunrises began to take effect, we could finally speak again. But there was not much conversation happening because we were stunned, and it was difficult to hear anything with the jukebox blasting oldies: Patty Page, Johnny Ray, Judy Garland, Teresa Brewer, and lots and lots of show tunes.

While sipping sticky cocktails we silently stared into the underbelly of this underworld trying to take it all in, and mindlessly filled an ashtray with butts, until Linda finally leaned in and yelled, "Okay. This is enough for my first visit. I'm ready to leave now."

"Amen! Halleluiah Jesus! Guide me from the shadow of darkness and into the light."

"I just have to use the bathroom. Do you mind?"

"Mind? No," I said to appease her. Meanwhile I'm thinking, *Yes, I mind being left alone in this hellhole.*

As I watched her disappear into the womyn's restroom, a smarmy little brown man with a scrawny penciled mustache, who looked like a miniature Mexican John Waters, approached from the other direction. Assuming he was heading to the head to piss, I moved aside, making room for him to pass, but instead of passing he lurched over and solidly planted a sloppy kiss smack on my lips, and shoved his slimy, smoky, disgustingly beer-basted old-man tongue deep into my mouth. I never saw it coming.

The rest of the dried-up old fruits without any dates erupted into laughter as I shoved him away and went running for the door. Once safely outside, I spit the taste of nasty old man and used beer out of my contaminated mouth, "Phew, phew!" But when I'd reached the car it was locked tight, and I automatically fell back on my Catholic training. "Dear God, save me," I implored, while scanning the parking lot for posses of perverts, certain I was going to be the victim of another (homo) sexual assault.

Linda finally moseyed out, while still mindlessly prattling away. "Now, that wasn't so bad, was it, honey? What happened to you anyway?

THE GAYS OF OUR LIVES

I come outta the bathroom and you weren't around. Why didn't you wait for me, honey?"

"Linda! Unlock the damn car and let me get inside. Soon as you left, this disgusting old man came up and shoved his nasty tongue in my mouth, all the way down to my tonsils. It was disgusting! Phew, phew," I said, spitting the taste of him out again.

"What? How could that happen? I was only gone for a couple minutes."

"I think he was waiting for you to leave, because he showed up the very second you left. They were all laughing, like it was some kind of joke."

"I was wondering why they were all laughing when I come outta the bathroom. I'm so sorry, honey. Are you sure you're okay?"

"Yes, I'm fine. I just need a Listerine rinse and a long hot shower."

"I'm so sorry, honey."

"Just get us the hell out of here, will you? And quick."

Linda placed the stick into first gear and crept back toward suburbia. "Did you notice, honey, other than that waitress there weren't any women there, just those old men? How am I supposed to meet a woman? I'll have to go back when there's more people, and some women. After that I'll be all right going by myself."

"Wait a minute here. You are *not* asking me to go back inside that snake pit again, are you? Don't you remember, less than five minutes ago I was molested by a Mexican masher who attempted to swipe my tonsils? I barely made it out of there with my virtue intact, and now you are asking me to go back inside there to be manhandled again?"

"Please, honey, just once more? Please...I'm so lonely." Then she began to cry.

Forgive them Lord, for they know not what they do. The following Saturday evening Linda picked me up, right on time, and she was totally transformed. Her luxurious long blonde hair was sheared off and styled into a short boyish bob. Sing along with Herman's Hermits: "Her long blonde hair...lying on the barber floor...doesn't need it anymore..."

Linda was so totally transformed that I scarcely recognized her. With her boyish cut, slight frame, and tiny boobs, she looked like an adolescent churchgoing grandma's boy. Perhaps this was her way of molting an old skin, coming out, and displaying her masculinity, while seeking femininity.

When we returned to Sodomy and Glam-more-ah, we found the shitty parking lot full. From inside the car we could feel the thump, thump, thumping from the old jukebox. It was Saturday night, and that joint was jumping.

The bulletproof steel security door was propped open, and the bar so overcrowded that the only way to get two more people inside was to rub them with Vaseline (the preferred homo lubricant) and shove them.

The hippest click of synchronized syncopated finger popping was coming from the crowded dance floor as the jukebox bubbled and blasted out the Blackbyrds' rhythm anthem "Walking in Rhythm." Everyone elegantly floated, rhythmically moving in sync like one organism. They did not merely dance; they glided and performed just like on the *Lawrence Welk Show*. This shitty place had an unmistakable presence, and clearly it was the crowd.

The disco era had splashed on the scene a few years ago, but it was a recent introduction here because Motown still ruled this jukebox, and Flint was Motown's slutty little sister. Here rhythm prevailed.

I was amazed there were this many queer people in this city, or even the state. I never dreamt it. For years I suspected I was only one, and afraid someday someone would see right through me to expose my deepest, darkest secret. Well, my secret was safe there. When you're among your own kind there's no need for secrets. They weren't big and scary, for the most part; they were pretty normal looking, without horns or tails. In fact, you could hardly tell them from normal people, except most were better groomed, smelled nicer, and some were even quite stylish. And everyone was having a really good time.

These people knew how to have a good time, and this was probably the only public place where they could be themselves and do just that.

Here, among the queer, they could be who they truly were and be accepted. Inside this alcohol-centric sanctuary they could feel safe expressing affection to their same-sex friends, dance together with their spouses, and let their hair down among like-minded people.

As we squeezed our way to the table we occupied last time I scanned the swarming sea of same-sex seekers for the lecherous little Mexican masher who attempted to swipe my tonsils. Thankfully I did not see him here tonight.

Sin-d ambled over, recognized us right off, and said, "Hi-ya. Good to see yous twos again. Oh, an' looky you, you went an' got all yer purdy hair cut off. Looks real cute, too. You twos want two more Tequila Sunrises-es, eh?"

"Fur sure."

This time nearly half of the patrons were women, *well*—sort of. There were some tough-looking gals in buffalo plaids, for sure, but some were "normal" and some resembled my Aunt Lenore, with bad haircuts, stretchy polyester pantsuits, and oversize purses. There were factory workers, teachers, nurses, secretaries, and mothers, and Linda was simply delighted.

When Sin-d brought around the next two drinks we felt much more relaxed. But then we were rudely interrupted by an old geezer who stopped by to inquire if Linda was a young man, which made her just beam.

In the meantime we sipped cocktail, smoked, and watched two women in blue factory work pants playing pool. They seemed to be having a real good time of it while swilling beers, smoking fags, and joking. Linda, being more broad-minded, was intently watching the women shooting stick, and I followed the dance floor and the elegantly dancing dicks. In all my life I had never seen two men dancing together like that, and there was a dance floor full of them. It was sensationally scandalous.

Linda seemed to take an immediate shine to the little Latina playing pool. Her brand-new blue cotton work pants had six inches of cuff rolled up as if she was expecting a flood soon and her clean but well-faded chambray shirt had the sleeves rolled up, revealing muscular arms that were accustomed to doing manual labor. Shiny black eyes twinkled when she laughed, and a broad crooked smile revealed pearly white teeth that sharply contrasted her cinnamon skin.

"Hey, I got a joke for yous guys. What did the one potato chip say to the other potato chip?"

"What? You don't know? Okay, here it is. The potato chip says, 'Are you free-to-lay?' Get it, 'Frito Lay'?"

Everyone within earshot laughed—including me, because we were eavesdropping, and the joke was just plain corny. Linda beamed from ear to ear, shining at the little brown-skinned woman with the crooked grin, and she smiled back just as warmly. The rest, as they say, is her-story.

Less than a month later Linda had moved into Rose Sanchez's little red, white, and blue mobile home in Bridgeport, where they started their blissful lesbian lives together, and raised a strange little family of nervous diabetic Chihuahuas and abandoned stray cats.

The Summer of My Disco Tent

$\mathcal{L}$inda and Rose were happier than two people were entitled to be. You couldn't wipe the disgusting smiles from their beaming faces. After a year of connubial bliss, their odd little family consisted of two lesbians, three mangy disabled strayed cats, and two overfed diabetic Chihuahuas.

Linda left Flint—and her drug-selling job—to move into Rose's little red, white, and blue trailer in Bridgeport, a low-rent suburb of Saginaw. There she started attending junior college, hoping to earn a degree in musicology, something she'd always wanted to do. She just loved her music. Her lovely Spanish Rose supported and encouraged all her endeavors, as any loving spouse should.

I commenced my second year of college, carrying a large course load of twenty credits, while still selling drugs at Baker's, which made my life quite busy. But there was a silver lining to all this hyperactivity, because now all my prerequisites were fulfilled and I could choose elective courses, classes I actually wanted to take, and painting was my first choice.

For the longest time I had looked forward to professional instruction in painting. I'd already taken just about every painting class, artsy summer workshop, or craft-making class taught in this tacky town. I even took the "Draw Bambi" art test from the back of a magazine and did so well that they sent a recruiter to our house. For the most part, those were small-town classes intended for amateur artists, mere arts and crafters. I was in the big league now—art school, college, among other wannabe artistes, and I wanted to know it all.

At the junior university I hoped to receive the kind of instruction that Leonardo da Vinci, Rembrandt, and Michelangelo received. I wanted to learn the time-honored traditions and work with the methods and mediums of the artistic gods. In fact, I took this all artsy stuff so seriously that I even decided to change my middle name from Leon, which I'd always detested, to Leonardo, because it sounded much more artistic. Don't cha think? Henceforth it shall be, Denial Leonardo Murphy.

On the first day of class I sat clutching a yellow legal pad and blue ballpoint pen, poised to write down the secret formulas that would transform me from a mere small-town paint-by-number amateur into an artiste extraordinaire and a learned member of the art world.

Room 101, commonly called the Painting Room, had a lived-in look and smelled of linseed oil, turpentine, and stale cigarettes. Back then you could smoke in class, because smoking was a civil right. Mott Community College's art school was a long and low international-style building with north-facing floor-to-ceiling windows, which allowed indirect sunlight to flood in all day. Heavy metal easels were scattered around the room, along with mounds of trash, deserted cups with dribbles of unidentifiable brown fluids, ashtrays heaped with stale butts, and a pile of jacketless 33-rpm records atop a radiator.

Along the short west wall were several vertical drying racks made of two-by-two yellow pine firing strips, used to store paintings in different stages of completion. At the opposite end was a filthy stainless steel slop sink with an impossibly stained top. In the corner sat an odd collection of junk: an enormous split-leaf philodendron with gnarly tubular roots spilling from a crusty terra-cotta pot, a bent wire birdcage teetering on a stand, miscellaneous mannequin parts, and an old floor lamp sitting atop a round oak table with crystal ball-and-claw feet. This collection of clutter was either crap used to create still-life arrangements, or a pile of trash ready for collection, a close call either way.

A diverse group of twenty-five people madeup the class, with a wide variety of races and ages. While most were young, like me, some were very old—in their thirties and forties—and all of us were chatting nervously while awaiting the arrival of our professor, Thomas Dolittle. But he was already ten minutes late, and the artsy crowd was getting restless; soon the cigarettes came out, windows were thrown open, and social hour started. Early September's weather was picture-perfect, sunny and warm, so nearly everyone's attention went back outside while smoking, chatting, and lustfully gazing at the luxuriously green, sun-dappled lawn just out of reach.

A striking young woman with wavy copper hair and clear green eyes spontaneously sprang out of her seat and began working, all on her own. Dressed way too nicely for the pigsty of a classroom, she didn't seem to fit in with this group of factory workers, misfits, and hippies.

Placing a clean white lab coat over her classy clothes, she got right down to work. Carrying in an oblong wooden frame, constructed of two-by-two pine strips and measuring three feet by four feet, she laid it on the big work table, cut off a length of canvas, laid it over the frame, started methodically stretching and pulling it tightly around the frame, and tacking it in place with her pretty pink hammer. Silence fell over the room while her classmates watched her work, and she naturally began to narrate.

"First you stretch canvass over the frame and then pound a tack in the center of all four sides. While making sure you're pulling the canvas good and tight, begin putting more tacks in on both sides of the center tack, moving toward the ends, make a hospital corner, and then tack it down real good."

"It looks like you've taken this class before," someone said.

"No, I just transferred here from Kendall, in Grand Rapids, and that's where I learned to make stretcher frames and cover them with canvas." Everyone watched Darlene as if she was the professor, until someone else asked, "What are you doing now?"

"I'm priming the canvas. This thick white glop is called gesso, and it's a mixture of chalk and glue that acts as a barrier. If you don't prime the canvas with this stuff, the paint keeps soaking in and you'll waste a whole lot of expensive paint. Personally, I like to put on three good coats. First paint on a coat, dry that, and then sand it smooth. Then put on the second coat, dry and sand it, and then do a third. It'll make your canvas smooth as a baby's butt."

The class chuckled.

"Usually I'll use a hair dryer to speed things up, but I forgot it today."

Twenty minutes later Professor Darlene was ready to paint her stretched and primed canvas, when we were distracted by the creaking of a door and a sudden gush of hot summer wind that flew through the room. But the open windows had created a vacuum, which sucked the door shut with a thunderous *kaboom*, rattling the windows and scaring the shit out of everyone.

The sonic boom was caused by an incredibly disheveled young man with wildly unruly, just-slept-in hair, and wiry mustache sprinkled with food crumbs. He slowly lumbered into the room. Big bushy eyebrows were perched over his crossed crooked eyes making me think of young Albert Einstein, if he were cross-eyed, homeless, and spoke like Sylvester the putty tat.

"Tho thorry I'm tho late. And thorry 'bout the thlammin' door, too. Got here late lath night, drove all the way from California, and overthlept. There's that three-hour time-change thing. Anybody got a thigarette?" he asked, while squinting and scanning the classroom for contraband.

"Anybody got a thigarette?" he asked again, till finally someone handed him a fag. "Anybody got a light?" he inquired, while frisking his body until handed one. Lighting it, he took a deep drag, exhaled, and absentmindedly put the "borrowed" lighter into his wrinkled pants pocket.

"So thith it the painting room, huh? Look real nith. I'm your in-thuctor. Name is Thom, and you can call me that." Reaching over and lifting a waxed-paper cup from a pile of trash on the work table, he brought the cup extremely close to his crossed eyes, examined the deserted contents, sniffed it, and then threw back the cup, downing the long-abandoned fluid in one fell swoop. It was brown. I couldn't tell if it was coffee, old soda, or used turpentine.

He certainly didn't look very professorial, dressed in a horizontally striped black-and-white collarless shirt that looked like it belonged to a homeless gondolier who'd been sleeping in it for a week, and three-inches-too-short crumpled black cotton pants.

"Tho, thith is Painting 101 and 102, look real nith. Now, ath far ath I'm contherned, you can do whatever kind of painting you want. I don't care if you youth thick paint or thin, work modernly or clathi-cally, all I ath ith that you complete four painting by the end of the themester. You can paint at home if you'd like or here in clath; doesn't matter to me."

Spying an abandoned bagel lying in the same trash pile as the mystery liquid he just finished swilling, he lifted it, held it up to his crossed eyes, and examined it closely. "Thith belong to anyone?"

There was no response but perplexity. That damn thing was pet-rified, weeks if not months old, hardtack. No one said a word as he sniffed it and then bit down really hard, snapping it in two as if it was a dried twig, and sending crumbs flying. Completely oblivious to everyone's revulsion, he continued prattling away, and crunching while spewing crumby shrapnel around the room.

"Tho, what you got goin' here, anyway?" he asked Darlene.

"I'm preparing a canvas for painting."

Crunch, crunch, crunch. "Okay. Look real good, too." *Crunch, crunch, crunch.* "I gotta go now, tho everybody who ith here check your name off the lith before you leave here, tho I'll know whoth here and not. I'll thee you next, when? When doth thith clath meet anyway?"

"Tuethday and Thurthday from nine to noon," someone offered. Without saying a word, he exited and absentmindedly left the door agape, and the vacuum immediately sucked the door shut with another thunderous, earsplitting sonic boom, startling the shit out of everyone and making the two Vietnam vets jump right out of their chairs.

Once the classroom was settled, we returned our attention to Professor Darlene, who was sorting through a pile of dusty warped records. Finding one she liked, she used the sleeve of her sanitary lab coat to wipe off the dust and pursed her lipsticked lips to blow off the rest. Placing it onto the turntable, she lifted the arm, dropped the needle, and Crosby, Stills, Nash and Young began to harmonize for us.

"*Love*...is coming, coming to us *all*..."

⟩ ⟩

Still operating on California time, Professor Thom made regular tardy appearances in class, always disheveled, usually famished, munching down any unattended or abandoned food morsels, and downing any deserted drinks within reach. We learned this was his first teaching job, but Darlene did most of the real instruction, teaching us where to buy lumber for the stretcher frames, how to use the radial saw to miter the wood, and construct the frames. We also noted how confidently she went about executing her paintings, with a whimsical abstract expressionist flair and commercial polish.

Way before attending college, I'd learned the basics of painting—color mixing, perspective, and shading—from reading books and traditional instruction. Art school exposed me to scale. In college you did things big: big paintings, big sculptures, and big mistakes. Somehow the larger your works were the more legitimate you were. Intense artistic debates about how much paint you should be using—thick vs. thin; oil paints vs. acrylic—and which school of painting you adhered to—classical vs. minimal, abstract, abstract expressionist, or blazing your own path—were constantly ongoing, and it was all so very important.

Then much to everyone's delight, the sonic booming door was propped open to stop it from slamming. Apparently the open door was inviting, because soon a Mr. Coffee machine appeared, then a toaster oven, and the unofficial art-student lounge was born. The buzz of conversations and the smells of cigarette smoke and coffee brewing, and the rhythm from records playing attracted all sorts. Maybe it was the more relaxed California concept introduced by Thom, or the times, but something was working in this uninhibited and inviting environment, and quality artwork was being produced.

Two weeks into the semester a critique was called. For those of you who don't know, that is an endless masturbatory discussion. It could be about the painting you were currently working on, the one you've completed, or the artwork you were thinking of doing someday down the road; basically a circle jerk sales pitch. Thom would usually show up late, completely disheveled, smoking up the abandoned butts and drinking down any leftover lifeless liquids, and holding hold court in the crummy burgundy, no-hair mohair chair.

I was proud to exhibit my first completed canvas, a realistic rendering of a large school of tarpon swimming in crystal clear water, painted in fluid blues, silvers, and yellows that looked like you were under the water swimming with the fishes, only in a good way.

Thom listened intently as each student presented his or her painting and discussed its many merits. He was quite encouraging, telling you to try a little of thith or that, and asking if you were familiar with the work of thith perthon or that the other. But he never really instructed. His method was more about self-discovery, letting you figure it out yourself, like driving from Flint to Florida without a map. Jump in, head south, and you'll get there eventually.

— ~ —

Chuck, a childhood acquaintance from grade school at Saint Luke's, was also in the class, and he was quite an accomplished artist, gifted at rendering and painting. Being buddies, we naturally worked on easels right next to each other.

"Hey, Den, you ever see that movie *Reefer Madness*? It's playing this weekend at the North Flint Drive-In."

"No, I've never heard of it. Is it supposed to be good?"

"It's ancient as hell, from the thirties or forties, I think, and supposed to be a real hoot. It's showing in a triple feature along with *Boxcar Bertha* and *Easy Rider*. Doesn't that sound like fun?"

"Sure does," said the tall guy standing next to Chuck, with the curly white-boy afro. We both laughed, because Randy had apparently been eavesdropping. An older man of maybe four or five years, he'd served in Vietnam before attending college on the GI Bill. He seemed comfortable with the group, was kind of goofy and his laughter was infectious, and people enjoyed being around him. The girls all seemed to like his piercing blue-gray wolf-like eyes and long lashes. And it seems he'd invited himself into our conversation and plans for Saturday night.

"What the hell, the more the merrier," I said.

"Sure, what the hell," Chuck agreed. "It'll be a hoot! We'll get twisted and laugh our asses off."

— ᴖ —

When Saturday evening arrived, and my drug-selling shift ended (I'd graduated from alcohol to drugs when Linda left), I called Chuck to let him know I was on my way.

"Hold up, dude. Sorry, but I'm goin' to have-ta bail tonight; all this shit just came down at the last minute and I gotta stay home. But hey, Randy still wants to go. Said he can drive, too, so give his a call, dude. Maaaan, I sure wish I was going."

Ten minutes later a muscular '71 Malibu Super Sport V-8, burgundy with black leather bucket seats, shiny chromed wheels, and dual chromed exhausts, came chugging into the parking lot. The heavy passenger door automatically swung open.

"Hop in," Randy commanded.

"Too bad Chuck couldn't make it, it's supposed to be a hoot," I said. After stuffing two bottles of too-sweet wine and several salty snacks into the backseat, I closed the door, and it rattled with a resounding thud. Randy placed his rod into gear and demonstrated what his muscle car was made of.

"Nice car," I said, as I felt G forces lay me back in the cushy Corinthian leather seat.

Arriving late, we found the first movie playing. Approaching the tiny carnival-looking ticket booth, he pulled out his wallet and automatically paid for both tickets.

"Here you go," I said, passing him a fiver.

"Fuh-get about it," he said in Three Stooges style, pushing the money away.

His low-hung street rod chugged in, searched the back row for a secluded spot so we could safely drink our outlawed alcohol in private, and backed in.

"You want the Annie Green Springs or Boone's Farm Apple? They're both sweet as pop."

"Hell, it don't matter to me, buzzed is buzzed. Just give me one," he said, taking the apple.

With the speaker inside and movie playing, we unscrewed our own bottles—so we wouldn't get cooties. *Boxcar Bertha* was already playing, so we tilted back the bucket seats and enjoyed the movie.

Randy reached into his pocket and pulled a pregnant marijuana joint out, held it up, broadly grinned and said, "I got wacky tabackee. You cool?"

"Absolutely."

Sparking the fatty up, he took a long leisurely drag, laid his curly mop on the leather headrest, and held the smoke inside his lungs as long as he could. Then he slowly exhaled the spicy intoxicating smoke, and it lazily circled and danced about the spacious cab, and surely smelled good. Unlike Bill Clinton, I inhaled deeply.

"Hey! *Easy there*, sport," he said in warning. "That's not a cigarette, ya know. That's called lung buster." Less than a second later I knew exactly why they called it that, as I attempted to hack my lungs onto the car's shiny metal dashboard.

"*Hack, hack, hack,* good stuff," I affirmed between fits of crying, laughing, and hacking. Between coughing fits we chatted about painting class and Chuck, laughed a lot, and barely watched the cheesy movie. Strangely, after sharing an entire joint and half bottle of sickeningly sweet wine, I couldn't relax and didn't get buzzed, because something about him made me nervous. His presence was palpable. He felt close inside this spacious cab. And he smelled really good, clean like soap.

Every so often I sensed him gazing at me, and when I'd glance in his direction he'd meet my gaze and smile back, like the mischievous cat smiles at a pretty peach canary singing inside a locked cage, while holding the key in his clenched paw.

I will admit it was a nice face, handsome even, with sapphire blue "bedroom eyes." And he was over six feet tall. Being vertically challenged, I'd always wanted to be tall. Yes, I'd noticed him.

Suddenly I felt a hand on my thigh.

It was not mine.

I glanced at the hand, and then up to Randy, who was now grinning from ear to ear.

"What are you doing?" I asked...after an extended awkward delay.

"You're kidding, right? You don't need to play dumb with me, because I know about you."

"What?"

"I saw you there."

"What? What are you talking about?"

"It's all right with me, because I was there, too."

"What?"

"The Pink Poodle, I saw you there."

Oh my God! "No, no, no. You don't understand. You're making a big mistake; I was there with a friend, Linda. I'm not like that."

He kept smiling, and all the while slowly easing his big warm hand farther up my thigh, inching up my leg, inching, inching, inching, and stopping perilously short of my danger zone.

I felt paralyzed.

I could not move.

I didn't breathe.

At the same time I felt myself becoming aroused, my slacks growing taut.

Homo-erectus.

My lips may have been saying no, no, no, but I could not hide the forming erection.

Randy saw it, too, smiled even more, and moved his hand one last time.

I did not protest.

— —

For the longest time I wanted something like this to happen, but I never thought it would be like this, or here, and with him.

"I saw you there."

Et Tu, Bubba?

"Denial?

"Hey, Linda."

"Is everything all right?"

"Yeah, everything's fine, how 'bout you?"

"What are you doin' here?"

"Having a few beers. Is Rose here?"

"*Well, yeah!* Now, I've asked you twice, what are you doing here?"

"I'm sorry, Linda; let me introduce you to my *buddy* Randy. He's in my painting class."

"Hi, Randy. Haven't I seen you here before? Aren't you friends with that hairdresser, Nick?"

"Why yes, I am his friend. It's nice to meet you, Linda. I've heard so many nice things about you. And this must be the lovely Rose. Nice to meet you, too," he said in his charming way, extending his hand and smiling warmly.

"So, honey, you got somethin' you wanna tell me, or what? Out with it."

Randy bent down from his six-foot perch and pulled me closer, placing a wet smacking kiss squarely on my lips. Nuzzling his curly blond mop on my shoulder, he said, "Out with it, Den. Do you have something to tell her...well do ya, do ya?"

THE GAYS OF OUR LIVES

"Randy and I...are...sort of...seeing each other."

"Really? When did this happen? Why didn't you tell me?"

"I just found out."

"Complicated, isn't it?"

"It certainly is. But Randy helped me feel better a lot about it, if you know what I mean."

"Rose, would you like to dance?" Randy said, trying to escape the awkward inquisition.

"No, thanks," she politely declined.

"Well it sounds like a great idea to me," I said, quickly accepting his offer and fleeing.

Randy, taking my hand, led me to the dance floor, and we were off. I didn't know it at the time, but he was one of the elegant dancers whom I'd admired the second time I was there. And as you may have heard, the third time is the charm. Disco dominated The Poodle now, and Randy could really do a lusty hustle. He slid a satiny arm around my twenty-eight-inch waist and rested it on the big white belt of my burgundy bell-bottomed slacks; pulled me closer, and we became one on the dance floor.

Luckily, platform shoes were the rage then, because they made me a full three inches taller, which topped me out at a whopping five feet nine. Now tell me, what man doesn't want three more inches? But even with my elevator shoes set on penthouse, and my biggest feathered-back *Saturday Night Fever* disco hair, I was still inches shorter than Randy.

When "The Hustle" finished playing we joined the girls, to make on big woman. "You guys looked just like the dancers on *Lawrence Welk*," Linda said. "Now sid-down, Bubba, 'cause I got a *whooole* lotta questions to ask you."

So she proceeded to grill me in depth, as to who said what to whom, and when? Then she asked me where this was going, and where we were registered? Womyn look at relationships differently than men do. Christ, Dyke Linda and her Spanish Rose were hitched after dating for only three weeks, and they registeres at Farm and Fleet. While as I was being grilled, Rose and Randy became acquainted, bonding over Budweisers and discovering they worked in the same plant. Small world.

Evolution revolution. The interior of the Pink Poodle had changed significantly in the year since my last visit. Motown had moved out, and disco moved in. The rickety red vinyl booths were replaced with sleek, round, black-topped café tables with chromed legs, and black metal chairs with black vinyl cushions. The dance floor, although still front and center, was now elevated a full ten inches, and even more important than before. But even more lofty was the disc jockey's station, and that pissy queen's throne towered a full foot above the commoners on the dance floor.

The ten-inch-tall dance floors' platform was constructed from clear Lucite panels. From within the stage came a rainbow of flashing multicolored lights in shades of red, blue, yellow, and green that pulsated in sync with the driving disco beat. Intermittently eerie strobe lights would pierce the smoky darkness, creating hypnotic fragmented dreamlike sensations, and adding to the illusion.

Everyone was on the stage now. Everyone was in the spotlights. Everyone was a star.

Overhanging this flashy platform was a twirling twinkling disco ball covered with hundreds of tiny mirrored tiles, and when hit with a white-hot spotlight, the glittering spinning orb sent a myriad of rainbows dancing around the smoky bar. The tacky tin foil ceiling was replaced with real mirror tiles, and the jukebox was replaced by the disc jockey. Now the DJ was the center of attention, spinning the nearly recent records and controlling the lights.

Way in the back, in the very, very back, the very scary bathrooms were renovated, too, with sunny yellow ceramic tiles on the walls and floors, and a sparkling white porcelain urinal replacing the tacky old tin pissin' bin. A glistening new porcelain throne was installed for the queens, and a sparkling white sink with chromed stiletto legs, to wash their dainty pinkies. Floating above the pissy urinal and high-heeled sink was a plate glass mirror, onto which some prankster has written a message in cock-sucker-red lipstick: "Blow jobs fifty cents, with lipstick a dollar."

Few women in this establishment wore lipstick. Linda and Rose certainly didn't wear any. They were two old married women by now, and just when were having fun they called it quits.

"Pussies," we said.

"Queens," they replied. "Now, 'member, Bubba, you got some 'splainin' to do."

"Come on, Linda. Let's leave those lovebirds alone," Rose said, mercifully cutting Linda off.

— —

Later that night...

"Well...would you look who's queer—it's Nick. You remember my friend Nick, Denny? But you probably don't know we took dance classes to-gether at Arthur Murray's, over on Corunna Road."

"Hello, Nick, it's nice to meet you. I've seen you and your brother walking your dog in the neighborhood quite often. I live around the corner from you, on Pierson Street."

"Yes, I remember you, too. You're the munchkin who lives above Frieda French, aren't you?"

"Hey Randy, I just love this song, 'Love Hangover.' Let's you and me tear up the dance floor. Excuse me for stealing your boyfriend, hon," Nick said, fleeing with Randy in tow.

As they floated effortlessly around the illuminated stage it became immediately apparent they were professionals. The crowd parted, leaving them the floor, and they elegantly twirled as if it was an ev-eryday thing, like going to the grocery store. Seeing them glued to-gether dancing that way I suddenly felt a twinge of jealousy, because clearly they had history. Was I actually threatened by this skinny, old, bleached-blond disco queen?

After a rousing round of applause from adoring onlookers, and several bows from Nick, they flopped back into their chairs, completely drenched with sweat, and gulped down their cocktails in an effort to cool off. And while wheezing and panting, they lit up another cigarette.

"Waitress! Waitress! Jesus, you can never find that blind midget cunt when you need her. Where the hell is that old lesbian Sin-d, anyway?" Nick demanded.

"Did you miss me, baby?" Randy said, stooping to plant a cool and salty kiss upon my lips.

"You two really looked good out there. Really—everybody said so."

"I'd like to thank all the little people," Nick said, standing and waving a paper napkin to the crowd, and acting as if he'd just received an award for his performance. "Just throw money!"

"Oh God! Speakin' of money, that reminds me of a story, I've *got* to tell you guys this terrible thing that happened to me the other day. One of my dearest old clients, Mary Lou Whitney—filthy rich, ya know, been with me for just years. Well, she up and died on me."

"Right in your chair, Nick? My God, that's so terrible," Randy said.

"Not in my chair, silly boy. Now shut up and quit interrupting me. Now, as I was sayin', old Mary Lou had been sick for the longest time; had the cancer, ya know. *Well*...she was in to get her hair done, and as I was dyin' her, she told me she was dyin'. It was so sad. So sad. Then she asked me if I'd do her hair one last time. 'Make me beautiful to meet my maker, will you, Nicky?'

"*Well*, I broke down and bawled like a baby. I was so distraught that Stewart had to finish her up, I was just a blubberin' mess." He was welling up just retelling the story.

"So, last night, during that fucking thunderstorm we had, I headed over to the House of Diggs' Funeral Home to do Mary Sue's hair for the very last time. Well, I'd stupidly lent my beauty travel-cart to someone so I didn't have it, and I had to borrow one. So there I was, hauling all my beauty supplies in a pink plastic piece of shit, through a fucking hurricane, and getting completely soaked.

"Well, I was beating on the door and screaming like a goddamn crazy woman trying to escape the asylum, when finally the door creaks open, and there stands Lurch. Without saying a word he leads me through the dimly lit funeral home, down the stairs, and into the dungeon. Now you remember, I'm soaking wet, and I like it cold, but it was like middle of fucking January down there. Then he leads me into the dingy room where they fix up the stiffs, and there was bony old Mary Sue, dead as a door nail and lying on a stainless steel slab, and naked as a jaybird. Well I was mortified, but she woulda been more mortified if she'd a known I saw her dried-up old bacon strip like that, *Jesus!*

"*Well*, the first thing I did was take my leopard-print beauty smock and covered-up all her wrinkled old business up, so I wouldn't have to look at that nastiness while I was working on her. Now remember, I was the only living soul down there, completely surrounded with dead people, and it was excruciatingly quiet. The only sound was the annoying buzz of those hideous fluorescent lights, and as you well know, they are the worst thing there is for putting on your makeup.

"Now, I had to do her hair *and* her makeup, and she looked just ghastly; the cancer, you know. That's when it hit me, and I got really sad, because I'd just lost a client, friend, and a nice fat check every week. Well, I started to bawl. 'Damn it,' I said, 'I'm not going to do this, I am not going to cry. I hate it when I do that.' But I blubbered away anyway.

"I could hardly see through my tears as I was putting on her false eyelashes, finishing-up her makeup, back-combing her hair, and dousing it with a goddamned good coat of hairspray, because that 'do was going to have to last her an eternity. Then the lights flickered. And then they flickered again.

"'*Jesus!*' I shrieked. *Well*...they nearly got another stiff, because my heart nearly stopped beating, right then and there. Before the lights could flicker again, I hightailed it for the goddamn door, but I didn't make it before the lights went completely out. Jesus! There I was, trapped in a dungeon full of dead people, on a stormy night, and screaming bloody murder. '*Help*! *Help*! Somebody help me!'

"*Well*, I screamed like a Sunday schoolgirl bein' raped by the devil himself, but nobody ever came to my rescue. Was nobody there but the stiffs. Then I sat down on the cold cement floor and bawled like a baby, and I hate it when I do that.

"*Well*, I sat there bawling for a good five minutes before I remembered I had a lighter in the pocket of my beauty smock, and a joint I was saving for when all this bullshit was over. What the hell, if I was gonna die, at least I was gonna die happy. So I took out the lighter and sparked the fucker up.

"*Well*, I puffed and I prayed, puffed and prayed, but nobody ever came to my aid. But then my nerve medicine started to kick in, and I started feeling a little better. Then I had an illuminating idea: I'd use the lighter like a flashlight to find my way outta there. *Well*... I had to keep switching hands because it was burning my thumbs; it was just terrible, I tell ya. Just look at these blisters, would ya."

He proudly displayed both slender thumbs for everyone to inspect the invisible warmed spots. "*Well*, I made it safely to the door only to find another dark room. Somehow I made it safely through that room without touching any dead stuff, just to find another pitch-black room. And you'd better believe I was sayin my prayers the whole way, 'Dear Jesus, get me the hell out of here alive and I promise I'll be good. I really meant it this time. *Really*.'

"And wouldn't you know it, right before I made it to the exit the lights came back on. 'Thank you, Jesus!' *Well*, you'd better believe I got right back in there and finished her up right damn quick, I kissed her on the cheek, said goodbye, and got the hell out of there. *Jesus*!"

— ◆ —

He kept us entertained all evening by sharing silly stories and telling off-color jokes. He'd definitely missed his calling, and should have been on the stage or in the movies. But I'm fairly certain, that in his mind he already thought of himself as a star. Between jokes and stories he danced the evening away—with anyone who asked—man, woman, or...whatever.

That night he was looking particularly fetching, in a monochromatic beige suede leisure suit ensemble with a bolero jacket, stove-pipe slacks, and shoes dyed to match. And everything was the exact same shade as his big blond hair. But I no longer felt threatened by him, because I noticed he had his baby blues set upon a certain someone—his handsome, hunky, ebony dancing partner, Dick Shaft.

Mr. Shaft was looking pretty sexy that night as well, in a two-piece Kelly green leisure suit. But his bolero jacket and white polyester disco-shirt were unbuttoned all the way down to his fat black belt, revealing his taut muscular blue-black chest, and this dramatic juxtaposition of blue-black against white formed a big arrow that pointed down to his well-rounded crotch; highlighting his more than generous "personality." The two of them were practically giving off smoke while dancing, appeared to be joined at the hip, and having full-out sex on the dance floor. He could really do a mean down-and-dirty, that Nick Clark. They were that good, sssssssssssssssssssssssssssssteamy.

"Look at the two of them. There oughta be a law," Randy said. And then he yelled, "For Christ's sake, get yourselves a room," even louder.

Bam-Bam, Ma'am

Usually I would run into Kim at the Saint Vincent de Paul, Goodwill, Salvation Army, or one of the other thrift stores that littered Flint back then. Hooked on the junk, he was. I could tell...'cause I'd acquired a taste for the stuff myself.

You really couldn't miss him, because he drove a bubble-gum pink Volkswagen Beetle with the "Dental Depot" logo splashed all over it, and jokingly refer to himself as "the Tooth Fairy." His job was picking up dental impressions around town and delivering them back to the lab. He often whined it wasn't very challenging; in fact, he often complained he hated the job, but his impressionable job made it possible for him to visit every thrift store and yard sale in the city while making his daily appointed rounds. Strangely, we both gravitated toward the similar items, each appreciating midcentury modern and skank (fifties furnishings with severe angular lines).

Belying his nickname, the Tooth Fairy had an unusually deep, coarse, and raspy voice, sounding like someone who smoked and drank for a lifetime. And with sort of mismatched features, he looked kind of unusual. Not displeasing, mind you, just peculiar. Always a dapper dresser, he exclusively wore "period clothes" from the 1940s instead of the seventies. Imagine spit-shined vintage shoes paired with high-draped pleated pants, a coordinating rayon jacket, and a shirt ironed with a crease so sharp you'd cut yourself if you weren't careful.

Warm brown, nearly black eyes and a coarse mop of slicked-back, shiny-black, closely cropped hair made him look Mexican, but he was Irish, dark Irish. Being an anxious nervous sort, he couldn't sit still; had what my dad called the "Saint Vitus Dance." But he had an excellent eye for junk.

Kim could home in on anything of value, buy it, and blow out with the goods before anyone else even knew they were there. With an impressive knowledge of periods, brands, and manufacturers, he was like a sponge absorbing data relating to junk. He was great fun to go junking with, too, making it festive by bringing along a shiny chrome shaker of cocktails and salty snacks. But you'd better watch him closely, because he'd run you over and wrestle you to the ground while trying to get at something he wanted. Rutting and digging, he'd search for diamonds in the rough, and more often than not, find them. There were few others were attuned to his particular frequency. He was a junk savant with an avant-garde flair.

When I first met Kim, he was twenty-two and still living with his parents. I may have been a flaky fruity artist, but when compared with him, I was a Republican ultraconservative. Although he was polite and respectful, he was certainly no wallflower. His look was always edgy and extreme, attention grabbing and flashy. You couldn't miss him, he made sure of it. He was smart, funny, and attractive, and yet strangely insecure; had an excellent eye for style and design, but was a bad judge of character.

During the late seventies I was working in the display department of a major department store, and Kim was hired, at my request, as holiday help. For some odd reason the management liked him, and he was hired as the trimmer for the men's department. Kim absolutely adored working in visual display, or VD as we lovingly called our occupation, and especially in the men's area, because while working he got to ogle all the handsome male patrons. But he also had a severe case of ADD, and he often gawked more than he worked, being easily distracted by a handsome face or manly cut.

We were not the only twits working in the store either; there were others. Bucky, the odd British hunchbacked dandy who worked in the men's fragrance area, was a *big ol'* fagela, and the management asked that he please be kept *behind* the counter at all times. Old black Sam sold men's suits and told the filthiest jokes you've ever heard; but you'd never have guessed he was "that way," because he was "on the down low." Then there was Mark, the weird lecherous hillbilly who measured inseams for trousers. He was just plain weird. But in his defense, he was from Ohio and probably couldn't help it. There also were a couple of "for-sures" in the beauty salon—duh—Uncle Peter in housewares, Uncle Marge in display—duh, again—and there were one or two hummers in the restaurant's kitchen, too.

Kim enjoyed being "out in the mall." From atop a ladder he observed the high life and thought things looked better from up there. Soon he was getting lofty ideas about himself as well when he began hanging out with what he considered to be an exclusive crowd. To him the party life was the beautiful life, high fashion, high drama, and high all the time; drinking, drugging, and sexing became his favorite new obsession. Work just got in the way.

Dressing to the nines each night, he would crawl the seedy nightclubs celebrating with his chic new clique of trendy friends, and after the bars closed he moved to the even seedier after-hour clubs to carry on till dawn. That's where he felt most alive. Buzzed by drink, emboldened by drugs, he had plenty of energy for dancing, partying, and staying up all night and screwing. What the hell, he could always catch a few winks in a secluded stockroom at work the next day.

—✦—

"Hey, Den, have you ever had sex with a midget?"

"*What?* No. In fact, I don't believe I've ever met a midget, Kim."

"You probably won't believe this, but I met me this midget in the tubs (gay bathhouse) last night, and his goddamned dick was dragging in the dirt. I swear to God, Denny, I never saw anything like it. His torso was normal-sized, like a real mans, but his arms and legs were short and midget like; they called him tripod. Maaan, I am fuckin' exhausted."

"Kim, we have to move the entire menswear department today, so don't go crawling into some stairwell to sleep it off when we have all this work to do."

"Jesus Mary, who died and made you queen anyway?"

But then he started hanging with an even trendier group, Detroiters, big-city faggots. He so wanted to belong to a posh posse. But those discriminating groups often ruled by exclusion rather than inclusion. Gay-on-gay discrimination is quite common. They're NOC—Not Our Crowd. No fats, fems, phonies, oldies, or uglies wanted. Acceptance and approval were the carrots hanging in front of the cart, and the ones he could never quite reach. The approval he sought was an elusive and continually moving target, and never granted. The acceptance he sought was denied, and it is such a small thing to give.

For reasons I don't understand, he desperately needed to be accepted. Whatever the current trends were, he recognized them and used them to his advantage. He had the biggest glam-rocker hair, longest sideburns, and the boldest eye-catching clothes in the loudest prints. When platform shoes were the rage he had the tallest ones—with goldfish in the heels—and when bell bottoms were the rage he wore low-rider, hip-hugger elephant bells, paired with the widest belt with the biggest and brassiest buckle. You get the picture. He was an extremist, and a victim of his own excess-es.

Definitely having a distinctive style, he followed the current trends and cleverly adapted them to fit his thrift-store expense account, always looking smart, chic, "interesting," and most unusual. But he wasn't completely self-centered, because he had a genuinely generous side, too. If you collected some-thing, such as china elephants, he'd pick them up, and before long you'd have a collection of over two hundred, even though you never bought a single one. He often gifted you with small tokens he thought you'd need or could use, and was quite thoughtful that way.

Often we would swap and share clothes, like girlfriends do, because we wore the same sizes. But he'd get really pissed when he found vintage shoes in my size, because he couldn't borrow those. He'd buy them for me, just the same. I still have a pair of black-and-white spectators he bought me nearly forty years ago that are in mint condition, but how many occasions do you have that call for those? I will admit they were a hit at trendy New York loft parties.

— —

In the early eighties destiny beckoned and Kim followed his star west to tinsel town, Hollywood; land of swimming pools and movie stars. Fleeing Flint in one of the mass migrations of the early eighties, he left around the same time that I departed for New York City.

Kim hitched a ride way out west with a fruitcake nutcase named Paul and his artistic boyfriend, Phil, and the ménage et twits moved using money that Paul collected from an insurance settlement. Now, Paul claimed that an elderly man—on his way to church one Sunday morning—careened around a corner, lost control of his Chrysler Cordoba convertible, and T-boned it into his pink Edsel sedan. But what he forgot to mention was that *he* was driving home, drunk and sleepy after partying at the Pink Poodle till closing and then slithering in an even seedier after-hours club called the Last Dog Hung.

Now, Paul claimed that the accident—which involved a minor head injury requiring a Hello Kitty bandage—caused him to become queer. In an attempt to convince the jury he was once straight he brought in his *former* high school girlfriend and used her as a witness and alibi. She solemnly swore on the Bible that they were once paramours, and even had "you-know-what." Promiscuous prom pictures taken with his alibi/witness/date only added further proof of his former heterosexuality. But it was a good thing the picturers were black-and-white, because they were dressed in coordinating purple outfits with their hair dyed a lovely lavender shade to match.

Paul proceeded to proselytize to the court about his strict religious upbringing, and repeatedly reminded them that his pop was a Pentacostal preacher. He also proudly professed his former athletic prowess and gladly provided Polaroids of him wearing his junior-varsity letter sweater. But he never once mentioned that the letter was earned for cheerleading.

Slouching at six-two, he weighed maybe 101 at the most, was painfully skinny, awkward, and twitchy. An enormous beak of a nose dominated his pale peaked face, making his other features look tiny and puppet-like. An anemic patch of hillbilly hair—which you couldn't quite call a goatee—sat on his puny pointed chin, and when paired with a nearly invisible adolescent boy's-size mustache, baby-fine dish-water-blond hair, alabaster skin, and gray-blue eyes, he nearly appeared albino.

Hell, he was so goddamned swishy that his portrait appeared on the queer three-dollar bill. Anyone in the courtroom, including the blind stenographer, could see he was fruity as can be as he gaily pranced around. He even had the audacity to wear a floor-length raccoon fur coat and skin-tight turquoise spandex stirrup pants—without any legal briefs (commando). His garish pink paisley shirt was impossible to miss, but in case you did, an armful of brassy bracelets and bangles bounced from bony elbow to limp wrist, clinking, clanging, and noisily banging away like wind chimes in a cyclone as he wiggled, wriggled, and twitched, so you constantly heard him even if you couldn't see him.

But I do believe the clincher came to a climax during courtroom recess, when he pulled out a big black, smelly overripe banana, slowly and sensuously peeled it, and performed fellatio on it before consuming it. This abhorrent performance made it abundantly clear there was no question at all he was totally queer. The dispute was never whether he was a faggot or not—that much was painfully clear. Was the "accident" the cause of the homosexuality abnormality? *That* was the question here.

A jury of twelve good God-fearing folks decided he was definitely damaged, and quite clearly queer, and paid him some money to get him the hell out of there.

So, after packing his pink-and-gray Rambler station wagon with vintage treasures, they took the funny money and headed west. While winding through the wilds of western Wyoming on scenic Route 66, Paul spied a burly cowboy driving a rusty turquoise pickup truck with his wooly white poodle sticking his head out the driver's side window, and finds the vision inspirational.

Paul arrived in Hollywood divinely inspired, with a pile of queer money in his purse, and the dream of becoming famous and rich, just like everyone else. Luckily he found a vacant storefront on Melrose just before the area becomes trendy, opens his inspirational store, and calls it Cowboys and Poodles. His chic new boutique exclusively sold "vintage" clothes, and for those who don't know the term, that means old clothes, many being decades old, and some still having the original packaging.

Poof... they were an instant success, become big poofs, and are embraced by the fashionable trendies and quirky natives. Instantly the hipsters, celebrities, and wannabes begin flocking into their trendy boutique to buy high-priced fashions from yesteryear, from tinsel town's latest immigrant queer. Their ultra-chic resale boutique gets critiqued by fashionable magazines and, just like in the movies, they became overnight successes.

"*They Say*" that people move to California to become someone else, so they do just that; Kim becomes Bam-Bam, Paul becomes Whitey Mandingo, and Phil become Philppe. And then they all pretend they are rich and famous.

Kim—excuse me, Bam-Bam—called me in New York City from time to time, and usually at three in the morning, to report his accomplishments, acquisitions, celebrity sightings, and boast about the latest lavish Hollywood parties he'd attended.

"Denny, you won't believe who was in the store yesterday, so I'll just tell ya: Goldie Hawn, and she was in with that hunky, hot-assed boyfriend, Kurt Russell. Damn, he's so fucking hot, *ouccch*! Oh, oh, oh, and I saw Zsa Zsa, and I saw Cher, and I saw Tina, and I saw Bette, and I saw, and I saw..." Christ almighty, you'd think he was a goddamn lumberjack with all that sawing going on.

Well, it seems life was one amazing adventure after another for Bam-Bam, and him a kid in a candy store with a pocket full of pennies. But wait...*Whitey* had made it big; it was *his* money, *his* idea, his old clothes and *his* fabulously fruity store. But Bam-Bam rode the wave of celebrity, too, just a few notches below Whitey. His photogenic puss often appeared in magazines and he attended the trendiest Hollywood parties, too. And after tasting and embracing the limelight, he was bitten and smitten.

"Denny, you won't believe it; I got my picture in *Italian Vogue,* again! They were at the store doing *another* fucking article on Whitey, so naturally I got myself all dolled up, just in case. And I was lookin' real pretty like; too, you shoulda seen me. I had me this bitchin' buffalo fur vest on, just like Sonny Bono wore on their album *Look At Us,* had me spit-polished, pointed-toe, black Beatles boots, peg-legged pants with a slimming vertical pin stripe, and a purple paisley print Monkey shirt with white cuffs and collar. I tell you, I was stylin' and smilin'.

"As usual Whitey was blabberin' on and on about him shit, so I borrowed me a pink French cigarette and went outside to smoke it. So, there I was, leanin' on a vintage muscle car and puffin' away, when this Italian stallion comes up and says, ''Cues-a me. May I take a peek-sure of Jew and chore Otto-mobile, senor?'

"*Hell*, I don't know who the hell's Otto-mobile it is, but I say, 'Hell yeah, snap away, José.'

"*Bam!* Next thing you know, there I am in *Italian Vogue,* Bam-Bam lookin' fuckin' fabulouso! I couldn't read what the hell it says, 'cause it was in Italian, but I was lookin' damn good in American." And it seemed as if that sort of thing was happening to him all the time. A star was born.

Still being an avid partier, he'd creep around LA's seedy underbelly at night, and consequently he made a mess of new lowlife friends.

While frequenting the underground lounge-lizard party circuit, he befriended many of the waiters who serviced the big Hollywood parties. So he'd often dress to the nines and arrive at a glitzy gayla through the back door, carrying a tray of pate. Once the festivities got going real good, he'd stroll out of the kitchen and into the most fabulous parties ever thrown, with free food, free booze, free baste, and quite often end up getting his pictures in another glossy publication. Always well put together, he was artistic, interesting to look at, and photogenic.

But ego problems quickly arose, because there was room for only one star in Whitey's lofty universe. Consequently he and Bam-Bam had a bitchy little purse fight and parted ways. Not long after separating Whitey made it even bigger, became even more self-aggrandized, found a newer store, nicer house, more outrageous car, older clothes, and a younger twenty-something, hunky male hooker boyfriend named Crotch.

⋯

P.S. Whitey and I are not that friendly anymore either. I will admit he was a very creative individual, but he was also an abusive asshole. At one time I worked with him, but our association ended when he said my duties included having sex with his bony, freakish ass. Just to let you in on a little secret, when I finally had enough of his bullshit I socked him in the jaw, knocking his pasty white, haughty hillbilly ass across his lovely art deco coffee table. We still speak, every twenty years or so.

To tell you the truth I'm surprised he's still alive at all and that someone hasn't killed him dead, because he could be so downright obnoxious. Quite like Al Capone, it was the IRS that finally shut him down for unpaid taxes, taking away his fabulous midcentury-modern home, vintage cars, and both of his businesses, Cowboys and Poodles and his second satellite location affectionately referred to as Cow Poo Two. Last heard, his Crotch left him, and he was living in the jungles of Guatemala exploiting the natives. *Bendiga su corazon* (bless his heart, in Spanish).

Being resourceful, Kim-Bam managed to land on his feet, and stumbled across people with money who wished to do business; together they opened a bizarre new boutique a few blocks from Cow Poo, and called it "Skank World." This chic new showroom was also on Melrose, but here's the kicker: instead of selling old clothes, they retailed used furniture. I'm sorry, vintage furniture; mint-condition preowned home furnishings, and chic recycled accessories. It was another instant success.

"You gotta see it, Denny—it's fuckin' fabulous; I painted the whole fuckin' thin', outside and in. I painted the inside with a chalky chartreuse, and then I spattered it with Necco Wafer pink. And then I painted and granitized the cement floors to make 'em look like black, white, and gray granite. Then I painted the outside this shockin' bubblegum pink, and used a shiny black for the trim. Then I had this black-and-white-striped awning made for the front, with the name 'Skank World' written on it in big blood-red letters. Then I put a bunch of shit ontop of the roof to make it look like it's fallin' off; there's a pink nylon frizze chair and a chartreuse sofa, sittin' cockeyed on the corner. Fuckin' fabulous.

"You should see the amazing furnishings I'm finding, too, fabulous fucking furniture from the forties, fifties, and sixties, Heywood Wakefield, Herman Miller, Eames, Knoll, and Peckerwood; I'm tellin' you, it is skank-a-licious stuff. I'm having several pieces reupholstered in these bitchin' vintage fabrics I found at the Rose Bowl flea market. You should see it, you'd love it."

"I'd love to, Kim. In fact, my partner, Debby, and I are scheduled to come out in the spring, to open the new Saks Fifth Avenue Store in Carmel a couple months from now; I will definitely look you up and check you out."

Three months had passed before we made it to California, and by then Kim was no longer associated with Skank World. Oh, the store was a smashing success and doing just fine, because now they had a concept and merchandise, so they didn't need him and he moved on. Of course he was dejected when he was rejected, but he bounced right back, because he knew he could always rely on his impressive junking skills and become a supplier to them.

Cruising the Valley in his rusted-out '62 rusty beater pickup, he'd spend afternoons scouring estate sales, yard sales, and thrift stores, searching for unsuspecting loot to pluck up and resell. He made a decent living buying and selling junk, high-end junk, and he knew how to tell the difference.

"I don't have any license plates on my truck anymore because I can't afford the fucking auto insurance. So now I drive around with the tailgate flopped down, to hide the missing tags. Then I had to bleach my hair blond, too, because they'll stop you sure as shit if they think you're a Mexican, and they will fuck with you. Hell, I got stopped all the time when I was black-headed. And Denny, let me tell you, I'm havin' *waaaaaay* more fun bein' a blond. Uh-huh."

Bam-Bam had always been a pretty hardy partier, but now he was embroiled in a big-city party circuit, and way out there in tarnished tinsel town, there was a *whole* lot more trouble to get into. He'd entered the big league now, hard booze, hard rock cocaine, crack, crank, methamphetamine, THC, and ecstasy—it was all good, ya see. Unlike his hipster, badass pretty posing posse back home, those were really hard-core people out there, and this was serious, scary, life-and-death snuff stuff.

When we worked together it would piss me off when he would party all night and then crawl into work the next day, all hungover and useless, and sneak into a storeroom to sleep it off. Or he would sweet-talk Jenny, the needy supersized girl in the kitchen, into giving him a diet pill to stay awake. She was always good for a go-go pill or two. But now that he freelanced and answered to no one, he could arrange his schedule to accommodate his party life. Party all night, sleep all day, and buy and sell some junk in the afternoon when he needed money. It suited him.

Now, I've known Kim for many years and watched him go through many metamorphoses. First there was his fabulous forties vintage look, then a bleached blond beach boy period, glamour rocker, and then a pretty punkster, but his latest incarnation was his most memorable. He referred to himself alternately as Juan Wicky or Cochise, and always as Bam-Bam. Eccentricity suited him.

— —

Debby and I arrived in sunny Southern California from chilly New York City, and I called Kim.

"*Hola*, Juan Wicky speakin'."

"Kim, it's Denny. We're in California."

"Kemosabe, where the hell you bin? Tank Got you're here. Oh my Got, you won be-leaf-it, oh my Got, the biggest fuckin' party of the seas-on is happening to-night, and I can get us in; through the fuckin' frond-ore and ever-thin'. Really, I know the homeowner, and I'm actually invited. You guys gotta go with me; hurry up and get your asses over here."

On our drive from beautiful Beverly Hills to the wilds of West Hollywood, I tried to explain Bam-Bam to my business partner, but where did you begin? I had sort of a love/hate relationship with him—I loved him but hated to think what he'd be up to next. Bless his poor mama's heart.

Bam-Bam was living in the "boys' town" section of West Hollywood, and his bungalow was located near the Oki-Dog Diner, on Fairfax near Santa Monica, a well-known male hooker hangout. That seedy establishment had thoughtfully installed a convenient take-out section, for when you had those late-night cravings for something tubular and meaty. As we were pulling up to the curb and parking in front of Bam's place, I suddenly heard Debby shouting.

"My God, it's coming this way! Get back in the car and lock the doors. Hurry!"

"Kemosabe!"

I looked up to see a drunken Indian reprobate shuffling toward us wearing a ratty brown-and-tan Indian blanket bathrobe that was dragging the ground, and old leather bedroom slippers. "It" was Kim-Bam. Cochise was smiling warmly while wearing a shoulder-length, pitch-black, pin-straight, blunt-cut wig with a purple kerchief tied around his forehead like an Apache Indian. A dozen chunky necklaces were draped around his neck, making him look like a queer Mr. T. Holding a large green glass bottle of Tanqueray gin in his outstretched arm; he slowly shuffled over to me. "Give me some lovin', dude. Ah, it's so good to see you," Kim said, his mischievous black eyes becoming misty as we embrace.

"You too, buddy, you too." Mine were as well.

"Love them glasses, Debby, *mucho bueno*. You know, you're really very pretty. Denny never mentioned how pretty you are. Most of his dyke friends have moustaches, wear buffalo plaids, and drive pickups."

"Thank you, I guess," she replied, still unsure. "You really had me scared there."

He led us across the street and approached what could possibly be a house, although that wasn't completely clear, because the one-story building was totally obscured by a fourteen-foot-tall wall of over-grown privet hedge. A narrow opening was carved through the thicket that led to a rusty chain-linked gate. As he slowly opened the squealing Gothic gate a menagerie unfolded before us.

We spied a shingle-shedding, paint-peeling house with a junky yard that was overflowing with unusual things. To the left of the rusty ornamental security door lay a stack of sparkling multicolored bowl-ing balls twinkling in the hot dessert sun. To the right was a mound of sun-bleached critter bones: horny steer skulls, jawbones, longhorns, and big leg bones with big balls-and-socket ends. A dozen chromed wheelchairs with black vinyl seats sat rusting against the chain-link fence. And next to those were stacks of jagged multicolored glass, bro-ken chunks of marble, hunks of rusty twisted metal, and lots of unique and broken things that had a previous life.

"Denny, I had me the best fucking cocktail party here a couple weeks ago. You shoulda bin here. We's all tuned up on gin and coke, and coke, and had us a game called crippled croquet, where we got one of those wheelchairs and used a leg bones as a mallet to drive a bowling ball down the sidewalk from here to the back door. It was a fuckin' laugh riot. Come on in, it's so good to see you. Just look at you, all grown up in your little suit, Denny, jeez."

Kim was currently sharing this three-bedroom freak show with his legitimate French wife, Demon, and her illegitimate tattooed six-gun-toting outlaw boyfriend, Nemesis. Supposedly he was a "filmmaker" who made {snuff} films. But his was strictly a marriage of convenience, because he had a convenient room to rent, and she conveniently had $3,000 to exchange for US citizenship.

It was hard to believe, but the interior made the outside look almost suburban. His living room walls and ceiling were painted with a shiny acid green, and the room actually vibrated, radiating an eerie anxious energy. Thank God he'd painted the fireplace black, to give your assaulted eyes a place to rest, but then he offended them further by staging a grotesque black altar upon the mantel. A coiled-up East Indian cobra lies ready to strike, while giving the snake eye to a stuffed green parrot perched on a twisted branch. To the left of center sat a giant chunk of lead crystal shaped into a life-size human skull. A fancy bronze funerary urn stood next to that, completing the aberrant display.

To the right of the macabre fireplace sat Salvador Dali's first TV. Somehow the television's plastic housing had melted and drooped over the edge of a blond boomerang-shaped end table with black wrought iron hairpin legs. "Sit down and make yourselves comfortable, but be careful you don't slash your leg on the jagged edge of my new coffee table. I just made it today. Can you guys believe that somebody actually threw those beautiful broken shards of jagged glass away?"

"Unthinkable. What happened to the television, Kim?"

"Isn't that cool, Denny? You know, most people back home think it's hot out here all the time, because it's a desert. Well, let me tell you, it gets pretty fucking cold out here in the winter sometimes, and this place doesn't have a fucking furnace, so I burns me some wood to stay warm.

"Denny, have you ever burned a wooden box? Well, don't ever do it, because I damn near burnt the fuckin' house down doing just that. I'd found me this beautiful little balsa wood box, all clean and pretty, just sittin' in the alley an' waitin' for me. So I picks it up, takes it home, puts it in the fireplace, and sets it off with a click of my trusty Bic. It takes off real nice like, crackin', poppin', an' glowin' real pretty like. Then all of a sudden, *poof*! This big ol' ball of fire comes a rollin' outta the fireplace and goes shootin' halfway across the room, hits the TV, and melts it. Fuckin' cool, eh? Still works."

He proudly turned on the television to demonstrate, as the "A mind is a terrible thing to waste" anti-drug commercial was playing. Perturbed, he switched it back off.

"Where'd the cobra come from? Is that real?"

"Hell yeah, it's for realz. Well, at least it was at one time. Isn't it cool, Denny? I got that and this here snake-bone necklace at this dinosaur professor's retire-mental sale. Look at this thing. It's made from the bones of a real snake. A piece of wire runs through all the vertebrae to hold it together, and it makes a complete circle. See, his tail's in his mouth. Pretty fuckin' cool, huh? Say, would either you guys like a cocktail? I got gin, the good stuff, too," he proudly restated, while holding up the bottle. "I got nose candy, too, if you want some."

The audacity of dope.

"Just make it two gin and tonics, thank you."

As he swung open the squawking door, and disappeared to fetch the refreshments, I got a glimpse of the disaster inside his kitchen. Then I gazed back to Debby, who had developed a blank stare. Being raised by Republicans in West Bloomfield, she wasn't prepared for all this; it may have been too much. Quietly perched on his preposterously purple boomerang-shaped sofa, she was gazing across the chaotic room to a pile of animal hides heaped on a cowhide-covered chair: zebra, gazelle, snake, giraffe, and leopard. And the bungalows aroma made you think all those animals lived there, smelling like a musty and dung-filled locker room full of used jockstraps and dirty ashtrays.

"Better make 'em good and strong, Kim," I said, winking at Debby.

When the squealing door swung the other way Bam-Bam returned, carrying a shiny chromed art deco tray with orange celluloid-handles, and three slender sherbet-colored cocktail glasses were riding upon it. The ice cubes tinkled loudly as Bam dropped the tray on the slasher coffee table, plopped down upon Barney's big couch right next to Debby, and placed his hand on her knee. "Hello, gorgeous, ya wanna see some of my pick-tears?"

The way he posed his query worried me, because I knew he had some very peculiar pictures, such as the baby photo he carried in his wallet and claimed as his own. Some innocent baby's picture was swiped and then photo-shopped to superimpose an extralarge, adult-sized penis onto his naked little torso. He just loved showing that around.

Beads of nervous sweat were dotting her upper lip as she took a sip of her gin-and-ice cocktail. Suddenly she started coughing profusely, exhaling alcoholic jet trails. While completely ignoring her distress, Bam pulled out a cellophane-covered photo album and began flipping through photographs and explaining.

"This chair with the cowhide on it was in the movie *Pretty in Pink*. I sold them tons a stuff, like this atomic-vintage fabric with the boomerangs all over it. I found me a whole bolt of that shit at the Rose Bowl flea market, for mere peanuts. They used the shit outta that shit. This here light fixture was in the movie *Frankie and Annette Go Back to the Beach*. And this here Sputnik-shaped thing is a grave marker for a dead dog. I had this guy I know, named Eddie Dodson, weld it for me, and that damn thing went all the way to Italy, really. This here coffee table here went to dead Ingrid Bergman's house."

"Wow, that's really interesting, Kim-Bam. Did Den tell you we're going to Carmel tomorrow?"

"Oh my God! I forgot all about *the party*! You guys have *got* to go with me, because it is *the* party of the season. This fabulous fucking party is happening tonight in the Valley, at a friend's house. She's got this tri-level home where they used to put up movie stars during filming, and it's completely vintage; a fuckin' time capsule, I tell you. I sold her all kinds of incredible stuff and helped decorate; practically furnished the entire interior, and I did the yard, too.

"You'll like her, too, Debby, 'cause she's a thespian, writes songs for people like the Pointer Sisters, and stuff like that. She's a damn good artist, too. Shit...why can't talented people just be good at one thing, and give the rest of us a chance?

"Does that sound like fun, Debby, going to a fabulous Hollywood GAY—LA?"

She was clearly overstimulated all ready.

— —

Rows of huge, expensive, lifestyle-defining shiny cars lined the streets in both directions as far as we could see. Handsome uniformed valets helped us out of our insignificant rental and parked it, and then escorted us to the door. All the lights were on, everyone was home, and the excess beautiful people were spilling into the yard. To serenade those hipsters lounge music drifted over the red tiled roof from speakers located near the backyard's turquoise guitar-shaped pool and Polynesian tiki bar.

The entire house had Kim's imprint, making it into a movie set. While all the conventional neighboring homes had green, grassy manicured lawns, this outstanding trilevel had a desert-scape out front made of differently-colored pebbles artistically arranged into interesting amoebic shapes. Glittery bowling balls were added for a little unexpected bling, and carefully clustered cacti configurations were added to create colorful points of interest. Here and there, among the prickly pear, sun-bleached skulls were added just for dramatic effect.

Still wearing his Apache wig and bathrobe getup, Bam-Bam proudly held up the invitation for the burly muscle-bound bouncer to inspect. Assuming he was just another eccentric long-haired musician, he let him in. "They're with me," was all it took for us to tag along.

The sprawling time-warped space capsule was swarming with important-looking people, unique people, artsy-fartsy, tanned tattooed flashy-trashy people—and definitely not a sophisticated New York crowd.

"Oh my God, Denny, there's my friend Paul. Come on, you two."

"Who?"

"Paul. Paul Reubens."

"Who?"

"Paul Reubens, Pee-wee Herman. Jeez, Denny."

"Kemosabe, *lookin' good*, give me some lovin'," Pee-wee said, hugging him affectionately.

"Dude, how's it hangin'?"

"To the left, dude, to the left."

"Hey, dude, these here is my friends Denny and Debby. They's artists from New York shitty, come out here to visit me."

"Nice to meet you two. Bam-Bam always has the most interesting friends. Say, I just love those glasses, Debby."

"Thank you. Nice to meet you, Paul," Debby replied.

"We watch your show every Saturday morning on Fire Island, and we just love it," I add.

"Aw, shucks," Pee-wee said, feigning shyness.

Tonight P.W. was going incognito by wearing a charcoal beret rakishly tilted to the side, and a loosely belted trench coat with the collar standing straight up. A tiny triangular soul patch rode upon his puny pointed chin, and a pencil-thin mustache sat under his impish nose; quite unmistakably French. Wee-wee, Pee-wee. While Paul and Debby made bicoastal small talk, Bam-Bam escorted me around the set and identified the furniture, artwork, and accessories he'd purchased, and gave me the detailed acquisition story. Provenance.

"I found me this Heywood Wakefield chair in the Valley, Oxnard. Hell, I had to wrestle it from a damn Mexican who thought he wanted it. Shit, he didn't even know what the hell it was."

This thoroughly modern/retro movie set/home was filled to capacity with glitterati, important-looking people. Reportedly, the musical group Devo was here tonight. Then we met another friend of Kim's, Bud Cort, who claimed the crowd also included Barry White and Angelyne.

They say, "The bigger the hair the closer to Jesus," and suddenly a heavenly body was heading right toward us. What a fleshpot she was. The big-haired bleached-blonde bombshell had *the* biggest breasts I'd ever seen in my life. I mean to tell you, those puppies were the goddamned Grand Tetons. I could not take my eyes off them and could barely resist the overwhelming urge to reach out and touch them; they were so unbelievably gargantuan.

This doll of the Valley was dressed from head to toe in titty pink, with shoes and stockings dyed to match. Her micro mini dress was so itty-bitty her nibbles were barely covered by the flesh-colored fabric that was struggling mightily to contain those mammoth mammalian mounds. Her low-cut and highrise doll-size dress was so unbelievably short she needed a hairnet instead of panties. When viewed from a distance {billboard} she was smoking hot, but she was well aged in close proximity, and the illusion dispelled.

Our conversation was much too brief to tell if she'd crafted her dumb-blonde act to perfection, or if she was frighteningly stupid. Either way, I'm certain it was those enormous titties that got her the big billboard on Sunset Boulevard. Debby was quite taken with her generous gifts, also, but she helped me resist the urge to reach out and touch them.

"Den, quit staring at those. And no, you can't touch them. Behave yourself."

"Ah, Ma, and just when I was startin' to have fun."

Then, just like in the Hollywood movies, a reporter with a flash camera came swooping in. "May we have a few pictures, Miss Angelyne?"

Flash, flash, flash! OMG, *People* magazine, and we were included in the photographs. "If they could see me now, those old friends of mine, I'm eatin' fancy chow and drinkin' fancy wine..."

No matter how exciting the evening was it was getting late and we were still operating on East Coast time. We were tired, and Debbie had made it abundantly clear that we would *not* be staying with Bam-Bam tonight at Chez Menagerie, despite his persistent offers. He recommended a lovely motel that was not far away, called The Tropicana, which straddled the Beverly Hills and West Hollywood border. And with a well-lit, cool blue facade, and gracefully arching palm trees, it looked like a postcard from Hollywood in its heyday.

But behind the serene tinsel town facade it was a dilapidated dump, a fucking false-front prop, and a flophouse. This roach motel had mushrooms growing in the grungy shower, and the filthy carpet slithered. But we were so fucking exhausted we stupidly stayed—not for long.

At three in the morning we were bolted awake by bloodcurdling screams as someone went running past our room, desperately pleading for help while being chased and shot at repeatedly. For five minutes we lay paralyzed while hearing bullets ricocheting, glass breaking, screams, and finally police sirens. Lying perfectly still atop the filthy bed, still dressed in party-going clothes, we didn't know which would be worse: diving onto the slithering floor or just lying there and taking a slug. As soon as the police showed up, we got our shit, hit the highway, and headed north to Carmel.

— —

Weeks later, when safely back in civilization, a.k.a. New York City, the *People* magazine article hit the newsstand, and sure enough, there was Angelyne and her big-old tits, front and center. Debbie's right hand was included in the right-hand bottom corner of the photo, easily recognizable by the heirloom sapphire ring she wore. I, unfortunately, was cropped out of the picture altogether.

About a year later the phone rang at three o'clock in the morning, waking me. I hoped it would be Kim, because no one else called me at that ungodly hour, unless someone had died.

"Denny? What's the matter with you? You sound all funny."

"I'm sleeping, Kim. It's three o'clock in the morning here; that's when people sleep."

"Guess where I am right now? Oh hell, you're never gonna guess so I'm just going ta tell ya. I'm at Bette Midler's house right now. She's in her kitchen frying me up a hamburger, while I'm granitizing her very own, personal, la-di-da, piss-elegant bathroom."

Granitizing was Kim's term for a top-secret speckled paint finish he accidentally developed. First he painted a base color, usually a gray, and then he took different-colored spray paints, such as black-and-white, and poked a pin into the valve of the nozzle, which would make it spittle droplets instead of spraying. That's how he did his *granitized* finish. You didn't hear it from me.

"Sounds like you'd better open a window, bud. You've been breathing too many paint fumes."

"It's the goddamned gin. She's been serving me cocktails all evening, sheesh."

"You'd better level out there, bud, 'cause it sounds like you've reached your cruising altitude."

"There's another reason why I'm callin', Denny. I got me another paintin' job out here, and it's a big one, but I can't do it by myself. I'd take the job if you'd promise to come out and help."

"Kim, you aren't a painter, you only have two finishes in your entire repertoire. But I have news for you, too. I'm moving back to Michigan. Maybe it could work; I'd would get out of the cold for a couple weeks, and help you out at the same time. Sure, I'll help...*if*...it all pans out."

"*Fuck*, now I lost my goddamn {not straight} pin. Shit. I need that thing to prick the spray nozzle. Fuck, here she comes with my burger and I'm blabbing long distance on her damn phone. Gotta go. Thanks, Denny. I really mean it."

Act Two

"We got us a bitchin' place to stay—and its right at the house we're working on. Plus we got us a badass burgundy Catalina convertible to drive, and all the Mexicans we want to help. You should see this fabulous hillside house, the pool, gym, and guest quarters; that's where we'll be stayin'."

Well, you never really knew with Kim, it could be amazing, or just as easily all fucked up.

So we drove though the lovely curving streets, past well-manicured hillside homes, and looked like the Mexican landscapers in his rusted-out truck with the tailgate flopped down, to avoid arrest. As we climbed higher up the mountain all the shit in the back of his pickup started rolling out, and bones, pebbles, rocks, wheelchairs, and bowling balls went tumbling down the street. We climbed up and up, winding around, switching back, and zigzagging until coming to the tippy-tippy top. Driving along the mountains' very spine, we can see the giant Hollywood sign almost within reach, just over the next foothill. Lake Hollywood's sparkling blue reservoir twinkled below us like a tranquil desert oasis.

Bam-Bam directed his decaying truck to the dead end of a cul-de-sac and parked in front of a sign reading: "No parking, keep out. Yes, this means you, Kim." Massive and ornate hand-hammered art nouveau iron gates stood between us and Ingrid Bergman's old home. She was dead by then, bless her heart, but she once lived there, and that still counted in holly-would.

Matte black river rocks set into matching mortar were used to pave the drive. All those well-rounded rocks radiated from the trunk of an ancient live oak, whose stately sprawling canopy provided shade to a gleaming red Ferrari Countach, yellow '69 Corvette convertible, and black stretch limousine. Peering through the massive art-nouveau-riche gates, we spied a sprawling hacienda with an outdoor living space, complete with an upholstered furniture grouping centered on a fireplace, all nicely nestled under a shaded portico draped with sweet-smelling jasmine.

Layers of lush tropical greenery surrounded the sprawling ranch, obscuring it from prying eyes. Palms trees towered above, swaying in the warm Santa Anna breeze. Trickling water was heard spilling into a distant fountain, drowning out the city's noises and creating a calming, cooling oasis within this desert city. Kim nervously danced around while repeatedly pressing and repressing the intercom, trying to summon the house.

"*Hello*," was the curt and irritated response.

"Hello. It's Bam-Bam. And I'm here to see Norm."

"All right. Please wait while I call him. And *do not* push the buzzer anymore. We heard you the first ten times."

"This place is amazing, Kim," I said. Suddenly lights come on above a set of French doors, illuminating the veranda, and the massive gates magically jerked to life, opening and granting us entry.

"I've sold this guy all kindsa stuff over the years. He just got divorced and wants to change every fuckin' thing in the house. So you just let me do all the talking."

"Kemosabe! *Que pasa?*"

"Not a damn thing. Not-a-dam. Hey, Norm, I'd like you to meet my amigo, Denny."

"Pleasure to meet you, Denny. Kim tells me you're a pretty good painter, huh? And you're visiting from New York City?"

"Yes. I'm a fancy-schmancy painter. Here, I brought my portfolio along, if you'd care to look." Flipping through photographs for less than a minute, he quickly looked up. "Nice, very nice, yes. Please come with me, and I'll show you around."

Escorting us from the kitchen, he then led us into the spacious great room, bedroom wing, and through the remainder of the sprawling ranch. The piece of geography was absolutely amazing, and the view priceless, but the house definitely needed major renovation. It was dated, and not in a good way.

The hascienda was perched high above Los Angeles; the entire city twinkled below us, and sprawled into the distance as far as we could see. Hundreds of acres of undeveloped hillside and the pristine Hollywood reservoir made this property feel like a giant nature preserve in the heart of the city. The surrounding hills were covered with dried amber grasses and sprinkled with wildflowers such as datura, sunflower, and cow-tongue cactus. Stately silvery eucalyptus trees with gracefully drooping gnarly branches framed the views to the north, where the Cahuenga Pass sliced through the foothills, revealing the entire San Fernando Valley; but their aroma was oddly astringent, like cat piss. Our closest neighbors were Griffith Park Observatory, Universal Studios, and Forrest Lawn Cemetery.

"On a really clear day you can see all the way to the ocean, but we don't get many of those, maybe only once or twice in twenty years," Norm informed.

"See that house right there? It once belonged to Howard Hughes. That one was once William Frawley's—you know, Fred from *I Love Lucy*. John Schneider, the blond guy from the *Dukes of Hazzard*, lives right down the street."

"Which house is his, Norm?" Kim said, suddenly becoming interested again.

Norm explained that he wanted to change everything, which made Kim extremely nervous. This was a large-scale commitment that practically overwhelmed him, but it didn't faze me nearly as much because I was used to working on projects that took months or years to complete.

You see, Bam-Bam was more of a hit-and-run artist. He'd hit the job and do a couple of hours of work, and then run back to his room for a couple of cigarettes, couple of cocktails, and a couple of hours of rest. He was another ADHD-accredited decorator. To say the least, our work ethics clashed.

Our first project was the renovation of the large but narrow dining room. Since there was an amazing view of the Hollywood sign at the east end, which you couldn't see, we suggested removing the wall and replacing it with a bank of French doors, to take advantage of the million-dollar hillside view. Once the wall was removed an outdoor terrace was created, so we added a table and chairs, to enjoy morning prayers and coffee, and all were nicely shaded by a green canvas roll-out awning.

Norm suggested we paint the room a verdigris green finish, something like the oxidization on the sculptures in his yard, and sort of a blue-green bread-mold color. When I suggested the room should have more than one finish, he agreed, and we also incorporated silver leaf. Two large round art deco tables with silvered bases adorned with stylized cabbage roses were already in the room, so we topped them with thick plate glass tops to keep the room light and open, and paired them with clear Lucite chairs, to give the room some sparkle.

Then I appropriated the cabbage-rose motif and incorporated it into a trompe l'oeil border that was painted around the room, and dropped a few inches from the ceiling. By using several increasingly lighter shades of a similar color, we created three imaginary receding rectangles on the long and narrow ceiling, which gave it the illusion of a stepped art deco tray ceiling. The room was quite lovely when finished, and we were asked to continue on.

Renovating the great room was our next project. Previously it was painted a formal dove-gray color and held two matching sofas that were upholstered in a pretty pearly papillon pattern that the ex-wife had picked. Kim did not do pretty. Since Norm already owned many significant art deco, art, and furniture pieces, and the house had significant Spanish colonial bones, we decided to merge the two styles to create a form of Southwest deco.

The muscular Mexican laborers harvest a dead eucalyptus tree, debark it, and secured it to the room's cathedral peak to create a faux ridgepole. Then smaller three-inch saplings were split lengthwise and nailed to the ceiling, flat side down, to create the ribs that radiated from the center spine. The entire wood-clad ceiling was then paint-washed with a dusty earthen color, giving the different tones uniformity and creating a warming, rustic, Southwest feel.

The formal chamfered wooden wainscoting was removed, and all the homes' hard corners replaced with well-rounded bull-nose trim. The walls were finished with an adobe-like texture and painted with a blend of warm earthen tones such as terra-cotta, pink, caramel tan, clay, and ocher.

Then the formal fireplace mantel was removed and reworked by an amazing mason named Ernesto, who helped Bam-Bam convert it into a sculpture in stone. Mr. Mason was a sturdy but sweet Mexican man who spoke very little English, and yet they managed to communicate quite well, and transform the red brick fireplace.

Bam-Bam had scoured the San Fernando Valley's stone yards for weeks until he found enough flagstones embedded with fish fossils to cover the entire fireplace and create his fishy sculpture. Some of those chunks had fish fossils six inches long; a few had schools of tiny minnows measuring two to three inches long, and one gnarly whopper measured nearly three feet long. Epic.

Kim arranged the fishy fossils into a "dog eat dog" formation, with the whopper at the far left chasing a school of bigger fish, which were chasing midsized fish, and they were chasing the minnows. Art was imitating life. The beautiful blond stone not only covered the fireplace, it had spilled over and completely incorporated the entire twelve-foot wall adjoining it. And when hit with three fish-eye spotlights, it was a unique sculpture in stone.

＊　＊

Recognizing that Kim was "sick" happened a while back, when he first asked for my help. He never would have done that before, because he was so fiercely independent. But he also had a delicate ego, was insecure and easily threatened; consequently we never talked about his illness. That would be his prerogative. But it was becoming obvious he was getting worse because he looked waxy, with crusty fungus-riddled nails, and lifeless hair with two inches of black roots and fried yellow ends.

Now that we were living together, I became privy to his personal life and saw the huge valise filled with herbal remedies, holistic aids, prescriptions, and assorted personal care products he needed to stay well. Each morning he'd sort and swallow a handful of pills large enough to choke a horse.

"She-it, I don't have any room left for food after takin' my fuckin' pills. I can't keep much of anything I eat down anyway, and what I do manage to keep down usually comes out an hour later like the Hershey squirts. *Hell*, I could shit through a screen door and never even hit wire."

For the first few months he did fairly well, but as the debilitating disease began taking its taxing toll, he steadily deteriorated. Working less and less, and sleeping more and more, he retreated inward. I made no mention of this, because he would discuss his condition if, and when, he wanted. Truthfully, it was easier getting things done with him sleeping. Often he didn't feel well enough to work, but he was threatened when I did, and worried that Norm would know who was doing what. Explaining that he didn't care who did what, just the end product, I tried to alleviate his fears. But that did little to ease his anxiety, and he was anxious all the time.

Before long the entire house was under reconstruction, per Norm's instruction, and we were changing everything from the cedar-shake shingles on top of the house to the servants' quarters in the bunker-like basement. Consequently, the homeowner had moved into one of his other homes for a few months to avoid all the constant noise and mess.

By slightly altering the home's floor plan, I changed the front entry to create a new foyer, and this new configuration also added a much-needed powder room. By connecting the homes east side to the detached garage, we created a family room and additional guest room, which serendipitously created a three-sided outdoor courtyard.

Five Mexican *muchachos* were working on the project, much-o, and they were the first to arrive each morning and last to leave at night. Taking two semis to Mexico, they purchased tons of terra-cotta tiles for the home's transformation. Red clay Saltillo tiles in six-inch hexa-gons, twelve-inch squares, and four-inch slabs were used to cover the floors of the kitchen, family room, and all of the exterior porches, patios, sidewalks, and areas surrounding the pool. Red-clay tiles now covered the roof of the house, new additions, guesthouse, and the ga-rage, too. They practically bought out Mexico.

While the workers were busy finishing the house, Kim was slowly withering. Getting up later each day, he'd put in a few hours work, when he could, and sleep for the rest of the day. He had lost interest in do-ing anything except sleeping, and was turning into a hypochondriac;

having all sorts of maladies, both *real* and *imagined*. At thirty-two he looked aged. Slowly losing weight, he appeared skeletal, except for his distended belly.

When waking late in the afternoon, his hair hurt from sleeping on it wrong. His bowels gave him trouble continuously; one day it was constipation caused by the codeine for pain, and the next day it was explosive diarrhea from the terribly toxic medications. He told me all about it, in great detail, daily. His teeth were rotting away from past cocaine abuse, and he'd constantly be digging at them with a toothpick, matchbook, pen, pencil, or, even worse, your pen, your pencil, your keys, or your former matches. He often tried expelling leftover food particles from his rotting teeth by forcing air through his mouth and making his lips flap something fierce, and sounding like a horse whinnying. And this disgusting disgorgement would send food particles flying in every direction simultaneously. Ick.

With long and crusty yellowed fingernails distorted by invading fungus, he resembled Howard Hughes at the end. White spots of yeast, candida, and thrush were now growing on his smoky tongue, and he was more than happy to show them. *"Ahhhh!"* No one had said the word yet, but it was AIDS.

Smoking continuously, he heaped every ashtray in the house with butts, but never emptyied them, and errant ashes coated every surface. He now slept in, lounged in, worked in, and lived in that Indian blanket bathrobe getup, clunky necklaces, and slippers. He'd laid claim to the garishly tropical floral-print day-bed and made it into his lair, creating a rat's nest heaped with unworn period clothes, papers, and magazines. A huge verdigris coffee table was withing easy reach of his gay-bed, and it was also covered with crap: overflowing ashtrays, empty pizza boxes with bits of food still clinging, pill bottles, sticky copies of *Honcho* and *Colt* magazine, and a plethora of personal care products.

One evening during all this mayhem, Bam-Bam and the burgundy convertible mysteriously disappeared. Somewhere around two thirty in the morning he returned—with a mystery "date." I was trying to sleep in the next room, and there was nothing noisier than someone trying not to be quiet. Around two thirty the following afternoon, he finally showed up at the worksite.

"Hey! Why are you doing that, Denny?"

"What? Do you mean painting the walls?"

"We never decided what color we were doing in here."

"I decided this morning, while you were sleeping it off."

"Fuck you, too, Denny."

"Kim, I don't mind doing more than my share of work. In fact I've been doing it for over six months now. I've noticed you seem to have enough energy to party and screw around, but not enough to work. We're getting paid the same wages, but it seems you're getting paid to fuck around while I'm doing the work. So don't ask me who picked the color. Be here when the decisions need to be made."

"Fuck you, too, Denny!"

That uncomfortable evening I stayed on my side of the room and silently read, while Kim sulked in his lair, watched TV, smoked, and smoked more. Thankfully the night was unseasonably warm, making it possible to have all four sets of the French doors open, allowing the fumes to escape. Warm Santa Anna winds came blowing through those open doors, carrying the eerie sounds of coyotes yipping at the silvery moon just now rising over the reservoir. A nightingale sang her melancholy tune, and the perfume of a blossom-laden plumeria floated in, replacing the fumes.

"*Shut the fuck up*, motherfucking bird. Jesus fucking Christ, can't a fucking-body get some motherfucking peace and quiet around here? Fuck," Kim screamed, using his outside voice.

Suddenly I heard the whooshing sound of a champagne bottle being hurled out the open door and smashing on the blacktop below. The mocking bird momentarily silenced her sweet song, and then quickly resumed.

"Shut the fuck up!"

⸺ ⸻

As the weeks passed, his health continued to deteriorate even further, and even faster. Desperate for a cure, he started to incorporate holistic treatment as well as traditional Western medicines. By now our place looked and smelled like a perfume factory's sickbay, sweet from the plumeria's perfume and medicinal from the stinky salves, toxic pills, and greasy ointments. A bulky atomizing machine used to administer breathing treatments of Bactrim and Pentamidine, and ward off pneumocystis pneumonia, was shoved into the corner.

At the urging of a friend, Kim began attending Louise Hay's sessions on healing your body through positive affirmation. He read her books and affirmed, but continued to diminish. By then he was deteriorating quickly and becoming worn down from constant battle to thwart off the ever invading infections. Becoming desperate, he latched on to every possible cure that came along, that he could afford.

One of those trending remedies was a restorative powder derived from sick eggs. In theory, foul eggs {duck or chicken} were inoculated with various infectious agents {antigens}, which thereby made them make antibodies. After an incubation period, those eggs were dehydrated and the newly produced antibodies extracted. This powder was then orally administered to patients with compromised immune systems, and *in theory* it would help bolster the body's immune system to help fight-off the invading opportunistic diseases. Even though he used the product faithfully, his condition continued to worsen. Anything giving a glimmer of hope was considered, no matter how far-fetched or expensive. Before long charlatans began appearing offering promising and yet unproven lifesaving treatments, which were often prohibitively expensive.

Worn down from the constant battle, and tired of losing every skirmish, he started reading Dr. Elisabeth Kübler-Ross's *On Death and Dying*, and that's a difficult thing to do when you are thirty-two. At the last, when he admitted *to himself* he was losing the battle, he returned to Flint. And Kim was fortunate that his parents took him in, because many of our peers were shunned by their families and left to die alone. How tragic.

Act Three

Six months had passed before we met again. When he did he was holding his own, but he looked ancient and sort of disgusting. His waxy
face had several days' of beardy stubble clinging to concave cheeks, and
his yellowed and nicotine-stained nails were thick, crusty, and fungus riddled. His lifeless hair still sported an overgrown two-tone flat-
top, with black roots and straw-like yellow ends, which made him look
like a towheaded baby doll that'd been dragged through the dirt and
loved too much for her own good. Hiding somewhere deep inside dark
sunken sockets, his once mischievous twinkling black eyes no longer
had their spark.

— ~

"So...how do you like my new store, Denny?"
"You always have such interesting spaces."
"Fuck you, too, Denny. 'Interesting' my ass."
"So you're a half-assed blond again."
"Yeah, I am, and I'm not having any fun at all."
"How are you feeling?"

"I feel just like I look, *like shit*! I got all kinds a strange shit happening to
me now, with new shit happening every day. I've got a nasty case a thrush
growin' on my tongue now, look at these fucking white dots, *aaaaaaaaaahh-
hhhhhhhhhhh.* I got fungus on my finger and toenails, and an asshole that's
either raw from having diarrhea, or it can't shit at all because I'm consti-
pated from the codeine for the constant pain. My teeth are falling out,
my hair hurts, I can't eat, all I do is sleep, got no money, got no life, it's
winter, and I'm living in Flint with my parents. Other than that it's all
good.

"Enough of that bullshit, I don't want to talk about that shit. What's
happening in California? Tell me all about that."

"You really haven't missed much. All the projects that were under
way when you were there are pretty much completed. The tile roof is on

the house, and the family room is finished. Here, I brought pictures. Everyone says to say hello, and they ask about you all the time."

"Yeah, well, fuck them, too."

"So tell me about your new store. How's business?"

"Denny, you remember when this place used to be Bob and Ethel's Rib Crib, don't you?"

"Yeah, it still smells kinda smoky in here from the wood fires."

"Well, that's how I got the name, Art Crib. Like it?"

"Clever."

"As you can see, I got this place chock-full of premium product. Everybody's leavin' this town, and the city is chock-full of great junk. The thrift stores are overflowing with treasures and its really good picking, and cheap. But nobody's buying the crap; hell, I can't sell the shit I've got now because nobody's got any money. And to tell you the truth, I just don't have any interest in doing this anymore."Pulling a bulky woolen sweater tightly around his bony frame, he escorted me through his store. Acting like a proud parent, he introduced me to his carefully selected wares. They were his treasures, he'd saved them from liquidation, marked them as special, and it was an amazing collection of stuff.

By cleverly creating vignettes, he'd constructed room settings and arranged the store as if it was a home. There was a kitchen housewares department, a women's room with hand-knit sweaters and coture dresses, men's things, children's items, artwork, pottery, and slightly used pornos; behind the counter, just ask. Natural fibers such as silk, wool, linen, and cotton filled the racks, as did handcrafted jewelry, both cosmetic and real. Unique and handmade items filled the store; things of substance, quality, and treasures otherwise overlooked in the thrift stores were prominently displayed here.

"You know, Denny, I get some really interesting people in here, but they're mostly college kids that don't have any money. Hell, I end up giving a lot of this stuff away—just because I like them. You know, they kinda remind me of us when we were young." He was only thirty-three.

Kim pulled his sweater tighter around his scrawny frame and shivered, while sitting so close to the open flame of the space heater I was afraid his ratty old Indian blanket bathrobe, which he was still wearing, was about to spontaneously burst into flames.

"Fucking Michigan, Jesus, I'm freezing all the time. I hate living in this goddamned icebox."

"I miss the sunshine. It's always gray and gloomy here."

"Denny, do you remember when we used to spend all weekend junking, and go up to Saginaw to fill your old Skylark with treasures? Boy, those were some of the best times. You know, I never hear from the old group anymore, and I tried so hard to belong. I kissed all their asses for years, and now I don't hear a word from any of them."

"Kim, you don't need those people, or their acceptance. You had the ruby slippers on your feet all along, and you didn't even see them. You're a talented artist who went out into the world and made your art. Just look what you have done with your life. Hell, they have never left even the city limits, and they're disapproving of you? Fuck 'em. You're worthy; can't you see that?"

I don't think he ever did.

Postscript: Kim died three weeks later.

He was cremated, because that was his wish, and his ashes placed inside the fabulous bronze funerary urn that sat on the mantel of his freakish Hollywood bungalow, between the stuffed green parrot and striking cobra.

God bless you, Buddy. I truly miss you.

Uncle John

"Is this seat taken?"

"No, go ahead. I'm just waiting for a friend."

"John."

"No, David."

"No, I'm John. *My* name is John."

"Oh, I'm sorry."

"Well, it's nice to meet you, Sorry. And what is *your* name?"

"Oh, Den."

"So, O'Den, do you come to the Monster often? I don't recall seeing you here before."

"Sometimes I'll stop by, usually earlier in the evening, just to get out of the place. When you live and work in the same space it can get claustrophobic. I like to get out, maybe have a drink."

"Let me get this right. It's claustrophobic at home, so you come to a crowded bar?...I see."

"I'm here to meet my friend."

"That's right, David. So, O'Den, is David a 'friend-friend,' or just a friend?" he asked, while making air quotes with his slender fingers.

"A friend. We have been friends since seven; we're from the same hometown. He's an actor."

"Actor? I see! And just where *is* home?"

"Michigan, Flint."

"Flint, Ah yes, *Roger and Me*—Roger Moore."

"Close. Flint, yes, but it's Michael Moore."

"I saw the movie, and the place looks absolutely abysmal."

"Yes, it certainly is a good place to be *from*."

"So, what brings you to New York City, Den?"

"Fame and fortune, just like everyone else. It's a long story, and I wouldn't want to bore you."

"Oh, please do, darling, bore away. I've nothing better to do this evening. Bore me to tears."

"Now remember, you asked for this. Okay...basically I'm an artist, and my work has led me here. My partner and I moved here about a year ago, and we started a new business."

"Partner, oh, I am so sorry to hear that. I guess you are taken then. The good ones always are."

"If it's any consolation to you, my partner happens to be a lesbian."

"Oh, that is *soooo* good to hear. Please, *do* tell me more. But not about the lesbian."

John was quite an elfin guy, with twinkling blue-gray eyes surrounded by lots of laugh lines. Small and mischievous, he looked like Barry Fitzgerald, the tiny matchmaker from the 1952 John Wayne movie *The Quiet Man*. John went on to explain that he'd moved The City at the tender age of sixteen, and had lived there nearly all his life; he didn't volunteer how long that was, but considered himself to be a naturalized native New Yorker. Not interested in talking about himself, he only touched on his rural Indiana youth, because we were not just having a barroom chat—I was being interviewed.

His thick brush-cut platinum-gray hair, and a flock of crow's feet beginning to gather around his eyes from smiling too much, gave some subtle clues to his age. It was a pleasant face, clean-shaven and well moisturized, ruddy. Sporting timeless gold wire-rimmed glasses, he looked quite conservative.

"So, just what is it that you and your partner do, anyway, O'Den?"

"We are artists and we restore artwork in historic homes, churches, and public places; and also designers, and fine artists. Currently we're supplying Saks Fifth Avenue with commissioned artwork."

"You're all that huh? And isn't it a small world. My friend Frank, from back home in Indiana, he supplies artwork for Macy's. He lives over in SoHo, on Spring Street."

"Talk about a small world. I live on Spring, too."

"66."

"66."

Saying it at exactly the same time, we lifted pinkies and interlocked them as if we'd been doing it all our lives. The City can sometimes be a small place, and our six degrees of separation were quickly removed. David never arrived that evening. A couple of days later I finally reached his roommate, who reported he'd been admitted to Saint Vincent's Hospital, and tragically, he was dead a week later. Yes, it was AIDS, and he was one of the first I knew to die, gone at twenty-eight, in 1983.

For the next two hours John continued our interview, and his skills were well honed. The only thing he volunteered about himself was that his apartment was on Christopher Street. And he repeatedly stated, "No, the street was *not* named after Christopher Isherwood, despite his persistent claims." But he did let it slip that he'd been living in the same apartment for nearly thirty years.

His Zen-like, shoe box–sized apartment overlooked the Hudson River; if you stood on the stool, gazed out the tiny bathroom window and crooked your neck severely to the left, you could see it, and in New York real estate terms it was a river view. But his itty-bitty pied-à-terre did have an underground parking space, two storage lockers, and cost a tenth of what we were paying for our SoHo loft.

"Three hundred a month, darling, it's called rent control, and it's a perk for staying where you are put. Garbo's one of my neighbors, see her all the time; lives just down the street. I'm just sayin'."

With alcohol lubricated lips, I explained about my industrial-strength childhood, artistic career, and star-crossed romance with my paramour back in Michigan, Mike. Listening patiently, he never interrupted, only asked more probing questions. "When did you first start feeling this way, Den?"

Johnny Slattery and Denny Murphy, two wee Irishmen sitting side by side on well-worn stools in a Greenwich Village gay bar, drinking beers and lamenting lost loves. It sounded as if he'd had quite a charmed life, here in what he called "The Emerald City," and I could tell he'd taken a shine to me.

When he asked for my phone number I willingly gave it, because I believed I'd made a friend that evening. From that night forward he would call about once a week to schedule an appointment of sorts, and we'd book time to do something special. John was adept at finding interesting things to do that were both engaging and affordable, or even free. By living frugally, he enjoyed the luxury of his abundant free time. If time were money, he would be a rich man.

Quite often an outing would be as simple as a stroll through Greenwich Village, or having dinner at one of his favorite vegetarian restaurants, such as Buckwheat and Alfalfa, Dirt Candy, or Dojo's on Saint Mark's Street, in the radical East Village. Sometimes we went to an ancient two-hankie movie, such as *An Affair to Remember* at the decomposing Saint Mark's Theater. Maybe we would go to a free concert in Central Park, attend a museum exhibition, catch a stage play, or just leisurely stroll through the always-interesting city streets.

During spring and summer he enjoyed visiting the areas gardens, such as Brooklyn's Botanical Gardens, the Oyster Fields and Planting Fields on Long Island, or have a stroll through Central Park in spring when everything was bursting into bloom. He loved nature, and sharing his secret green places was his pleasure. We often visited the Cloisters way up in Harlem, on the Hudson River by the George Washington Bridge, and other out-of-the-way gardens, such as Gramercy Park's iron-gated garden, or the tiny victory garden plots over by NYU. These little bits of nature inside the city were his favorite getaway places, and I probably never would have experienced them without his invitations.

On these appointed afternoon outings we would often share secret stories about his past loves, lust, and Antonio, the one he never got over. He excitedly told me about the year he'd spent living on the beach in Hawaii with his first lover, Dean, when they were teenagers, and how they survived on coconuts, food stamps, and laughter, before finally returning to reality. He even went to Woodstock.

Sharing his stories from the dark ages—before gay liberation—he spoke of the seedy sexual underworld that existed in The City before the advent of AIDS. In almost reverent terms, he told about the boarded-up warehouses and abandoned piers at the end of Christopher Street, on the Hudson River, as if they were holy hushed cathedrals. "Sun-dogged light beams came streaming through the jagged broken windowpanes, illuminating the dusty darkness. And there, within those silent sacrilegious spaces white doves took flight, as men, on their knees, gave service to fellow man." His unvarnished tales of lusty bookstore escapades were likened to church confessionals, where the needy men of the seedy city went to commit sin, and absolution was both given and taken in the sweaty silent darkness.

Uncle John made a point of introducing me to the proper people; the ones he thought could open new horizons or help advance my career. As I now reflect, he was the one true friend I'd made while living in the city. Because so much of New York life had to do with competition—how much money you made, whom you knew, and where you lived—friendship was measured by a sliding scale that measured looks, wallet size, dick size, and your perceived overall importance. You were allowed to prosper, but you shouldn't do better than your contemporaries.

It was not like that in Flint, where soup to nuts ended up in one place and worked it all out. In New York you specialized, by selecting the particular niche or archetypal watering hole that best suited your self-image. There were the suit-and-tie preppy bars for Republicans, piano bars for the off-tune Democrats, and drag bars for the fiercely independent. They also had bars for Asians, blacks, Latinos and

Blatinos (a black and Latin hybrid), muscle men, sissy boys, leather and lace, and transplanted cowboys, too. Plus there was an array of bars for women as well, every sort, lipstick to collar-and-tie.

The problem for me was I never seemed to fit into any of those slots. On this Fantasy Island the choices for queers were seemingly endless, because there were gay bookstores, restaurants, boutiques, clothiers, travel agencies, doctors, lawyers, and a plethora of gay bars, too. In the West Village the gays had created a sort of gay immersion, where an entire section of the city had been annexed as a queer-centric environment. Real or imagined, those gay-tolerant boundaries pretty much stopped at the bridges and tunnels, and they didn't pick up again until you reached the Pacific shore.

But New York City was also a great finishing school, because it gave me a better idea of who I was and where I fit in the larger picture. That exposure allowed me to discover how my talents rated against the best of them, and that was a valuable lesson. Uncle John made a point of exposing me to the right people, saw that I traveled in the correct crowd, and introduced me to gay authors such as James Baldwin, Oscar Wilde, Armistead Maupin, Truman Capote, and Andy Warhol.

Making a special effort of pointing out who was who in the queer community, he introduced me to important gay people he knew, such as the prominent AIDS activist Larry Kramer, and the writer and actor Charles Ludlam of the Ridiculous Theater Company. Taking an interest in my business affairs as well, he introduced me to the correct people, such as the legendary dowager decorating diva Dorothy Draper, and the head of the American Institute of Architects.

John also had a knack for giving thoughtful and practical gifts, the kind of items you'd find yourself using every day. Thirty years after his passing, I still use the red-handled kitchen scissors he gave me, and the kitschy little red tomato timer, too. Hearing the peaceful Woodstock wind chimes he gave me clang as the wind stirs, making their tranquil offbeat melodic tunes, reminds me of him, too. Along with those utilitarian items, he also gave me a small brass joint-carrying case that cradled three rolled marijuana cigarettes. He strongly encouraged the use of pot daily, for its many medicinal and metaphysical properties, and claimed that pot helped him become a better human being.

"Darling, God gave us the grass. Certainly it was his intention for us to use the stuff."

It has taken thirty years for society to catch up to his thinking. He had many opinions to share. "You know, for practically forever we queers have been thought of as merely sexual creatures, and that is mostly because as homosexuals we are defined by the act of homo-sex. But darling, we're so much more than that. I never have sex anymore, but I'm still quite gay, *thank you very much*. And you know, those straight people would certainly be living in a boring, ugly, and unentertaining world without us, now, wouldn't they? And as you well know, queer things have come a long way in the last few years, especially since we've gotten rid of that goddamned orange juice queen, Anita Bryant."

"You got that right, sunshine."

"Amen. See that building over there, Den?"

"You mean the bagel shop?"

"Yes, the ghastly red one. Well, that's where Stonewall started. You see, years ago it was a queer bar, and back then the police thought they could just raid the sissy bars whenever they felt like it. Hell, they'd do it just for kicks, because they were bored, or needed some extra pocket money. *But* on that night, June 28, 1969, they'd bitten off more than they could chew. I remember it well because it was so close to my birthday, and also around mayoral election time, and that sort of thing, clearing the streets of perverts and devaites, well, that stuff goes over real big with the self-righteous types.

"So, that night they decided to raid a couple gay bars and stir up a little trouble. Well, let me tell you, it was just like throwing a rock into an already agitated hornets' nest. You see, Judy Garland had died that week, and the raid happened on the night after they'd had her her funeral. She was beloved by the boys, you know, especially the drag queens, because they'd just lost one of their biggest idols.

"*Big mistake,* and *baad* timing on the part of the police. Well, the drag queens, dressed in head-to-toe black, were in deep mourning and drinking heavily, lamenting the loss of one of their most revered icons. And most everybody else just wasn't in the mood to be fucked with anymore. So when the raid started, those grieving drag queens, in their best little black dresses, stood up on their stiletto heels and fought the fuckers back. With their mascara running, they pounded on the police and pushed them back, drove them out of their bar, into the streets, and right on out of their neighborhood."

"Wow, I never knew that. I thought it was more of a political thing."

"Well, darling, I should know, now, I was there. Just pissed-off drag queens was all it was."

"I never knew."

"But truthfully, darling, it was also the first time that us gay people stood up for ourselves and fought back against systematic oppression. Now, you'll have to understand, these were turbulent times for everybody, with us still being in Vietnam, having the active draft, campus protests, street riots, and black power. That was the summer of Woodstock, and the man on the moon."

"I was in ninth grade when all that happened."

"You're just a child. Do you see that building there, the ugly place on the corner? That is *the* diner pictured in Edward Hopper's painting the *Nighthawks*. You can still see its rounded profile."

"Oh my God, yes, I recognize the silhouette. Even though it's plywooded over now, you can see where the curving plate glass windows used to be."

"At one time Hopper actually lived across the street in those row houses, right over there."

"Yes, I remember seeing the painting of them in art history class. They havn't changed a bit."

For three years we were friends, because he made that happen. Most of my "artsy" friends just tolerated him, but I felt differently. He'd wriggled his way into my life, and into my heart. By the time I'd spent a couple of years living in the city, I wanted to, and could afford to, secure a summer getaway, and Fire Island, the queer sandbar paralleling Long Island's coast, was the logical choice. Many years ago it was annexed by the gays as a seedy seaside resort, and Uncle John, of course, had been summering there for many seasons.

On Flaming Island there was a rigid pecking order based upon how close you lived to the shore, which lane your cottage was on, which neighborhood you lived in, how good you looked when packed into a Speedo, how much money you had access to, and how big a party you could throw.

With both of us being of Irish extraction, we'd often spend hours on the beach hiding from the sun, or quiet afternoons curled up by a crackling fire reading and drinking tea. I liked spending time with John at his cottage because mine was so overcrowded. The only way I could afford a room at all was to purchase "a summer share," And that meant you were selected {by a persnickety committee} to share a bedroom with another man (not of your choosing, and no touchy-feely) and share the bathroom, kitchen, and rest of the cottage with seven men, every other week and weekend.

On major holidays such as Memorial Day, the Fourth of July, and Labor Day weekend, there could be as many as sixteen sissies staying there, with all of them trying to outdo each other decorating, exhibiting chic attire, displaying culinary expertise, gossiping, and displaying their dateability. Most Saturday mornings would find eight men gaily huddled around a TV to watch *Pee-wee's Playhouse,* because a housemate did animation for cartoon segments. Laughing and singing along with the TV, eight grown men instantly reverted back to boys: "Meka Leka Hi, Meka Hiney Ho."

On quiet weekdays, when all those noisy boys were back in the city, there was time for tea and sympathy on the big weathered deck, with long heartfelt conversations and leisurely walks along the sandy shore.

"When did you first realize you were gay, Den?"

"I'm not really sure, John. I guess I've been this way all of my life, that part hasn't changed. But, as you've said, being gay isn't all about sex. I was exposed to homosexual sex at an early age by older boys who lived next door to us at our first house. So I knew about sex. But my first adult experience was when I was about eighteen."

"My fucking uncle was the one who first used me for sex, when I was about twelve. And you don't need to hear about *that*. But—as you know, with gays there's always a *butt*—but there was this boy who lived on the farm about two miles down from us. He was a couple of years older than me and we were real close, and we did all kinds of stuff together. Everything was fine until my dad found us doing stuff in the hayloft. Let me tell you, I got my scrawny ass kicked something fierce. Then he told me to get my goddamned queer ass the hell out of there—to spare the family further embarrassment—and never come back. That's when I moved to New York. I've never been back."

"Wow. That kind of rejection must have really hurt."

"I got over it."

"What was your friend's name?"

"Billy, Billy Knudsen. Big beautiful Billy boy. He was tall, tanned, and handsome as hell; sort of a Sterling Hayden looker, with wavy sun-bleached hair, twelve-pack abs, muscular arms, and he was an incredibly good kisser."

"Do you ever hear from him?"

"Oh, heavens no. By now he's probably married to some homely woman from back home and had an ugly family. He's probably fat, bald, toothless, and broken down from a lifetime of farming and alcohol abuse. That's enough about me. What was your relationship like with your father, Den?"

"Difficult. I think he knew about me, you know, being queer, even before I did, and didn't like it. And because he didn't want me to be 'that way' he kept trying to make me into a man, saying: 'comb your hair like a man; stand up straight like a man, go hunting and fishing like a man.' Like those things would change the way I was wired. But I guess that was his job, wasn't it?"

"Did he ever come right out and ask you if you were queer?"

"Well...there was this time when we were at the cottage, and he had a few beers."

"*Well*...what did he say?"

"He asked if I liked Barbara Streisand."

"Ha, ha, haaaaaaaaaaaaaaaaaa." John laughed so hard he nearly fell off the designer couch. "Thank you for that, it was really good, and I needed a good laugh."

"And you—what about your dad?"

"I was the puny runt of a son who just couldn't cut the mustard. I had seven bossy older sisters, and then came lil ol' me, the *'other sister.'* I was the only boy on a big farm in Indiana and nothing more than a child slave. That stone-hearted bastard never showed me an ounce of kindness, ever; wasn't that kind. To him I was useless as a farmhand, a huge disappointment as a son, and we never related, at all, ever. When I left there I never looked back."

"Don't you keep up with your family at all?"

"No, I left them all. My father forbade any kind of communication with me. They totally shunned me, were ashamed of me, and wanted me out of there. But I do have one sister I was kind of close to; she was closest to me in age, and she gave me her hope chest money to escape there. We still write, and she's visited a couple times, but she has her own life and family back there. I left all of them many years ago, and made my own family of choice, here, and you're a big part of it."

"Thanks for including me."

"Wouldn't have it any other way, darlin'."

Uncle John had been spending summers in the same salty seaside shack for several seasons, and every year he hosted a gay-la. That year's theme was *"All About Eve."* Glossy invitations stated, "Fasten your seat belts, ladies and gentlemen; it's going to be a bumpy night. Every guest *must* come dressed as a character from the movie, and no one will be admitted without a costume."

*"P.S. I will be *Eve*, the one and *only* Eve, and there will be no others. Love, John."*

Well you better believe, those top-notch twits really competed to out-costume each other. Glamorous gowns were couture made, with arm-length gloves the exact same shade to conceal their hairy forearms, pails of pancake makeup purchased to covered their burly beards-up, and gallons of glitter were added, too, 'cause a girl needs to have her bling. Birdseed built-up bulging bosoms, big wigs dressed their balding heads, and high-heeled shoes the size of gunboats bedecked their big flat feet. Jus add enough alcohol, and it's all good.

Later that summer, during a walk on the sandy shore, a foggy sea-driven mist turned into a drizzly rain, and the gray oppressive day turned the conversation serious. Blue eyes crying in the rain. John explained that he had volunteered for a hepatitis B testing program a few years earlier, and he was told that he was infected with the HIV virus. It certainly was not the kind of news you wanted getting out, especially when they were threatening to quarantine those who were infected.

"You know, Den, when I first learned I had it, it stopped me dead in my tracks. After recovering from the shock I did everything I could to help my body become more fit and fight off this dreadful disease. It's funny, because I feel just fine, and even have this little potbelly I can't get rid of no matter how hard I try. But I can feel it there, lurking inside me."

"I don't know what to say, John."

"Don't need to say anything, darling, it's all right...just be there for me."

"I'm here."

"Thank you. You know, Den, really, I've had an amazing life. Who would have ever imagined this little snot-nosed brat from the wrong side of the cornfields would ever make it to Oz, let alone see the things I've seen, and have the amazing life I've had. I've been truly blessed. Life can be so rich and beautiful, and you can make yours exactly what you want it to be."

"Thank you for that pearl of wisdom, but I have to point out that you're not gone yet."

"I know. But none of us are going to make it out of here alive. We all die eventually, I just happen to have my expiration date. I'm not doing that well now, my T-cell numbers aren't good and they've been steadily going down; it's only a matter of time. When I first learned that I was positive I became a complete vegetarian and have remained that way for nearly four years, I quit smoking, quit drinking; hell, I quit doing about everything except having a little pot now and then. May as well be a monk. And even though I did everything I could to clean up my life, I know the grim reaper is still coming for me. I can feel him lurking, Den, and I'm just waiting for the other shoe to drop."

"John!"

"*What*? You've seen it happening. One by one our friends are slowly vanishing, they are either just getting diagnosed as being HIV positive, in some stage of the illness, or already dead, and the rest of us are walking around marked for death. I've been lucky so far. Since being diagnosed I haven't had any serious symptoms, but now I need to have surgery to remove some cancerous lesions from my back. It's Kaposi's sarcoma."

"What can I do, John?"

"Just be a friend."

It was true; many of our contemporaries were succumbing to the dreadful plague. After much soul-searching I made the difficult decision to be tested. And quite unbelievably, my physician advised me agaist it. In spite of his very questionable advice, I was tested anyway, and thankfully learned I was HIV negative. That was when I really began to examine my life.

I understood why John made every day count, because he knew his days were numbered. And even though I may not have been sick at that time, he made me realize my days were precious and numbered as well.

"Don't postpone happiness, Den. Follow your bliss."

But as you may know, bliss is a difficult thing to follow. One of my blissful unfulfilled dreams had been to live a simple life in tranquil rustic surroundings and support myself creating art; an idyllic,

Thoreau-like life. I never dreamed of living in The City, it just happened. But something had shifted in me after witnessing my contemporaries prematurely dying, and a form of survivor's guilt set in. Why did so many die, why was I spared, and what was I supposed to do with my life?

Later that year I left New York City and returned to Michigan, to begin my new "smaller life." Uncle John took my leaving particularly hard, but also understood why I was departing. As luck would have it, we saw each other later that same year, on the other side of the country, while I was working in Hollywood with Bam-Bam. Uncle John had been scheduled to attend LA's Pacific Design Center's Spring Design Market, so we made plans to rendezvous while he was there.

John, and Anya, his high-toned client, climbed the mountain to Ingrid's place for an afternoon tour, and they were very impressed. After having the big reveal they wanted something to eat, and not being familiar with the local epicurean possibilities, I asked Bam-Bam for advice. Big mistake. His recommended Hell's Kitchen, the greasiest spoon in LA, and a filthy hole-in-the-wall located in the most notorious gay prostitution district of West Hollywood. This slippery eatery just "happened" to be located right next door to a seedy male hooker bar called The Cockeyed Optimist, making it easy for patrons to have a disgusting dinner and then something fruity and infectious for dessert.

"You know, darling, I've lived in The City for nearly all my life and known some pretty low-life characters, but this friend of yours, this Bam-Man, he *is* without a doubt the lowest form of life I have ever met," John announced. He *was*, however, impressed with Ingrid's place and the work we were doing there. Like many others, he could appreciate Kim's artistic endeavors, if not his proclivities.

The following summer John arranged a visit to Michigan. When picking him up from the airport I noticed he'd diminished, had aged over the year, was smaller, but he still possessed that wonderful warmth. His was a glowing I'm-so-happy-to-see-you smile that demonstrated his unconditional love, such as I would have received from a gay father.

Uncle John had so much fun on his visit he booked two weeks' vacation for the following summer, and this time he invited two dear friends to join him; Lahr the mischievous Scandinavian scamp who worked with him in the city, and Felix the Kat, from Key West. Both of these friends had also attended the "All About Eve" party, with Lahr appearing as Celeste Holmes's character, and Felix appearing as the housemaid from the French version of *La Cage aux Folles*, a part which was *not* in the movie. Wearing a short black ruffled French maid's outfit with black fishnet stockings, and carrying a feather duster and whip, he was sort of an S&M maid. "Clean it up—*or else!*"

Felix was an elegantly long and exotic ebony man, a dancer who slinked along, catlike. Articulate and distinguished sounding, he'd acquired the upper-crusty accent while living in *Mary* Olde England for years with one of Princess Di's queer cousins; and like most fags, he simply hated name-dropping. But his coserative way of dressing, infectious upper-crusty accent, and proper manner only belied his wicked ways. He was from Dayton, for Christ's sake.

While visiting I treated them to a local production of *Sweet Charity*, which was performed on a sultry August evening in the historic, and not air-conditioned, Manistee Ramsdell Theater.

"Darling, *I* was seated in the audience for the Broadway debut of *Sweet Charity*'s, and let me tell you, it was absolutely *electric*. There will never be another Fosse," Felix said, sitting erect and wearing a black velvet tuxedo jacket. When the play ended he stood, soaking wet and politely clapping, and announced, "Well, bless them for crawling out of the woods and putting this on for us."

He certainly knew about the theater, because he was a true thespian, having appeared in the original cast of *Hair* and *Pippin* and played Aubrey, the man-eating plant from *Little Shop of Horrors*. Then he married a queen from England and moved abroad. But that silly show about the bloodthirsty plant was still running for years after he'd left. Every once in a while Felix would shout out "Feed me", and make the whole house crack up, especially Lahr. He was tall and blond, slim and Nordic, and had a cute speech impediment. But he was trouble, especially when paired with bad cat Felix.

At their lovely lakeside retreat, Broadway show tunes played on a borrowed record player all day long, cocktails were consumed, and cigarettes smoked from the moment they dragged out of bed late in the afternoon till they finally passed out in the wee hours of the morning. Their only reason for going to town was to get more cigarettes, booze, or sweet corn. I never saw people eat so much corn.

"Do you guys realize that there are over three dozen ears of corn in the fridge already? Quit buying it every time you go out," I said.

"But, darling, haven't you seen the *delicious* farmhand who's selling that *sweet* corn?" Felix said, as if I was completely ignorant. "Lahr just can't seem to get enough of that corn."

They only visited the beach briefly, or occasionally went for short woodland walks and a bit of fresh air, because they weren't there for the air or scenery, they wanted to see each other one last time. They cherished their time together, dear friends at different stages of "the illness," and they were all gone within two years, including Uncle John.

— ~

"Mr. Murphy? This is the Manistee County sheriff, and we are calling you because a Mr. John Slattery has been in an automobile accident, and asked that we call you. He was just sent to West Shore Hospital, and you will find him there."

"Oh dear God. Is he all right?"

"Yes. He seems to be, but he's quite confused. Nothing appears to be broken."

— ~

"John, I got here as fast as I could. Are you all right? What happened?"

"I'm not sure, everything just went black. They say I hit a power pole."

"But you're all right?"

"Yes, yes. But I'm kinda confused. I don't know what happened. They made me take a goddamned Breathalyzer test, because the assholes thought I was drunk."

"But you're all right? No cuts or scrapes?"

"A couple little ones. I had to tell them to be careful of the blood. I don't think they've ever seen anyone in here who was HIV positive."

John was all right *physically*, but still quite confused, and the two-week-old car they were "borrowing" was wrapped around a telephone pole on Main Street, and I felt responsible for that. Thank God no one was hurt.

Another vehicle was rented and two days later we were headed toward the Mackinac Bridge, because John and Lahr were still planning to go to the Grand Hotel on Mackinac Island and check on their decorator friend Carleton Varney's handiwork. They'd both made a shitpile of money selling him coordinating wallpaper and fabrics to overdecorate the stick-built lakefront palace, splashy and geranium-themed, it was gay, gay, gay as could be; chintz, chintz, chintzy.

Uncle John and I shared a toot-suite, a sunny vision in daffodil-yellow, overlooking the side yard and woods; not the best harbor view, but a roomy suite with two enormous beds and comfortable sitting area. Aunt's Lahr and Felix shared an adjacent room, and we didn't need to hear all of *that*.

That evening while they were busy having a rip-roaring private party in their chintzy room, John was slowly going blind in ours. "Den, I'm scared I'm losing my vision. I'm getting these strange blank spots in my field of vision, and I'm pretty sure that's what happened when I crashed the car. It all went black."

"How long has this been happening?"

"Off and on, for quite a while now. I can't even see enough to button my clothes anymore. My hands don't work right. I've been dropping things, and can't hold utensils. Its little stuff, but it's adding up. I feel like Bette Davis in *Dark Victory*—I feel it coming and I can't do anything about it."

"Let me know if you need anything."

"Can you help me get dressed? I can't even do that."

"Sure. Don't you worry."

"Den, when the time comes, and when *I* decide that I am too far gone, I want to go on my own terms. Can I count on you to help me?"

"Are you talking about helping you, like Jack Kevorkian 'helps' people?"

"Yes. Will you promise to help me go when I decide the time comes?"

"I'll do what I can."

But I could not do that, even when he asked. And he did.

His final wish was to die quietly at home, in his little corner of the world, the itty-bitty studio apartment that was his home for over thirty-five years. He left this earth free of pain, comfortably, and on his own terms.

— —

John was truly a giver, and he cherished each day of life; probably because he knew he was living with a death sentence. Acting as a catalyst, he came into my life at an important time, and helped me to understand what was truly important, too, to love, be loved, live in the moment, and experience life's abundant richness. Achieving fame or amassing a fortune did not interest him, because: "Your worth has nothing to do with a decimal point."

His parting words to me were, "Darling, you can't take a thing with you but your memories. And I will remember you most fondly."

"Goodbye, my dear friend."

He'd figured a way to have a high-quality life on a shoestring, lived frugally, and had abundant time to experience the rich cultural venues his wonderful city had to offer. His was a prickly kind of friendship, but an unconditional kind of love. When it's my turn to meet my maker, I am certain that he will be among those present to welcome me home.

Bless his dear soul.

Lee the Flea

oving from Manhattan to Manistee was monumental, mercy me. This life-altering migration, from a large metropolitan congregation with nine thousand people living in one block, to a mostly wooded wilderness with nine thousand people in the entire county, was a real adjustment. Departing New York City in the late eighties, I left to find peace and quiet, and *boy* did I get it, big-time. One minute I'm a big man in Manhattan, making movies with Charlie Sheen,* and the next thing you know I am chatting it up with the chipmunks in the forests of north Michigan.

*Before leaving Manhattan I had a split-second appearance in the movie *Wall Street*, where my partner and I were hired to portray decorative painters. The part was so small that it did not qualify me for my fifteen seconds of fame.*

Arriving "up north," as the locals say, I scoured northern Michigan for nearly a year before finding the perfect place—a lovely little lakeside cottage in a sleepy little Lake Michigan shorefront town called Manistee. Manistee is a Chippewa Indian word meaning "spirit of the woods," and that was an appropriate name, because the Manistee National Forest is the largest in the Lower Peninsula.

By working diligently, my latent dream became reality, and my cozy lakefront cottage and smaller life became comfortable and settled. Once settled I set about finding a "community." Fully realizing there probably would be very little *gay life* in the north woods, I was prepared to make the necessary lifestyle adjustments, just the same. Bring 'em on. But still being young and idealistic, I hadn't entirely given up the idea of possibly finding romance in the backwoods, or at least a like-minded lumberjack with loose morals.

Finding a milieu was going to take some work. So I did my research, networked, and found organizations. Back in the olden days, before Al Gore invented the Internet for computer dating, there were mailbox organizations for rural gay folks with cute anachronistic names like Rural Fag Delivery (RFD) and Sons and Daughters (SAD). These "monthly visitors" were mimeographed newsletters that worked as a primitive form of networking for us gay folks in far-off places, and they included articles on health and politics, poetry, recipes, hair trends, and even some personal ads; for same-sex seekers who were searching for similarly love-starved singles in similarly secluded sections.

"People...people who need people...are the luckiest people...in the..."

According to my fag-rag fact-findings, in the late eighties there was not an officially "outed" community to be found in this entire section of the state, and the closest gay bar was a two-hour drive to the south, outside Muskegon. This was disheartening, to say the least.

Back then, Bob Dameron published a paperback guide called *Gay Places in America*, which listed the bars, restaurants, and known cruising areas in your neck of the woods. Pathetically, the only queer thing listed for northern Michigan was Dignity, a "gay-friendly" Catholic group, an oxymoron, and my last resort. So, in the dead of a snowy January night, after having several beers, I wrote them.

"Dear Dignity, I am contacting you...because I have lost mine."

About a week later I received a short handwritten reply explaining that the local Dignity chapter had closed due to lack of interest. How very sad. But they thoughtfully forwarded the PO Box number of a sister organization and suggested that I contact them.

The group was called "Friends North," and their meetings were held in Traverse City, the largest city in north Michigan. They thoughtfully sent along one of their cheery Cherry City newsletters that were mailed monthly to areas gay and lesbian, transsexual, transgender, and gender-blender peoples; and that included the Upper Peninsula. This loosely organized social group hosted monthly meetings, mixers, dances and socials, canoe trips, cookouts, camping outings, biking tours, and gatherings where people got to know each other, without becoming alcoholics in the process. Sign me up.

These "Friends" were my introduction to northern Michigan's gay society, and to my liking, they were a very diverse group of enlightened young professionals, quite like myself; an attractive active group.

There were also "bears" in the north woods. Bears were fat, hairy old men who got together regularly for potluck dinners, as well as bodily fluid and recipe swaps. There were several subspecies, such as the polar bears, the really old, fat, and raunchy white-haired ones. Black bears were the fat, hairy, dark-skinned urban ones with big "personalities," wink, wink, and cubs were the fat, young, and hairy inductees. There's a crooked lid for every crooked pot, and probably a den in your area. Grrrrrr!

Usually the problem with scenic but remote places always comes down to geography. Most of the people, events, and organizations for gays were over an hour's drive away. But there was another way of finding fresh fruit in your area—as Sheriff Dullard from the 1995 movie *To Wong Foo, Thanks for Everything! Julie Newmar* did, use gaydar to seek them out. Sniff the air for expensive colognes, hairspray, and bronzer and you'll surely find their dens of iniquity; seek out florists, theater people, hairstylists, decorators, antiques dealers, mechanics, bankers, undertakers, lumberjacks, and big, burly firemen. This would take some work.

In the meantime I adjusted to the straight world I found myself living in. My new/old cottage had been around for over a century, and it was a fixer-upper with a lot of potential. But you know what Dr. Phil says about potential? "Potential means you ain't done it yet." But I was young and optimistic, idealistic, and knew that this rustic Cape Cod clapboard cottage, just a few miles out of town, was the perfect place for me. Four wooded acres were nicely nestled on a small spring-fed lake, with a cozy cottage that was just the right size for me, and a big old barn for a studio. Perfect.

When the renovations were completed I wanted to furnish my home with comfortable, cottage-style décor appropriate to the rustic feel and age of the place; so naturally I looked for antiques. The local newspaper was running an article touting the opening of a new antiques store called Victor's Victorians, so I decided to drive into town and check them out.

"May I help you?" the haughty man with the prissy pencil-thin mustache disapprovingly said while looking over his half-lens glasses, clearly irritated by my very presence. When translating from gay to straight language, that meant; "Who the *hell* are you, and why are *you* in *my* piss-elegant store?"

Admittedly, I was wearing a ratty red-and-black buffalo plaid woolen Mackinaw jacket and matching Elmer Fudd hat, because I'd just stopped into town right after painting and plastering, and looked like shit. Seeing as I was wearing my wabbit-hunting attire, and had a couple days' stubble, he probably mistook me for local and straight; and while watching me park my rusty-but-trusty beater truck, he'd already sized me up, assessed my net worth, and summarily dismissed me.

"Yes. I'm looking for cottage furnishings, things from the thirties and forties. Stuff like that."

With his nose pointed at the tin ceiling, and without looking up from his bookkeeping, he said, "I'm sorry, but we only carry *fine antiques* in here. I wouldn't have any*thing* like that in *my* store. No."

Got your number, Stella.

But...since I was already in town, and in need of a haircut, I decided to take care of that. The tiny newspaper was also running an article about the grand opening of "Lee's Glamorama," reportedly "the newest and hippest salon in town." The "Glamour-room" was reported to be opening on River Street, and with downtown being three blocks long, it wasn't hard to find.

My stylist was a tall and good-looking man with a heaping head-full of prematurely platinum hair, sitting atop a suntanned and youthful face. A Marine Corps tattoo adorned his well-toned upper arm, and he was quite a striking man. Sometimes the package does not match the contents. Lee was handsome as hell, scattered as the wind, and dingy. He should have been born a blond.

While hacking away at my dwindling hair, Lee began to prattle away endlessly and mindlessly. Not paying any attention to measuring or precision at all, he went at it willy-nilly with scissors flying, lips flapping, and happily barbering and blabbering until he accidentally clipped my earlobe.

"Oh jeez, I'm so sorry. I don't have any Band-Aids either. Here, hold this perm-wrapper paper on it, sorry," he said. And after making me look like Van Gogh he handed me a tiny two-inch piece of tissue to soak up the blood hemorrhaging from my severed earlobe.

"So, what's your name again, Dean?"

"Den."

"You're not from around here, are you, Doug? So where'd you say you live again, Dan?"

"I just bought a cottage on Canfield Lake."

"Why'd you wanna move way out there, Dave? I never go out there, because I hear that lake has the swimmer's itch."

"Really?"

"You know, Dick, you should be careful ou there 'cause I hear people drowned in that lake all the time. So whatcha do for a living? Married? Wife? Kids?"

"I moved here a couple of months ago, from New York City. I'm an artist. And it is Den." "New York City? Artist? Really! What the hell'd you move here for, Dale?"

"It's beautiful here. Den."

"I keep telling you, it's Lee. Oh my God, ya know what? I'm getting a tanning booth, and I wanted to paint the room all tropical; you know, palm trees, bananas, and lush and green. This place is painted gray and it looks like a funeral home, and that tanning booth looks just like a coffin. So can you do that? How much would that cost? And what the hell made you want to move to Manistee?"

"I wanted peace and quiet."

"Well, you sure moved to the right place for that, 'cause we got *lotsa* that, and that's about all we got lotsa, besides lotsa trees, and lotsa water. So what about painting this tanning booth, Dennis?"

"Sure."

I believed I'd made a local fruitcake friend that day. He was dingy as hell but genuine, sweet and childlike with a heaping head of snowy-white hair. Blabbering endlessly away, he told his life's story, including having a brain tumor removed while in the Marines. After being discharged early, he received a monthly disability check, which he gave to his white-haired, widowed mother. What a nice boy. I assumed that the tumor had something to do with his simpler ways. He was unaffected and trustworthy, and we easily became friends. Like many fruitcakes, he was fond of his junk, so we became yard-saling, and barhopping buddies, because those were our common interests.

Identical-Lee had a twin sister, living in Florida, but the rest of his large and extended family still lived up there, and it was a good place to call home. His older brother and sister-in-law, Jim and Diane, ran the Sunrise Bakery, the local luncheonette and heartbeat of town, dink-tank and roundtable, where the locals went daily to solve the world's problems over coffee, cigarettes, and doughnuts. After getting to know them, they asked me to paint a mural for them, so I painted something a little "Norman Rockwell-ish," and from then on I was known in town as "the artist."

Eventual-Lee I met the entire extended fam-a-Lee, brothers, sister, aunts, and uncles, and they were a nice Polish-American family that treated me like they would any other Polack. Most Thursday nights we'd join the girls after bowling league for beers, billiards, and barhopping, the local wintertime traditions, which were traditionally done while intoxicated and on a snowmobile.

During this period I was also commuting back and forth to California, and alternately working with Bam-Bam on Ingrid's home and my enchanted cottage. While I was working way out west, the prissy antiques store queen, Victor, and his cute but dumb boyfriend, Dicky, befriended Lee, and they become well acquainted. Innocent-Lee, mistaken-Lee, and stupid-Lee accepted a loan from them for $3,000 that was practically offered as a gift, and lent without any mention of the terms of repayment.

The fly was stuck in the web.

He happy-Lee used this borrowed money to gay-Lee make cosmetic changes to his chic new salon, going complete-Lee black-and-white; most striking-Lee, don't you think? Well, the usury loan quickly became a millstone around his neck. He'd never dealt with unscrupulous people like these two, and was blindsided by the Shylock loan shark. Victor began to make Lee's life miserable, just because he could. He threatened to call in the loan and take possession of the chic salon, when he knew full well that Lee was unable to pay. Caveat emptor.

— —

Now...I had been around a bit more than Lee, and seen a sociopath in action. Lee, on the other hand, was more of a babe in the woods. When I returned from California, Lee reintroduced me to the antiques queens, who fortunately did not remember me. And after shaking hands I needed a wet wipe. "So, just what is it that you do when you're out in California all the time, anyway, Don?" Victor, the older part of the May-December relationship, asked, pumping me for information.

"The name is Denny. And I'm working on a home renovation."

"Sorry, Lee's been calling you Don. So, Den, this house you're working on, is it yours?" "No, it's a client's home."

"Oh, a client, I see—you have clients. Just what is it that you do again, Den?"

"I'm an artist and designer, decorative painter and restoration artist."

"All that, huh? Well, ya know, my parents live out there in sunny California, and I'll be going out to see them at Easter. Maybe I should just look you up when I'm out there, and check you out."

"Wouldn't that be fun," I said, trying to keep a straight face, but I couldn't. Well...I guess curiosity must have gotten the better of him, because three days later he just happened to stop over and blatantly searched through every nook, cranny, cupboard, and closet in my cottage, to assess my net worth. I just let him look, and dismissed him as being a busybody.

My precious time in Manistee disappeared all too quickly while I happily labored on my lovely lakeside retreat. Shortly after returning to the Hollywood project, the butler called me on the intercom and informed me that I had a call.

"Den? This is Vic. I'm out here in sunny California visiting the old folks, don't cha know, and I just thought I'd just drop by and visit you. Now, wouldn't that be fun?"

"Who is this?"

"*Vic*, I'm from Victor's Victorians. You remember me—from Manistee? I *own* the antiques store."

"Sorry, I didn't recognize the voice," I said, thinking, *what is he calling me for?* We met twice.

"Well, I'm out here and thought I'd look ya up ta say hello. So *hello*, ha-ha, ha."

"Back at cha." I was most surprised to hear from him, to say the least.

Within an hour he was buzzing the gate. Maurice, the butler, escorted him into the family room, made him comfortable, and called me on the intercom informing me I had a visitor.

"You son of a bitch," Victor whispered so loudly the neighbors heard. "My God, would you look at this fabulous fucking place, with a butler and maid, gardener, and chauffeur. And, oh my God, would you look at that fucking million-dollar view. The Hollywood sign's practically in your yard."

"Nice to see you, too, Victor."

As I escorted him through the house, I could actually see his pointed little head running an accounting actualization of the home's contents and net worth. Scanning the house as if it was a store full of merchandise, he looked at everything—over and under—searching for signatures, labels, and dates. I will admit the place was furnished with museum-quality pieces: Ruhlmann furniture, Tamara Lempicka oil paintings, Icart statuary and lithographs, René Lalique art-glass pieces, a rosewood Steinway grand piano, Tiffany lamps, Erté sculptures and prints, the good stuff, the real stuff, and he was completely blown away.

"Is this him? Is the man in this photograph the homeowner?"

"Yes, that's him; he's standing in front of his house in Hawaii. It's an old mission church that sits right on the ocean."

"You son of a bitch, he is scorching hot, *ouch*! You're fucking with him, aren't you? You lucky fucking bastard. Is he a movie star? Who is he? Well, look at you, bein' somebody *after all*."

When I returned to Manistee I discovered he'd blabbed his big mouth all over town about my huge mansion in Hollywood and the incredibly handsome, rich, and big-dicked Italian movie star that I lived with. He also reported that we had a staff of maids, butlers, gardeners, and chauffeurs who drove us around in big black stretch limousines, plus giant swimming pools, great big saunas and gyms, "and the views...don't even get me started."

"Most likely he's been relocated by the FBI witness protection program, and living undercover, don't cha know. 'I mean, why else would someone move from Manhattan to Manistee and also have a mansion in Hollywood?' Well...Victor made the story sound so convincing that they wanted to believe it, and completely bought all that manufactured malarkey.

Unbelievable-Lee said, "Vic tells me your mansion in California is fabulous, a great big castle, and you've been dislocated by the eyewitness news program. Ya know, by looking at you you'd never guess you was so rich and famous, because you just don't seem to give a shit about what you wear or how you look. Vic says that you've got a staff-a maids and butlers, and gardeners, and a Ferrari, and a swimming pool, and a, and a, and a…" He prattled on and on as if he had a severe stutter.

"That's not my house, I'm just working there."

"Vic says that you're living with this really rich, hot Italian movie-star boyfriend with a really big dick. You'd a never thunk it looking at ya. Rich, huh? So, you wanna get married, or what?"

"Or what!"

Lee never wanted to believe otherwise. He preferred lies to the truth, because it sounded so much more appealing. "How big is his dick? You can tell me, Den. Is it like a beer can?"

But by now he was totally embroiled in the invisible web Victor had spun, and while squirming to free himself he became more entangled with each movement. Vic enjoyed watching him struggle, he moved in for the kill, and seized the savvy salon. So now the Glamorama belonged to Vic, and Lee was working for him. *Well*, small towns have nothing to do but talk, so they did, and about this. Before long a tempest was brewing at the coffee shop and the locals were justifiably on Lee's side.

The spider emitted a single silken thread, very fine, and extremely strong. The invisible threads were joined, a web was spun. The unsuspecting fly was caught, drained of its vitality, and discarded.

He may have been old enough to have snowy-white hair, but he was still a babe in the woods who had never experienced anything like Vic-tor-mentor before. He'd never dreamed people could be so mean-spirited, manipulative, and downright evil.

"To the Victor go the spoils." Supposedly, Vic had spoiled other businesses as well. It seems he was quite industrious, and a sociopath; operating without a conscience, lyin', thievin', and smilin' all the way.

I'd seen it before, he was in cahoots with the devil, and so crooked he had to screw his pants on each morning. Before long his trail of misdeeds and wicked ways began to catch up with him, and the first domino to fall was his beloved Dick, the pretty but dumb young man he'd shared a home and bed with. He finally had his fill of Vic's shit and left. Victor went into nuclear meltdown, was violently outraged by his lover's rejection, and set about seeking extreme revenge.

Now, allegedly both men were already "tainted fruit."{That was an inside eighties euphemism for being HIV positive}. But then victim Vic filed suit in court vindictively accusing his once-beloved Dick of intentionally infecting him with HIV. And his cute but not so smart young boyfriend never saw it coming, the venom of the scorned spouse. Dick was immediately arrested, incarcerated, and placed in quarantine in the county jail, where he remained for several solitary months. Eventually his case went to trial, was dismissed, and he was released with time served. After being released he quickly fled the state and returned to his home, and died less than a month later.

Meanwhile Vic went about playing the valiant victim and visiting area schools preaching abstinence, and warning students of the consequences of having promiscuous and unprotected sex. He'd perfected the part of the defenseless victim quite convincingly, but he was far from innocent. Capitalizing on his newfound notoriety, he made appearances on television and was often quoted in newspapers, but this public lip service did not mitigate his misdeeds. Be it good or bad, he enjoyed them talking about him; and they're talking about him still, over thirty years later.

"Allegedly," there were several other actions pending against Saint Vic as well. There were a couple of your basic bread-and-butter, slip-and-fall accidents. In another case, he'd been accused of importing tons of marijuana using his antiques store as a mule. In yet another case, he was allegedly being sued by the USPS for filing fraudulent loss-and-damage claims.

And yet another "misunderstanding" occurred when he was sued by an insurance company for filing a fraudulent loss claim. *Now*, he "claimed" his "claim" was a stolen Mercedes, but in reality he had hidden the car inside a leased barn and pocketed the reimbursement. Then, three years later when he thought the coast was clear, took it out and sold it to some unsuspecting schmuck for an irresistible price. Talk about chalking up your bad karma. Cha-ching.

Well, the dirt piled up until Vic had a mound big enough to start a ski slope, Mount Vic. So he packed up the antiques store, closed the salon, and fled town when he smelled the tar cooking and saw the flaming torches coming his way. Slithering away under the cover of darkness, he departed with his new lover, Rob Thecradle, and they moved to California to become someone else.

Lee never did figure out exactly what happened, but he went back to being happy-go-lucky Lee and working at another salon. As long as he had a pack of cigarettes and bottle of soda pop, he was good. Somehow the bills got paid.

Ya see, Lee was truly a fam-a-Lee man at heart, and lost without a committed relationship. He needed structure, routine, and a babysitter. Believe it or not, he had one relationship lasting fourteen years, and another nearly ten years long, and when it ended badly he was completely lost. Not knowing what to do, restless-Lee went searching for his new life. In one year alone he'd moved a total of sixteen times; there were a couple of moves into and then out of Manistee, into Ludington twice, then to Flint, Chicago, Traverse City, and Muskegon twice, too. And that's when we started calling him Lee the Flea, because he'd hopped around so much. Final-Lee he landed in sunny central Florida, near his identical twin sister, Glee, who helped him get established.

Lee's last stop on his way out of town was my cottage. "Bye, Den, I'm leaving for Florida." But before splitting he spray-painted the rust on his beaten-up Pinto periwinkle, and left me with six empty paint cans and blue paint dust all over my garage, pickup truck, and the once-white laundry hanging downwind on the clothesline.

With his periwinkle Pinto packed with paraphernalia—a few parcels of personal possessions, some household items, and a couple of boxes of clothes—he arrived in sunny central Florida two days later. Thankful-Lee he had exactly $2.37 to begin his new life, so he did.

"Hell, Den, I started out with nothin'—and I still had most of it left."

He didn't even have enough money left to buy a pack of cigarettes. So, he bummed a cigarette and bought an off-brand soda pop and an instant scratch-off lottery ticket.

BINGO!

He'd won $10,000. So that very instant-Lee ran right out and purchased a mobile home for $7,000. Then he spent the remainder on furniture, accessories, and artwork to pretty up the peaked old place. First he painted it a pretty periwinkle blue, with coral trim, then he purchased a shitload of pretty plants to beautify the tiny yard. He fixed the shit out of the trailer, creating a nice, comfortable, and paid-for home. The next week he was broke again and had to borrow money for a pack of cigarettes.

Immediate-Lee, and I mean the very day he arrived in Florida, he was hired at the local Wal-Mart Smart Styles Salon, hit the ground running, and did very well. Since ADHD ruled his life, he was not meant for precision work, but he excelled at volume, and turning out ten good enough haircuts an hour. He was always personable and chatty, frequently requested, and continuously busy.

The problem was he was ease-a-Lee bored, so he would regularly quit the Wal-Mart's to seek the greener pastures and monetary rewards that supposedly awaited somewhere else. When he didn't find the green he was seeking, he'd just quit the new place and return to the Wal-Mart's, and they just kept hiring him back—thirteen times now, by our count.

Everybody liked Lee in spite of his proclivities, and he was always busy. Truthful-Lee he was an asset to the salon because he had an amiable personality and turned out good enough work for most of Wal-Mart shoppers. Central Florida was full of Q-tipped, hair-helmeted old ladies, and they loved Lee, because nobody could rat a head of hair higher, or faster, than him, and his well-lacquered dos lasted through a whole week of humid hurricane weather.

When not in the salon Lee spent his leisure time fixing up, decorating, and making trailers pretty. So once his prize-winning trailer was fixed nicely and decorated within an inch of its life, he quickly became bored with it and sold it for less than he'd paid for it. Feeling the need for yet another crafty project, he bought another decoratively challenged shit shack of a trailer and made it pretty, too. Then he sold it for less than he paid for it, and bought another mess and made it pretty. Again and again Lee the Flea hopped around the park, making pretty trailers out of shit shacks, until he was broke and homeless—and the trailer park was fucking fabulous.

On and on Lee the Flea happily hopped around the Happy Days mobile home court, until nearly every single trailer was beautified— except for one—a teeny, tiny, and torpedo-shaped 1938-vintage coral pink travel trailer that sat under a spectacularly sprawling tree. Lee thought the trailer was darling as could be, and before long it actually was. He loved new beginnings and had a knack for painting, decorating, and making shitty things pretty, inside and out.

Kenny Rogers sang "You decorated my life," as painter-Lee made the outside a Tootsie Roll brown, added geranium-red window boxes, painted the trim and shutters a spicy mustard yellow and the front door and decorative accents a tasty avocado. A sign warning "Don't come a knockin' if the trailer is a rockin'" was hung by the back door. But something wasn't quite right, because he'd made the place look Bavarian and not Floridian, like Hansel and Gretel's Florida getaway.

But the thing he loved most about his tiny trailer was the exotic sprawling tree that sheltered and shaded it. You've never seen such a fabulous tree. Lacy little chartreuse leaves covered its canopy, and in early summer it would be so completely covered with colossal clusters of purple petals it would stop traffic on Highway 92. Being unfamiliar with Florida flora and fauna, I asked him the tree's name. Lee had no idea, but said the redneck locals called it a nigger ear tree, because of the curly black seed pods. He just thought it was pretty as could be, and when in bloom it truly was glorious.

*P.S. I later learned that this exotic purple tree was a called a jacaranda.

"Den, this place is so darned small I have to go outside just to change my mind."

That much was true. The tiny travel trailer tucked under the pretty purple tree had dwarfed proportions. It was not a mobile home at all. It was a miniature movable mansion made for midgets. Lee stood over six feet tall, and I am five-six, and I had to scrunch while using the lovely coral pink tub and shower. Rotten-egg-smelling, rusty, not-well-water continuously leaked from a corroded chromed faucet, making a permanent skid mark down the pretty pink tub. What the hell did he care? The stinkin' water was provided free by the park, so he had no incentive to fix it.

Every single surface of his house was completely covered with crap, filled with collectible stuff, and looked like a time capsule or museum. His trailer was so small there wasn't room for anything, and he had everything. Separating the living room from the dollhouse-sized kitchen was a round table with three blond chairs around it, because there wasn't room for a fourth. A contact paper—covered side table had a stained-glass lamp sitting on it, right next to a honey-maple armchair with the cushion skirted in a rust-, gold-, and forest green-striped fabric. A pretty trapunto pillow made with calico prints sat on the chair's back, a gift from his elderly mom.

A petite loveseat was covered in chic sage chenille and pushed up against the west wall; the back draped with his mother's hand-crocheted, warm woolen throw, in harmonious shades of rust, gold, orange, sage, and cream. One of her patchwork quilts, in similar shades, sat on the sofa's arm.

Really, the aged trailer was quite cozy, fit his needs, and he was happy there. Contented-Lee he worked at the Wal-Mart all week, spent Saturday night watching reruns of the *Lawrence Welk Show*, and then gay-Lee went across the highway to the queer bar. What more could he want?

Entertaining-Lee hosted many festive get-togethers, and most of them were held outside on the "lanai." Under a big aluminum carport/awning there was plenty of room for drinking and smoking, arts -and-crafts making, barbecuing, laundering, and gardening; he liked to be busy. The one and only bedroom was equally small, and had barely enough room for a full-size bed; it wouldn't hold a queen. There was not room for a sidepiece or even a chair, just the bed. His favorite color was red, and he'd painted the bedroom red, *again*. Do we see a pattern here? *Definite-Lee*.

He liked to refer to the living room, dining room, and kitchen combination as the "great room," even though it measured a mere eight by ten feet. He had covered the walls with the most wonderful white birch bark wallpaper *ever*, which was purchased from Wal-Mart's, and it took only one roll to do the entire room. The windows, doors, and trim were painted red, because he *loved* red. Then he covered every inch of the paper with a plethora of paraphernalia: paintings, prints, and pretty china plates, wise-cracking plaques and nifty knickknacks, shelves chock-full of tchotchkes and tiny figurines, and an old oval mirror that'd lost its sheen. So much shit covered those trailer walls you couldn't see the paper at all. But it was his little paid-for tin can, and he was a happy man.

But during the night, while Lee was slumbering in his lovely nest, some mischievous prankster had snuck into the trailer park and repainted the sign, changing the *D* in *Days* into a *G*, and making it read, "*Happy Gays Trailer Park*;" which was certainly truth in advertising, because this fabulous mobile-homo park was located just across the highway from the local gay bar, The Cockeyed Cowboy.

The queer bar was a bombproof bunker built of cement block, with its front door permanently propped open. A green felted pool table was prominently placed—front and center—and both kinds of music playing on the jukebox, *country* and *western*. A non-lifelike "Billy the Buck" rubber-necked deer head was proudly mounted on the western wall, and for dollar deposits it would move its fake rubbery lips to sad hillbilly drinkin'songs. Drag shows were performed every Friday and Saturday night, if you liked it or not. *Not.* Their patrons were a rough-and-tumble rednecked crowd of citrus workers, blacks, brown-skinned migrants, bent locals, misguided snowbirds, manly women, and sun-scorched men.

One terrible summer Central Florida had three hurricanes blow through one after the other, and Lee's part of the state was hit particularly hard. I couldn't reach him for days but finally found his twin sister, Glee, who lived just twenty miles away. She reported that the entire back of her double-wide had been ripped off, but she, Earl, and the hounds were fine. When I finally reached Lee, he was fine, too.

"Hell, I rode out the first two hurricanes inside-a my little trailer just fine, and about the worst thing that happened was the 'Don't come a knockin' sign' and the flock of pink plastic flamingos went flying away. But that last hurricane started shaking this trailer something fierce, and when it rolled me into the neighbors' lot and I lost TV reception; I figured I'd better go find some shelter—with cable.

"So I crossed Highway 92 during the hurricane, and went over to the queer bar. Things wasn't too bad over there till the power went out, the beer got warm, they lost cable, and ten inches of stinkin' swampy water came flooding in. I had to sleep on top-a the pool table that night, and let me tell you it was suffocating, stinking, and hotter than hell, without any air-conditioning."

One wicked winter I was most fortunate to be working in sunny Florida, about two miles from Lee's little love nest with a hitch, and renovating a four-thousand-square-foot lakefront home. Lee, living nearby, would often visit the jobsite to offer his unsolicited advice. One day he showed up with an important announcement.

"I'm quitting the hairdo business, Den. I'm sick of it, sick of dealing with people, and I'm going to be a decorator, *like you*. After all, I've got the Home and Garden Channel at my trailer now; I have been watchin' all those decoratin' shows, and I can *definite-Lee* decorate much better than those taste-free people. You seen my trailer, Den. Ain't it purdy? I want in on all the fun."

This was my profession, not what I did for fun, and against my better judgment he began to work with me. Did you know? It is difficult to tell someone who knows everything, anything. Definite-Lee. He was good for bull-moose labor and broad strokes, but didn't have the focus needed to execute precision craftsmanship, or the interest in seeing projects through to completion, and that's what I do.

Ruled by ADHD, he was good for only a few hours each day. But he added his two cents to the project so many times he helped me singlehanded-Lee corner the copper market, thus becoming a rich man. He insisted we needed more drama repeatedly, and I would frequently remind him I run a drama-free workplace. Needless to say, our management skills clashed. The very next day he returned to Wal-Mart's salon, *again*, and according to our counts that was the fourteenth time.

"I was *so* over working with that Den, jeez; what a pissy queen. It was his way or the highway. And he had such boring beige taste. Who died and made him queen, anyway?"

Gleaning, however, was in his nature, and he couldn't turn off the overwhelming urge to shop. Lee was a gatherer and not a hunter, and for him each gathering day would begin with a ritual of strong black coffee and cheap generic cigarettes, followed by a greasy breakfast of fried sausage links, runny-yolked eggs, and well-burnt white-bread toast. Soon as vittles were over, he would hit the thrift stores. Visiting the top-tier merchants first, he'd hit the Salvation Army, Goodwill, Habitat for Humanity, and then the faith-based thrift stores. Next he would hit garage sales and yard sales, and all the while he'd be constantly scanning the curb for cast-off treasures. If empty-handed, but still possessing some cash, he moved on to the lower-tier merchants: Big Lots, Ross, and Family Dollar.

His day was not complete unless he'd returned home with some vintage article, pretty print, darling doodad, funky piece of furniture, or antiquated accessory for his miniature mobile homo. He did have a real knack for arranging his junk, and he was arranging and rearranging it all of the time. But the trouble was, he was continuously starting projects and never finishing them—another ADHD-accredited decorator.

"I'm so poor I can't even pay attention, Den."

"You got that right, brother-Lee."

"I'm so pissed, Den, because I just spent my last dime at a yard sale buying this beautiful oil painting—that goes with absolutely everything I already own—but I don't have any room left to hang it on my walls because they're completely full of stuff all ready. That pisses me off so much, because it would look real pretty in here. Don't cha think?"

"Why yes, Lee, it is beautiful for a swamp scene. Maybe you should hang it on the ceiling. You don't have anything up there yet."

"Oh my God, Den, that is such a good idea. How'd I do that? Never mind, I know—hot glue!" Final-Lee he was finished decorating his tiny trailer and it was finely furnished, just the way he liked it, all comfy-cozy, homey as hell, and pretty as can be. It seemed like a snapshot from the past because everything was preowned, relaxed, familiar, like something you'd once owned, or a memory.

Out on his lanai, Budweiser can wind chimes clinked and clanked in the sickeningly sweetened southern breezes that drifted from the orange juice processing plant, located just a block away, making sweet music for his country company. Under the big aluminum awning there was more furniture than inside the trailer, a burgundy pleather sofa, two corduroy green Lay-Z-Boy recliners, and an oxidized brass coffee table with a coordinating knickknack étagère. And cleverly centering his elegant plein-air grouping was a colossal cut crystal chandelier that was collected from the curb.

It surely felt like home. Home sweet mobile homo.

A dented early American—themed rusted tin storage shed, with a black plastic eagle proudly displayed above the door, held a combination arts and crafting area, washer, potting shed, barbecue, and slop sink. A solar clothes dryer {lines and pins} and purple picnic table completed the hardscape.

Lucky-Lee lived there quite comfortable-Lee for one of the longest periods of his adult life. He predictable-Lee worked all week at the salon, and on Saturday nights he would have a big dinner, watch *Lawrence Welk*, and go to the queer bar and tie one on. It was a good life.

But then...a catastrophe occurred one sunny summer's day, and tragic-Lee the travel trailer romance was ended. It wasn't a hurricane that took the tiny trailer and ended the love affair, and it was not a tornado either—it was lots, and lots, and lots of tiny little bugs: termites. Oh yes, there had been plenty of evidence of their existence all along, because he swatted at them as they flew around during mating season, and each morning he would sweep up their little brown frasses,{ pelleted excrement} from the bedsheets, floors, counters, and tabletops and throw it out the squeaky screen door.

But eventually those pesky little cellulose crunchers caused a major calamity. It happened on a sunny afternoon, when his regular Tuesday, Thursday and Saturday after-an-AA-meeting bud stopped by to conjugate a few verbs. And it was during their conjugal commiseration, while lost in the throes of phonics (*in flagrante delicto*), that the vintage four-poster bed fell through the rotten termite-riddled floor with a crashing thunderous boom. *Whoosh!* They laughed their asses off, so did the neighbors in the trailer park, and they're laughing about it still.

So his darling dainty trailer, along with most of its bug-eaten contents, was abandoned and left to the termites, and Lee was homeless again. Deserting the sawdust pile, he bought another termite farm starter kit, right on busy Highway 92, and began again. Easy come, easy-Lee gone.

Lee the Flea didn't think before he leapt. If he felt like it he leapt, because his life was ruled more by emotion than intellect. That meant he was always starting over, and that tends to become more difficult when you're over sixty. But he needn't worry, because I have often heard that God watches out for fools and babies, and apparent-Lee, Lee, too. He was always blessed with luck and winning money at the casino and on lottery tickets came easily to him.

Perhaps he was more intent on the journey and not the destination. Last I'd heard, he'd left Florida, again, and moved back to Manistee. Come home —all is forgiven.

His most admirable quality was his ability to be in the moment— that, and a genuine childlike innocence, generosity, and gentle trusting nature. He didn't look very far ahead and tried not to look back, never even thought that way. He enjoyed the here and now. Lee will probably never have any wrinkles, because he had so few worries; didn't worry about money or the lack of it. God provided.

God bless his generous, distracted heart.

Château Ghetto's Estate Gardens

This gardening thing had really grown on Nikki. For the first time in his life he was seeing gratifying results in his landscaping efforts, and he was simply thrilled. He desperately wanted more.

As anyone who gardens knows, there is something life affirming about growing things, and to see life's reemergence each spring is among the most marvelous of miracles. Tiny slumbering seeds lie dormant during the many miserable months of cold and snow, while patiently waiting for the sun's warming rays to return and encourage new life to spring forth. And those tiny quiescent seeds know they were meant to be a marigold, marjoram, mustard, or a mint; it's nothing short of miraculous.

Now, Nikki was not at all interested in nurturing seeds, because that took way too much time. "You've got to be kidding! Yeah, that's all well and good for you old hippie types, planting seeds and then waiting three goddamned years for them to turn into a plant. Forget that shit."

He, instead, preferred gardening by Visa and having his plants arrive fully grown and in full bloom. Just dig hole and insert plant. Until now his backyard was nothing more than a sloping, shady, debris field used for overflow parking, with a few pathetic patches of parched

THE GAYS OF OUR LIVES

anemic grass that had pushed up amongst the mounds of trash the lazy renters threw out and never bothered to pick up.

But his peculiar parcel was practically landlocked, and you could access it only through a gravelly alley that ran between two houses on a side street. Turning sharply ninety degrees left, and then heading north about fifty feet; you took another sharp left turn and headed due west along an ancient two-track wagon train trail that ran alongside a rusty old chain-link fence.

On the riffraff-renting-neighbors' side of this fence grew ancient gnarly Persian lilacs, with towering twisting trunks that reached skyward a full fifteen feet before gracefully drooping over the fence and into his yard. He let them fall where they may. In springtime they were completely covered with intoxicatingly lavender blossoms, and that was Nikki's favorite scent; spring lilacs, because they reminded him of his grandma Effie. His second favorite smell was freshly minted money.

A minuscule patch of dirt measuring barely four feet wide by thirty feet long ran alongside the rusty fence. This sunless trash-strewn overgrown strip was filled with brambles, brush, trees, and lots of debris, making it totally unsuitable for planting. Chiquita, wielding the mighty chain saw, cleared the copious underbrush and took down a couple of good-sized box elders, a big dead mulberry, and a few scrappy monkey-love trees, too. Suddenly light came streaming into the yard.

Rustic fieldstone retaining walls, standing over three feet tall, were unearthed in the clearing of the urban frontier. From the looks of it, they were created to shore up the sloping soil and keep the driveway in its place. Three stone slab steps intersected with the rock wall and gently transitioned you from the drive down into the sunken backyard. Two crumbling sidewalks were also discovered under the leaves and debris, which led to a walkout basement and a potting shed that was hidden beneath the bedroom/sun porch and totally obscured by overgrown grape ivy.

Now the yard had an English garden feel, with its rustic fieldstone walls, stone steps, and red brick, ivy-covered potting shed. "First thing I want to do is get some kind of a privacy fence back here, because I just detest having all these riffraff neighbors gawking at me every time I'm working in my yard. They have nothing better to do all day than sit on their fat asses, on their front porches, while drinking malt liquor, smoking cigarettes and reefer, and watching me slave away."

"They probably think of it as having a live gardening show, the Better Homo's Garden," I said.

"Ha-ha, ha, you're so funny, but looks aren't everything. So what do you think, Den? I've been thinking of putting a white vinyl fence up; they always look good—clean and fresh. What cha think?"

"Oh, you're so right, plastic fences always look so pretty. There's one around my mom's trailer park, and it looks real nice. *No*, I don't like *plastic* fencing. What about something real? Wood, rustic, or maybe stockade?"

"Ooh. You can be so bitchy sometimes, trailer park—harrumph! Wood...real...rustic. Say, whatcha think about a cedar tree border, you know, something live and green?"

"Brilliant. Why didn't I think of it?"

"Because I did. Now, I've also been thinking I need a water feature; you know, a focal point and something lovely to gaze at, a pretty pond with waterfall, water lilies, and maybe even a few fabulous fishies. You know, that one at your cottage is just phenomenal, and I love gazing at it."

"You need a pond? No, you *need* food and water. You mean you *want* one, right?"

"Oh, no, honey. You really are a simple thing, aren't you? You don't understand at all, do you? Well, let me explain it so *even you* can understand. You see, if you want something *long* enough, and *hard* enough, a want can turn into a need, and then you'll *need it*. Oh, yes, you will actually need it to survive. Oh, yes, I definitely need a pond and fish, and gobs of pretty plants, too."

"First thing you should do is give the yard some structure, maybe make more rock-lined beds, and bring in some rich planting soil. This dirt is definitely deceased. Your yard has a natural slope so you should take advantage of that topography and do some terracing. You're going to need help."

Nikki's law was "Anything worth doing is worth overdoing," and his gardening plan was to do exactly that. Murphy's Law kicked in next: fix one thing and the thing next to it looks shitty; fix that, and so it goes. The master plan for the backyard's renovation was drawn up, and Nikki was attacking the puny plot with a vengeance. The only thing not being changed was the location of the drive, and that was spared because it was a deeded access and not changeable. But he considered it nonetheless.

Once all the decisions were made, and the cash was laid, in came a parade of flatbed trucks and the "beep, beep, beeping" from them backing up was deafening. Mega-rocks the size of Rhode Island were mechanically lowered into place by boom and chain fall—and dropped exactly where he wanted them, and some were placed exactly where he wanted them several times.

"Everything looks better in black," he decreed, and another deafening "beep, beep, beeping" blast woke the neighborhood again, as dump trucks began backing up heaped with the blackest soil available and dumped their riches into the new rocky beds.

The very next morning the entire neighborhood was again awakened by ear-piercing beeps, so they rose from their cribs, and moved to their falling-down front porches to watch as every truck in the fleet of the Weed Lady's landscaping company backed up toward Nikki's. The racket was deafening. He had ordered two hundred eight-foot arborvitae shrubs, at $55 a pop, and they were being delivered to make his privacy of greenery; he was never one to do anything in a small way. "Go big or go home" was his motto. This was certainly overkill, considering his itty-bitty shitty city lot measured only fifty feet wide by one hundred feet deep. Beep, beep, beep.

"Nothing succeeds like excess." That was his mantra, and his garden plan, too. Excess. After he painstakingly selected each privacy tree he instructed the landscapers to plant them as close as can be, because he did *not* want to see a single thing through that hedgerow, at all. *"Got it?"*

"Got it."

"They will grow, you know," Fern, the Weed Lady, said. (You could make suggestions to him, but you couldn't *tell* him anything.)

"I don't care if they will. I want them up tight and I mean right now. I don't want to see a gap as thin as a dime. Am I understood? I'm tired of having all the neighborhood porch monkeys gawking at me every time I'm slaving in my own backyard! Not one of *them* works, and they have nothing better to do all day than sit their fat asses on their front porches and watch me work."

"These newly planted trees will require massive amounts of water to become well-established. An automatic irrigation system would be highly recommended, and that has to be installed before the trees can be planted. You can set it on a timer, and you'll never have to drag that hose around again."

"Well, yes, Fern, that is a brilliant idea, and yes, I do hate dragging that dirty old hose around, but I have an even *better* idea. You see, I just read in the latest issue of *Whore-to-culture* magazine that you can get a FertiGator, and that, my dear woman, is an irrigation system that fertilizes at the same time as it waters. That is what I want. *Snap.* Make it happen."

So it was said, so it was done. Beep, beep, beep, and more beeps. The very next day, a green truck loaded with big black pipes bounced down the two-track trail and a hunky man in a tight-fitting uniform jumped out, walked up to Nikki's back door, and started knocking, and hard. *Well...*one look at him made old Saint Nikki's oversize heart skip a teensy beat, so he sucked in his sizable gut, threw back his head of store-bought blond hair, and answered the door.

"Mr. Clark? My name is Mr. Gorton, and I'm here from Pipe Layers to install your new irrigation system." Nikki looked him up, and then looked him down, while pausing for an extended period in the midsection, because like Will Rogers, he never met a man he didn't like.

"Very good, Mr. Gorton, *very good*," Nikki purred.

"It looks like you've taken on quite a project here, Mr. Clark."

"Yes, Mr. Gorton, I certainly have messed things up. Please call me Nikki."

"Certainly, Mr. Clark, uh, sorry, I mean Nick. You may call me Jeff."

"Well, Jeff, I understand you've spoken with Fern about all of this, and you *do* understand that I don't want a *common* old irrigation system? I want a FertiGator, a system that fertilizes as it waters."

"I can see you're up on the latest technology, sir. When shall we begin?"

"Dig in, Jeff. Let's get dirty."

Handsome, hunky Jeff got right down to business. Unzipping the fly of his bulging pile driver, he plowed into Nikki's moist thatch. Nikki swooned while watching him skillfully manipulate his impressive tool, lay pipe, and get downright dirty. By working diligently for the better part of a week, and often staying till way after dark, he completed the job on time. He even brought his well mannered kids along a couple of times, just so he could get the job finished on time.

Seeing this hardworking single father struggling so hard to keep his family together, Nikki's big ol' heart naturally went out to him. So as a special treat he surprised everyone and made dinner; if you counted picking up Kentucky Fried Chicken as making a meal. Well, the kids loved it, mashed taters an' gravy, and the entire family gathered around Nikki's grossly expensive MacKenzie-Childs table in his ultraextravagant kitchen; a picture of domestic bliss.

*A strange footnote to mention here. Later that very same summer, this nice young family man was arrested for committing multiple murders. When Chicago police were investigating the murder of a stewardess, the trail led them to Flint and the handsome man with the impressive tool. Our darling Jeff was arrested for murdering the flight attendant, and for also committing the infamous Margaret Eby murder at the famous Mott Estate, just a few blocks away.

This gruesome crime was one of the most notorious murders in Flint's history, which went unsolved for nearly twenty years, until our darling Jeff was arrested and convicted of committing it. Known as the "Panty Bandit," this unscrupulous uniformed young man allegedly absconded with an extraordinary amount of unmentionables and undergarments from many unsuspecting women, and had ultimately amassed an impressive pile of pillaged panties numbering well over one thousand pairs before being apprehended and incarcerated.

— ~

"My God, Chiquita! Did you hear about that darling irrigation man being arrested for committing multiple murders?"

"*Did I hear?* For Christ's sake, Stella, *yes* I heard. It was on the national news! That was a close call."

"You know, I even I had him and the kids over for dinner a couple of times and *everything*. And what a shame, he seemed so nice. Didn't look like a murderer at all."

"You was sweet on him, wasn't you, Missy?"

"Well...there's nothing like a tight man in a uniform. And he was really good with tools."

"Have you checked your unmentionable drawer to see if you're missing any panties?"

"Can you imagine some strange murdering maniac pawing through your pretty panties?"

"Just imagine."

— ~

So, after a week of trenching for the irrigation system, the yard was a rutted muddy mess, and once again Nick was most displeased. Now it was time for his arborvitae privacy fence to be planted around the yard's perimeter, and that displeased him, too, because the bushmen were digging another fucking trench. But this time it was even worse, because the bitch had to be painstakingly dug by hand because of the copious rocks, roots, and debris found while excavating.

Murphy's Law Number Two: Everything will always take longer than anticipated, and cost more than estimated. Time dragged on, costs escalated, he became exasperated, and more confounded with each cost-compounded day.

Finally, during the third week of the urban oasis transfiguration, the landscapers were able to begin construction of the water feature. Handel's "Water Music" was piped into the backyard for the workers' inspiration, and green glass bottles of effervescent Perrier administered to prevent dehydration. He only wanted water with good taste.

As Fern explained it to him, "Picture us creating especially for you a wonderful one-of-a-kind water feature. Imagine a crystal clear stream gently flowing alongside the drive while daintily dancing over pretty pebbles, gaily skipping over well-rounded rocks, and carelessly meandering downstream. Then the gentle rivulet rounds a bend and gathers up speed, rushes, and gushes until it becomes a cascading waterfall and plunges three full feet into a peaceful pool, nestled in the lower lawn."

"I don't know if that's going to be nearly enough for me. I was picturing something much splashier. Have you ever been to Vegas?" Nikki said most sincerely, not at all certain that would be enough. Then he inquired about the surrounding plantings, lighting, aquatic plants, and exotic fish.

"I'll need to make a shopping list, won't I? I should begin by purchasing some substantial pieces of sculpture for pertinent points of interest, because, as you well know, significant statuary is vitally important to the overall impression of a garden's true aesthetic. And, of course, the water feature will have to be illuminated, from within *as well as* without."

The entire week the pond was under construction, it decided to downpour. Daily deluges of dismally cold spring rain only dampened the process and added misery, mud, and mayhem. Next a huge semi-truck loaded with large flat gray river rocks, which were hand harvested from a riverbed in upstart Connecticut and shipped while still live, were delivered to create the pond.

The stoned truck driver stupidly dropped the rocks by the pond, for the workers' convenience, but it was also right in the middle of Nikki's driveway, so he couldn't park his Jag. This displeased him immensely, because he had to park on the street like a commoner. But if you want to talk about being inconvenienced, the miserable pond makers had to dig the basin, run the plumbing, electricity, install the rubber membrane, and stack the heavy rocks while working in a chilly spring rain.

Each night after work Nikki would conduct inspection. While standing under his big Burberry plaid umbrella and shivering, he'd be lamenting the lack of progress, bitching and complaining about how slowly things were going, what a mess everything was, how much it was costing, and acting as if someone was holding a gun to his head and *making* him do all of this.

Being one who was always willing to share his feelings, he did. "The whole fucking backyard is a ripped-up muddy mess from stem to stern, shit is lying everywhere, it's costing me a fuckin' fortune, and it's *not* pretty. Not pretty at all! Damn it!" he bitched. And really, it wasn't pretty, not pretty at all. He'd bitten off more than he could chew this time, and bawled like a baby robbed of his candy.

Most miraculously, Monday morning mercifully arrived, and the pond maker's truck was gone. The irrigation system was finished, and the installer gone, too. The hedgerow/fence was planted, and the landscapers were also gone. Suddenly the sun appeared from behind a cloud, and there it was, all that he'd imagined, the yard of his dreams. Nikki's private Eden was surrounded by an eight-foot-tall, tightly packed, green arborvitae hedge, and watered with an automated irrigation fertilization system. But the pièce de résistance was an amazingly lovely stream, waterfall, and fuckingly fabulous pond.

He'd have to spend the rest of the summer cleaning up the monumental messes they'd created, and the rest of his life paying for it, but his dreams had become true, and he was pleased. For now. As soon as the pump was connected the stream started to flow, and the soothing sound of water spilling into the tranquil pond instantly blocked out the gnarly urban sounds of gunshots, car wrecks, sirens, and gut-wrenching screams, and transformed the inner-city ghetto yard into an urban oasis. Serendipitously, it also began to attract exotic birds, squirrels, coons, and kids.

This was such a costly venture, this gardening and landscaping hobby, but so very rewarding. But he was finished yet. The workers left him with an unsightly mess, and what was left of the lawn was trampled beyond redemption by those inconsiderate workmen.

"I can plant grass seed and grow a lawn if you'd like," Chiquita stupidly offered.

"You have *got* to be kidding, seed my *ass*, we need *SOD*. It will make it instantly fabulous."

So it was sod, so it was done. Beep, beep, beep, in came more trucks, as he shelled out more bucks, and long flatbed trucks began backing up heaped high with rolls of sod. The trampled grass, which was certainly trashed, was replaced with a luxurious thatch installed like wall-to-wall carpet. "Now, *this* is more what I had in mind," Nikki said, while slipping out of his Gucci loafers and plunging his fat flawless feet into the brand-new grass, wiggling his chubby toes into the freshly laid lawn, and loving it, loving it, loving it. Taking himself for a leisurely stroll in the cool, damp grass, he mentally scratched another line off from his lengthy list of tasks—and added another hefty bill.

"Now that tired-assed old drive just looks like shit, doesn't it? You know, I have always hated that wagon train driveway, and all that loose gravelly shit that flies every which way when they mow. As you well know, everything looks better in black, so I think it would look absolutely fabulous blacktopped. Much more finished and clean. Whatcha think?"

Was that a question or a proclamation? We didn't know which, but we were certain the drive would be the next project undertaken upon *his* lengthy list. Sure enough, Monday morning, at eight sharp, the offensive stench of hot tar cooking, the beep, beep, beeping of trucks backing up, and the shrill screeching of air brakes announced the blacktop installers. With another episode of the *Better Homo's Garden* about to begin, the neighborhood porch monkeys got up—without any coaxing—found their coffee, cigarettes and reefer, and plopped their fat asses on their front porches to watch.

Blacktopping the two-track trail was an incredibly stinky and noisy process that took forever to complete, and that displeased Nikki immensely. It even offended his delicate nose. So he chose to flee the stinking inner-city and have a spa day instead. A complete manicure and pedicure, spray-painted tan, massage, exfoliation, and a south-of-the-border waxing was in order. Much to his delight, when he'd returned, looking most fabulous—"Don't I look simply fabulous?"—he found the drive finished. Instantly the yard was transformed from the ghetto to the suburbs, looked significant, purposeful, planned, and a place you'd really want to spend time.

"Now, this is just ridiculous. How can even enjoy all this? I need a patio table and chairs out here, so I can have my morning cappuccino and gaze upon the fabulousness I've worked so very hard to create?" So it was said, so it was done. Beep, beep, beep, and it weren't cheap. A brand new patio was constructed behind the Château, beneath his lovely boudoir window, so he could gaze upon the loveliness from the comfort of his lovey nest. Then he purchased a gilded patio set with four golden chairs, and a stunning, sun-shunning umbrella.

Someone stupidly suggested using the river rock left over from constructing the fish pond to create the new patio. "Oh, heavens no, that will never do, it's way too dark, drab, and dreary for me. I want something bright and cheery, with sparkles. I saw a stone I kinda liked, called Idaho Silver and Gold; make it happen!" So it was said, so it was done. Beep, beep, beep, in came more trucks, and he shelled out more bucks.

Now that the big-bones bull work was completed, the fun part—the planting—could begin. Now he had another reason to shop, oh yay, oh yay, a foliage foray, a plant acquisition expeditions to purchase the prettiest plants possible. This botanical buying binge began by visiting every nursery in this part of the country and purchasing a plethora of perfectly potted plants, and all magnificently mature specimens in spectacularly full bloom.

Scouring every exclusive designer gardening catalog known to man, he ordered only the most exotic and exquisite specimens available. Then he carefully contemplated the perfect place to position each plant, and plunked it in the garden. But those poor plants were planted and replanted so many times they suffered from motion sickness and had to be watered with Dramamine.

Clearly Nikki was hooked on the hard stuff now, and mainlining Martha Stewart, because now those flowerpots from his old apartment seemed way too insignificant for this grander landscape he'd created. He needed bigger pots—much larger pots. Pots so big they had to be brought in by crane and lowered in place—cement urns and enormous estate-sized cast-iron craters. He was never accused of doing things in a small way; it was over the top for Nikki or nothing; go big or go home.

Nikki's dear frienemy, Joany, was always happy to share gardening tips and yardly advice with novice yardman Nick. As a wee lassie in Scotland, she'd learned traditional gardening methods, which she employed in the lovely gardens surrounding her stately estate. "You'll need structure, statuary of course, and several interesting *objet d'art* lying about, a weathervane, finial, birdbath or gazing globe, and even a strategically placed rock could nicely do."

She happily shared her prized perennials, as well as her well-guarded gardening secrets, and sent him home with a trunkload of starters, which he just detested and rejected. "Baby plants, phfft, who the hell has the time to wait around for plants to grow? Forget that shit."

Objet d'art...now there was something he could get his nicely veneered teeth into—more shopping. He now had permission to scour every upscale gardening shop for sculptures, benches, birdbaths, and gazing-at balls, and attend every artsy fairy in the area to gather yardly embellishments. After a summer-long search, and when nearing retail exhaustion, he came upon the darling decorations made of cement and rerod, and fell in love with them. But buying a single cement toadstool eventually mushroomed into a collection of over thirty, making an entire fun-guy patch. And the purchase of one darling dancing nymphette statuette eventually turned into an entire chorus line of the high-stepping, lead-footed little trollops. Anything worth doing was overdone—and repeatedly.

Nikki had read in gardening books the strategic placement of *objets d'art*—that's pretty stuff other than plants—was vitally important to the garden's aesthetic. Realizing this essential element was absent from his estate, he was prepared to make some serious and significant acquisitions, and took out another credit card.

But also being pretty persnickety, he'd have none of this local gardening store, crafty resin shit. He wanted estate-sized statuary made of stone, bronze, cement, and substance. After another summer-long search, he'd settled upon a stately set of cast-concrete putti, which represented the four seasons. The fleshy quartet of cherubic babes stood well over seven feet tall when they were placed upon their lofty pedestals, appeared as if they'd been outside a crumbling castle for centuries, and were truly were lovely. They must have cost a fortune.

One just never knew what he'd take a shine to either. Just when you thought you had him figured out, he'd surprise you. Although he usually went for bold and bright bordering on gaudy, at times he was most traditional. For instance, one day while snooping around Chiquita's yard he came upon a rambling rustic path he'd made from salvaged *junque* and simply adored it. Crafted from rocks, bricks, gravel, and other bits of scrounged debris, it was thrown down to keep his feet from getting muddy. Well, Nikki just adored the antiquity, and wanted Chiquita to install one in his yard, too.

"Make me one exactly like it, only different. Have it ramble through the woodland shade garden. Make it happen!" So he commanded, *snap*, so it was done. So Chiquita scrounged around for more old junk, bricks, rocks, and interesting "architecture arty-facts" that he thoughtfully "cleaned up" from the local abandoned homes, and transformed the rubbish into an artsy walkway that looked as if it had been there for ages; for a modest sum, of course.

"*Well*...it's what you'd call a win-win stipulation," Chiquita explained. "One of my cleaning clients paid me fifty dollars to haul that busted-up old rubble away from her yard when they knocked down her old chim-lee. So I used that crap, plus a few interesting unattended things I sort a found lyin' around the neighborhood not bein' used, hauled all the rubbish over ta his house, and charged him a pretty penny ta arrange the 'architectural relics' into a pretty path for his yardly pleasure."

So Nikki checked the rambling path off his lengthy list and moved to the next item: purchasing pretty pet fish for the pond. Ordinary goldfish simply wouldn't do, nor would common comets like the five-for-a-dollar feeder fish I had. He wanted splashy spectacular specimens. So he went to Something Fishy first, because they had the most exotic aquatics in the area, flashy hybrid specimens such as platinum fish, koi, and shubinkins. He'd read up on the fishies, too—ichthyology.

But he wasn't the least bit interested in starter fish, the tiny two-inch hatchlings. "Starters? You've got to be kidding," he said. "I want full-grown, foot-long, fabulous fancy fishies with flowing fins and translucent tails." But those golden fish cost well over $100 each. But nothing was too good, or too grand, for him. Spending well over $700, he hauled home ten of the most spectacular specimens you've ever seen; tuna with good taste.

While driving home with his impressive cache of resplendent fish, he was thinking up clever names for them. "Now, let's see, there's Cleo, Cher, Diana, Bette, Ethel Mermaid, and Cally for the beautiful blue-and-red-speckled one that looked like Grandma Effie's calico quilts." He was so happy to be having a fishy family, and proudly placed them into their pond. It displeased him immeasurably that his pond was still murky. The pond people told him it would eventually clear up. It just took time. Oh, how he hated those four words—"It just takes time." He wanted everything *now*!

The next morning before leaving for work, while it was still dark, Nikki grabbed a cup of his exotic Kopi Luwak coffee and went for a meandering stroll through his lovely moonlit garden. "It's lovely,

lovely, lovely," he said, while breathing in the floral perfumes, perusing the pretty plants, and visiting his fishy family. "Good morning, girls, Mommy's here with breakfast."

"Dear God in heaven," he shrieked. The eerie light emanating from the pond illuminated seven bloated bellies bobbing at the top; the fish were dead as doornails, and fins pointing straight to heaven. Well, he sat down in the FertiGated lawn and bawled like a baby. Tears streamed down his cherubic cheeks, streaking his bronzer, and sobs heaved from his lovely chest. "Why, why do I even try?"

Well, he wailed wildly, wallowed in the wet thatch, and wept for the perished Pisces; that, and the fucking $700 bucks that just went gurgling down the goddamned drain. He needed professional assistance. So that very day he hired James Pond, an aquatic troubleshooter and pond maintenance man, who'd visit once a week and tend to the water's features, adjust the pH, clean the filter, and do whatever fishermen do. Nikki was only interested in gazing at the pretty pond and overfeeding his fishy family, and not getting wet or dirty in the process.

He quickly replaced the floaters with suitable substitutes, before anyone could tell they were goners, and was once again a happy man. Each morning he'd greet them, "Hello, girls, Mommy's here! Miss Cleo Fantastic-tail, you are looking fantastical, and Cher, you're looking simply Cherific." Soon they recognized him, associated him with food, and instantly surfaced with their mouths gaping, greedily looking for more, and quickly growing to look like watermelons with fins and tails.

Each night while on his way home from work, he would stop in front of his magnificent miniature mansion, his beautiful petite Château, and gaze upon the loveliness he and Visa had created. One such summer's eve, he did just that—stopped his shiny new leased Jag right out front, rolled his power window down, gazed out, and smiled broadly. The lovely lavender impatiens had filled in so nicely they were standing nearly three feet tall, thanks to being fed with straight plant steroids and having nowhere to go but straight up.

"Now, you make damn sure you're planting those impatient things good and tight now. I don't want to see any dirty old dirt showing in between them when they're planted. Am I understood?"

Understood.

The poor impatient things were laid straight out of the flat like wall-to-wall carpet, grew to be luxuriantly colorful, and from that year on those flashy flowers were the backbone of the annual beds, and the the most difficult decision was the choice of color, with coral and lavender being his perennial favorites.

The flashy impatiens performed magnificently for several summers. But then, one day tragedy struck. The flowery mound began to slowly implode; collapsed, withered, and melted into a disgusting slimy pile. Outraged, he called the Weed Lady to pitch a royal bitch, and demanded that she fix the problem. "Well, you're the one who sold me the defective vegetation. Don't give me any shit, fix it."

After taking one look at the slimy mound, she immediately diagnosed the problem. "This yard has been contaminated with *plasmopara obducens*. Mildew spores have infected those plants with a downy mildew, which is sucking the life right out of them, and it will ultimately kill them. All those infested plants will have to be removed and destroyed, and the beds treated with toxins to eradicate the spores. But the *really* bad news is, you won't be able to grow impatiens here for the next five years."

"*What the hell?* I've been gardening for three whole years and never heard of such a thing. Why, why, why do I even try?" Nikki wailed. Lying down on the FertiGated lawn, he blubbered and bawled. "This just burns me up. There went sixty-five flats of flowers, and $650 worth of pretty plants has been turned into a slimy oozing mess that's not even suitable for compost." On his next day off he removed and replaced them.

More correctly, he ordered Chiquita to take out the disgusting slimy remains, chemically treat the beds, and plant boring, common, pink wax begonias. The yard would never be the same. And for the record, he detested those wax begonias, and counted the days until he could replant the splashy impatiens again. He was only beginning to learn of the dangers that lurked in his very own backyard; for gardening is fraught with peril.

So each night he would conduct a curbside inspection from the comfort of his air-conditioned Jag and look for trouble. One night while doing just that, his well-trained eyes noticed light flashing from something metallic moving in the backyard. Pulling forward a teensy bit, and stretching his delicate neck like a turtle to see what it was, he quietly peered into his yard unobserved.

"What the hell?" he screamed, using his outside voice. Three little brown boys were back there fishing in Nikki's platinum fish pond. "Hey, hey, HEY! You little bastards get the hell out of there!" He was really steamed, red-faced, nostrils flaring, pulse accelerating, and yelling like a mad woman with her ass set afire. Immediately dropping their poles, they shot out of there like a lit bottle rocket, and ran for their lives. Nikki stomped on the gas and swerved down the alley, screeching into his drive, but they were already goners. "Goddamn it!" He threw the Jag into Reverse and backed out, leaving rubber on the road, and took off in hot pursuit of the miniature fish snatchers.

Not one of those boys was over ten years old, but they sure could run like the devil. Scrambling like hell, they jumped the fence to safety on the next street over. Nikki swerved around the corner to head them off at the pass. Spying him coming, they frantically raced back across the street and jumped the fence to the next street over. Now he was really steamed, turned a deeper shade of red, and went screeching off in hot pursuit, screaming at the top of his lungs.

"Goddamn it! I just bought those fucking fish, and they cost me a fucking fortune. You little sons-a-bitches. I'm so fucking mad. *Damn* it, *damn* it, *damn* it!"

But he finally gave up when he realized he wasn't going to catch the pilfering little bastards. And what would he have done if he had? So he went home to assess the damage. Carelessly tossed on his lawn was two halves of a cane pole, both rigged with red-and-white bobbers, hooks, and wriggling earthworms. But what was even more infuriating was that his newly planted garden had been trashed in their search for worms to use as bait to catch *his* luxurious fish.

Now he was really stea'med, mad as hell, and attempted to snap one of the poles across his knee. It didn't break; it snagged his good pants and gave him a big black-and-blue bruise on his beautiful knee. Then he stopped dead in his tracks and started to bawl, because lying limply in the lawn next to the pretty pond was his favorite, Cher, in all her glittery glory, languishing. Opening her lovely lips widely, greedily gasping for air, she was pleading for help, and barely alive.

Tears rapidly gathered in his baby blues as he gently lowered her listless little body into the cool pool, and tenderly massaged it. Unable to move, she stared at him wide-eyed, desperately beseeching him for help. He'd gladly have given her mouth-to-gill resuscitation if he could, but with one feeble flop she was a goner. Nikki plopped down in the grass and bawled. "Why? Why? Why do I even try?"

Nikki, the poor thing, he was perilously close to the edge and nearing complete exhaustion from the constant craziness going on in his backyard, and desperately needed a break. Sympathetic to his plight, I suggested he spend a weekend at my lakeside retreat for a refresher, and he quickly accepted.

Jumping into the Jag, he punched it to the floor and gaily headed north at ninety miles an hour without ever looking at a map (I lived northwest). Consequently he got completely lost, arrived hours later than anticipated, and was royally pissed. It took the rest of the day for him to unwind, but finally he adjusted to the slower pace of northern Michigan, where it was low-key and one could listen to the birds, go for long meditative walks in the woods or down by the lake, smell the roses, and eat dessert whenever you felt like it.

My cozy century-old Cape Cod cottage was quite comfortably nestled in the woods, resting on the shore of a small spring-fed lake, and just a mile from big Lake Michigan. It was a quiet, spiritual, and rustic retreat where you can get up late, and don't give a shit about what you wear.

Nikki greatly admired my landscape with a shimmering lake out front, surrounded by mature woodlands, abundant wildlife, exotic birds, and a pond stocked with five-for-a-dollar goldfish. Upon closer inspection he started noticing the details. "I just love your Italian terra-cotta statuary, and I'm definitely going to get me some for my yard. And this fern you've planted everywhere is absolutely fabulous, so green, luscious, and thick. Where'd you buy it at, honey?"

"Silly boy, I didn't buy them. God planted them. That's a native plant, a woodland fern that grows all by itself."

"*Really!* All by itself, you say?"

"Absolutely."

"Well, it's absolutely fabulous. Do you think it will grow in my yard, honey?"

"No, that is a runner-root fern that only grows in sandy acidic soils. You'll need a perennial fern with a crown, such as an ostrich, cinnamon stick, or rabbit's foot fern."

"Are there any of those around here, honey?"

"Down by the Sable River there are hundreds of them growing in the rich wet bottomlands."

"Oh, goodie, goodie. Can we go get me some? I need some for my yard. When can we go?"

"We're going to the market this afternoon to buy sweet corn for dinner and red haven peaches for a pie. The river is near there. We can go anytime you'd like."

"I'd like now."

Fifteen minutes later he was leisurely pushing an overstuffed grocery cart through the Garden of Eat-in Farm Market as if he owned the place. "Oh, this looks awfully good. Don't you think we should have some of these sweetie rolls, honey? Don't we need more bread? This cheesy bread looks awfully yummy, honey. And oh my, doesn't this blueberry pie look simply scrumptious, sweetie?"

"I'm making a peach pie for dessert. We don't need to have peach and blueberry pie, too."

"*Well, why not?* We can have blueberry with our afternoon coffee. Yours won't be done till dinner."

"It's useless arguing with you, isn't it?"

"I'm so glad you are beginning to see things my way. And we'll need some ice cream to wash our pies down with, don't cha think? How about butter pee-can? Do I hear a yes, Mr. Grumpy?"

With the Jaguar loaded with enough produce to feed a third-world country, and the ice cream already melting, we headed for home with one wee pit stop, to plunder plants.

It was getting late in the afternoon as I removed the shovel from the trunk. Searching the mucky riverbed for an access not too mushy to cross, I was immediately surrounded by a million bloodthirsty mosquitoes that began biting me mercilessly.

As I dug in the stinking muck collecting ferns for his yard, Nikki sat inside the air-conditioned Jag munching on chilled black sweet cherries, while watching me get eaten alive.

"Is that enough?" I asked, knowing full well there was never enough for him. Rolling the power window down, he spat out a fat cherry pit and said, "Just a few more honey; after all, they are free." Then he quickly rolled the window up to begin swatting at an impudent mosquito that had the audacity to try to bite him. I dug a couple more ferns up and threw them into the trunk, and fled the stinking swamp because I was quickly becoming anemic.

"Just look at you, honey, you look like a connect-the-dots game with all those nasty red welts all over you. Ya know, ya really shoulda worn long pants and a jacket. Thanks for the starters you gave me, too. I'll be sure to plant them soon as I get home," he said, knowing full well it was a big fat fib.

He was having such a wonderfully relaxing weekend, he returned home on Monday, instead of Sunday, when he was *supposed* to, and was completely rested and refreshed. I, on the other hand, was totally exhausted. Most of my guests did not require nearly as much structured activity or attention.

Four full days after returning to Flint, those ferns were still sitting inside his Easy-Bake Oven trunk on the blacktopped parking lot, baking to a crisp, before he instructed Chiquita to take them out and plant them.

"You ditzy queen, I can't plant those plants, they're completely cooked, composted, a stinkin' rottin' mess, and dead as doornails. Just how long have those ferns been roastin' inside-a that trunk anyway?" Chiquita demanded.

"Only since I was up to Denny's place," he remarked, all innocent and schoolgirlish.

"Well, that was four days ago, missy. They're useless now."

"*Shit*, I really wanted to plant them in the new flowerbed beneath my bedroom window. Do you know how much those damn things cost in the gardening centers?"

"Well, yes, I know, you ditzy queen. Answer me this, do ya think *you'da* survived if you was shut up inside-a that trunk in the blazin' sun for four days without any water?"

"When ya put it that way you make it sound like I'm running a vegetation concentration camp."

"Well, ya are, Blanche, ya are. But you know...if you still happen ta want some ferns, I just happen ta know where there are a few, not that far from here, and they're just waiting ta be liberated. Ya see...there's this old abandoned house with all these hostas and ferns in the yard that aren't being cared for. Why, why, why they're abandoned, rejected, and orphaned with no one to care for them. My heart just goes out to those poor parentless plants."

"When you put it that way, it sounds like it's our duty to rescue them, liberate them, care for the poor orphans, and give them a decent and loving home. Don't cha think?"

"Absolutely, absolutely; our solemn duty as Christian women."

"Can we take your Jag? The trunk's already filthy."

"Oh, don't you worry about that filthy trunk, honey. You won't ever have to clean it, because the people I lease it from will just come out and clean it for me whenever I call them."

Victorian and sorry, the squat, sprawling thing was for sale and not abandoned, and it was only two blocks from their homes. The heavyset house with a massive fret-worked wraparound porch had once been a lovely home, but now it was run-down, neglected, and badly needed repairing.

"We can't take these plants, Chiquita. This house is for sale."

"Oh no, it's been abandoned, just look at it. Look how sad and neglected it is, nobody's lived there for just years. Anyway I know the homeowner, Mrs. Tremaine, and she said its fine to take 'em."

"Really? Oh, well then, that's different if you have permission."

While they were loading the third trunkload of pilfered plants, the problem arrived. Red flashing lights surrounded them as a police car pulled into the drive and blocked their escape route. Nikki and Chiquita, spying the officer at the same time, stood frozen like deer caught in the headlights.

"That's them, Officer, those two rights there. Arrest 'em both, and throw the book at 'em. They already took two trunkloads outta here before you *finally* got here," said Gladys Crabass, the nosy old neighbor. She'd been hiding behind her ruffled Priscilla sheers spying on them and quickly called the coppers on the suspicious plant pluckers who were pilfering plants from the neighbor's yard.

"Thank you, ma'am, I can take it from here," the imposing officer said. But she stayed planted right where she was, dyed hair in curlers, arms tightly folded over her flowery polyester housecoat, and her wrinkled red puss uselessly smeared with a shiny beauty treatment.

"May I see some ID, please, ma'am?" the officer demanded, looking right at Nikki.

"Oh, Jesus, I don't have anything with me, Officer. I don't even have my wallet. I just live down the street. I'm so, so sorry."

"And you, what about you?" the policeman said, looking Chiquita squarely in the eye.

"Me neither. I'm in my gardening shorts. Came with her."

"Just what are you two up to, anyway?"

"Well, as ya can see, Officer, this house is for sale, and Mrs. Tremaine said we could have some of these here flowers," Chiquita said, lying, and acting as if he actually believed what he was saying.

"Noooo way, Officer! The homeowner isn't Mrs. Tremaine," yelled Mrs. Crabass. "It's Johnson, Irene Johnson. Arrest 'em, Officer! And throw away the key."

"You two should know better. Do you live in the neighborhood?"

"Yes, sir, right down the street, both of us," Chiquita offered, talking to the ground.

"Well, you two just turn around, take those plants out of your trunk, and put them right back where you found them." Scowling at them, he watched as they scrambled around feverishly replanting them in a most uncomfortable silence.

"Now, I don't ever want to see the two of you again. *Am I understood?*"

"Yes, sir, Mr. Officer, sir," they both groveled, with their heads bobbing up and down like advanced Parkinson's patients. Completely humiliated, they drove home.

"Jesus Christ, Chiquita, why the hell did I let you talk me into doing this? I'm going to prison, I just know it," Nikki lamented.

Once safely inside the house, they sat at opposite ends of the over-size red velvet sofa and shook like Chihuahuas left out in a blizzard.

"Just what the hell have you two been up to, anyway?" Rob asked, when walking into the room. "You two look like you just saw a ghost."

Chiquita was opening his mouth, and about to make up another teensy little white lie to explain their prickly predicament, when he looked out the window and spied a car slowing down in front of his house. Flashes of light suddenly went shooting into the parlor's big bay window.

"Oh dear God!" Chiquita shrieked. "It's Gladys Crabass and the nosy neighbor citizen's patrol. They're documenting the abducted vegetation from the first two trips."

Nikki and Chiquita looked at each other in utter shock, terror-stricken.

"Oh my God! They're headin' ta your house, Stella," Chiquita screamed. "And they're takin' pictures of the snatched plants at your house, too. Oh God, they're walkin' in-ta your backyard now."

"Sweet Jesus, what've we done? I just know I'm going to prison. You got anything to drink, honey?" Nikki pleaded. He never drank. We all knew it. He despised drinking.

"Come to mention it, I could use a good stiff one myself," Chiquita chimed.

"Just what the hell have you two been up to?" Rob demanded again.

Nikki and Chiquita looked at each other, hooked pinkies, and howled with laughter.

"Let's take this little secret to our graves. Whaddya say, Stella?"

"Make mine a double, Chiquita."

Nikki Has "A Little Work Done"

Nikki had lived with it long enough, that tired old face of his. For well over the past half century, more than fifty-some years, he'd been looking at it, he'd thought about it a long time, and now he was ready to take the plunge. He was going to have "a little work done." Not the entire face, mind you, because something that lovely would require only a few minor tweaks.

Now, Nikki tended to, and pampered, the rich. By working his magic he made them look more attractive, and from nearly fifty years spent on the front lines of the beauty battle, he knew full well that becoming beautiful was damned hard work and cost a *whole* lotta money. After all, that's how he got to be so stinking rich. He also knew that most of his wealthy old ladies, and even some of the young ones, had a teensy little secret—they had "a little work done" from time to time, all along, and they called it maintenance. Well, it was his turn now, so step aside, bitches.

Prying the carefully guarded secrets from his cash-heavy clients, he persistently pumped them for information. "*Who* did you go to anyway? *What* does that sort of thing usually cost? *When* you had that done, was it terribly painful? *Where* do you go to have that sort of thing done? *Why,* is he the best?" Diligently doing his homework, Nikki discovered that the best refacing surgeons were located in the metro Detroit area,

Troy, Birmingham, and the hills of Bloomfield and Rochester. Several top-notch specialists were solicited for their expert advice, and he seriously considered all their learned opinions, before finally making his painstakingly difficult decision.

The Deux Visage Clinique DeTrois was selected to do the reconstruction, sorry, the refreshment. Now...he was just planning on having a little chin job, and maybe a teensy bit of liposuction here and there, to smooth a few things out, and perhaps even a partial eye job to remove those annoying laugh lines he'd grown; but not the complete face-lift. After all, he was practically perfect the way he was, he just knew he could look "better." In reality, he wanted to look sixteen again, but would settle for forty.

"Dr. Noir, thank you for seeing me. I must say, you come very highly recommended. It was hard to even get an appointment to see you. First off, I'd like to get rid of this little excess chin skin I've just developed lately," he innocently remarked, while wiggling the sagging, flaccid, mango-size wattle of skin hanging under his chunky chin from side to side. "It's just shown up in the last couple months."

"Mr. Clark, I am a busy man, so let *me* give *you* the facts. *You* have been working on that sagging flaccid jowl of yours for many years now," the surgeon sternly replied. He had a gruff and authoritarian presence, and you dared not challenge his pronouncements. Nikki was taken aback.

"But...Doctor, I really don't want a complete lift, you understand—just a little freshening up."

"Yes, I understand all right. But what *you* don't understand is that it's a very good thing you came in to see me when you did, because it's nearly too late for you. This would be the correct time to address the critical geriatric onset problems you have developed and neglected for years, because they are now at a grave stage. Your face is literally collapsing because your skin has completely lost its elasticity, and when gravity wins it's a fast and ugly greased downhill slide.

"To tell you the truth, I'm totally surprised you've been able to stand it this long; it's a testament to your very tenacity. I recommend the total overhaul. After all, you're already having your eyes, chin, and neck done, and a little liposuction; you're practically there, it won't cost much more, and you'll be amazed at the results. This marvelous face-saving surgery will actually push back the hands of time. Really. It's the best gift you will ever give yourself. And you deserve it."

"Yes, I do deserve to get it, don't I, Doctor? Work your magic, make me young and beautiful!"

"I'll do what I can."

"The entire procedure is performed right here, at our state-of-the-art facility. Afterward you'll have several light days of recuperation/vacation at home. Most clients are back to work in two weeks, with no one ever suspecting a thing. You'll just look rested, refreshed, and everyone will think you were off on a wonderfully relaxing vacation. But I assure you, you will be a brand-new... ma... ah...person."

Nikki was completely sold. Now he had permission. Why, why, why, it was beyond having permission—it was absolutely mandatory, and practically a matter of life and death. He didn't want to have a face-lift; he absolutely needed the reconstruction or his entire face would slide right off. This was an honest-to-goodness case of a want truly becoming a need, right then and there. And this marvelous miracle worker could put everything right back where God intended it to be, and make him into his most perfect-est and beautiful-est, self. What the hell, he went for the works.

The top-secret surgery was scheduled for a month from the date of consultation, and he was given a lengthy list of things to do in preparation for going under the knife. First he'd have an EKG to see if the old ticker could take it, and have his blood sugar and pressure tested, too. Hell, he was given an entire phone book—sized pamphlet listing all the medications and herbal remedies to cease before surgery, but he didn't bother reading that shit; phfft, that crap was for other people.

The test results came back, and yes he did have a heart, which was in good shape. His blood sugar and pressure was fine; all systems go, right on schedule. Clearing his calendar for two weeks, he told his clients he was going on a spiritualistic journey to Nepal, to visit with his dear friend, the Dolly Pardon, and they just believed him, because he was always flitting all over the globe.

So in total secrecy, under the cover of darkness and in the wee hours of the morning, Chiquita whisked his impatient patient, Nikki, to the surgical center. After the dirty deed was done, he'd secretly shuttle him safely home, and hopefully be unnoticed by the paparazzi. The heavy lifting was going to be completed in the clinic as outpatient surgery, and everything was very hush-hush, because this definitely was not the kind of thing you wanted getting out. It may be a symbol of status being able to afford plastic surgery, but it is understood by those who can that you keep that sort of thing quiet.

Post-rebeautification, the surgeon reported that everything went well, and he was sent home later that day with his brand-new face. By late afternoon he was home and resting comfortably in his downy bed, and wrapped up like Boris Karloff in *The Mummy*, with only his nose holes exposed.

By early evening it was becoming apparent that something was a teensy bit wrong, because he began to swell, ever so slightly. When asked if he was in much pain, he responded by rolling his head from side to side, meaning no. Being completely stoned on horse tranquilizers, he passed out and slept comfortably for the rest of the afternoon. Chiquita was concerned about his puffiness, but not overly alarmed, and the powerful anesthetizing drugs kept Nikki knocked out the rest of the day.

As Nikki drooled, snored, and moaned, he looked as if he'd gone through a windshield in a head-on crash. Later that evening, Chiquita reawakened him to administer another dose of powerful narcotics before going to bed. Immediately passing out again, he resumed his snoring like a grizzly bear in deep hibernation. Chiquita "borrowed" one of Nicky's "vitamins," stayed for the night, and snoozed in the leopard high-heeled chair sitting next to the giant playpen bed, just in case.

In the wee hours of the morning, Chiquita awoke needing to have a cigarette. When he gazed at Nikki, tears spontaneously filled his weak mole-man eyes, because overnight he'd turned purple, black, and blue, from the tippy-top of his bald head to his bulbous belly. Swelling terribly, he looked like a ripe plum sitting out in the hot summer sun, about to split its skin. Quite frightening, he was. Chiquita raced to his bedside and tried to wake him from the drug-induced coma.

"Stella, wake up! Oh…you don't look so good, honey. *Stella!*" he screamed, trying to awaken him, but Nikki couldn't come to consciousness. When he did, his swollen, recently enhanced lips would not cooperate because his entire face was distended and blackened, turgid, distorted, and his eyes were swollen shut, purple puffy pillows.

"Oh dear God, Stella, something's terrible wrong with ya, honey, we're goin' ta have ta get ya right back to that damn two-faced hospital, and right quick," Chiquita said. Quickly grabbing the phone, he immediately dialing the clinic. "Listen here; somethin's gone terrible wrong with that new face you stuck on Mr. Clark. So get ready, 'cause I'm bringin' him back for a refund."

"Pack him in ice to reduce the swelling," the doctor commanded. "This is most urgent! And get him here as quickly as possibly. Hurry, because it sounds as if time may be of the essence!"

So, at four thirty in the morning, Chiquita frantically scrambled around in search of ice. Quite unbelievably, there wasn't one single cube in Nikki's entire freezer; it was completely empty, except for a box of Skinny Cow double-fudge ice-cream-sickles. Running back to his own house, he was dismayed to discover he didn't have any ice either. "Shit!" he screamed. "What the hell am I goin' to do now?"

As he blankly stared into the freezer, he thought really hardly, and there, staring right back at him, were two big bags of fresh-frozen sugar snap peas, a bag of French-cut green beans, a container of crunchy-crust French fries, and a bag of frozen strawberries, with no sugar added. What the hell, they were icy and self-contained. Snatching them up, he ran back with arms full of frozen foods.

Carefully laying Nikki back in the seat, he took the frozen fruits and vegetables and delicately placed them onto Nikki's shiny swollen face, neck, and chest while trying not to touch him. He looked absolutely frightening, oozy, swollen, and sore. You couldn't tell where his chin ended and chest began, because he was nothing but a black-and-blue blob from his head to his bulging, blackening belly.

But the friggin' frigid fruits and fries kept slidin' off his swollen cheeks and chest, and wouldn't stay in place. So Chiquita frantically searched for something to secure them. Deep inside the glove box he found a roll of tan Ace bandage that Nikki used to wrap his wrists when they were sore and limp. So he secured the icy produce in place with the Ace, and left his nose holes exposed, so he could breathe. He looked like Boris Karloff in drag, a fruity mummy wrapped in a Carmen Miranda frozen fruit and vegetable turban...quite ridiculous.

Saying his prayers, at least as sincerely as he could (it had been a *very* long time), Chiquita punched the pedal to the metal and rocketed Nikki's shiny black Jag-u-lance to the two-faced clinic. He was scared to death, praying, and fighting back the tears the whole way. "Dear God in heavenly, why the hell didn't I call a fucking am-balance? Please, God, don't let him die before we get there. Dominoes and biscuits, ramen. Dear God please save him, and I swear I'll be good. And I really mean it this time."

Dr. Gupta, the night watchman, was waiting under the portico to receive Nikki when they arrived. (He spoke with a strong East Indian accent.)

"Oh...Mista Clock, just look at Jew. Jew are a mess. Can Jew hear me?"

"Unnnn," Nikki grunted pathetically, as they wheeled him into the brightly lit surgical center.

"Oh...Jew are bleating belly, belly badly. We must try to find-out why Jew are bleating."

"Uhhhhhh," Nikki pathetically grunted from inside his frozen fruity turban.

"Are Jew a drinker, Mista Clock. Do Jew drink?"

"Nnnn!" he angrily grunted.

"Are Jew a bleeder? Do Jew take blood thinners?"

"Nnnnnnnn."

"And Jew stopped taking all meditations two weeks prior to sue-jelly, like we asked Jew?"

"Uhhh," he moaned in affirmation.

"Did Jew stop taking aspirin and ibuprofen as well?"

"Ad-fill," he grunted, trying to make his new lips move, but they were too swollen to cooperate.

"Advil?" he questioned again.

"Uhhhh." Nikki moved his head up and down in agreement, making his strawberries slide off.

"Mista Clock, you have ben taking Advil? That is a aspirin product. That is the problem. Jew blood is too thin and it is making Jew bleat. Now that we now know what the problem is we can make Jew better. We will give Jew something to help Jew rest. Don't Jew worry, Jew will be just fine."

Chiquita stood by Nikki's bedside weeping like the slave girl in *Odalisque*, because he was certain it was window treatments for his patron.

Quite unbelievably, and most irresponsibly, they sent him home that very same day after getting him stabilized, medicated, and drained of the excess accumulating pustulant fluids. Four days after sue-jelly, I stopped for a visit. This was neither encouraged nor appreciated. Chiquita secretly slipped me in through the servants' side entrance.

Wrapped in those ooze-stained bandages, he looked truly gruesome, like a battered Barney, purple from his well-plucked eyebrows to his belly button, and blackened everywhere except for the tippy-tippy-top of his shiny bald head. This was the first time I had ever seen him without his hair, and he did *not* like to be seen this way. Thankfully his eyes were swollen shut so he couldn't see the horror on my face. He didn't have any neck at all, just a shiny purple mass from chin to chest, and clear on down to his nether regions.

I could not stop staring at the unusual apparatus that was strapped to his head. A flimsy white appliance was fashioned from fabric, draped under his swollen neck and chin, pulled over his chunky cheeks, taken to the top of his bald head, and snapped together. This ridiculous device kept his new face in contact with the old one, so they could re-attach. Apparently the swelling had caused a problem with that. Ick. Chiquita jokingly referred to this contraption as "the face bra."

But this was no laughing matter; it was serious life-threatening business. Every day for the next two weeks Chiquita shuttled ghastly Nikki to the clinic to have his new face, neck, and torso drained of the nasty puss and weepy fluids that had accumulated overnight. This re-pugnant process was torturous to witness, and an even worse treatment to experience. Heavy-duty antibiotics were administered daily to stave off infection, diuretics to eliminate the ever-accumulating fluids, and serious narcotics to deal with the constant pain. Christ, he was given a regular medicine cabinet full of pills to take daily.

⚬ ⚬

"Are you in much pain, Mr. Clark?" Dr. Noir inquired during his post-surgery examination.

"Nnn," Nikki grunted. But then, he suddenly felt a sharp shooting pain emanating from the center of his back. It was Chiquita's bony finger, poking him, and damned hard, too.

"Why, he just cried somethin' terrible all the way down here, Docker," Chiquita said. "He's in terry-bull pain, terry-bull, I tell you. Moans and wails constantly all the time, even in his sleep."

"*Certainly* I'm in pain, for Christ's sake, just look at me!" Nikki sputtered through swollen, yet well-enhanced purple lips. The doc-tor immediately wrote out a prescription for 120 Vicodin pills. Once safely back inside the Jag, Nikki handed the script to Chiquita, saying, "Here you go, honey, enjoy them with my blessing. But on your own time, now, damn it."

Dear Chiquita, bless his heart, he certainly needed a break, be-cause for the past two weeks he'd been doing absolutely everything for Nikki, driving him everywhere, accompanying him to all of his ap-pointments, and singlehandedly nursing him back to health. He was a regular Florence Nigh-ting-gay. Each day he would change his bloody bandages, feed him low-sodium, low-fat chicken broth, and help him get into and out of bed, and to the bathroom, too. He nursed, kept house, and kept him company until he was once again well. He simply couldn't have survived without his loving assistance. Nikki was indeed a friend in need, and Chiquita was a friend, indeed.

By the end of the third week of his confinement, Nikki was greatly improved and only had to be drained every other day. On the upside, after not eating for two weeks, he'd lost over fifteen pounds of ugly fat, and that was an unforeseen dividend from his self-induced shit storm. Still, he was black, blue, and purple from the top of his bald head to his not-as-big belly button, but now a few yellowish, greenish, and brownish areas were starting to appear because he was beginning to heal.

Already bored with staying home, he wanted desperately to get back to work but was unable to drive, so he asked Chiquita to chauffeur him to the mall.

"What?" Chiquita squealed. "Are you outta yer cock-a-maybe mind? You actually wanna go out in public lookin' like a crash test dummy after a car-wreck?"

"Take me to the mall. I want to go to the cosmetic counter at Hudson's. Perhaps they will have something that could help me conceal these hideous black-and-blue bruises." He was right, those nasty bruises just would not go away, and he simply couldn't leave home looking the way he did. Soon as the cosmetic counter girls saw him they shrieked. Stepping back inside their beauty cubicles, they clutched their ample breasts, while suppressing tears.

"Oh my Gawd. What happened to you, darlin'?"

"Was a terrible car wreck...The wife didn't make it. I have to go to her funeral today."

"Oh ma Gawd! You poor thing, does it hurt terrible bad?"

"Excruciating. But listen, I really need your assistance. I'm looking for a concealer to hide these terrible bruises. Do you have anything like that in my shade?"

The counter girls began falling all over themselves trying to be helpful, but they were afraid to even touch him. Handing him several vials of viscous fluids, of varying fleshy values, they stepped back fearing he was contagious. His face was so badly swollen he could barely stand to touch it himself, but one after the other he tried them. The cosmetic queens valiantly held back their tears as they looked on in horror at this fifty-something man trying to hide the painful-looking bruises, but nothing covered his blackened and bruised body.

"Maybe you should try one of them theatrical makeup places, you know, get ya some pancake makeup like they use in plays," suggested the perky blonde. That got his wheel to turning. Thanking the girls, he wrapped his head back up in the coco cashmere shroud, put his giant Gucci movie-star shades on, and had Chiquita escort him back to the Jag, just like a scene from a melodramatic movie; Prognosis negative. Other than doctor visits, this was his first outing in two weeks, and the first time he'd his hair on, and while glad to be out, he certainly didn't want to be seen this way, especially by the paparazzi.

Suddenly Nikki had a magnificent idea, and said, "Take me to the House of Diggs."

"*What*?" Chiquita shrieked, jerking his head around 360 degrees like Linda Blair in *The Exorcist*. "Have you lost your cotton pigeon mind?"

"Just start the goddamn car and drive. Damn it."

He obediently did as he was told, and drove to the funeral home in a most uncomfortable silence. Of course Nikki knew the owner because he'd done his wife's hair for years, plus he'd also been there a few times to do the final "dos" for a few special clients. But this time he *insisted* on going in alone, and was in there for the better part of an hour before finally returning, *concealed*. While still wrapped in his cashmere shroud, he turned to Chiquita for the big reveal.

"Well, I think I've finally found something that will work. And don't you *dare* say a thing about this to a living soul. You got me?"

"Uh-huh," Chiquita hummed, while gawking at him in disbelief, and crossing his fingers behind his bony back. Chiquita drove him gaily home, parked the car, got him out, got him inside, and into bed for the night. Then he ran across the street and immediately called me. "Stella, are you sittin' down? Well siddown, 'cause I took Nikki to the funeral home today."

"What?" I shrieked.

He laughed so hard it brought on a coughing fit. Once recovered he explained about the cosmetic girls, funeral home, cover-up for dead people, and how Nikki looked like the "*Bride of Frankenstein.*" It was funny as long as you weren't the one with your face falling off. But we both laughed anway because we knew that Nikki was healing and coming out of the woods, returning to his old piss-and-vinegar self. Four full weeks after sue-jelly Nikki resumed work. After delicately shaving his swollen face, he applied the oily pancake makeup over the bruises, pulled the face bra over his unattached but definitely less chubby cheeks, and snapped it together on top of his hairpiece. He looked absolutely ridiculous, hideous, ghoulish, and scared the shit out of the girls at the salon.

So his carefully guarded little secret was definitely out of the bag now, and it was abundantly clear something was terribly wrong. So... depending on the circumstances, and the client, he'd either been in a hideously disfiguring auto accident, or was recovering from having "a little work done." Needless to say, he booked very light days for the next few weeks.

It was a full two months before he looked somewhat normal again, and after six months had passed you'd never have guessed he had anything done at all. He just looked better, rested, refreshed, and happy to still be alive.

Bromance

God never has such a good laugh, as when you tell him your plans for the future.

Once upon a time... in the dark ages of the last century, before the invention of the Internet, and during the reign of "Ronald the Reagan" in the early 1980s, things were getting bad here in Buick City. The acting president's "trickle on" theory of economics had not yet made it this far down the ladder, and we were still bone dry here in Flint.

Flint had been hit particularly hard by this economic downturn. We were witnessing the end of the factory system as we once knew it. For over one hundred years this had been a one horse powered town built upon the auto industry, and when General Motors made the calculated decision to vacate the city we died. We'd been fucked. And after having their way with us for over one hundred years, and using us completely up, they were "pulling out."

This seismic shift signaled the start of the mass migrations out of Flint, and as a consequence we had lost half of our population in less than twenty years. The factories closed, the jobs disappeared, and the workers left with them. The end of the industrial era brought about another dust-bowl type of population shift with folks fleeing

Midwestern rust-belt cities such as Flint and Detroit and heading to areas of warmth and opportunity. Times were getting tough around here, and the bumper sticker that best summed it up read: "Will the last person out of Michigan please remember to turn out the lights?"

Foolishly swimming against this steadily outflowing tide, I returned to Flint after earning my bachelor of fine arts degree in Ann Arbor. During those young and lean, hungry years, I was struggling financially while exploring different career options, such as teaching, visual display, and sign painting. I even tried being "a real artist," and making artwork to sell at art fairs and galleries, but it wasn't easy selling art to jobless people living on food stamps and welfare cheese; consequently I did a lot of bartering, and ate a lot of grilled cheese sandwiches.

At the tender age of twenty-five I found myself floundering in Flint, and barely keeping my nose above the polluted water. Working three part-time jobs still did not generate enough income for me to support myself, and that was after having surrendered my phone and cable services, dropping health insurance, selling my truck, and taking on a roommate to share expenses. I couldn't have downsized myself anymore or I would have completely disappeared.

But a glimmer of hope finally appeared on my smoky-gray horizon when a friend from college wrote and told me they needed a painter on a restoration project she was working on in Ann Arbor. So I immediately jumped on the Greyhound bus and headed south.

After meeting in a painting class, Debbie and I became friends and started hanging out after school as well, eventually becoming confidants. Most likely, we gravitated toward each other after sensing our same-sex inclinations. She'd confided that she was a lesbian, and I shared my deep dark secret that I was gay, which I think we both already instinctively knew; it's called gaydar.

Joining Debby, and the ongoing restoration project, I worked in A2 weekdays and commuted to Flint on the weekends. During the workweek I shared Debby's modest apartment, and we even shared the same bed. We were that close.

That project went well, another began and I was asked to continue on. Our next project was the restoration of the parlor in a historic home on the National Register of Homes, in Marshall, Michigan, known as the Honolulu House. That job lasted several months, which helped get me back onto my feet financially, making it possible for me to purchase a used car, resume phone service, and secure health insurance again, which made my mother feel a lot better.

Once outside Flint, I discovered people were having normal lives, doing mundane things like going out for dinner, shopping, taking vacations, and even buying new cars; but hard times prevailed back home with food stamps, welfare cheese, and long unemployment lines. These were the *Roger and Me* years for Michael Moore and Flint.

While commuting back and forth from Flint to the outside world, I couldn't help but notice the Grand Canyon–size rift growing between the haves and the have-nots. The world outside Flint was definitely different, and better. People actually gave a shit about where they lived, had pride in their communities, were involved with the arts, culture, education, and cleanliness. Flint was, and still is, one trash-riddled shitty city. For Christ's sake, people, get up off your lazy asses and throw *your* trash into a receptacle. Give a shit about where you live!

Thrown a lifeline, I was grabbing it and getting out of filthy old Flint while I still had the chance. But wait—there are flies in paradise, too. Living on the road meant that I was working, traveling, and sharing meals and lodgings with Debby, and Carla—my new boss. She was continually disgruntled; it was like living with a drill sergeant mother-in-law with a constant bad toothache. She did not like men at all, not even a close facsimile like me, and she made that abundantly clear. So boo-hoo, cry me a river. She was my boss for Christ's sake; I wasn't supposed to like her. But it was a decent job and a ticket out of Dodge, which I took without looking back.

For the next three years we lived on the road while restoring historic homes and public places throughout the country. Moving on from Michigan, we restored the decorative paintings in an Italianate residence in Portland, Maine, then cleaned and embellished an antebellum estate in Nashville, repaired the Gothic mansion in Connecticut where *Dark Shadows* was once filmed, and refurbished the graphic trompe l'oeil paintings in the historic First Congregational Church on the picturesque island of Nantucket, Massachusetts.

Merciful God must have intended the Nantucket job as blessed payback for the three years spent living on the road, the backbreaking labor and having to work through holidays, and dealing daily with Carla's dirty disposition. On the postcard-perfect island we shared a well-weathered cedar-shake shack sitting on the sandy shore of Nantucket's natural harbor, comfortably nestled into a private cove, and lying directly across from the Coskata-Coatue Wildlife Refuge.

A winding sandy two-track trail split from a blacktopped road and disappeared into a darkened thicket of scrubby piney woods, creating a shady woodland tunnel. Emerging into the light, you spied the storybook cedar-shake cottage with a latticework lean-to porch that was completely covered with barely pink climbing roses. On the harbor side of the seaside shack, two big rows of dinner-plate–sized French blue hydrangeas flanked the central screen door, thriving well in the sandy acidic soil.

Our cozy beachfront bungalow was comfortably nestled into the secluded cove, surrounded by a backdrop of scrubby woodlands, and it felt far removed from the outside world. A fieldstone fireplace, white wicker furniture, and shabby-chic furnishings made it feel homey, familiar, familial, and the fact that it was provided rent free by the congregation made it even more ideal. The only downside to the deal was that we had to share the shack with our surly boss.

She eventually revealed much more of herself than I cared to know, and she was a real piece of work. Damaged by an abusive event early in her childhood, she'd been scarred for life, making her resentful, distrustful, and defensive. She was also jealous, passive aggressive, lazy, manipulative, and suspicious, and those were her good points. Somehow she went from being abused to becoming the abuser. Anyone could tell she was unhappy, because it was written all over her.

Throughout this prolonged period of working and traveling together, several magazine and newspaper articles were published about the projects we restored together, and she seldom mentioned our names or gave us credit for doing the work. She would just boss us around with her church-lady disapproving mouth eternally puckered, pursed, as if she'd just sucked off a lemon.

Working around her became increasingly difficult, and finally nearly intolerable, so we arranged our schedule to avoid seeing her. Starting at five A.M. and working through lunch, we'd finish by two in the afternoon and spend the rest of the day at the beach. Most days our schedules would overlap two hours, and at times that was too much to tolerate.

There were many nasty, backbreaking, toxic, and hazardous aspects common to this line of work. While it certainly wasn't fun removing and carrying away heavy chunks of wet and moldy, one-hundred-year-old horsehair-and-lathe plaster, it wouldn't kill you. *However*, abating lead-based paint, making and applying caustic lime poultices, using toxic cleaners and industrial-strength solvents to remove ancient grime, and handling Rhoplex adhesives and other toxic plaster consolidators on a daily basis probably *would* kill you, eventually. And when we were asked by OSHA to participate in a {limited} lifetime study on the effects of hazardous chemicals in the workplace, we were through.

Debby had enough of her duplicitous ways as well, so when our contractual obligations were fulfilled we left restoration altogether and joined forces, to begin a new decorative painting business in New York City. And in the fall of '82 we became the Isle of Manhattan's newest artists in residence.

Sing along with me: "If I can make it there...I can make it anywhere...it's up to *you*... (big finish now) *New York*, New...York!

Moving to Manhattan, we leased a loft that would've been every artist's dream space. Our three thousand square feet of sun-drenched wide-open space, had polished blond maple floors, and twenty-foot-tall cast-iron Corinthian columns, that held-up a whitewashed pressed-tin ceiling. A fifteen-foot-tall bank of east-facing windows looked down on Crosby, by the corner of Spring Street, in the heart of SoHo before it was trendy, when real artists lived there, with our neighbors being people such as Andy Warhol, Robert Lee Morris, and Robert Mapplethorpe.

The summer of 1982 I turned twenty-eight {28} on 8-28-82. The numbers seemed to align, and so did the stars. And quite unbelievably, our first job in New York City was painting, marbleizing, and gold-leafing in George Hamilton's Park Avenue apartment. But even more unbelievable, while working there we met the silent movie star Buddy Rogers, and the former Philippine First Lady Imelda Marcos, who was actually carrying shoe bags—I kid you not.

Triumphantly returning to Flint, I'd planned on spending Thanksgiving and Christmas with my family, packing, and then leaving Flint for good. That's when Nikki called.

"Hey, Murf, I heard you was back in town. Whatcha think; should we get all dolled up and go out and paint the town one last time, before you leave to become rich and famous? Who knows, if you are lucky you may never have to come back to this gutbucket town ever again. Whatcha think?"

"Sure, let's make a night of it."

Plans were made to rendezvous and go downtown, to the Copa, Flint's newest and nicest nightclub. This was a big-city-looking-and-feeling disco, with a much more attractive and select crowd than ever graced the Pink Poodle. The pulsing disco beat thump, thump, thumped all night long, as multicolored lights flashed on and on, and wall-to-wall pretty people partied hardy.

Being a bon vivant, Nikki quickly deserted me to cha-cha-cha the night away and entertain the locals. But I didn't care, because I had noticed a certain someone off to the side, standing all alone and leaning on a mirrored column. When I first saw him my heart skipped a beat. He seemed wholesome, and wore a long-sleeved oxford button-down shirt with the sleeves rolled up, in an unusual shade of lavender, which made his ruddy face take on a suntanned appearance.

While spying on him from afar, I was contemplating if he was out of my league and trying to work up the nerve to speak with him, because no one else was. He had dark curly hair and a James Franco look about him, and was ruggedly handsome. After two more brews I'd worked up the courage.

"Would you like to dance?" I awkwardly asked, trying to break the ice.

"No, but thanks for asking."

"Don't you like to dance?"

"Yes I do, but I can't."

"You can't dance?"

"I have a wooden leg."

"Oh my God, I'm so sorry. I feel so stupid."

"I'm sorry, too," he said, laughing. "That was mean of me. Hi...my name is Mike."

"Den here, and it's nice to meet you, Mike."

Smiling broadly, while still chuckling at his joke, he extended a hand. I accepted. It was warm and his grip firm; these were workingman's hands. He was nicely built, with broad sloping shoulders, a narrow waist, and the cutest little butt you'd ever seen. As I leaned in closer to hear him speak, I could feel the warmth radiating from him, and he smelled so damn good, as if he'd just stepped out of the shower. I just wanted to stand next to him and inhale.

"Have you been to Florida recently? You look tanned."

"No. I hardly ever make it out of the county. My dad has a horse farm near Vassar, and I'm outside a lot. So, where do you live, Den?"

"That's a little difficult to say, Mike; because mostly I'm living out of a suitcase. I'm going between New York, and Flint. I have a home here, but I'll be moving there after the New Year."

"Wow, how exciting, you must be really excited. What do you do, anyway?"

"I'm an artist...of sorts. What about you, what do you do?"

"I guess you could say I'm a painter, too. Because I paint Buicks, Oldsmobiles, and Cadillacs as they roll down the assembly line at the Buick, Oldsmobile, Cadillac Group in Lake Orion."

He went on to explain that he'd come with a friend from work, Andre, who was currently off seeking a mandate. I, in turn, explained about my imaginary friend Nikki, who was off on a similar mission. We chatted for quite some time getting to know each other, and I liked what I saw and heard.

When Andre finally returned, Mike introduced me to a handsome, energetic, well-dressed, caramel-colored man with an unexpected mop of curly blond hair."Den, this is my friend Andre."

"Hello. Nice to meet you, Andre."

"Same here and thanks for entertaining Mike this evening. As you've probably noticed, I've really been neglecting him tonight. Say, who is that brassy blond guy over there? Is he your friend?"

"Yes, that's Nikki. Would you like to meet him? Because I'm sure he'd like to meet you. His favorite flavor happens to be chocolate."

From that moment on they were all smiles, danced the night away, worked up a serious sweat, and we barely saw them. Mike and I talked the rest of the evening, and his genuine warmth, openness, and sincerity melted my big-city defenses. His voice was pleasing, his manner warm, and his lips very kissable. As he fondly described his folks' farm, I could imagine the fine-legged horses in green grassy fields, feel the cool spring-fed ponds where he talked of skinny-dipping, and picture the shady woodlands where he rode horses, took long meditative walks, and drove dirt bikes.

The night disappeared as we chatted, suddenly the lights came on, and they kicked us out.

"Murf, where've you been all night?" Nikki demanded, glistening with sweat and smirking.

"I never moved from this spot, except to pee a couple times."

"Well, Andre here wants to come over and look at my painted ceilings," Nikki announced.

"What?"

"*Hellll-ooo*, he's from out of town, ya know, and he can stay with me tonight if you can put up what's-his-name there. Now, you wouldn't want me to be deprived of male companionship and have to suffer all alone tonight. Now, would you?"

"It's up to Mike, really. I'd love it if he stayed at my place tonight; if he wants to, that is."

"I don't know. I don't usually do this sort of thing," Mike said. "Maybe I'll take Andre's car and come back in the morning."

"I'm so glad we have *that* all figured out. Bye-bye, see you two later. Don't get caught doing what I'm planning on doing," Nikki said, fleeing, and his laughter bouncing off downtown's walls.

"I'm sorry. I didn't mean to put you on the spot like that. I just thought..."

"I would love to come over. Yes."

And then he reached over and kissed me, sensuously, right there on Main Street.

— ⌒ ⌒

"Wow, this place is really colorful," Mike said, surveying my house and studio.

"Chartreuse is for new growth, maroon for compassion, pink for love, and black for grounding. Each color has a metaphysical manifestation. Would you care for a beer?"

"Sure, thanks. Your place is really cool. Are any of these paintings yours?"

"Yes, this one is mine, and my friend, Linda, did these prints. Come over here and sit down. I want to read you a story that I just illustrated. It's called *Amanda Panda* and it's about a little girl who was lonely until she got two kittens." He sat next to me on the cabbage-rose sofa, I open the book, and it straddled our laps. Listening intently as I read aloud, he carefully studyied the mixed-media pictures, and snuggled closer.

When he snuggled up to me, that's the moment I fell, right then and there, that very first night.

"*Oh*, that was so cute, I just loved it," he said, genuinely meaning it, and snuggling even closer. "That was so good. What are you going to do with it?"

"I'm taking it to New York when I go and trying to peddle it."

"Cool. So when are you leaving?"

"First of the year, January."

Then he reached over and kissed me again, but this time it was passionate, velvety, and romantic. He was an excellent kisser, and that was so very important to me, because it told me what he wouldn't say—how passionately he felt about me, releasing all those feel-good endorphins.

By now it was getting late, so I led him to my colorful bedroom, where life-size cutout figures of cowboys and horses, props from an old store display, adorned the royal blue walls. Covering the bed was my boyhood chenille bedspread that was gaily decorated with a cowboy wearing brown woolly chaps riding a bucking bronco. His shiny six-shooter and holster were sitting atop the pillows, and a rusty-red barbed wire border ran around the perimeter as a pretty decoration.

"Wow, this is really fun. Did you do all this, too?"

"Yeah."

After I switched on the Conestoga covered wagon nightlight, next to the blond bird's-eye maple bed, the room began to radiate a warming amber glow. Lighting a lavender-scented candle, it began to flicker, smolder, and fill the air with its clean scent.

Slowly we began to explore each other, awkwardly at first, touching, kissing, loving, unfolding, and holding one other as close as humanly possible. Liplocked, I felt his velvety tongue exploring my eager mouth, heavy breathing, skin against naked skin. All night long we lay glued together basking in the candle's golden flickering glow. Caressing, embracing, and falling asleep in each other's arms.

Broad shouldered and narrow at the hips, with a well-defined chest, he had the type of muscular arms you'd get from doing manual labor and not the kind you'd get from going to a gym. Warm black close-cropped wavy hair and a matching mustache were complemented by deep semisweet-chocolate eyes. His smooth olive skin simply invited touching, but it was his smile that was so disarming. When he smiled I felt his genuine warmth, and it melted me. I instinctively felt he was a good man worthy of loving, and for the first time in my life I let myself fall for a man.

Mike was not your typical shop rat. Even though he was working in a factory at that time, he'd earned a BA and was attending graduate classes in business administration. He was smart and funny, lovable, and would considerately call on his coffee breaks to ask how my day was going, tell me he thought of me often and wanted to be with me each night, which only encouraged me. I so wanted to hear those things from him.

For the next five weeks we saw each other every stolen moment we could find, each night and every weekend. On our first Christmas together he helped decorate holiday shortbread cookies, as well as a crooked Charlie Brown Christmas tree with the vintage ornaments I'd collected.

For the first time in my life I felt love was reciprocal, because he declared it in the shower, just before I left, and it was magical and bittersweet. Finally I'd found love, but I was committed to another life, in another state, and with a woman. For the longest time I'd hoped to find someone like him, and when I finally did, I was leaving town. Ain't life a kick in the pants?

Once committed to loving him, I did not want that to ever end, because I was young and naive I wanted a forever kind of love, and thought it was possible with him. Before Mike I'd never let myself fall to this degree, but I felt he was worth loving and able to love me in return. And just like in a sappy old movie, I was willing to love him even if he wouldn't love me as much.

When January came and it was time to move, it was torment. Before I even left my heart ached because I missed him so. But Mike was so good at sending cards, letters, and calling often. He was very tenderhearted and never wanted to hurt anyone's feelings and I loved that about him.

For three difficult years we carried on a crazy long-distance romance, spending every chance we could to be with other. He loved coming to see me in "The City" because it was brimming with energy and excitement, alive, and prospering, unlike Detroit, which was quickly going to shit.

Being an avid reader, he was up on the latest pop culture, movies, plays, and popular music. Knowing he loved Broadway shows, I saved my leisure time to share those experiences with him. He just loved the musical *Cats*, and I hated the dreadful thing, falling asleep during the boring third act, but knowing he loved it I sat through it again. He also loved visiting the many unusual stores, shops, and unique boutiques The City had to offer, and I did not care for shopping; but because he found those things enjoyable, I would accompany him and share his joy.

I loved visiting him in Michigan, where I could once again find comfort, peace, quiet, and a sense of home I never experienced while living in Manhattan. Back home I could drop my shoulders and my defenses to where they belonged, see lush, green wide-open landscapes and breathe clean, unleaded air once again.

This was way before cell phones were invented and computers commonplace, so between visits I wrote, penning volumes and volumes, and we spoke on the phone often. When we were reunited there was always a tinge of sadness, because we knew our limited time together would be ending soon, we'd be apart, and I would be missing him again. Longing and separation became familiar feelings, and like those sappy old Irish drinking songs, our relationship seemed cursed by geography and timing. "Oh, Denny Boy, the pipes, the pipes are calling."

Homosexual relationships have always been difficult to orchestrate, because they needed to be completely covert, *if you wanted to live*. Existing underground, they were unsanctioned, out-of-the-box criminal love affairs, considered to be sinful—going against all the laws of God, nature, and the state.

But loving him was difficult at times. I felt he loved me more by the passion he demonstrated during love-making than anything he ever said, because he was stingy with the word *love*, and I wanted to hear that word from him unsolicited. Like many men, he was emotionally distant, and many times I felt he was pulling me closer with one hand and pushing me away with the other.

People don't come with warning labels; you have to figure them out yourself. He didn't know he was bipolar and manic when we met, and I didn't either, but he was. He also had epilepsy and was troubled with seizures. Those kinds of extreme mood fluctuations were unpredictable, unexplainable, and often people with those kinds of swings are difficult to be around.

In other ways I realized my relationship with Mike was similar to my dynamic with my father—difficult. With my father I felt I had to try harder to get him to recognize and accept me, and to earn his love and approval. It was difficult for him to praise me, or accept me as I was, and ultimately I think he sensed I was gay and disapproved of that. But my being gay was not something I could change, and we never really found common ground.

There was a familiar dynamic with Mike. I wanted him to love me, and say it unprompted, but he was so stingy with the word *love*, as if saying it was a sign of weakness. As time passed, our having a future together began to look less likely, because our new business was becoming successful and I was committed to Debby and New York. And he was unwilling to transfer his job with General Motors to join me in the city, and we knew something would eventually have to give.

Never desiring another, I was faithful to him the entire time we dated, and that was fortunate, because it may have saved my life. This was the early eighties, and also the beginning of the terrible AIDS epidemic, which had its epicenters in New York City and San Francisco.

After carrying on a crazy long-distance love affair for three difficult years, it was Mike who eventually found another, and that didn't make it any easier to accept.

"Oh, you'd like him, Den; he's a lot like you. His name is Denny, too, and he's a *doctor*."

Just shoot me now and get it over. Who needs to hear that your replacement is just like you, only younger, a bodybuilder, a doctor, *and* an artist, too? *Whoopee!*

For the next ten years I went on with my life without him, and I made a pretty good one. Mike and I did not communicate during that time, but our time apart did not change the way I felt about him, because he still held a special place in my heart, and I pined for him. But in reality, I know I yearned for what he represented, a loving relationship and home life with a man whom I loved.

Nonetheless, through the terrible dark years of the AIDS epidemic, as more friends died, I prayed that God would keep Mike safe. Secretly I hoped that one day he'd come to his senses and we would have a life together. Often, when I watched a romantic movie, read a mushy greeting card, or had an amorous thought, it was him I imagined. There were others in between, I was not a nun, but no one ever had the same gravitational pull he had upon me. I never got over Mike, and wondered what my life would have been like if we had lived together. I never did "partner" with anyone else, ever.

—～

During the dark ages of the eighties, while living in New York City, I witnessed many of my contemporaries dying from the new gay plague, AIDS. Many dear friends passed away, and it was a catastrophe in the gay community with so many bright young and talented people dying in their prime. Realizing I was not immune, I was tested, because I wanted to know if I was marked for death or not.

Learning I was HIV negative only left more questions, and a strange form of survivor's guilt. Why was I spared, and what was I supposed to do with my life? Life becomes much more serious when contemplating your mortality, especially at such an early age. Like Thoreau, I longed for a simpler life than the one I was living in Manhattan, a small life, not asking for much, just a cottage where I could make my living by creating art and be one with nature. Like Saint Francis the Sissy.

A few years later I had made manifest that dream by moving back to Michigan and finding my cozy Cape Cod cottage on quiet Canfield Lake. And it was there that I created my home and studio, and lived a small, peaceful, and orderly life.

— ⌒ —

A decade later, Labor Day weekend, and the phone rang.

"Murphy's Bed-and-Breakfast. How may I direct your call?"

"Den?"

Immediately recognizing the voice, I reached for a chair, and sat down.

"It's Mike. Are you busy?" he said, clearing his throat. "Hope I'm not interrupting anything."

"No, that's okay. I was just cleaning up after having company."

"I hope you don't mind me calling."

"No. Actually, it's good to hear your voice again. It's been a really long time, Mike."

"I know. But I didn't know if I should call you, or not. Over the years I've attempted to call you lots of times, and to tell you the truth, I'm not really sure why I finally did."

"I'm glad you did. It was stubborn and stupid of me to not call. I've really missed you."

"I've really missed you, too, Den. Really."

"There were so many times when I wanted to call you. And after so much time had passed and I hadn't heard from you I became worried that you might not have made it. I've lost a lot of friends."

"Me too, and I'm really glad to know you're still here. You know, Den, I have to tell you this... no one has ever loved me the way you did, I mean unconditionally, with my warts and all."

"I never stopped loving you, Mike. It was you that quit."

"I want to see you. I need to see you. How do I get to you?"

The four longest hours of my life were spent nervously cleaning; my house had never been so spotless. When finished scrubbing, I paced, wearing out my hardwood floors, anxiously awaiting his arrival, nervous, excited, and scared to death all at the same time.

When he finally arrived, we fell into each other's arms, out in my driveway, for God and the world to see. I held him for the longest time not wanting to let him go. Then I looked at him. I mean seriously examined him, and he'd clearly aged. His Roman nose finally fit his handsome face, and his once-black wiry hair was thinning, graying, and receding like mine, but he was still very handsome, only now in a more mature, Richard Gere kind of way.

Talking for hours, we caught up on all those lost years, and because his lips were lubricated by the six-pack he'd admitted drinking while driving there, he was very talkative. Later that evening, as I stood at the sink washing salad greens for dinner, he walked up behind me, wrapped his arms around me and nuzzled his head on my shoulder, and I melted like a stick of oleo in the August Arizona sun.

"I have missed you so much, Den, you have no idea."

The world around us disappeared as we entwined arms and bodies. His kissing was hungry, desperate, greedy, and passionate, and we could not let go of each other. I began to cry, feeling safe again, home.

"What's this, are you crying? Are you all right?"

"Never better. Hold me tighter."

———

By the next morning the honeymoon was over, when Mike went on to explain about his very complicated life and the ten-year marriage to the doctor, which ended badly a year earlier. Then he explained about his current disastrous living arrangement.

"It seemed the doctor's family didn't approve of his alternative lifestyle, and that would be me. He was supposed to be receiving a substantial inheritance soon, and his loving family let it be known if he'd consider marrying a nice, young, Christian woman, and preferably one with a ready-made family, they'd be more inclined to give him the straightening-out money. So after we'd been living together for ten years, he came home one afternoon and announced: 'Thanks for the memories. Now pack up your shit, get the hell out, and don't let the screen door hit you in the ass on the way.' Then he married some unsuspecting war widow with a couple kids."

"I'm sorry to hear that, Mike."

"I was really blindsided, Den. I mean totally devastated. I'd never had the rug pulled out from under me that way before. I really thought we were a couple, and I thought he felt the same way."

"Mike, I can see this has hurt you deeply. But in another way, I'm glad you have such deep feelings, because you've never admitted to having them before."

"Well, I'm admitting it now, and that's why I want to be straight with you. It was selfish of me to come here yesterday. I shouldn't have come at all, but I really missed you, and I needed a friend. The guy I'm living with now is a jealous hairdresser, and my fucked-up life is pretty much sex and drugs, and I don't know how to escape. What I need is a good friend, and you've been the best friend I've ever had. I wanted to see you badly, and you wanted to see me, too, but I know I can't ever give you what you want. I just don't have it in me. And I'm afraid my depression will ruin your life, too, just like it's ruining mine. At times I get so depressed and hopeless, and I don't want you to have to live with that. So please, just be my friend."

Then he went outside and searched through his car, returned with a yellow straw suitcase, and emptied the contents on the chenille bedspread. The satchel held all the cards and letters I'd sent him over the years. He'd kept them. The bed was covered.

I was touched and embarrassed, because this looked like the writings of an obsessed person. I had no idea I'd sent him this much mail. We began opening the yellowed envelopes and examining the past. All those feelings I once held for him were dragged back out and reexamined, and for me many of them were the same.

But he was wrestling with other feelings, other demons, and other substances.

After our trip down memory lane, Mike went on to confess that during the ten years we were incommunicado he'd developed a rather serious substance abuse problem. Self-medication is quite common in depressed people, and his abuse problem began with over using alcohol, progressed to cocaine, and eventually moved to abusing prescription drugs. His problem eventually became so serious that he went into an addiction recovery program. But he also confessed that he'd suffered a small heart attack just a couple of weeks earlier, and that was what must have really put the fear of God into him.

After our cataclysmic reconnection, we returned to our separate realities, but we both wished to remain in contact. Speaking frequently and visiting when possible, we remained "friendly," because he was in a relationship and living in Detroit, and I was living four hours away way in northern Michigan.

During this difficult retrograde period, he somehow managed to keep his GM job, even though he commuted fifty miles each way, each day, to make that possible. There were several unexplained accidents during this period, with two cars being completely totaled. But no tickets were ever issued for these miscellaneous wrecks, because he looked so "normal," like the suburban father next door, and no one ever suspected he was stoned on prescription drugs such as Xanax, Oxycontin, and Oxycodone.

But then, on one lost weekend he was stopped by the state police at four in the morning, while driving the wrong way down the expressway and stoned out of his mind on prescription drugs. After being stopped he complained of intense pain from having kidney stones and was taken to the hospital, knowing full well they'd show up on X-ray. And after finding them, he was given even more drugs and was released, without ever receiving a ticket. When I learned what had happened, I yelled at him so loud the entire neighborhood heard.

"What the hell were you thinking? Being fucked up like that you could have killed someone!"

"I didn't even get a ticket."

"Mike, you can get fucked up and kill yourself if you want, but I know you wouldn't be able to live with yourself if you took out an entire family while you were doing it."

When we first reconnected, I stupidly thought he wanted me back, like in some sappy romantic melodrama. After twenty years he finally realized it was me he had loved all along, and we would be reunited. But he didn't feel the same way. He wasn't dealing with any romantic fantasy—he was dealing with a serious life-and-death reality.

When his relationship with Raun finally did implode, he moved back to his folks' for sanctuary, and that is where he stayed for the next few tumultuous years. While living on the farm he stabilized and slowly healed. During his downtime he helped out by mowing and gardening, caring for the horses, and helping his grandmother; it was good for him. Once he was grounded, his overall life improved.

When he was once again whole we started dating again, and saw each other for nearly a month. Things seemed hopeful because for the first time in a decade we were both living in the same state and he was unattached. I thought we were happy together. But he must have felt differently, because while I was in Greece with Nikki and Chiquita for three weeks, he met Bill online, and that exposed another aspect of his addictive personality: his computer dating compulsion.

Mike talked quite frankly about his relationship with his new friend. Apparently, going through addiction treatment must have made it easier for him to communicate his true feelings, because he was not able to communicate like that when we dated. But he must have felt even more comfortable with expressing his emotions in writing, and he composed me this Dear Denial letter to clarify his feelings about me and his new friend, Mr. Bill.

> Dear Den,
>
> I want to start by saying thank you for putting up with all my shit over these past few years. You are the one person who knows all the dirty details of my life,

and has stuck by me. I wish I could understand why you feel about me the way you do. When I look at myself, all I can think is that I am not someone a man like you should be serious about, I am not good husband material. I think that is why I choose men who aren't available; when the relationships fail with them it's not such big a deal for me. I guess the last relationship I was in, with Raun in Detroit, was a 360-degree reaction to the rejection I felt after my marriage with The Doctor failed. I guess I took up with Raun just to have a good time, but boy...was I wrong about that.

When I met Bill online a few weeks back, we really clicked. He lives just twenty minutes from me, and we have so much in common. He's an elementary schoolteacher, and he says and does things that give me a sense of hope about having a serious relationship and even a future together; but it might be all bullshit, too, because he is also in another relationship and having the best of both worlds.

Somehow I see my whole life being played out with him in a way that I never have with anyone else. With Bill there is some sort of cosmic force at work. We seem to have so much in common—our music, obscure cinema, art. But he also could be my cosmic payback, because I have truly fallen for this man, and he may not be there for me at crunch time.

I know that these are things you probably don't want to hear about, because I'm talking about feelings I have for someone else, but it's something you are going to have to deal with if we are going to be friends. And I want to be your friend, in your life, because you are one of themost together people I know and I'd hate to lose that. I have so few friends left. With you, you see something else in me that I don't see in myself, and it's very hard for me to deal with that. My feelings about myself are what keep me from being able to respond to you. You'll make a great catch for someone who wants the same things you do. You need to find someone who will return those romantic and sexual feelings that you need and want but that I don't have for you.

I do want to be in your life. You've been a very good friend and I would hate to lose that. I think you are very talented, and I enjoy seeing the work that you continue to do, and yes, I still think you're cute, too; but the feelings I have for you aren't romantic or sexual. But I do love you in my own way, and I'd like to have you along for the ride.

Love, (yes, love) Mike

The truth hurt me deeply, but I saved his letter to remind myself that even when he had the chance to be with me he chose to be with some -one else. This "Dear Denial" letter was the only letter I kept, except for a Valentine he sent when we were romantically involved. That prophetically read, "Love isn't always about the destination, it's about the journey." I burned all his other correspondences a long time ago trying to remove him from my heart. They made a lovely flame, but it didn't extinguish the warmth I continued to feel for him. Throughout this tumultuous time we remained friends as best we could, because after more than twenty-some years we had a long his-story.

Not long after receiving this "letter of rejection" my mother died, and I was thankful Mike was there for me. He offered what comfort he could, but he wasn't in good shape, was always anxious, had developed a slight tremor, and was just plain tired.

When given enough time, things did not work out the way he'd wished with his romance with Bill, and Mike became seriously deflat-ed, the lowest I'd ever seen him. I wondered how the sensitive, whole-some, conservative man I once knew had turned into this defeated and addicted man. And as a friend, I wondered what I could do to help a loved one in serious trouble.

After many years spent struggling against the current, he eventually gave in to the flow, and joined AA. To maintain sobriety he joined a Gay AA group that met twice weekly at Woodside Church, and my dear friend Gigi Mitzvah became his sponsor. He was slowly getting his life back on track again. Adonai, bless her caring heart.

— ~

Sobriety for some is an ongoing struggle.

— ~

"Den, this is Mike. Can you pick me up from rehab? I don't want to bother my parents. They've been through too much already."

"What time will they be discharging you?"

— ~

"Thanks for coming to get me, Den, I really appreciate it."

"I'm certain you'd do the same for me."

"And I want you to know that I appreciate your sticking by me through all this. There aren't many people left in my corner anymore."

"I don't have any choice, Mike. You're my friend. What happened to you this time? You look exhausted, and not ready to take on the world like the last time."

"I *am* exhausted, tired of all this, and I just want to get to my own apartment and get some rest."

"I'm exhausted, too, Mike. Your addiction has taken its toll on the people who love you. And while I certainly don't care for the things you've done, I still love you, Mike. I want you to know that."

"I thank you for that."

Reaching over, he took my hand and we both began to weep.

Driving north in somber silence we passed through a barren winter landscape that was cold, gray, and bleak, with snow blanketing the frosty ground and ice covering the frozen lakes. There would be nothing but gray sunless skies for many months to come.

— ⁓

The following weekend it snowed six inches, making it look more like Christmastime than nearly Thanksgiving. On this wintry afternoon I was having my family over for turkey dinner with all the fixings, because we were going separate ways for the holiday this year, and this was a chance to get the family together. The windows were frosted over when we sat down to eat, and wouldn't you know it, just as we did the phone rang. I let the answering machine do its job, because this was time to be with family. When the meal was finished and the family gone I retrieved the message. *Beeeeeep.*

— ⁓

"Denny, this is Jo Ann, Mike's mother. Have you seen Mike? We can't get him to answer his phone, and I'm real worried about him. Please call me when you get this message, it's very important."

Her voice was cracking. There was panic in it, and I could tell this was serious. I phoned her.

"Hello, this is Den, is Jo Ann there?"

"She can't come to the phone now," was the curt reply.

"She just called and left a message asking me to call her right back. It sounded serious."

"Hold on, honey, just a minute."

"Den...we lost him...we lost him..." she cried, and then she let loose with a deep guttural wail.

"What?"

Her speech came out in short, halting, and breathless spurts. "I knew something was wrong... when I called you...I could just tell...so I sent his dad...over to check on him...They found him... slumped over on his computer desk...heart attack. We lost him, Den. We lost him..."

May God bless his beautiful and troubled soul.

— ⁓

My sister, Mary, and friend Bette accompanied me to the visitation in Vassar. I knew I wouldn't be able to attend the funeral without melting down, and I didn't need a lot of people who didn't know me wondering why I was carrying on so. And that is part of the price you pay for living a closeted life. By the time we arrived at the funeral home, the viewing room was filled with family and friends who had come to say goodbye to Mike. In spite of the bumps in his later life, he was close to his large extended family, well loved, and remembered as being kind, considerate, and generous with his time.

When I finally summoned the strength to look at him, lying there in the casket, I was totally shocked because he looked just ghastly, swollen and bloated, like Joseph Stalin, and not my handsome Mike. I know he would have hated being seen looking like that, because he was always so particular about his appearances.

While numbly walking up to the coffin, I was greeted by Mike's father, who reached out to me with two big and warm work-worn hands. He clasped my hand tightly and shook it firmly, "Hello, I'm Mike's dad, Joe. And you are?"

"His friend Den."

Somehow that seemed woefully inadequate to describe what Mike had meant to me, but how was he to know about me, or us? His father had the same kind of warmth Mike possessed, and the same disarming smile. I was overwhelmed with emotion, choked up and lost for words. When turning to leave, I was stopped by Mike's mother, Jo Ann.

"I'm so glad you could make it, Den. I know you was a real close friend a Mike's, and I want you to know that we appreciated everything that you done for him."

"I am so sorry, Jo Ann, I can't begin to tell you how sorry I am for your loss."

"Thank you, Denny," she said, clasping my hands and gazing knowingly into my eyes.

"This is my sister, Mary, and friend Bette. They came with me tonight."

"Thank you both for coming, and Bette it's nice to finally meet you. I've spoken with you on the phone a few times over the years, about Mike and his sobriety."

"It's nice to finally meet you, too, Jo Ann. And please accept my deepest condolences. It's not supposed to work this way, you know, burying our children."

"We are all so sorry," Mary added.

"Thank you for coming. And Den, we'd like you to be one of Mike's pallbearers."

"I'm afraid I won't be able to do that, Jo Ann. I hope you understand."

"Yes...I understand." On that reply, I had to turn and leave.

I could not stay for the prayer service because I was too emotionally overwhelmed. Unable to stop it, I started to bawl, and didn't need a room full of witnesses. Mary and Bette followed me out.

Driving off in somber silence, we passed through a miserably black night, with the only sounds being the pinging of tiny icy pellets on the windshield and the squawking of windshield wipers trying to remove the accumulating clumps. Bette finally spoke up.

"Could it possibly be a more miserable night? With that relentless bone-chilling wind coming right out of the north. Oh, Jesus. Oh God! *Look out*—there's a dog running into the road!"

Thump, thump, thump, yelp, yelp.

"It just ran into the road. I couldn't help it," Mary exclaimed in her defense.

"I saw it, too. That dog darted out of nowhere, you couldn't help it," Bette confirmed.

"You'd better pull off the road; I'll call 911," I said.

As we pulled in the drive, a van coming from the opposite direction ran into the poor animal again and hurled the carcass farther down the road. Red brake lights flashed onto the icy pavement, and the minivan pulled into the next driveway down.

"911. What is the nature of your emergency?"

"We are on M-15, just south of Vassar, and there is a dog in the road that has been hit three times now. The traffic won't slow down enough to get the poor thing off from the highway."

"Please stay away from the road, the sheriff is on the way. We don't want you getting hit, too."

Suddenly a wiry young woman, without any coat, climbed out of the minivan and went running toward the commotion. "Oh my God, that's our dog, Tipppppppppppy." Then her three young children, strapped inside her van, began to wail along with her. "Tippy, Tippy, Tippy."

"She must've got out and tried to find us. Oh my God. What am I going to do? She's the kids' dog...I just got divorced...we just moved." Then she began to lose it, big-time, hands clasped to her temples, chest heaving, and tears streaming down her shiny red cheeks.

"Ma'am, the sheriff is on the way. I can hear a siren coming. Please don't go near the road."

Appearing out of nowhere, Bette sternly said, "Ma'am, I am a therapist. You will have to pull it together for the sake of those children of yours. They're traumatized, and you'll have to be strong for them. Go and comfort your children, tell them it's going to be all right."

"You're right, I'm so sorry. Thank you."

"You will probably need to talk to someone, so here is my phone number. I'm very sorry about your dog, but the children are your real concern now. Go and comfort them."

It was all too awful.

— ～

Mike's unexpected death hit me extremely hard. In the depths of my grief I moved down to Flint, because there aren't many places more miserable than Flint in winter. I spent that winter holed up in my trailer, lost in grief, overwhelmed emotionally, and weeping.

And just to make things worse, I called his cell phone a couple of times to listen to his voice message play, because that was all of him remained, and after a few weeks that disappeared, too.

Three weeks after he was buried, Mike's mother called informing me they were cleaning out his apartment and there were a few of his belongings she wanted me to have…if that was all right. A large box arrived containing a watercolor portrait of Mike that I'd painted some twenty years earlier, a blue glazed ceramic wall decoration set of *The Man in the Moon* and two stars that I'd given him, and a yellow straw suitcase filled with cards and letters.

The winter following his death was the darkest of my life. I cried until completely drained of tears, felt limp, listless, and devoid of feelings. And even with my family living close, I felt alone. Most people didn't know what Mike had meant to me over the years, and that was mostly my fault, because I had not included them in that part of my life. So how were they to know that I loved him deeply, and how much I grieved his death?

God bless your lovely troubled heart, Mike. I love you.

Travels with the Queen

"We simply *have* to begin our vacation in Venice. *Have* to, end of sentence, period. We'll fly from Detroit to the European continent, Amsterdam, *you see*, and that way we'll rack up frequent-flier miles. Then we fly from Amsterdam to mainland Italy, for more frequent-flier miles, *you see*, and then it's off to the isle of Venice. Oh, I tell you, Venice, there is no place like it in the entire world."

Nikki was misty-eyed, with a wistful far-off look in his pale blue eyes and sentimental smile upon his lovely, newly restored face. This trip would be the unveiling for the world to view his new, surgically enhanced loveliness. Brace yourselves world, here it comes.

"We'll fly into the Italian mainland because there isn't any room for an airport on Venice—it's completely filled with lovely little luxury shops. Then a posh polished yacht picks us up at the airport, and whisks us off to our fabulous island destination. For over half an hour we speed through the briny sea, surrounded by nothing but gray-green water and gray-blue endless sky, while hearing seagulls cry, and feeling the cool morning mist. Then you slowly begin to glimpse her.

"As our yacht begins to slow down, lovely snippets of architectural antiquity seem to appear out of the misty moist. Buildings seem to suddenly rise from of the ethereal fog-shrouded sea, grow larger and lovelier the closer you get, and suddenly there she is, Venicea, The Queen of the Adriatic. Oh, it's breathtaking, I tell you. There is nothing like it in the world. And I should know.

"Okay girls. Now, speaking of the world, here's our itinerary. I've picked a suitable place for us to stay while in Venice. It's on the Grand Canal, not too far from Saint Mark's Square, and yet within easy walking distance to all of *my* important shopping destinations. Now, it only has four stars, but this is just a little side trip to pick up a few pretty things. As you well know, *I* always stay at the Gaudy Palace when *I* am there, but you poor welfare bitches can't afford that place, *believe you me*!

"So we'll have four fabulous days in Venice to see the sights and do some shopping. Now, I know you like old churches, Murf, and you'll be glad to know they've got all kinds of old and moldy holy shit there. One day we'll go to Burano, a cute little island where they make lovely lacework and doilies, and we'll go to Murano, too, where they make those artsy glassy thingies I so dearly lovely.

"After spending four dazzling days of resplendent luxury and ornate opulence in Venice, it's back to Amsterdam—for more frequent-flier miles, *you see*. Then we're off to ancient Greece. Ah, antiquity! We will fly into Athens, and then take a puddle jumper to our Grecian island destination, Mykonos. Oh and there's that teensy little side trip to Turkey, to pick me up a few rugs.

"Just wait till you bitches see the coop-de-villa I rented for us in Grease. It sits right on the Aegean, and it's fucking fabulous. I found it in the *Architectural Digest*, and it's obscenely expensive, sheesh. Now, I know you two are coupon clippers, and that's all well and good for you poor bitches. So here's the deal: I'll pay for the villa, and you two ghetto girls will only have to pay for your booze, recreational drugs, male hookers, penicillin, meals, entertainment, and stuff like that.

"Now, remember, we're going to be on a teensy tiny island for nearly three weeks, and that's a lot of time to be spending on a dot a dirt, so I figured, since we're so close to Turkey, we should drop over and visit them for a couple days, just to be neighborly, ya know. That'll break up the boredom of being with you two bitches for two weeks, too. After all, we're practically already there all ready, and I hear they're having fabulous deals on carpets since having that nasty old earthquake; they're desperate for money, practically giving the stuff away, and I desperately need some good cheap carpets.

"Now, we'll fly from Mykonos to Athens, Athens to Amsterdam, and Amsterdam to Turkey. That way we rack up more frequent-flier miles, *you see*. After spending three or four days there, we'll fly back to Amsterdam—for more miles—then it's back to Athens—for more miles—and finally back to Mykonos. After resting up for a couple of days, we fly back to America via Mykonos, Athens, Amsterdam, Detroit, and bingo—more miles. It'll be fabulous, don't cha think?"

His description reminded me of a pinball machine in motion, *boing, boing, boing*. My head was spinning. Detroit Amsterdam, Amsterdam Athens, Amsterdam Venice, Amsterdam Italy, Amsterdam Turkey, and then Amsterdam and back to Detroit, whew! I'd never been to Amsterdam, but now I was going to be there six times—and I would never see anything except the inside of the airport terminal. Yes, I wanted to go to Europe, but not to accompany him on his insane acquisition expedition.

"I don't know where to begin, Nikki," I said. "That's a lot to take in..."

Cutting me off midsentence, Nikki relaunched, setting his newly reenhanced lips back into motion."Well, as you know, Chiquita's been such a dear friend, helping me with all of my ordeals, the surgery, recovery and all, and I want to repay him. This is a small way I can do that. And Den, you've been a dear friend, too; you have never been to Europe, and you really should see those aged crumbling churches and museums before they completely collapse. You know, it might even help you with that little paint-by-numbers business of yours. You simply *have* to go, and I won't accept no for an answer.

"Now, I'm going to pay for Chiquita's airfare and the coupe-de-villa on Mykonos for the three of us. So Murf, you'll just have to pay for your airfare, meals, and the cheap little four-star places we're staying while in Venice and Istanbul, and the Villa in Grease is my little gift to the two of you, because I love you both. Doesn't that just sound fabulous?"

Chiquita and I stared at each other, dumbfounded. "Well, hon, that sounds a little extravagant for me. I'm just a scrub woman, ya know."

"Well, yes, *I know* that, but I *want* you to go. I *want* you to do this, and I'll help you both if you need it. But I really *insist* that we all should go. Murf, what do you think?"

"Beware of Greeks bearing presents. I've wanted to go to Europe, but to other destinations. This trip sounds amazing, but dizzying."

"Nikki, I just gotta ask ya, hon, did ya really think you was dyin' when you had that whole face-fallin'-off thing?" Chiquita asked, in all seriousness.

"Shush now, and behave yourself. Now, I'm not taking no for an answer. I've already checked on flights and reservations, and everything is ready to be booked. We will leave the second week of September and be back by mid-October. You'll have plenty of time to get your passport, syphilis shots, and you will probably want to pick out a few new things to wear, Murf, 'cause I'm gettin' kinda tired of lookin' at that Salvation Army shit you usually have on. Now, you two think it over. This will be the trip of a lifetime, and I want both of you to be there with me. This could possibly be my last trip," he said, and then he started to tear up. And as I told you earlier, I can't stand to see an elderly woman cry.

Later that same day...

"Where the hell did that come from, Stella? The Queen Mother was turnin' on the waterworks and ever-thin'," Chiquita said, while pouring vodka gimlets into well-chilled glasses, just pulled from his freezer. "'This may be my last trip.' Jesus, Stella, give us a break, such theatricals. She's pullin' out all the stops, ain't she?"

"So what do you think, Clara?" I asked.

"Ya know the old sayin', if somethin' sounds too good ta be true, you're probably screwed? Well, I think that may be the case here. Ya know, she's exhausted or outlived his travelin' companions, an' you an' me are the only ones left. Aunt Ronnie can't go anymore 'cause he's dead, and all he ever had to do was do everything Nikki wanted, whenever he wanted to, and Nikki paid for everythin'."

"You're preachin' to the choir, Brother Chiquita. I've traveled with him before, ya know."

"Say...did you ever see that Agatha Christie movie, I think it was *Death on the Nile*? Well... Bette Davis was this bitter old lesbian spinster, and she was travelin' with a snivelin' old downtrodden companion, I think it was Maggie Smith. Well, she was just hoary-bull to her, and always treatin' her just terry-bull. Somehow I imagine this trip to Greece to be somethin' like that. We're meant to be nothin' more than his royal toters and floggers."

━ ～

A month later Rob was dropping us off at the airport, and I'm certain he was more than happy to be rid of us. For three weeks' vacation Nikki took four bulging and matching Louis Vuitton steamer trunks. Chiquita took two boxy brown and tan vintage Samsonite leather suitcases, and I had one black nylon duffel bag stuffed with Salvation Army clothing.

Traveling was much easier in this pre-9/11 world, but nonetheless we had a grueling schedule to keep. During the first twenty-four hours, we rode three different planes, had six hoary-bull meals, saw three terry-bull movies, and listened to several bawling babies.

With the Greek gods blessing us, we arrived in Mykonos as the swollen setting sun was sinking into the azure Aegean. And a Maxfield Parish evening sky was blending indigo into velvety blackness and slowly becoming studded with a thousand twinkling stars when we touched down.

The tiny airport was a wide-open pavilion without any windows or doors, hot, reeking of aircraft fuel fumes, and making me nauseous. We surely looked like refugees from a war-torn third-world country as we collected our bags, completely exhausted from twenty-four hours of hauling ass.

"I don't know what this Mark guy looks like. I've only spoken with him on the phone a couple times while making the arrangements, but he sounds kinda cute. I sure as hell hope he gets here soon, because I'm starving, tired, and goddamn sick of traveling."

"Do you have all your bags, Missy?"

"Why yes, Chiquita, and thank you for helping me."

"Oh yes, Missy, I's happy to hep. Happy ta hep."

Suddenly someone was tapping me on the shoulder. "Mr. Clock?" Turning around, I spied a suntanned Greek god with the bluest eyes I have ever seen, like a bottle of window washing cleaner. His chest full of muscles was attempting to break out of a low-cut, peach-colored wife-beater tank top, and everything on his person was bulging—arms, legs, chest, crotch—and he looked like a gay Arnold Schwarzenegger, only good-looking—handsome, in fact.

"I am Mr. Clock," Nikki shouted, suddenly feeling reenergized, hurdling over a pile of steamer trunks, shoving me aside, nearly trampling me, and pushing his fat ass up to the front. "You must be Mark?" Nikki gushed, all atwitter.

"My God, Mr. Clock, what a big piece of blonde hair you have," Mark said, speaking directly to the hairpiece. No one *we* knew dared say anything about the big "you-know-what." But Nikki giggled like an infatuated schoolgirl when Mark spoke to his hair. Introductions were made as our luggage was crammed into the tiny Jeep, and we were off like a dress on prom night.

"You know, ever since I ran that advertisement in the *Advocate*, I've been really busy with you American gays. After you guys leave, there's another group of gay guys coming in from Galveston."

Chiquita turned to me and whispered loudly—out the wrong side of his mouth—"*Advocate*? He told us it was *Architectural Digest*. Harumph."

"One of those queer fagazines that start with an *A*," I whispered in reply.

"So, tell me, Mark, do you live here all year *long*?" Nikki innocently inquired, as he tilted his head provocatively to the side and twirled his store-bought hair with his index finger and thumb.

"No, I am only in Greece for the summer season. I'm from Switzerland, where my family owns the Madre Horny ski lodge. I reside there in the winter. I am head manager."

"I bet you're good at it. And you must speak German."

"Ya. *Sprechen sie Deutsch?*"

"Oh, heavens no. I can't talk Dutch. I can barely manage English."

"I speak English, French, Italian, and German, because I live where the Alps come together and these people are my neighbors."

"Well, your English is very good. You almost sound American. Do you speak Greek, too?"

"Yes, I do, and some Polish, too, because a lot of workmen here are from Poland and Albania."

After leaving the well-lit airport, it suddenly grew so thoroughly dark that the only lights left in the world were the headlights of the jeep and a multitude of twinkling stars. The nicely paved road near the airport quickly gave way to bumpy, rocky, rutted, twisting two-track goat paths. Shoved way in the back, with the Louis Quartet, I was mercilessly tossed about and nearly gassed to death by the exhaust fumes pouring in through the windowless tailgate.

"There she is," Mark said, as he screeched on the brakes and stopped at the top of a rocky ridge, just before it plunged five hundred feet into the churning ocean. Our Villa, Malacka, stood silhouetted against a low-hanging full moon, which was just now beginning to rise out of the Aegean. Beyond the villa, two distant islands floated on the shimmering moonlit sea, making this dreamlike black velvet panorama more breathtakingly beautiful than any photograph could ever express.

But the Aegean in moonlight was nothing when compared with Mark's incredible home. Precariously perched on a rocky ridge, at the very edge of the world, this villa's three floors of organic architecture were literally carved from the jagged rock ledges. From the road all you saw was a pebbled rooftop with three parking spaces and solar water heater, but gazing beyond you saw the curving stone steps that descended to an expansive outdoor terrace.

The spacious terrace offered breathtaking views of the glittering moonlit panorama. Our villa's main floor had four sets of rustic French doors opening onto the veranda, which made the living room levitate, like an open-air pavilion floating above the ocean, with an infinity edge. All the interior walls were curving, rounded, and freshly whitewashed. Serpentine sofas with white canvas cushions hugged those meandering walls, and canary-yellow pillows were tossed about to add a perk of primary color.

A compact kitchen was nicely nestled at the back, with just the basics. All the appliances were tucked under the counter, with open shelving above. The islands countertop was crated from a single stone slab that was softened by centuries of relentlessly pounding surf. Well-rounded rocks that were harvested from the seashore, were stacked and cemented together and used to support the massive stone-slab, and a bank of rustic yellow pine drawers supported the other end.

Warm ocean breezes blew continuously through our open-air pavilion, making its white linen window panel's flicker and dance about. So we flitted about as well and explored our expansive villa. First we find graciously spiraling stone steps that descended to a lower level. Downstairs we found two roomy bedrooms with rustic French doors opening to private logia's that offered breathtaking ocean views. And antiquated clay pots spilling over with scarlet geraniums added a perk of color to them.

All the floors were rock, all the rustic furniture made from warm yellow pine, and there was not a hard edge or straight thing to be found; everything rounded, natural, and timeless. Colorful hand-woven cotton rugs enlivened the bedroom and kept delicate feet from the cool stone floors.

"I get this room," Nikki delighted. "It's the prettiest, and it has a yellow bedspread, oh goodie, goodie." Of course it was also the larger of the rooms. Immediately throwing the French doors open, he stepped onto his private terrace, spread his wide arms as if he was Evita, and started throwing kisses to the ocean. "My people, I have arrived. Thank you for coming to greet me, muah! I love you. Just throw money," he said to an adoring audience of hovering seagulls.

"Murf, do you want the other bedroom? 'Cause I'll take the upstairs couch," Chiquita offered.

"Nope! I'll take the upstairs and you can stay down here with *her*, thank you very much."

Across from the spacious bedrooms we found a set of hand-hewn yellow pine saloon-style doors that opened to reveal a grotto/bathroom with rocky ceilings, floors, and walls. At the back we found a shower with a handheld wand, delivering water warmed by the rooftop solar heater. A notice posted in neon pink read: "For our convenience, showers should be taken in the afternoon when the sun had time to warm the precious water."

This grotto bounced noises and amplified them greatly, which was not a good thing, especially if you were having a blowout, which Greek food could often do to you. The odd tin-can commode was nothing more than a stainless steel pot, such as something you'd find on a submarine, and next to the tin toilet was a lengthy listing of instructions, of which we were continually reminded by our host:

"Water is an expensive commodity here on beautiful Mykonos, so please follow the house rules concerning water usage.

*For Number One: Do not flush if you are only urinating. If it's yellow, let it mellow. Please help us conserve water, because it is a rare and *expensive* resource here on beautiful Mykonos.

*For Number Two: If you are full of shit you may use our precious water to flush. If it's brown, flush it down. Our water is not *that* precious.

*_This is also very important._ After wiping please discard the used *tissues into the stainless steel canister* next to the toilet. *Do not put any paper products into the toilet.

*For Number Three: If you are using feminine-care products, please place them into the canister."

"What the hell?" Nikki squealed. "I've never heard of such a thing! Jesus H. Christ, for what I'm paying for us to stay here, someone should be wiping my ass for me, and *they* can throw the damn dirtied tissue in the toilet and flush it for me. I don't know about you two bitches, but I'm going to take me a long hot shower to get the filth of traveling off me, and going to bed. I'm exhausted. Night, girls."

"Night, Queen Mother," I said.

"Night, Mommy Dearest," Chiquita added.

Twenty minutes later Nikki popped out of the shower, while still steaming. "Let's get all dolled up and go to town for breakfast in the morning. Whaddya say, girls?"

"Good night, Mommy Dearest."

— ∼ —

Awakening to the sounds of squawking shorebirds, I turned to see them floating past the wide opened terrace doors. From the divan I gazed beyond, to the sparkling Aegean, and for the first time viewed the panorama in daylight. Two distant islands, Santorini and Paros, appeared to levitate right in front of our villa. It was barely daylight and already warm, all the doors were open, and there was not a mosquito in sight. This surely had to be paradise.

Remembering that dear Chiquita had thoughtfully brought coffee, bless his heart, I found my way to the cozy kitchen, located the Mr. Kafes machine, and began brewing a pot. Warm ocean breezes swept the stimulating scent through the villa, down the spiraling stairs, and into the bedrooms of the sleeping booties. Upon smelling the coffee percolating, they ceased their synchronized snoring, dragged their tired old asses out of bed, and joined me on the terrace.

Nikki was the first to shuffle up. "I smell coffee, honey."

"Mornin', sunshine. Yes, the coffee's all ready, grab a cup."

I swear to God, he was *still* wearing that same old nasty, thigh-high, snagged-up, once-white terry cloth cotton robe; he needed to throw that damn thing away. Yawning and stretching, he smiled broadly while scratching his head and making his messed-up wig wriggle in every direction.

"*Oh my God*, would you look at that fabulous fucking view," Nikki said, clutching his arms to his chest and getting misty-eyed. "That's simply breathtaking! Can you bitches believe we are here?"

"That's right, Dorothy; we're not in Kansas anymore," Chiquita said, coming up the stairs right behind him, and laughing along with us.

There we were, three ghetto boys from Flint sitting on the Greek Riviera, having coffee, and taking it all in.

Magnificent.

Native Sons

℘recariously perched high upon a precipice of jagged rusty rock was our bella villa, Malacca. Breathtakingly panoramic views of rocky ledges, cloudless blue sky, and the deep Lapis Lazuli Aegean were interrupted only by two picturesque islands, placed on the horizon just to break up the boredom. Paradise, the island's gay/ nude beach, was a short distance away, within easy binocular-viewing distance, but not easily walkable. The other landmark on this side of the island was the stinking dump, which burned odoriferous trash continuously, and was located just upwind of our expensive villa.

Exploring our villa's expansive terrace, we discovered an enormous beehive grill neatly tucked into the far corner. Constructed of smoothed stones, the enormous cooker was large enough to roast an entire goat. At the patio's other end we found an ancient wooden dory that was slightly tilted onto its side, worked into the jagged rock wall, and cleverly converted into a comfy couch. The cushions were covered with white cotton canvas, and a few canary-colored cotton cushions were casually thrown about for a bit of perk...gay, gay, gay, gay, gay.

Eye-poppingly red geraniums were planted in ancient urns and strategically placed about the expansive terrace, adding color and life. Crusty old craters containing other heat-tolerant plants such as cacti, jade trees, and similar succulents softened the patio's corners. Overhead, to shield us pasty white boys from the punishing Greek sun was a rustic wooden pergola just dripping with the brightest fuchsia-pink bougainvillea you've ever seen; garish as hell, shockingly pink.

"I just *lllllllove* this pinky viny plant, Murphy," Nikki said, pointing heavenward in classical Greek form. "That color is absolutely fabulous. What is the name of that?"

"It's called bougainvillea."

"Oh dear God, would ya look down there," Chiquita whispered extremely loudly, suddenly becoming bug-eyed, while pointing to the terrace below. "It's Mark, and he's *completely* neck-ed."

"*Would ya look at that!* Sweet Jesus, just take me now!" Nikki swooned.

Our landlord was out watering the plants, and naked as the day he was born. Whoever said all men were created equal had not seen Mark naked. He was outstanding, "gifted," as we'd say in the business. Bronzed everywhere, his incredible muscled body had not one tan line, and I happened to know this because three people scanned it thoroughly. We were mesmerized watching him drag his hefty hose around while sprinkling the greenery, and marveling at his magnificent member.

"It was definitely the *Advocate*," Chiquita finally said, breaking the spell.

Mark looked up when he heard us drooling, and remarked, "Hello there, and good morning. I was wondering if you three were ever going to get up. Beautiful day isn't it?"

"Beautiful. Oh yeah, definitely beautiful." On that point we all agreed.

"Be-you-tea-full. Be-you-tea-full," Nikki agreed wholeheartedly.

"I'll be heading to town soon. Would you guys like to come along? You can pick up provisions and get scooters, if you'd like."

"Absolutely, we'll be ready in a minute," replied Nikki, acting as our self-appointed spokesman. But we knew better—it wouldn't be all that soon. Two hours later we arrived in Chara, where everyone knew Mark and greeted him warmly: "*Cristos*, Marcos."

This picturesque village was practically a movie set cliche, complete with a row of slowly churning fieldstone windmills, dressed with white canvas sails. A sleepy natural harbor was cluttered with brightly colored boats, some beached on the gravelly bank, and others bobbing in the indigo bay. Steep rocky hillsides were layered with whitewashed buildings, stacked upon each other, and capped with red tile roofs that popped against deep blue cloudless skies. Upscale boutique shops lined the winding cobblestone streets, offering luxury items to international tourists.

"Here is the currency exchange where you can purchase your drachmas, and there is the travel agency where you can arrange for your trip to Turkey. Why don't you exchange your money, and then I'll show you where you can rent scooters. You'll probably need to buy provisions and get liquored."

The scooter merchant was a friend of Mark's, and we could easily see why, because he was another Greek god, only younger, prettier, and more living proof that all men were not created equal. His bronze chiseled chest was muscled—but not too big—and he was buff as could be. We gladly surrendered handfuls of Greek Monopoly money for the privilege of riding his rods. Given a quick driving lesson, in Greek-speak and sign language, we were off to the races.

"Boosty," he said in parting, laughing as the Greeks so easily do.

"Boosty," we responded. Parting is such *a sweet...ass*, oh my God what an incredible ass, two perfectly round casaba melons bouncing inside an onion-skin bag; woof, woof, *woof*!

The tiny village's irregularly winding cobblestone streets were not nearly wide enough for a vehicle. Occasionally they were interrupted by another scooter, or an apple-faced doll of a grandma who was dressed in head-to-toe black, wearing a babushka, and hauling a dusty old donkey weighed down with brown burlap bags bulging with produce and woven hampers heaping with colorful cut flowers.

"Boosty," the old ya-yas said to us as we went scooting past and laughed.

"Boosty," we replied, smiling warmly. "Beautiful day, ain't it, Toots?"

The pace was slow and leisurely here, and the local such friendly, attractive people, always smiling and laughing whenever they saw us. Floating on the morning breeze were the ever-present smells of the briny sea, scooter exhaust, and the intoxicating aroma of fresh baking bread. So, like any good American would, we plundered the grocery store, meat market, produce vendor, and liquor store, purchasing way too much booty to transport home on three toy scooters.

Before making it back to the villa, I managed to crash my scooter into a parked Jeep, screwing up my elbow and thigh. Chiquita stubbed his toe, which was exposed by fashionable open-toed sandals, and Nikki's flawless flesh was savagely scratched when an inconsiderate person's scooter fell over on him. Somehow we managed to make it back, with the groceries and booze intact.

"It says here, in this here pamphlet, that the number one killer a tourists on the Greek Islands is scooter accidents," Chiquita announced, while reading the rental agreement once we were safely on the patio having cocktails.

Nikki, paying him no mind, walked to the terrace's edge, extended a fleshy arm, pointed, and made his royal proclamation: "That's the gay beach right over there. Best beach on the island. Why don't we have us a little light lunch, and then visit the meat market? Whaddya say, girls?"

"If we're gonna get back on them there death-wish machines again and drive down that darned mountain, I'm gonna need me another dose-a my vitamin water," Chiquita said, howling.

*An observation: There was a severe scarcity of trees on this island; shade was scarce as ice. Each minute it grew hotter, and ultimately reached well into the nineties by afternoon. But it was a dry heat. Still, it was the most ferocious sun I'd ever experienced, intense sun, as if *you* were the ant under the magnifying glass getting fried.

Slowly inching down the mountain, we made our way toward Super Paradise Beach, squealing the brakes all the way. Pathetically, we were being passed by ancient jack-o-lantern-toothed nanas, who were walking. "Boosty, boosty!" said the leathery old ladies, with wiry hairs growing from their warty chins, and laughing wickedly.

"Nice ass," we replied, smiling and waving like old friends. "Boosty."

Super Paradise beach was secluded, sheltered, and nicely nestled into a natural niche surrounded on three sides by high sloping rock walls. The shoreline was covered with rounded pebbly pieces of brownish rocky gravel, and not sand, making it difficult to walk in my new red Kmart flip-flops. This establishment was a commercial beach, and it was pay as you go. You could place a towel onto the gravelly rocks for free, or rent a lounging chair for not too much bucks. But if you were a rich American, like us, you rented a palm-frond-shaded cabana. You also could pee in the bay for free, or use the pay restrooms at the bar/grill/disco.

And everywhere there was skin, lots and lots of skin. There was a nude section, a clothing-optional section, and a please-cover-that-shit-up section. Renting lounge chairs, we located ourselves between the "cover it up" and the "let me see a little more of that" section, but within viewing distance of the "would you look at that" section. After all, it was a nude beach; we were old, not stupid. It was Europe and they didn't care who looked. Like I say, "If you don't want the business, don't advertise."

But even here, in laissez-faire Europe, Nikki's fetching beach ensemble was causing quite a stir as we trudged through the pebbles toward the shore. He was smartly outfitted in a pair of yellow Yves Saint Laurent crepe swimming trunks—with room enough for two—and a coordinating short-sleeved terry cloth-lined over jacket in the exact same shade of tart lemonade. Haughtily sauntering along with nose held high, his matching sling-back sandals were smacking like crazy and wildly flinging chunks of gravel at the unsuspecting beachgoers, right and left.

He was seductively shaded beneath a coordinated wide-brimmed yellow straw hat, and acting most aloof whie hiding behind Gucci movie-star sunglasses the size of a windshield. This outfit was pulled together oh so smartly by a retro-inspired plastic beach tote decorated with yellow-and-white daisies and it was gay, gay, gay, and gay as can be. But with his big blond wig, floppy straw hat, outrageous outfit, and perky bouncing boobies he was confusing children. They pointed at him and asked inappropriate questions.

"What is that, Mommy?"

"Shh," their mothers said, not knowing how to answer.

Sweltering for early October, the day topped out at well over ninety degrees, but it was easily tempered by several cooling dunks in the salty sparkling sea. Yellow water taxis chugged into the cove on the half hour, breaking the serenity, spewing noxious diesel fumes, and discharging more obnoxious people onto our private paid-for beach. A striking man in his early forties, wearing nothing but a worn-out straw hat and flimsy cotton wraparound tablecloth, was trolling the beach peddling body scarves. While watching him selling his woven wares to beachgoers, we prayed for a stiff breeze to shift his kerchief ever so slightly, because he made a most fetching model. Everyone seemed to have one.

"Lemme look at what you got there!" Nikki shouted, commanding him to appear from halfway across the beach, and oddly the sun-roasted man obliged him. It was obvious this beachfront merchant spent his days in the hot sun, because his sun-bleached dread-locked hair and matching dreadful beard made him look like a shipwrecked Robinson Crusoe. But that tissue-thin wraparound tablecloth made his taut, trim, and tanned torso look absolutely tantalizing. He made the sarong look so right.

His splash scarf was gaily tied at the right hip, which left his entire left flank exposed. Bare bronzed buttocks were barely draped with the sheer clinging cloth, and the see-through tissue revealed the salesman's more-than-ample "personality," wink, wink. We all purchased one of his "play-hos."

"Say, wouldn't these Play-hos make wonderful window treatments for my bedroom? And they are so cheap," Chiquita said. He loved cheap, so he bought six of them for the equivalent of three dollars apiece, American...such a steal.

"Boosty," the sarong man said in parting.

"Sarong," we replied in unison, waving like long-lost friends.

Back at the villa later, we had a vogue fashion show featuring our recently acquired play-hos. Chiquita, who was tall and slim, built like Kevin Bacon, was the only one who did not look completely ridiculous wearing one, I was too short and my wrap dragged the ground. Nikki was too well rounded, and the scarf wouldn't conceal enough girlish girth.

"You might as well take mine, too, you skinny-assed bitch. Hang it in your window for all I care," Nikki said, throwing the splashy teal-and-purple tablecloth at him.

"You might as well have mine, too," I said, tossing him mine as well.

That evening we got dolled up with our best going-to-town clothes, to dine at Little Eva's, a quaint outdoor grill and tourist trap with a treed canopy covered in tiny white twinkling lights, rustic tables dressed with white linens, and the most attractive waiters on the island. Fire-roasted lamb shank was served with fingerling redskin potatoes, grilled aborigines, and freshly baked crusty bread.

After our leisurely dinner we strolled through the village's narrow winding streets and window shopped, winding our way down to the picture-perfect harbor to watch the sun set. As darkness drew near it dawned on us that we'd have to drive the scooters back to the villa in darkness. Dim headlights barely cast any light upon the rutted goat paths as we slowly groped our way home, and it was darker than I'd ever seen it in my life, black-hole dark. Finally making it back, I stopped at the mountain's top and said a prayer, unhinged the metal gate, and descended the severely sloping drive with the scooter.

Once safely inside the villa, we laughed at our stupidity, and Chiquita and I soothed our ragged nerves with Jim Beam, generously poured over precious ice. Lounging on our veranda, we all marveled at the sparkling moonlit panorama stretching out before us, put our feet up, and made ourselves quite comfortable. Staying up until way after two in the morning, we shared stories of gays gone by, bared our souls; remembered friends now passed, and enjoyed being there, with each other.

"Would ya look at that fabulous fucking view, we certainly ain't got nothin' like *that* back in Flint, Missies. Can you bitches believe we've crawled out of that gutbucket town and ended up here, on the Greek Riviera?" Nikki said, while clutching his ample chest and getting misty-eyed.

"Thank you for making this happen, Nikki. It really is amazing," I said.

"You're welcome, honey. I'm glad we're all here together. And that goes for you, too, Chiquita, you're really a dear soul," he said, reaching out to clutch his hand.

"You're smashed, Stella," Chiquita snapped back, snatching his hand away.

"I am not; haven't touched a drop. But I'm still really glad we're all here."

"I still say you're smashed," he said again, and grinned even more.

"You're awfully quiet tonight, Murf. Are you all right, honey?" Nikki inquired.

"I'm fine. I was just thinking...about Mike. We started seeing each other before I left and I'm missing him tonight."

"Oh, you poor thing. Well, you just come over here and sit down with your evil old stepsister, and tell me all about it," Nikki said, throwing his ample arms open to offer a bear hug.

As I sat alongside him on the dory sofa, he pulled me closer, gave me a big old hug and sloppy wet smack on the cheek. "Is this the guy you were in love with a long time ago, honey? Is he the one?"

"Yes, he's the one."

"Well, honey, I'm happy for you. I hope it works out."

"I do, too."

"Rob is moving out," Chiquita blurted, seemingly out of nowhere.

"What?" Nikki and I shrieked at the same time. Then we linked pinkies.

"Yeah, he's already bought a house and says he's goin' to have the suburban dream, with three bedrooms and a two-car garage, a golden retriever, and apparently without me."

"When did this all happen? Why haven't we heard anything about this?" Nikki demanded.

"Just last week. Said he didn't want to live in that nasty ghettoized neighborhood no more. He's already bought himself a house in Flushin', and movin' before I get back. He said I could go with him if I wanted, but he wasn't very convincin'."

"Honey, I'm so sorry," Nikki offered. "You just come over here and sit with me too, honey.""Me, too," I offered. "I'm so sorry, Chiquita."

Chiquita sashayed over with his ice cubes tinkling, sat on the other side of the Queen Mother, and we all had a moment.

Greek Tragedy

By the third day of our fabulous Grecian getaway, we were practically natives, easily navigating through the village's narrow streets and having our favorite restaurants, waiters, and boutiques. Luring us seductively for days now was the incredibly appealing scent of bread baking; it lingered in the still morning air, we smelled it everywhere, and could no longer resist the enticing aroma.

Finding the fragrance too overwhelming to resist, we sniffed through the tiny village like bloodhounds searching for the source of those intoxicatingly yeasty airs. Finally we found them drifting from a wide-open weathered wooden door, with a set of well-worn steps that led to a rustic rathskeller. With our bellies overriding our brains, we crossed under the aged carved lintel stone and descended the spiraling stone steps into the hellishly hot underground chamber.

We were immediately slapped in the face by a blast of white-hot heat emanating from the big beehive oven blazing at the back of the bakery. The hellishly hot fire was being tended by a handsome, hunky, and shirtless Muslim man, who was glistening wet with sweat and hot as hell. We took great delight in watching him shoving his hard wood into the red-hot-hot slot, and poked and stoked the flames, making it hotter than it already was with each thrust.

"Sweet Jesus, would you look at that dough boy," Nikki sputtered, while ogling the Muslim masterpiece. The buff bakery boy stopped his stoking and put on a shirt, shit, and strolled over to sell us some of his hot stuff. Purchasing two loaves of his long, hard, crusty bread and several sweet and sticky pastries, we were unable to wait and devoured them right then and there.

"Have you ever tasted such a delicious blueberry croissant in your life? And that fucking bakery boy, two words, oh-my Gawd almighty! We shall visit here every day, I decree it! So it shall be!"

If that meant we'd have to overlook the collections of cockroach carcasses under the flour sacks, then so be it. Seeing the baker alone was worth the dough.

"Boosty," he said, laughing each time we left his bakery.

"Boosty," we said in reply. The natives were so very friendly.

Our leisurely morning of squandering time slowly slipped into afternoon, so naturally a light luncheon was in order. We chose to nosh at a quaint seaside café called The Sea Hagg, with what we unanimously decided was *the* most handsome waiter on the island. His name was Phallus, or something like that in Greek-speak. It was a pleasure to be serviced by him. Seeing us coming, he smiled broadly and said, "Hello American friends, please join me for lunch. I have lots of ice, and lots of butter," he said, looking directly at Nikki, winking, and taunting him.

"Come to mention it, I *was* beginning to feel a bit peckish. So, Denny, what are you ordering, and you, Chiquita? Well...maybe I could have just a *little* something," Nikki innocently said.

First the darling dimpled waiter brought us chilled green glass bottles of Coca-Cola, and glasses full of ice. To seduce us even further he presented us with a piping-hot plate wrapped in a white linen cloth, concealing freshly baked buns, and a chilled china bowl heaping with big butter balls.

"I have lots of butter for you, *Nikki*. You like the butter, yes, Paisan?" he said, smiling at Nikki, winking, and making him blush.

Delicately holding one of Phallus's hot hard buns, Nikki daintily pointed a pinkie, ripped it apart, gingerly smeared it with a huge hunk of butter, and quickly shoved it into his mouth to demonstrate his approval. "Mmmmmmm. That was just dee-lish-us, Phallus, thank you," Nikki said, smiling at the waiter with a most satisfied grin, and talking with a mouthful of well-breaded butter.

"Ya know, ever since I was a little girl I just loved the taste of butter, num, num-num."

"*We all know*, Stella. Now the *whole world* knows."

"Sounds like somebody is cranky and needs a nap, Missy. Okay, now, let's get down to business. I will have the long-weenie with greasy grilled Greek sausage, and maybe a little cucumber salad. Should we order some deep-fried calamari for the table?"

"I swear we have the hungriest table on the island. It's always orderin' somethin'. Chiquita said.

"And you, Murf? What are you having?" Nikki said, ignoring his smart mouthed comment.

"When in Greece...grilled seafood."

After our seven-course snack, we shopped for more unneeded provisions, and headed back to the villa for another afternoon at the gay /nude beach. That day the seashore was scorching, hotter than hell, so I rented a palm-fronded cabana to hide from the punishing sun. Meanwhile, Nikki and Chiquita, lying next to me on "choice lozenges" {as Chiquita would say} had slathered themselves with roasting oils and commenced to cook. From inside my solar shroud I heard them sizzling and popping, and saw smoke streams rising from their roasting carcasses.

With three play-hos completely covering me from head to toe, I was trying to hide from the merciless Mediterranean sun. My balding head was wrapped in a big beach towel with only my nose exposed—and that was uselessly slathered with a thick white coating of zinc-oxide paste in an attempt to keep it from molting even further.

The ferry chugged into the cove, dropping off another load of obnoxious and obviously American tourists; probably day-trippers from a gay cruise line, such as the *Everybody's a Princess Line*. Drunken, loud, and lecherous, they were creating a spectacle running butt-naked on the beach, laughing, shouting, and throwing each other into the drink.

We were just appalled by their outlandish hedonistic behavior, and could not take our eyes off them while expressing our disgust. "Thank God we're Canadians," I finally affirmed.

"Those Americans are so vulgar and crude, aren't they?" Nikki replied, in complete agreement.

"I second that emotion, and God bless the queen," Chiquita said, standing and bowing toward Nikki. "Bless you, Your Majesty, bless you, my Queen."

"Dismissed," Nikki said, waving him away like an annoying gnat.

Our afternoon of roasting and ogling mankind came to an oily end, so we dragged our well baked asses back up the mountain and parked the scooters on the rooftop. Covered with salt and sweat, we wanted to have our showers and remove the crusty coatings from our crispy carcasses while the solar-heated water was still good and warm.

Nikki, taking the lead, started descending the steep stone steps first. Somewhere around the third step he had a sling-back mishap, which was quickly followed by a complete blowout. Stumbling, he tried to recover his balance, but was impeded by his bag of beachy paraphernalia and meat-roasting lotions. As if moving in slow motion, he tumbled forward, dropped his excess baggage, and stretched out his delicate arms in an attempt to stop his impending fall from grace. Gravity sucked and ultimately won as he slid down the rest of the steps on his front side, and finished in a heap at the bottom. It happened in a millisecond.

Motionless, he just laid there. Chiquita and I flew down the steps.

"Oooooh," Nikki moaned.

"Are you all right, Stella? Oh, dear God. Can you move?"

Snapping back to reality, Nikki sputtered, "Yes, I can move, Jesus. I just scraped my knees. Help me up, damn it. Ugh, ugh, *owwwwww*." He winced when he moved.

We helped him up, he unsteadily hobbled into the villa, and we laid him on the divan. After, surveying the damage it was obvious he'd done more than scrape his knees. Both reddening hands had abrasions and were embedded with grit and gravel, his elbows and knees beginning to bleed.

"Nikki, it looks like we'll need to take you to the clinic."

"No, I'm fine; just let me lie here a minute."

There was no way we could get him to the clinic, even if we wanted to. We couldn't take him on those stupid scooters; we'd have to call an ambulance, or find Mark and use his Jeep. Searching but not finding him home, I tacked a note on his door explaining our predicament, and returned to the villa. A bug-eyed Chiquita met me at the door with a stiff cocktail, bless his heart.

Nikki piped up. "*Owwww*...my wrist is hurting kinda bad. Do you think you two tipsy bitches could spare some of your cocktail ice for my wrist?"

The darling little European undercounter fridge didn't make very much ice in its two tiny trays, so we sacrificed the precious ice from our cocktails. Filling a yellow linen dishcloth with ice, we made a makeshift ice bag and carefully wrapped it around his wrist, put purple rubber bands around it to hold it in place, and slid his arm inside a ziplock baggie to collect the drips from the already melting ice.

When searching the bathroom for bandages, I couldn't find a single one. But someone did leave feminine pads. What the hell, they were the closest thing I could find to a bandage, and sterile. So we wrapped the mini-pads around his scraped elbows and the maxi-pads around his bloody knees, and then secured them in place with purple rubber bands borrowed from the broccoli bunches. He didn't look so good. I was especially worried about his right wrist, which was obviously swelling.

Mark returned shortly after, took one look at pathetic Nikki, and immediately drove us to the clinic. Still wearing his lemon beach ensemble, he hobbled into the exam room like Grandpa McCoy, with his hair looking like tossed salad, and sanitary pads stuck to his booboos with purple rubber bands.

The Spartan clinic was clean and efficient, and within ten minutes they had the results of the X-rays. Prognosis: the right radius was badly broken. The bones would have to be set and his right arm placed in a cast, which should be on for six weeks or better. The left wrist—although not broken—was severely sprained, and the limp limb was placed in a sling for the next few weeks.

A few crocodile tears were shed, mostly by Chiquita and me, while watching his cast being applied in the lovely clinic overlooking the village, harbor, and now-setting sun. Chiquita finally piped up, breaking the silence.

"That pam-flitt also said that the second-leadin' cause a death ta tourists on the Greek Islands was flip-flop failure. Go figure."

"I'm afraid to ask what the third thing is."

"Please don't, because it involves goats."

With head held high, Nikki limped out of the triage unit, with real bandages on both of his knees and white cotton slings on his damaged wings. His arms were neatly crisscrossed over his chest, making him look very Egyptian and regal. Two appointments were made to make sure the arms were healing properly, and the entire bill came to only $250, American. Two prescriptions were written, one for an antibiotic to ward off infection, and the other for Xanax to ease the pain and help him sleep.

We had Nikki wait in the air-conditioned clinic while Mark, Chiquita, and I crossed the street to have his prescriptions filled. Quite unbelievably, they cost only three dollars each.

"Lemme see that, Stella. How many refills has she got for that Xanadu stuff, anyway?" Chiquita asked, snatching the script right out of my hand. "Three dollars for thirty Xanax, with two refills, and the whole bill comes ta two hundred and sixty-five dollars? That cinches it; I'm movin' here. Please forward my mail. Boosty!" Chiquita said, while laughing his skinny ass off.

"What did you say, Jim?" Mark asked.

"I'm movin' here," Chiquita repeated, laughing at his joke just as much, if not more.

"No, the last thing you said."

"Boosty? *H-e-l-l-o*, Mark! That means hello in Greek-speak. You should know that. Ever-body here greets us like that. It's a traditional Greek greetin'."

"No it isn't. It means prick-fag-queer," Mark said, busting out laughing.

"Oh, Jesus Christ, ever-body's sayin' that to us. So we've been sayin' it right back, and smilin' like idiots. Hey. Say, let's not tell her what that means, okay?"

"Chiquita!" I said.

"Well, I'm just sayin'..." Chiquita said, suddenly acting all innocent.

"Why are you guys always calling him her, anyway?" Mark asked, seemingly confused.

"Well, just look at 'er over there in that yella getup a hers," Chiquita quipped.

Mark glanced over to the clinic where Nikki was mysteriously shaded behind windshield-sized sunglasses, in his two-piece yellow beach ensemble, with a yellow straw hat with a hole cut out for his wiglet, coordinating sling-backs, and daisy tote clutched tightly to his side.

"Yeah, I see what you mean."

When we finally returned to the villa it was dark, we hadn't eaten, and we were exhausted. The smell of a pine scented cleaner immediately hit us when opening the door, telling us the villa had been recently cleaned, and the floor was still glistening to prove it. A stack of freshly laundered white towels lay neatly folded on the table, and the washing machine was sloshing away with another load.

"Goldilocks has been here, me thinks," Chiquita said.

"And I believe she still is," I replied. "Noises are coming from downstairs."

"G'day," came echoing from below.

Bounding up the steps, two at a time, came a handsome suntanned Aussie lassie dressed in khaki shorts and a stretched-out white wife-beater top. Wiry blonde hairs poked from underneath the pits of her unshaven muscular arms, and hairy athletic legs were tucked inside buckskin midcalf hiking boots. She was either an Olympic rock climber or a lesbian.

"Name's Deb. An' sorry I 'aven't finished cleanin' yet. Got ohm from the beach too late da-day, I did. But I'll be outta ear in two shakes, I will, so pay me no mind. Dearie me, watt 'appened to you, love?" she asked, looking at Nikki with both wings in slings.

Introductions were made, and the broken arms explained. Nikki was then medicated and hand-fed crusty bread, salty cheese, and fruit with thick Greek yogurt. Deb joined us for a glass of cheap local vino, while the last load of laundry was spinning.

While chatting we finished a bottle of wine, and then opened another. She was a charming girl, but her eyes were red and glassy; it was obvious she'd been smoking marijuana, and was our kind of girl.

— —

"I may be overstepping my bounds here, but would you happen to know where we could find some smoke?" I inquired.

"Smoke? You want a fag?" Deb asked, offering me her Marlboro Red box.

"No, marijuana, pot," I clarified.

"Well...what makes you think I'd 'ave anythin' da do with that?" she said, stone-faced.

"I...I...just...thought," I said, stammering and turning several shades of red.

Then she let out a full-bellied laugh, which brought on a coughing spell, and when recovered she pulled out a pregnant joint. Holding it up with two fingers, she smiled the Cheshire cat grin and said, "You means funk?" Sparking the joint, she took a long leisurely drag, smiled broadly, and passed it to Chiquita. "How much funk do ya need?"

"It looks like there may be a few funky weeks ahead, so you'd better get as much as you can for this," I said, handing her the Greek Monopoly money. She shoved it in her lesbian purse (the Marlboro Red box) and then stuffed it inside her hiking boot.

"I 'ave ta get it from the Albanians. I'll bring 'er around da-morrow. Cool, mate?"

"Cool." After our visit with MaryJane, the problems of the day seemed to ease just a bit, and the next few glasses of wine didn't hurt either.

"Oh, what the hell; pass that damn thing over here," Nikki said, even more irritated than usual.

"Stella! Have you completely lost your mental faculty?" Chiquita shrieked.

"Oh, Jesus Christ, I can't even hold the fucking thing. Put it up to my goddamn lips, will you, Murf?" Nikki demanded, and then he inhaled.

"*Well...Missy*, I'm shocked at you! Just look at you. You're usually so pious and disapproving of us drunken drug-a-dicks. Look at you now," Chiquita said, laughing his skinny ass off.

"Well, don't just sit there like you got two broken arms, Chiquita. Pass that damn joint back here," Nikki said, making everyone laugh. And believe me; we really needed a good laugh.

Talking Turkey

Sunrise arrived ahead of schedule as I slowly and regrettably crawled back to consciousness, while recovering from the evening's bourbon, marijuana, and Xanax anesthetizing combination. Last night, while helping Nikki, our "winged victory," get undressed, hosed down, redressed, and into bed, we realized we'd be doing a whole lot of assisting from here on out.

—　—

"*Well*...I've thought about it," Nikki announced during coffee and re-entry. "If I'm going to be laid up, what better place to do it than on this beautiful island, I mean, we've already paid for all this loveliness, so we may as well enjoy it. Don't cha think?"

"Answer me this, Stella. Are ya goin' ta be able ta wipe your own kiester, hon? 'Cause that's where I draw the line. I mean, a-friend's-a-friend and ever-thin', but I don't want ta be that kinda friend," Chiquita smart-mouthed.

"Well, yes, I can wipe myself; at least I *think* I can. But I want to stay here if it's all right with you guys. As you know, I'll need a little help getting dressed, bathed, fed, medicated, and little stuff like that, but

I'll do as much as I can by myself. You two won't have to do hardly a thing."

"*Well...?*" Chiquita said, looking to me for answers.

"*Well...?*" I replied, with none to give.

"Be a dear, will you, and get me some more coffee? Then spread a chunk-a that yummy blueberry croissant on some butter, and feed it to me. Will ya? You're such a dear," Nikki purred.

Chiquita and I looked at each other, stymied. "Okay, let's try and make the best of it," I said.

"Okay, now, as I see it we got three weeks left, and three refills of that fabulous Xanadu stuff, so that's thirty pills each, for three weeks. At least we'll be able to a-nets-ta-thighs our miseries while we're here. I'm in, too, Stella. What the hell, it'll be a hoot—pass me the pills," Chiquita said.

"Isn't someone supposed to be getting me more coffee, or will I have to die of thirst? And make damn sure it's good and hot, now. Don't you be bringing me any of that piss-warm, anemic swill!"

Our grumpy impatient patient, Nikki, was laughing out loud by the time we'd finished breakfast and cleared the table. Other than cutting his food, feeding it to him, and helping him drink his coffee, he did everything else himself—the chewing and swallowing.

"So, girls, are we still going to Turkey, or what? You know, I *have* to go there because I'm having the carpet ripped out while I'm here and the floors refinished. So I *have* to buy some rugs to cover the bare wood floors. Isn't that clever of me? I won't have to lift a finger, or move the furniture, deal with the dusty dirt, or the stinking stain and sticky varnish," Nikki said, beaming at his brilliance.

"Nikki, you just had the best wool carpeting you can buy installed not less than three years ago, and now you're ripping it all out?" I exclaimed, appalled at his extravagance.

"I never liked that boring beige carpet. It's too damn light and it shows every damn thing; it's always looking nasty. Plus I'm going broke just paying Chiquita to keep the shit clean. I prefer the aesthetic of beautiful hardwood floors and luxurious area rugs."

"*Well...*" Chiquita piped, "I'm not the one who's making your carpet filthy."

As you may have figured, Nikki was always one to get what he wanted. Three days later, at nine in the morning, we arrived at the Mykonos airport for our flight to Athens. Once there we would make a connecting flight to Istanbul; gaining more frequent-flier miles, *you see.*

Our flight was scheduled on Onassis Air Lines, which we discovered was notorious for being overbooked, running late, and making empty promises. Our luggage made it onto the plane, but we did not. While watching it leave, we were informed we'd have to wait four hours for the next flight, which arrived fourteen hours later.

Nikki was literally melting in the terminal, and rivers of sweat flowed from under his tousled toupee. After four days of not being attended to, blown, shaped, styled, or even combed, his towheaded snatch looked like the hair of a dirty-faced, mistreated doll.

Fourteen hours later, we finally made it to Athens, only to find everything closed for the night. We had been attempting to make our connecting flight to Istanbul for an entire day, and regrettably, the next flight didn't leave for another five hours. But looking on the bright side, Nikki could finally use his play-ho, because it made a perfect sling for his injured wing, with the purple, teal, and electric pink fabric blending nicely with his splashy Hawaiian shirt, which was clinging to his voluptuous melting torso so tightly it looked as if it was painted on. Despite looking the contrary, he was getting old and cranky. But I had to admit that up until then he'd been a real trooper.

"Jesus Christ, I'm absolutely roasting to death inside of this fucking place, and I can't stand it for another minute. Get me the hell outta this terminal and find me some air-conditioning before I'm terminal!" Nikki said, his face glistening with sweat and red as the devil's dick. Errant wig hairs were clinging tightly to his sweaty forehead and his cherubic cheeks were streaked by the rivers of sweat pouring from under his tousled toupee. And those damn damaged arms made it nearly impossible for him to blot away the sweat, making him a miserable, melting mess.

The nearest place of refuge was a pretty powdery-blue two-story hotel called the Tropicana. Translating from Greek to English that meant fleabag. But it was air-conditioned. Checking into a room, we asked for a six o'clock wake-up call, hoping to get a few hours' rest. But we needn't have worried about oversleeping, because between the commotions coming from the airport a block away and the clatter from the street traffic just six feet outside our window, no one slept a wink.

Thankfully our crack-of-dawn flight was on time, and uneventful. The help was easy on the eyes, and after a light snack and beverage we were there. Everyone was extremely helpful with our invalid, Nikki, assisting him in every way, and he loved the attention, playing the victim perfectly.

Immediately we were aware that we were in a very different place as myriads of minarets repeatedly punctuated the cluttered skyline of red-tile roofs precariously stacked on top of each other. And there were trees. I'd truly missed green, with Greece being so arid and barren.

Our bearded taxi driver, Said (sa-eed), who was obviously Muslim, never cracked a smile, ever. He never once stopped at a stop sign, red light, or intersection during our half-hour trip from the airport to our four-star luxury hotel in downtown Istanbul. We all held on tight as he intently hunched over the wheel and launched. Barely slowing down at any street crossings, he'd give the finger to the other three drivers and plow right on through the intersection. Bending his wrist, he'd give his bony elbow a hard shove upward and then shout something curse-like in Turkish.

*Here is an interesting cost comparison for you. Our water taxi from the airport on the Italian coast to the island of Venice cost over a hundred dollars; whereas, our half-hour ride from the airport in Turkey to our downtown luxury hotel cost twelve dollars. And that included a nice tip. One dollar was the equivalent to one million Turkish liras, so we were instantly rich Americans, with millions to spend, and Nikki just couldn't wait to bestow his newfound wealth among the local merchants.

"Now, we've already lost two valuable shopping days in just trying to get here, so let's drop off our luggage at the hotel and go do some power shopping; precious time is wasting."

When checking into the hotel, Nikki found, much to his dismay that the Grand Bazaar (mall) would be closed tomorrow and the day after because of some stupid Muslim holy day, so that meant he had only five hours to shop today. Period. *Shit.* Sensing the urgency, Nikki switched into crisis mode, changed into his head-to-toe Christian Lacroix camouflage ensemble, and we were off.

Charge! It.

"Okay, girls, here's the plan of attack, so listen carefully. I've been reading up on this. We're going to the Grand Bazaar, and for your information that is the world's first shopping mall. This place is fucking fabulous, six hundred years old, and absolutely mercantile Mecca. This mega-mall has three thousand shops under glass, a mosque, and a hotel, all interconnected by quaint cobblestone streets, and selling lovely handmade goods such as rugs, metals, silks, furs, and china. Did I hear someone say rugs?"

"Your royal toters await, Your Highness; and I, for one, can hardly wait to watch you do more power shopping," Chiquita sarcastically said.

"Sounds like someone could use a nap, Missy. You're getting cranky," Nikki sputtered.

The Hotel Merit Antique was located in the city center, close to the bazaar, so our concierge hailed us a taxi for the short ride. Women were noticeably absent from the city streets, and everywhere there was an unbalanced presence of swarthy young men. Some street corners had camouflaged men armed with machine guns. Other streets had piles of red bricks and timber sitting on sidewalks, either materials collected from recent earthquake damage or supplies to repair it. And the ancient structures that were still standing looked precariously unstable, as if they'd tumble down any time soon.

The smell of grilling meat came wafting into the taxi's open windows from families picnicking on a narrow grassy strip between the expressway and the commercial Bosporus. This seemed a peculiar place considering you were constantly being overwhelmed with exhaust fumes from the freeway on the right and diesel fumes spewing from cargo ships on the Bosporus on the left.

Ships of all sizes were constantly coming and going, and spewing black clouds of diesel exhaust into the air. Streets were extremely noisy, with honking horns, cursing men, and loudspeakers blaring foreign music. The nauseous smell of exhaust was overwhelming.

Immediately upon entering the Grand Bazaar we were dwarfed by the scale. Immense stone arches hold up glass-and-metal skylight ceilings, and ancient cobblestone streets are lined with shops. Tiered fountains at the street intersections added the soothing sound of water cascading into pools, and flocks of chirping birds were gladly drinking from them. They paused to eat the gifted nuts and seeds from the vendors, and then they shit everywhere. So you'd be advised to wear a hat.

Exotic and unfamiliar smells wafted from stall to street, beckoning us to sample something salty and pungent, spicy, and sweet. East met West here, with silks from the East, tourists from the West, furs from the North, hand-hammered brass, tooled leather, precious jewelry, fine-glazed ceramics and precious porcelain china; and everything was handmade by craftsmen carrying on ancient traditions. And with four hundred merchants to shop Nikki had his work cut out for him.

He really meant business, so he stopped dead in his tracks and commanded Chiquita, "Pull out my reading spectacles and put them on me. Then retrieve my little black book from my camo bag." He obediently obliged by putting on the glasses and holding up the book for Nikki to read.

"It says here we're supposed to go down two blocks and over three to find the rug merchants. Oh, would you look at that, and it's silky, too. Oh my, I've been wanting to get me one of those pretty what-ya-ma-call-its for just ages. Oh dear God, would you look at him. I'd like to get me one of those too, in large, and don't bother wrapping it. My, my, my, my, my. Mercy."

Indeed, as Nikki had noted, many of the men were handsome, and young. But the shopkeepers seemed to be desperate, because they were coming into the streets pleading and pulling on our sleeves. "Please, sir, come into my shop, I have the best deals. Please, sir, come this way."

Rug buying is an ancient tradition; caveat emptor (let the buyer beware). Block after block of merchant stalls appeared in front of us and Nikki's baby blues glazed over. A Mona Lisa–like smile of admiration and determination appeared on his lovely new face.

"Now, I'll be needing an eleven-by-fifteen for the great room, wool-on-wool most likely, and that should speak to the carpet in the conversation nook. I will also be needing an eight-by-eleven, or so, for in there. I was thinking silk-on-cotton, since that's not a highly trafficked area; naturally dyed most certainly, hand-tied absolutely, with a high knot count—indubitably. And for the foe-yeah, I'll need a five-by-three, and something splashy, because it's so dreary without any window in there."

Our merchant spoke impeccable English, while explaining he he'd earned an engineering degree from MIT, and afterward returned to Turkey and the family rug business. He was young, dark, and very handsome. Sizing up our trio, he immediately began fawning over Nikki, found him a chair, fussed with his comfort, and brought him hot tea in a clear glass—with a striped straw.

The first word of Turkish Nikki learned was *kaput*, which meant "I'm through, take it away, and bring me another." So two boys, not more than fourteen, began feverishly hauling in cumbersome carpet bundles; they wrestled, untied, unfolded, and presented them to the big blond Pooh-Bah.

"Kaput," he commanded, and they hurriedly hauled it away and brought him another. Those poor skinny boys were running themselves ragged, sweating, panting, and exhausted from presenting Persian parlor carpets to the big blond American; *I'm-impotant-tate*.

"Kaput," Nikki said repeatedly while waving his limp limb dismissively. He just loved saying "kaput," and did so repeatedly, delighted with his mastery of yet another foreign language. Lengthy discussions about the regions where the rugs came from, types of dyes used—natural as opposed to synthetic—fiber content, knots per square inch, and all that bullshit eventually gave way to gut instinct. *Do I like it, or not?* As in purchasing art, rug purchasing is a deeply personal decision, and he had to pick three. Kaput, kaput, kaput.

Watching him power kaputing for two hours, in six different rug shops, was too much for me to bear, and after drinking hot tea for two hours, I needed to use the restroom. When I inquired where they may be located, Muhammad sent one of the rug Sherpas to escort me.

"It id dib-occult to pine, sir," he said in broken English. Maybe being all of fourteen, he was practically running ahead of me. I was certain he needed to use the restroom, too, and quickly.

"Do Jew knee tiss-oo?" Now *I* was confused. He asked again, "Do Jew knee tis-oo?" Now I understood. Another boy, the restroom attendant's cousin, was selling toilet paper by the slice.

"Yes, I will," I said, and the stall jockey sold me each four-inch slice separately. It wasn't cheap. Purchasing an adequate amount for the job, I realized it may have cost less to clean with liras, because you would have gotten a million of them to every dollar. When shown to the stall I thought someone had hijacked the head, because all that remained was a hole in the ground.

A strange handlebar-like device was attached to the wall. I stared at it for a moment before figuring it out. Pull pants down, squatted, hold the handlebar, align ass over hole, and bombs away. The sold-by-the-slice toilet paper was two grits short of sandpaper, making it a very memorable experience. When finished I went to wash my hands and dried them with yet another paid-for towel. But the stall jockeys lingered around, looking hungry and making me feel I should tip them, so I did. Clearly they were in cahoots.

As soon as he saw me returning, Chiquita left the showroom. "What the hell took you so long, Stella? I need ta get the hell outta there and get myself a cig before I die a fresh air. Kaput, kaput, kaput. Jesus H. Carpet!"

"Chiquita, years ago I saw an old rug in a home in Portland, Maine, and I just loved it because it was old as hell, worn, and threadbare, but still lustrous because it was made of silk. That's what I want. Would you like to go with me while I look for a rug like that?"

"Oh sure, watching more rug shopping—what a novel idea. C'mon, let's leave that mad cow in there with her babysitter and go find you a rug. It'll be a hoot!"

Less than an hour later I was leaving Magic Carpet International with my beautiful antique silk carpet in lustrous shades of rusty red, warm tomato soup, pomegranate, and black, with an intricate central medallion. My merchant kindly placed it inside a nylon suitcase, which would travel as my second piece of luggage.

"Kaput, kaput, kaput, kaput." We could hear Nikki barking before even reaching the stall. "Where the hell have you two been hiding? I have vitally important decisions to make here, and you two are off shagging rug Sherpas. I need help—and I mean right now. Precious time is running out," Nikki said, flustered and red-faced.

Again we were served piping-hot tea in clear glasses, while watching a dizzying array of carpets go flying by in a blinding barrage of sizes, colors, and patterns. "Kaput, kaput—wait a minute...no, no, no, kaput. Maybe, what do you two think?"

Then—all of a sudden—all three of us gasped. "Oooooooooooh." Silk-on-silk, pastel, shiny, pretty. "How much?" Nikki demanded.

"Four thousand five hundred American," merchant Muhammad responded most meekly.

"Too much," Nikki instantaneously shot back and quickly countered with, "Fifteen hundred."

Muhammad slumped back into his seat, flabbergasted. After recovering, he stood, walked over to Nikki, took his not-too-broken hand, and placed it upon his chest, saying, "Please, sir, feel my heart. You are ripping it out."

Nikki set his jaw, snapped his hand back, and folded it across his chest, saying, "Fifteen hundred dollars American and not a penny more."

"Sir! Sir, please, just look at the workmanship. It takes four months to weave just a meter of this carpet. Please, sir, I have four children to feed. Please, sir, think of them withering."

Instead of acquiescing Nikki immediately stood and announced, "Let's go!" Obediently we, his loyal toters, obliged and followed him out. "Let's go look at more rugs. I'll come back later, and I'll bet you he'll be ready to deal with me then."

"Oh, goody, goody, more rug shopping. Kaput, kaput, kaput," Chiquita mugged.

"Cranky, cranky, cranky, someone needs a nappy," Nikki scolded.

Halleluiah! Two hours later Nikki had selected, paid for, and made arrangements to have two carpets shipped home. We headed back to the first rug merchant for the final showdown.

"Welcome, my friends. Please come in, please sit down," Muhammad said.

"Ding." The bell rang, starting the match.

In the *right* corner was poor old merchant Muhammad, who weighed 110 at the most, soaking wet. In the *wrong* corner, weighing in at somewhere around 275 pounds, from the US of A, was the reigning heavy -weight cham-peen, Nikki Clark. They sized each other up, and the velvet gloves are off. Wide-eyed and worried, the rug Sherpas pasted themselves against the east wall, scared shitless and sweating bullets, simply in awe witnessing Mr. Kaput in operation.

A horrible hour of haggling ensued, and it was not pretty, not pretty at all. Nikki, with both broken arms folded tightly to his lovely chest, defiantly scowled and gave him the stink-eye. The first person to speak was the loser. Muhammad, who was nearing complete exhaustion, finally broke down and admitted this was his *first* and *only* sale of the day. But he only acquiesced, knowing he was beaten by the best of them, and reluctantly accepted the measly $1,500 for his four starving children and their crippled and cancer-riddled mother.

Exiting the bazaar with our bizarre booty, we were instantly swarmed by a mob of desperate grasping people who were pulling at us urgently, talking excitedly, and trying to sell us something, any thing. "Please, sir, only the best price for you." While loading the taxi it quickly became frightening as they shoved trinkets at us—pots, pans, and rugs—while speaking excitedly and unintelligibly in foreign tongues, and pursuing us until the taxi finally sped away.

Other desperate and industrious people had small looms set up on the sidewalk outside the bazaar. For these street-side entrepreneurs, times appeared most desperate.

"*You know*, I think I coulda got him down even further if I'd a really tried," Nikki said.

"*Nikki!* I just saw you snatchin' that bread right outta his poor kid's mouth," Chiquita said. Because of his scalping, Muhammad refused to ship the carpet for free, so Chiquita and I were stuck schlepping it and the plethora of other impulse items he had purchased: a heavy hand-hammered antique copper cauldron that would become a container for a potted house plant, two sacred silk prayer rugs that would be turned into poufy pillows for his precious pampered pussy-cats to shred, and a silk baby-blue belly-dancing outfit bedecked with silver spangles, in women's plus-size twenty-four, which was *supposedly* bought for a "client." We didn't ask any questions, we just carried the stuff.

As Nikki paid the driver his chicken feed, Chiquita and I unloaded the taxi. "Would you like to get him back real good?" I asked Chiquita, who looked at me strangely but said nothing. We continued to unload the trunk *full of his* trophies, and I purpously placed the suitcase containing his silk rug under mine to obscure it from view, and waited for the taxi to leave.

"*Nikki!* Didn't you get your silk carpet out of the backseat? I don't see it here."

"I don't see it neither," Chiquita shrieked, playing along. "Don't look at me; wasn't my rug."

Nikki gave us a look of horror and bolted down the street after the departing taxi, flailing his sling and cast about frantically, screaming and turning a brilliant shade of scarlet. "Stop, stop, stop!" We let him get half a block down the street before stopping him, and nearly wet ourselves laughing.

"You dirty sons-a-bitches nearly gave me a heart attack," Nikki said, and then he laughed, too.

Meanwhile, back at our luxury hotel, an orthodox minister wearing a towering Byzantine miter was conducting a wedding service in the lobby that mingled East and West. The beautiful bride wore a traditional white Western wedding dress with a full crinoline skirt, adorned with crystal beads and seed pearls. Her unusual headdress looked Asian and stood a full six inches above her head, with a fringed veil of opaque glass beads obscuring her pretty face.

As we rode the glass-front elevator to our four-star room, she was presented to her guests. Joyful eastern music floated in from the reception until we fell asleep.

— —

Bolting us out of bed ahead of the crack of dawn was the wailing mournful call of morning prayers being blasted from loudspeakers located just outside our room. They announced the start of another day, and the Muslim world slowly began to stir to life. Being good Americans, we rolled over to sleep another hour, ordered room service, and watched the *Today* show from New York.

We planned on doing some sightseeing today and visiting and Topkapi Palace, the sultan's home; it was the first piece of real estate on Nikki's must-see list. The other was the Blue Mosque.

"Now, *this* is a house," Nikki announced as he strutted through the massive palace gates and into the sultan's compound as if he owned it, or was considering picking it up for a quaint little seaside getaway. Wide tree-lined streets of gray pea gravel connected a multitude of ancient ornate buildings topped with verdigris copper onion-domed roofs, and huge cantilevered overhangs.

Ceramic tiles decorated absolutely everything. Tiles organized into intricate geometric patterns embellished entire buildings, inside and out, covering walls, ceilings, and floors with blue, rust, white, green, and yellow ocher designs. The harem held forty rooms of opulently gilded grandeur; sitting right on the Bosporus overlooking Asia, and it was an amazing, sprawling complex. It was also dusty and moldy, and making Chiquita wheeze and sneeze. Nikki said, "I'll take it. Now have it painted yellow."

Back at the hotel, Nikki opted for television and room service, while Chiquita and I chose to explore the neighborhoods surrounding the hotel. I had seen the movie *Midnight Express*, so we didn't venture too far. Street-side vendors were everywhere, so we sampled the curbside cuisine. Going by smell and sight alone, we tasted their foreign fare, and it was some of the best food I had ever eaten. Stewed dishes with beans of all sorts, especially king-size lima beans, meat falling off the bone, and not at all spicy or hot as I imagined; mellow, melting in your mouth, and comforting.

This unusual city was oxymoronic, ancient and modern at the same time, because there were old buildings housing traditional halal foods with duck and goat carcasses hanging in the windows standing right next to modern shops selling cell phones, computers, and the latest Western technology.

Our trip was much too short to know what the place was really like, but I loved the taste.

Kaput.

Illumination

Practically everyone knows that Venice is an island floating in the Adriatic. They may also know this lovely little island has canals replacing streets, and gondolas instead of cars. But what they probably don't know Venice has 118 little sisters, and these other itty-bitty landlings lie in the sea right alongside her. Two of these picturesque islands are Murano and Burano, which are known for their artistry and handiwork.

A water bus shuttles common tourists to these lovely little luxury shopping destinations daily. But Nikki was not ordinary; he was an American big spender, so he hired a private water yacht to take him window shopping. So very early in the morning a slickly varnished cabin cruiser picked us up at our hotel and whisked us to the glass factories portal on the quaint offshore island.

Effortlessly gliding through the moist morning mist, our leisurely twenty-minute cruise took us past Lido, the beach of Venice, and several smaller islands the size of postage stamps with old homes, cemeteries, and other ancient crumbling and sinking water-soaked ruins. We arrive to find this quaint colorful island bulging with upscale boutiques, galleries, glass-blowing factories, and chic restaurants. But it was so unbelievably picturesque it looked like a Disney re-creation instead of a real destination.

Our beautiful boutique boat docked us in front of the *Costa-Lotta-Moola* Glass Studio because this was the sacred shrine where Nikki had previously made several significant pilgrimages. Two trim men in navy blue uniforms, with big brassy buttons, fawned over him while helping him out, and he just loved it, nodding knowingly in their direction.

Dressed in a fetching ensemble of head-to-toe natural linen, with a coordinating sling for his injured wing, he was definitely stylin'. Hiding behind those outrageously enormous, movie-star sunglasses, he tossed back his head of store-bought hair and strutted his stuff as if he really *was* somebody. They naturally assumed he *was* and act accordingly. Because of this air of self-importance, they thought he was an actor, movie star, director, or celebrity. I mean, who else but an eccentric celeb would dare go out in public dressed *like that*, and with hair that looked as if he'd stuck his finger into an outlet? Plus he traveled with those two devilishly handsome male escorts (Chiquita and me, duh).

Having an agenda, he was laser focused, and we were simply there for immoral support, nursing assistance, and Sherpa services. Our demanding docket included the purchase of a new chandelier for his upcoming kitchen renovation, and it would have to be something spectacular, and a catalyst for the entire rejuvenation. Reading glasses were on—this was serious work.

Our gorgeous guide provided us with a brief history of glassmaking and a demonstration of the glass-blowing process, which was followed by an exhibition of craftsmen creating works of art. I found this information interesting, but to Nikki it was just a waste of valuable shopping time. "Yada, yada, yada, seen it all before."

"These artisans have apprenticed for as much as fifteen years before being approved," our guide explained, while escorting us through the air-conditioned showroom bulging with extravagant things made of glass, which nobody really needed. Our guide was an exquisite piece as well, an athletic soccer player, and quite charming—in the Italian way. He introduced us to José, who was our sales associate.

"Good morning, gentlemen. And how may I be of assistance to you?"

I immediately turned around to see if someone had entered the room.

"Yes, I am looking for something for my upcoming kitchen renovation," Nikki announced with utmost authority.

"Very good, sir, and what did you have in mind; a sculpture, objet d'art, or maybe a beautiful chandelier? How may I be of assistance, Mr. Clock?"

"A chandelier."

"Very good, sir, please look around while I have some refreshments brought in for you and your devilishly handsome male escorts. May I get you some coffee, espresso, or perhaps some vino?"

"Coffee would be nice, and *black*," Nikki blurted out first.

"And for you two gigolos, may I get you something?"

"Wine would be fine," Chiquita said, innocently.

"Coffee please, with cream. Thank you," I replied, and José went away for the café.

"*Ouch*, that hurt Grizzelda," Chiquita yelped, after he was kicked by Nikki, and damn hard, too.

"For Christ's sake, Chiquita, its nine o'clock in the morning," Nikki said.

"It's practically five o'clock back home, I can tell,"Chiquita affirmed, as he rubbed his ankle.

Chiquita and I sipped our beverages while Nikki experienced a serious case of whiplash from thrashing his head about, and strained his eyes surveying all the lovely sparkling thingies. "Oh, that's exquisite, and oh my, doesn't that just take your breath away?"

"Well, the price certainly does. Sheesh, twenty-five thousand dollars! My whole house ain't worth that much," Chiquita said in disgust.

As Nikki scrutinized the unworthy wares, José kept one eye on us peons while making small talk and kept the other on Nikki, who was displaying a sour poker face, and having low expectations of finding something suitable for the Château Ghetto amongst the rubble.

"No, I am not Italian at all, I'm Cuban, and I have been living here in Italy for many years," José proudly stated, sounding quite like Ricardo Montalbán.

Suddenly Nikki stopped dead in his natural linen loafers. His lower jaw quivered and dropped, ever so slightly, and his eyes were glassy and transfixed. He was either witnessing an apparition of the Blessed Virgin Mary, or he'd found his chandelier. Silence fell upon the showroom, factory, and then the entire island, as all eyes focused upon him. With baby blues lifted toward heaven, he slowly walked toward his vision, eyes lighting up and a smile broadening across his lovely, newly remade face. He'd found his prize.

Of all the exquisite chandeliers in this expensive showroom, I would never have picked this one, because it was gaudy as hell. Irises fashioned with burnt orange, violet, yellow, and cobalt blue made the globes, and Kelly green stems curved around to make the leafy arms. It was garish as hell, and looked like the circus had come to town—but to him it was absolute perfection.

"Absolutely perfection. This is exactly what I have wanted. I have waited long enough, and wanted it hard enough, and now I need this. How fabulous!" Suddenly his head spun 360 degrees. "How much?"

"Four thousand five hundred dollars American, plus shipping," José replied nonchalantly.

Feeling emboldened after his recent Turkish conquest, Nikki shot back,"Nooo waaay, José. Waaay tooo much!" José looked at him, flabbergasted, and said nothing. Nikki gave him the stink-eye and stared right back. They sized each other up like sumo wrestlers about to wrangle, and my money was on Nikki, broken arms and all. The horrible haggling session continued for twenty minutes, and Chiquita and I, like frightened children watching parents fight, headed for the door. We were just about to make a clean getaway when Nikki threw up his one almost good arm and said, "Fa-get-about-it."

Instantly he lept to his feet to leave, and like obedient Sherpas we followed. José escorted us to the door like a gentleman. And we'd nearly reached the door when Nikki just blurted out, "Go and ask your boss if he'll take two thousand for that nasty old chandelier."

José looked even more amazed, stunned at his audacity, seemed puzzled, apprehensive, and confused; then he remembered his taxes were due, relented, and went to discuss the weather with the janitor in the coffee break room. Five minutes later he returned reeking of cigarettes and wearing a sour look upon his distinguished suntanned face.

"Okay, but *only* if you pay for the shipping. You must understand, at this deeply discounted price I am not making any commission at all. But I will only do this for such a good customer as you."

Now I was absolutely certain they had him confused with someone else. But Nikki quickly snapped back, "No! Two thousand and *you* pay the shipping."

A stunned José sheepishly departed again. Ten minutes later he returned reeking of cigarette smoke and cheap red wine. Deeply exhaling, he deflated himself and pathetically announced, "Okay."

Feeling even more emboldened now, Nikki stuck out his sizeable chest, threw back his head of messed-up hair, and said, "I'll think about it," and strutted out the door...*whoosh*. "Let's come back later. I'll betcha I can get him down to about fifteen hundred," Nikki said smugly.

So we leisurely strolled the antiquated streets and examined yet more glass factories, galleries, and showrooms full of shiny pretty shit that nobody really needed. To break up the shopping monotony we crossed over a cobblestone bridge on the main waterway and visited a cute canal-side café to lunch. A parade of sleek black gondolas went gracefully drifting by, while we enjoyed out little lunch.

After having our six courses of nibbles, Nikki bought a cute little impulse item, a homely little boudoir lamp costing $600. To me the thing was ugly as sin, and definitely not my cup of tea. With a yellow gourd-shaped base and powder blue drooping mushroom-cap shade, it looked like it was stolen from Papa Smurf's house, warped by the sun, and coated with powdered sugar. Thankfully he'd made arrangements to have it shipped home, so we didn't have to schlep it around and break it ourselves.

"I still want that chandelier, you know," Nikki stated with utmost certainty as we neared the showroom. When we rounded the bend we found José standing out front having a cigarette.

"Gentlemen, it is so good to see you again. It is so very hot today. Please come into my air-conditioned showroom and have some nice cool refreshments with me." He escorted us into the closing room for the rematch. Nikki asked for water—without any bubbles—while Chiquita and I requested wine. It was free; we were Sherpas, not stupid.

Silence fell upon the crowd; this was the final showdown, and the first person to speak would be the loser. Four excruciating minutes of deafening silence ensued as we scanned back and forth from José to Nikki, wondering who would be the first to crack. Nikki finally broke down and began to blab, "Well, ya see, I found the cutest little boudoir lamp—in one of the 'nicer' showrooms—and bought it. So, ya see, now I don't have the two thousand to spend on this little light of yours. All I have left is fifteen hundred dollars. So…I was wonderin' if you'd consider taking the f—?"

Nikki couldn't get the *F* out, before, *whoosh,* José leapt to his feet, cut him off midword, and with one grand gesture of his noble suntanned hand, had the goblets plucked from our lips and the mug snatched from Nikki's almost-good hand. Pointing emphatically toward the door, he said, "Please leave my showroom. *You* are no gentleman. I have prostrated myself in front of my boss just to get you that deeply discounted price, and now you come back in here trying to break a deal *we have already made.* Leave," he said, with his middle finger pointing toward the door for added emphasis.

He *really* meant it. Chiquita and I were already standing outside on the promenade smoking before he even said, "Pa-lease leave." But I must say that Nikki stayed behind and bravely took it like a…whatever. Twenty minutes later, a sheepish Nikki came out to fetch us.

"Come home, children, all is forgiven. Mommy and Daddy have kissed and made up." So we rejoined them to celebrate the gaudy light fixture purchase and finally have our well-traveled wine.

The harvest moon was completely full and dangling directly over the Grand Canal while we leisurely strolled the crowded moonlit streets, gazing at the lovely people, shops, and restaurants, *La dolce vita.* Stopping at a quaint canal-side café called Angelo's, we thought of Flint while having a delicious meal of eenies: seafood linguine with fried zucchini, a plate of spatini, rotini, cappellini, and veal scallopini, too. To finish this sup we each had a cup of sweetened espresso coffee, and for dessert tiramisu was served to two and crostini for the third.

Nikki, still having his designer pockets bulging with money, and a couple of items left to check off his impressive European shopping list, wished to do some window shopping, so we strolled across the Bridge of Sighs into the quieter neighborhoods farther removed from Saint Mark's Square, and the central city clatter. Suddenly he stopped dead in his tracks. A look of reverence appeared upon his new face as if he was awestruck.

"Thank you, Jesus. This is it."

"It" was a hallowed luxury linen boutique/shrine called Grossolanamente Exorbitante, and he was simply beaming beholding the breathtakingly beautiful luxe linens displayed in the window.

But when he attempted to open the door, much to his dismay, he found it locked. "Holy shit, they're closed. No, no, no, *how* could they *possibly* be closed? I came all this way," Nikki pleaded.

"All the way from Kansas," Chiquita added for emphasis.

"Oh, look. I can see someone inside there. Hello! Hello! Why aren't they paying any attention to me? Why aren't they answering the door?" Nikki wailed, and then kicked the door.

"Jeez Louise, don't break the glass. They're closed," I stupidly said.

"Well, I can see that," he shot back. "But it's me! Can't *they* see that?"

Chiquita leaned over and started talking out of the other side of his mouth. "You know those stupidly expensive sheets she buys? Well, this is where he gets 'em. Those damned re-dick-a-lust linen things have to be specially hand laundered, by little Vietnamese virgins, way up in northern Minnesota. Every week I have to bundle up a set of the soiled sheets—while wearin' a hazmat suit—and then send 'em off to bumfuck Mini-ha-ha-ha to be deloused, disinfected, and prayed over. I understand there isn't even a single soul in our entire state qualified to clean 'em. Ya know, he used to buy them fancy Frette linens, but when he found this lofty linen line, he gave those natty old rags to the rescue admission."

This sacred jewel-like luxury linen boutique was the only place Nikki ever bought his bedding, because according to Nikki, sleeping on their sheets was like having an orgasm, they felt that good. Apparently he'd ordered a cashmere foreplay throw, and it was ready for pickup.

"Hello, *hello*! Oh, why doesn't anyone answer this damn door? I just know they can see me."

"Obviously they don't know who they are dealing with. It's closed, Stella," Chiquita said.

"Obviously," I agreed.

"Don't they know who this is? I made a special trip here just to get this," Nikki pleaded.

"So that's why we came to Venice, to get you a new blankie?" Chiquita said, most irritated.

"She sees me now!" he yelled, jumping up and down and flailing his wings about. Magically a buzzer sounded, followed by a metallic click, and the door miraculously opened all by itself. We were silently escorted into the sanctum sanctorum, where Nikki was presented with the cashmere lap blanket.

"I have been deprived of this for so long, and now another dream is coming true."

The dream "throw" came in a color called I-v-o-r-y (pronounced eye-vo-ree). You see, beige simply would not do because it was too dark, oyster was way too gray, and white was much too crisp; but Ivory was the perfect shade. "Perfection," he said while heavy petting it. "Have it sent."

"What? You mean to tell me that we came all the way to Venice for that damn cash-smear kerchief, and you aren't even taking the dumb thing home with you?" Chiquita said, completely miffed.

"Well, I was only thinking of *you*, honey. I figure you two have enough stuff to carry already."

The following morning was misty, but we had breakfast on our hotel's veranda anyway, and watched as the sun rose over the Grand Canal. Few people were up so early, and the streets practically deserted, except for street sweepers. Moving side by side in a choreographed row, they slowly pushed bright blue soft-bristled brooms to clean up the debris from the previous day's tourist stampede. Well-scrubbed parochial school-children wearing ugly plaid uniforms solemnly strolled toward their prisons, and the smells of baking bread and seafood lingered in the moist morning air.

Served a hearty breakfast of orange yolk eggs on dry crusty toast, fried red-skinned potatoes peppered with pepperoncini flakes, salty prosciutto ham, creamy polenta, and strong black coffee, we were fueled for the day. In the morning we were off to the island of Burano, and in the afternoon we'd visit the Guggenheim Museum.

Taking the people's boat today, we were traveling like commoners to a distant dot on the horizon. The itty-bitty island of Burano was colorful and charming, but just a tourist trap/shopping destination, and cheapskate Chiquita was the only one who bought anything.

I was content to spend my time photographing the colorful canal-side houses. A heliotrope house sat next to a yellow one, then magenta, olive green, red, lime, mustard, puce against rust, and when thrown together they literally vibrated. The turquoise water coursing through the canal reflected back their vibrant colors, making them dance, amplifying their intensity, and a steely gray stormy sky added contrast to the vivid impressionist palette. Pop, pop, pop!

Pregnant past-due clouds told us rain was imminent. So we headed back to the water bus at the exact same time as everyone else on the island, making it tilt to the left. We didn't make it in time, and the heavens opened up, thoroughly drenching everyone. The boat arrived just as the rain let loose, and swarms of drenched tourists poured onto the boat, filling every possible nook and cranny.

Tightly pressed against the water closet, I was certain we were becoming overloaded. Chiquita held tightly to the lifesaving ring, bug-eyed and soaked to the bone. And I said my prayers as I held on to

Nikki, because he could not hold on to anything with those broken arms.

As the boat groaned and listed badly I took a deep breath of stinking diesel-laden air, thinking it could possibly be my last. Pressed body to body, the passengers looked like refugees, with nowhere to move, no air to breathe, and what air there was reeked of diesel fumes. Lightning flashed all around us as the wind fiercely howled, horizontally driven rain drenched the bitty battered boat and the raging seas rocked, rolled, and tossed the overloaded vessel about as if it was a toy boat inside a washing machine set on the spin cycle.

Soaked to the very core and blinded by sharp, stinging wind-driven rain, all 150 people on board the assaulted boat were praying for their lives to be spared and God to save them from capsizing and being devoured by the bloodthirsty sharks that were most certainly encircling the flailing ferry.

Merciful God must have heard our prayers because the storm finally ceased its relentless roar, we made it safely back to shore, and a collective sigh of relief was exhaled. A rainbow appeared in the heavens. Transferring boats, we disembarked at Saint Mark's Square, close to our hotel, De Palazzo Venier dei Leoni (House of the Dandy Lion). Chiquita and I went to Saint Mark's Cathedral to light a candle thanking God for sparing our lives, and after we returned to the hotel to find Nikki watching *Jerry Springer*. "When I miss home I watch an episode of Jerry, and it makes me think I'm back in Flint."

In the afternoon we visited the Guggenheim Museum, which was housed in Peggy's former home, a modern but oddly horizontally oriented structure, sitting right on the canal and overlooking the Bridge of Sighs. The long and low residences' very modernity placed it in direct opposition to all else on the antiquated and vertically stacked island. It was so unbelievably extravagant it even had a lawn and garden, which were unheard of on this damp dot of dust.

The exhibition was titled *Six Thousand Years of Works on Paper*, and it featured artwork that represented many of the major players through the history of art, with charcoal drawings by Leonardo da Vinci, pencil sketches by Michelangelo, an Andy Warhol watercolor, Rembrandt renderings, and a fine Jim Dine line drawing. Outside, on the estate's terraced and manicured grounds, lovely intimate spaces had sculptures strategically placed in quiet shaded places.

The thought of leaving this lovely little luxury landmark saddened us. And even though it was misting a bit, we had our last supper outside on our hotel's veranda, to enjoy the fairy-tale world one last time.

The moon, golden and full, rose over the Grand Canal, right on cue.

There Is No Drama without Conflict

Memories of our sunny days on Mykonos still lingered, but like a summer suntan, they faded more with each passing day. Vacation ended, and the realities of life quickly returned.

My antique Persian silk carpet, which I'd carried across Europe, was lost in transport and did not arrive in Detroit with our luggage. Apparently it felt homesick, because it was sent back to the rug merchant in Turkey. Eventually it arrived, in good condition, and looked amazing in my living room.

Shortly after returning to the States, Nikki visited an orthopedist {a boner specialist} who also happened to be a client. She confirmed that his arms were healing nicely, and commented that the work completed in Greece was top-notch. Regrettably, she also informed him that the cast would have to stay on for four more weeks. So...while recuperating, he decided to focus all of his excessively fruity energies into further redecorating the already overly adorned Château Ghetto.

Much to his displeasure, he returned to find the wood floors refinished, but not to his exacting standards. They were too dark, too rustic, and not at all what he'd hoped they would be. He was not pleased at all, and we heard about it—in great detail.

His precious Persian parlor carpets arrived, and were carefully placed into the greatest room, the not-so-great room, and the foe-yeah. But he wasn't nearly as thrilled with his Turkish conquests as he'd hoped he would be, and it really steamed him. Once again, he was greatly displeased.

"This displeases me immensely. I just hate the way sound bounces around in this big old barn of a room, with these hard plaster walls and those damn hardwood floors. It feels so cold and impersonal, not at all comfy-cozy like when there was plushy wall-to-wall carpeting. I am not happy, not happy at all. Plus, I've spent a goddamned fortune on these fucking investment carpets and I don't even like how they look now that they're laid. Damn it, damn it, damn it. Why do I even try?"

Two weeks later, the very best—and most expensive—carpeting you could possibly buy, in a luxurious leopard pattern of caramel-toasted brown, golden ocher, and rich warm black was installed over the recently refinished floors. Then the expensive handmade carpets that he made a special trip to Turkey for, painstakingly selected, and practically stole from poor old Muhammad—and his now-dead wife—were sent to the basement to languish in a luxury limbo. "Kaput, kaput, kaput."

The basement—excuse me, the lower level (as he continually corrected me)—warehoused the many magnificent castoffs from Nikki's impressive worldly collection. This overflow booty chest was housed in an old coal bin, and it was a permanent purgatory for precious paraphernalia, house dandruff, and priceless artifacts. Tables and chairs of gold and teak, Tiffany lamps, a vas by Lalique, large lavish artwork, and luxury items too lovely to part with were sent to this luxury limbo to languish. And very seldom did any of these deluxe discards ever find their way back to the light of day.

Already bored with his two-year-old, seldom-sat-upon, platinum sateen-quilted sofa, Nikki had purchased a bolt of green chenille to have it slip-covered. When recovered it did not meet his critical criteria, so the slippery sofa was sentenced to a damp cell in the dungeon for three long years, until it was given to me for my trailer. It took nearly a year for the smell of his cologne to dissipate, but I've never owned such a lovely piece of furniture; bless his generous heart.

Then the gaudy chandelier arrived from Murano, packed in a wooden crate the size of a fridge, and Nikki was so excited it hurt. "Oh my God, I'm so excited it hurts. I can't wait to see it up there, oh goodie, goodie, goodie."

Brad, his electrician and construction man, was responsible for removing the expensive and fragile monstrosity from the crate, assembling it, and hanging it. "This light won't be hung for a couple days, Nick, because it's arrived in a hundred pieces and has to be assembled. That alone will take a couple of days. And it's *really,* really heavy. I'll have to crawl into the attic to place a crossbeam on the ceiling joists, and then fish a threaded rod through that to support all this added weight."

"I don't know what all that bullshit means, just do it. Don't give me any shit, just *do* it."

Twenty-four hours later it was finally hung and illuminated. And it was spectacular, *to him.* To me it looked like the Las Vegas gay circus on steroids, with gaudily colored iris-shaped globes of bittersweet orange, heliotrope purple, and rich mustard yellow, and vivid slime-green spear-shaped leaves that wrapped around the chandelier's arms and connected to the flowery glass globes.

"Would you just look at that—it is absolute perfection I tell you. Worth every penny."

But poor Chiquita had to carefully wash each splendiferous, crystalliferous hand-blown piece and make sure the garish thing sparkled like Tinker Bell's tush. While washing each piece separately, and placing them on terry cloth towels for Brad to assemble and hang, he accidentally tinked a green leafy spear against the black-veined marble countertop, and it broke in two.

"Oh Dear God, I barely touched the thing, it was an accident," Chiquita cried, in his defense.

"You did that on purpose, *didn't you*? You just can't stand for me to have anything nicer than you, can you? Goddamn it, that pisses me off so much," Nikki screamed, while running out.

"Believe me—I did not want to do that. It *was* an accident!" Chiquita said.

"I can glue it back together, Nick; it can be fixed," Brad said, coming to Chiquita's defense.

"It was perfect the way it was, and now it's not. Damn it, this pisses me off. I know the factory in Murano can make another piece and ship it to me, but then I'll have to *wait* for it to be shipped, and on top of all that I will have to *pay* for it. Damn it, damn it, damn, it. Why do I even try?"

"Well, I will pay for it. It's not like I did it on purpose, it was an accident, ya know," Chiquita said, while sweating bullets. Brad glued the broken piece together, the replacement part was ordered, blown, shipped, installed, and eventually the chandelier was as good as new. Well...almost. Feelings were hurt, and time apart would do them both good. About six months.

—◆—

Chiquita decided this probably *was* a good time to get away from the "mad cow" (his words, not mine) across the street to visit his younger brother, in Mary-land, who also happened to be queer. Nikki was left in charge of pet-sitting Chiquita's precious babies, Miss Anne, the wrinkly old shar-pei, his two old house cats, Fido and Butch, and let's not forget Lusty, the horny cockatiel. Busty, the aged female, died last year, and now that she was gone he continuously humped the mirror instead of her.

On his first day pet-sitting, Nikki noted how shabby the place had become. He hadn't been in Chiquita's home since Rob moved, but he'd certainly noticed how he was letting the outside crumble away, and it really steamed him, because he was doing everything in his power to improve his home and lift the entire neighborhood. Shit was stacked everywhere. It was just plain filthy, disgraceful and certainly not the same spic-and-span space since Rob moved from the place.

It was late in the evening of the fourth day, while Nikki was uselessly slathering anti-aging cream on his repuckering old puss; he remembered he forgot to feed the pets. So he slid on old mules, pulled his heather-died mink car coat over his same old, snagged-up, once-white shorty bathrobe, and tiptoed his way across the street to feed the famished pets—hopefully unnoticed by the nosy neighbors. When he walked in, he discovered Miss Anne lying in her fluffy nest, peacefully slumbering.

Shuffling closer, he whispered to her, "Miss Anne, sweetheart, wake up. It's Auntie Nikki, and it's din-din time." But she would never be waking again—because she was stone-cold dead. He tried his hardest not to, but he began to bawl while placing a snagged-up old blanket over her wrinkly lifeless carcass, because he just couldn't stand to look at her another minute.

"Miss Anne. Oh dear God, what am I ever going to tell Chiquita?" Then he looked around for the cats. "Here kitty, kitty, kitty. Butch, Fido!" he called, between his heaving sobs. "Oh, where the hell can they be? They're usually right here getting fuzzy fuzz all over my good slacks!"

Glancing over to the big white Victorian wire birdcage, he nearly went into shock, because Lusty, the dirty old bird, was laying stone-cold dead on the bottom of his filthy cage, with his little feet sticking straight out, and his little pecker sporting a hard-on.

"*Oh my Gawd!* There's a goddamned gas leak in here—lllllllooooook oooouuuuuuuuuuut!"

Bolting out the door and speed-shuffling barelegged through the blowing snow in bedroom mules as fast as he could, he was heading for home and the phone to call for "*Hellllllllllp!*"

"911. What is the nature of your emergency?"

"Emergency, emergency oh thank God you're there! Please help! *Helllp!* There's a gas leak. Please hurry. The dog is dead! Hurry! The bird is dead, hurry. The cats are dead, too. Hurry, hurry. Oh, please hurry, because I'm certain the house is about to blow at any second!"

Red lights were flashing and sirens blasting as the emergency trucks pulled into the driveway. Suddenly the big red doors burst open, ejaculating big burly men wearing rubbers and raincoats. Nikki went speed-shuffled back to Chiquita's to meet them. *"Oh thank God you're here Officers, there's a gas leak and all the pets are dead!"*

"Step aside, ma'am."

Donning black rubber respirators, they swarmed through the wide-open front door. Nikki stood barelegged and bawling, while shivering and shaking, and biting on the sleeve of his shorty mink. "Poor, poor old Miss Anne. How will I ever tell Chiquita about her dying, and the cats, and the bird, too? Dear God, what will I do?"

A crowd of nosy neighbors quickly assembled, wanting to know what was going on, and no one claimed to know a thing, especially Nikki. Several minutes later two frightened felines went frantically flying out the gaping front door, scared shitless by the invading masked men.

"Thank you, Jesus! The cats are alive!" Nikki exalted, lifting his mink-clad arms heavenward, bawling, and clasping his hands tightly to his age-defying, tear-stained face.

Sweaty emergency responders lumbered from the house and took off their gas masks. Clearly irritated with her, one of them asked, "There's no gas leak in there. Did ya smell gas? Or what?"

*"Well...*I walked in and found the dog dead, and then I found the bird dead, and when I couldn't find the cats I just *naturally* assumed they were dead, too. I guess I must've jumped to the *logical conclusion* that they were all dead from a gas leak, and that's when I called you. I'm so sorry, Officer."

"Better safe than sorry, ma'am. And, it's a real bummer about your dog. Tough break."

"Shut the front door."

This is a fucking catastrophe, Nikki thought. *What will I do about those damn escaped cats? And what am I going to do about the bodies?* Since Jim was away for some time yet and it was the dead of winter, it would be easier to keep the stiffs preserved. He thought of calling his friend in the funeral business and asking what to do with the perished pets. Should they be buried now, or would Jim want them cremated? He was just verklempt.

Knowing how close Chiquita was to Miss Anne, and also how fucking cheap he was, it was a very difficult decision. Christ almighty, he'd hauled his own mother to the gas chamber, in a cardboard box, just to save a few bucks on her cremation.

Dirty old bird hardly weighed a thing, was light as a feather as he was lowered into the Jimmy Choo shoebox and placed high upon a shelf on the lean-to porch, where he'd be held in cold storage until Jim came home. Miss Anne weighed fifty pounds; what would he do with her? The porch/morgue seemed to be the logical place for the perished pooch, too, because it was the walk-in cooler for most Michiganders during winter. When Chiquita returned home *he* could figure out how to dispose of them. But he was completely done in now, and went home to cry himself a river.

In the morning Nikki located the cashmere blanket he'd purchased in Venice a little while back, and because those damn pampered pussies had shredded it up and completely ruined it he wanted to destroy the evidence. It was also the softest thing he owned, and he wanted to comfort Miss Anne. But she was stiff as a board now and her wrinkly old legs were sticking straight out like four table legs. He was practically blinded from bawling, but he tried picking her up and carrying her to the porch anyway. She was dead weight. And when he finally managed to lift her, those rigid legs kept knocking shit off shelves, and when she knocked a gallon of shocking pink paint off; dropping it to the ground, splashing it open, and spattering it in every direction, he fucking lost it.

"Why...why...why do I even try?"

Walking backward and dragging lifeless Miss Ann like a kiddy pull toy, he pushed open the door with his ample ass, laid her on the snowy bank, and went back inside to clean up the monumental mess. He'd managed to splatter pink paint everywhere on the porch, the pooch, his legs, and mules.

"Damn it, damn it," he lamented, while scrubbing the stinking pink paint from the porch. "Jesus Christ, just *look at me*! I'm cleaning the goddamned cleaning lady's house now. Why do I even try?"

Three days later, when Chiquita *finally* came home, Nikki tried to tell him what happened but he began to bawl instead, and the tears flowed like Niagara Falls after a heavy spring rain. "Waaaaaaaaaaaa, I'm so sorry, honey. I don't know how it happened, waaaaaaaaaaaaaa."

"Wha' happened? What are you talking about, Nikki?"

"There was a teensie-weensie little problem while you were away, honey. Waaaaaaaaaaaaaaa."

"What is it, honey?"

"It's...Missssssssssssss Aaaaaaaaannnnnnnnnnne."

"What's the matter with Miss Anne?"

Nikki couldn't speak anymore; he just blubbered into his lavender-scented hankie and shook like a bowl of Jell-O on a vibrator. "Awwww!"

"Is she gone, honey? Is that what you're trying to tell me? *Oh*...she was really old, ya know. She's already lived much longer than she shoulda. Oh, it's okay, honey," he said, tearing up while comforting Nikki as he blubbered.

"There's more," he heaved and sobbed. "Dirty Bird, awwwwwww, he's dead, too. I don't know how it happened. I'm so terribly sorry, honey, awwwwwwwwww."

"Don't you carry on so. I was tired of hearing him squawking and humping the mirror all the time anyway. It's okay, honey—now, don't you cry."

"Awwwwwwwwww," Nikki bawled, bellowing harder. "That's not all there's more."

"Wha?" Chiquita said, stymied, and looking at him, confused. "How could there possibly be?"

"Butch and Fido."

"Oh dear God, now, don't tell me you killed the cats, too!"

"Well...no...they're not dead...just missing. When the firemen came they..."

"*Firemen?* Just what the hell happened here anyway?"

"Well...the firemen came because of the gas leak..."

"*Gas leak?*"

"Yes, and that's when the cats escaped. They've been gone for three whole days now and I can't find them anywhere, and I've been driving the neighborhood and searching like a crazy woman off her meds looking for them; and yelling 'Fido, Butch, here kitty, kitty, kitty' till I'm hoarse."

"Oh don't you worry 'bout them cats, honey. I can get 'em. Let's just call it a night, shall we?"

"You have no idea what I have been through here, Missy! No idea at alllllllllllllll!" He bawled away, his fat face red and shiny and streaked with salty tears.

"Oh, it'll be okay, honey, it'll be okay. Thanks again, sweetie. You can go home now."

"Don't ever ask me to pet-sit again. I'm going home to bawl myself to sleep."

〜 〜

Chiquita thought, *Babysit what pets?* There weren't any pets left; the house was pet-free thanks to Nikki. But he still had to figure out what to do with the past-tense pets. Because he was living hand-to-mouth now, he didn't have the cash to bury them legitimately, so he would have to do it illegitimately. The next day he pulled a rusty shovel from the shed and removed three feet of snow above the frozen ground, but he couldn't get the shovel into the dirt because it was frozen solid. So he moved to plan B: build a fire, thaw the ground, and dig a hole big enough to accommodate two tiny pets; sounded simple.

He never dreamed it would take five days of continuously burning junky old furniture, apple crates, newspapers, charcoal, love letters, and anything else flammable before the ground softened enough to dig a burial chamber large enough to accommodate the deceased pets.

Chiquita gently placed Miss Anne, wrapped in Nikki's $3,000 cash-smear blanket, down into the icy burial chamber, along with the horny old bird she'd be spending eternity with, and said a prayer.

"Dominoes and biscuits, God bless 'em." He blotted his eyes, blew his nose, and threw on the dirt.

Ramen.

— ￫

Meanwhile, back across the street at the Château, the holidays came and went with their usual splendor. A magnificently mounded, ten-foot-tall Fraser fir was placed into the mammoth mirrored bay window of the grandiose room. The overtrimmed tree could barely hold its droopy branches up because it was so weighted down with opulent hand-blown ornaments that it appeared to be dripping glass.

This hoochied-up Hanukkah bush was the centerpiece of his holiday décor d'excess. The other element was a garland made from freshly harvested herbs, which was designed especially for him and nicknamed the "Saint Nikki Garland." This herbed holiday roping was made of silvery sage, yummy yarrow, tangy tansy, comfy comfrey, and bits of yew with berries of blue, and some fuzzy lamb's ear was added, too. This luxury potpourri also included sweet Annie, sweet grassy, rusty-red rosehips, red-berried holly, and fragrant boughs of cedar, by golly, making the house smell incredibly holiday. And several poinsettias were strategically placed, to add some color to the peaked old place.

Across the street, at Chiquita's, the season also came and went, only with fewer pets. He no longer put up any Christmas décor at all, not even one tree, or outside lights, because with Rob gone and being alone for the holidays, it just didn't make much sense.

When the holidays were over, winter's wicked death grip once again descended upon us, and Nikki needed a little project, a divertimento: the reconstruction and redecoration of the kitchen. He'd given this considerable consideration, and marble countertops were an absolute must. He also needed a cooktop for the contrasting marble island, double-stacked ovens, compactor, dishwasher, microwave, and a large-capacity side-by-side subzero refrigerator to hold his nibbles and the kitties kibbles.

But this was just a little spruce-up, you understand, because he mostly ate out. When he did cook he used the George Foreman Grill, because he didn't want to dirty up the kitchen. Nonetheless, this renovation had to be dazzling, because it was his crescendo, a complement to the gaudy chandelier. It's kinda like trailer decorator Lee said, "You always need a theme." Nikki had given this a lot of thought, and his theme was loosely interpreted as "excess," in the MacKenzie-Childs fashion. For those of you who don't know the names, you should. They are the two upstart artists from upstate New York who make the grossly expensive, pastel-painted pottery pieces that Nikki coveted and collected. Their high-priced housewares and pricy do-dads are sold at the Needless Markup store, and you really should consider buying stock in their company, because Nikki was constantly purchasing more pieces to replace the ones Chiquita was continuously "accidentally" breaking for Aunt Lucy's craft projects.

"*I* was thinking," Nikki began his decoration summation. "Since *I* already own all of these fabulous hand-painted MacKenzie knobs, drawer pulls, and handles, and every single one of them is a deliciously different pattern, *I* will use them on the cupboards when *I* renovate. Now, what *I* want *you* to do is take the patterns from each knob and expand that to cover the entire door. I'll use the buttons on the cupboards, the braided handles on the drawers, and the checkered fishies on the sinkbase cabinet doors facing each other and kissing. Whatcha think, honey?"

"Whoa, that sounds awfully busy to me. That's an awful lot of pattern."

"I'm so glad you agree with me. I think it's a fabulous idea, too. Next I was thinking I should paint a little border around the top of the room, and maybe use another MacKenzie pattern; I see floral. Wouldn't that be fabulous? Maybe I should do a little something simple on the ceiling, too, such as the Sistine Chapel, or the heavens with white clouds and *me* up there, painted as a pretty putti. And I just love that black-and-white-checkered thingie they do, too, so I'll work some of that in, too.

"Feel free to jump in and give me some input," he said, appearing quite irritated that I wasn't lit up like the Rockefeller Christmas tree at the very thought of painting his chaotic vision.

"Jesus Mary, that sounds like an awful lot going on in this little kitchen. Maybe you should use a little less pattern. I can dilute the colors so they will look watercolor-like, similar to the brushwork on your pottery pieces, and keep it low-key."

"Do I look like a low-key kind of person to you?" {He said while dressed in a green velvet one-piece jumpsuit.} "*No*, I don't think so either. So don't *you* tell *me* what I want, Missy! I want *everything*, and I *will not settle for anything less*. Now, as I was saying before I was interrupted, I want you to do something with the back of this boring old steel security door, too. Perhaps you can paint a giant crusty urn with a magnificent flower arrangement spilling from it. I just love gaily colored flowers."

"Maybe we should add a black-and-white checkerboard behind that; it's sounding kinda plain."

"Love it, love it, *loooove it*. Do it."

"I was only kidding."

"Well, I'm not, so you just add that to your little do-list, honey."

"That just leaves this boring old wainscot here untouched. Maybe we should paint it with a black-and-white check, too. Let's add one more thing in here while we're at it," I sarcastically said.

"*Ooooh!* I just adore that idea, honey. I just love their black-and-white check thingy, and I was wanting more of it in here. That's brilliant, honey, tell me more. And let's marbleize the woodwork, too."

"Nikki, that means that the only surface in this entire kitchen that doesn't have any designs painted on it is the floor, and that's way too much—waaaaay too busy."

"Oh, thank you for reminding me, honey. I wanted you to paint something on that nasty old wood floor, too. A black-and-white checker; or maybe I should do a stripe. Whatcha think?"

"Leave it be, please. Give my poor eyes a place to rest."

"Well, aren't we getting testy? Oh, honey, you are such a simple thing, aren't you? Well, you just put that on your little list, and paint that nasty floor with a rustic black-and-white checkerboard."

"About twelve inches?"

"Ooooooh, I would *love* twelve inches, love it, love it, lllllllove it."

The work was scheduled, appliances painstakingly shopped for and purchased, and in the meantime Brad gutted the old kitchen, updated the wiring and plumbing, and installed the new stainless steel sink, dishwasher, trash compactor, and appliances. Then it was time to get stoned. So, Nikki and I visited Mr. Gotrock's glamour-stone show-room to select his new counters.

"You know, I simply *adore* that blue lapis (doorknob-sized) pinky ring I got when we were in Greece. Wouldn't a dark blue countertop be absolutely fabulous? It'll match the chandelier, and I know how much you like that matchy-matchy stuff, Murf. Oh my, would you look at all the pretty stones they have in this place. This rock lot is huge, honey!"

"I know. Let's go see the salesman, Kurt."

"Oh, he's cute. Yes, let's ask him to show us what he has. Pretty, pretty please."

"Hello, Kurt, this is my friend Nikki Clark, and he's interested in purchasing some lapis lazuli stone for his countertops. Do you happen to have any?"

"Hey, Den, and hello Mr. Clark, it's nice to meet you. Let me just check the inventory. Ah, yes, here we go." Pulling a three-by-three, one-inch-thick chunk of the semiprecious stone from the safe, he handed it to Nikki.

"Yes. That's it! That is *exactly* what I'm looking for. How fabulous! *How much*?"

"Okay, now, since this is considered a semiprecious stone the sample you're holding requires a four-hundred-dollar deposit. I've checked stock availability and there are only two slabs in the country. I can tag them for you if you'd like. One is priced at forty thousand, and the other, which is slightly larger, is listed at sixty," Kurt said, unapologetically.

"Well..." Nikki nonchalantly volleyed right back, not missing a beat, "since I'm already here, let me just see what else you got."

"Please do look around, and let me know when I can be of assistance."

The airplane hangar–size building was filled with thousands of slabs of marbles, granites, slates, and quartz, in shades of red, yellow, blue, brown, and green. We each selected several suitable samples, and I chose several subtle stones. Nikki picked out bright yellow marble, bold black-and-white high-contrast granites, gaudy green malachite, glittery blue quartz, and not a beige one in the bunch.

For the main counters he chose a black, white, and dappled-gray marble with fancy flashes of blue quartz. A contrasting slab of white, with black-and-blue flashes, was selected for the island. The slabs still had to be measured, templated, fabricated, and installed, and the entire process would take about six weeks to complete. He hated waiting for anything. It displeased him immeasurably.

While he was waiting to get stoned, the rest of the renovation pushed forward. But all of this destruction made an unsightly mess which nearly drove him over the edge, and he was perilously close already. And with the kitchen being located on the home's central axis, one had to pass through there to access the great room, bedroom, den; both bathrooms, and the basement—excuse me, the lower level.

Gritty dust freely floated about and settled everywhere. Then the dust was pumped by the furnace blower, became springtime freshened, and distributed everywhere it couldn't reach on its own; the entire house was coated in white. It found its way into every cupboard, inside the bed, drawers, and the closets, too. You were constantly blowing sticky wads of it out your irritated nose.

This mess displeased Nikki immensely. And even though he didn't make the mess, Chiquita got the blame for its existence. After all, it was his job to keep the house clean, now, wasn't it?

— ~

So, after Brad finished his reconstruction, it was my turn, and my job was to embellish the shit.

First the walls were painted a lovely color somewhere between cantaloupe and peach flesh, and the cupboards done in a nice almond joy. The multitudes of patterns from the fancy-schmancy knobs were painted on the doors, and by keeping the colors light and semitransparent; it made the many colors and patterns have a cohesive look, similar to a quilt.

The ceiling was painted with soft and fluffy off-white clouds, and set against the palest of blue skies, making it subtle and pretty.

"You're not finished with that ceiling, are you?" Nikki quipped, fresh from work and still wearing his beauty smock.

"I thought I was, yes. It's a very low ceiling, and you shouldn't draw attention to it."

"Says who? This is my house, damn it, and I'll tell you what I want to draw attention to. *Everything.* I want more, damn it. And I don't like that boring vanilla shit you painted on the walls one bit. I want bold, bright, color, and contrast! Take this boring beige shit away and add fabulousness."

But by now I was sore and stiff, exhausted from standing on a ladder all day with my arms held above my head and painting the heavens, and not in the mood for his theatrics. "I thought it should be subtle. That's enough; I still have to paint a border around the room, the steel security door, wainscot, and the f—." I couldn't get out the *F* out before I was cut off.

"I am *not* subtle. I don't *like* subtle. I don't *want* subtle. I don't *do* subtle. I want a deep, dark, bold, and in-your-face blue color like on that chandelier. And paint some more vines around that chandelier, and make that ivy shockingly green, and have it trailing way out onto the ceiling," Nikki demanded, while pointing toward the heavens in classic form.

"Well, it's not happening today. I'll see you tomorrow."

"We are not finished here, Missy. I'm tired of paying too much and not getting what I want."

"I'm not the reason you're unhappy, and I am going home." Then I remembered tomorrow was his day off, and he'd be home all day. Shit. I hated conflict, especially between friends. But I was not going to indulge his theatrical, tyrannical behavior. This was a night for a long hot bath and a joint.

Thursday morning I dawdled, stopped to get coffee, and picked up paint before going to Nikki's. Luckily he was visiting the dry cleaner, pet groomer, spray-on suntanner, and manicurist, so I could paint in peace. When I arrived at the Château, I found a note taped to the door.

> Denial,
> Do not do *anything* until I get back from the dry cleaners, about nine o'clock.
> Nick.

Uh-oh. *Denial*, not Den, Denny, Midge, Murf, or even honey; this was the equivalent of your mother using your entire name. When mothers were particularly pissed they'd yell out all three names when calling you home, and you knew you were in deep shit. It was nearing nine and he would be back soon, so I cleaned up, organized, and prepared to paint the border. Seeing the Jag pulling into the drive, hearing the car door close, and the kitchen door open, I braced myself.

"Morning," I said cheerfully.

"Morning," he drolly responded, as if I'd just told him he had terminal cancer. "Let me put this dry cleaning away and then I want to speak to you." I felt my face flushing, as if I were about to go to the principal's office. How bad was it going to be?

"Back. Now, do you see how dark that blue is in that chandelier? Well, I want you to use that color for the sky, deep, dark, in-your-face blue, and not that baby blue crap you painted. The greenery for those leaves needs to be an in-your-face green, too, and work in some more of that bright orange somewhere, maybe berries—or a butterfly. I want this color *intense*. I am not a subtle person."

You certainly got that right, Stella, I thought to myself.

Then he reached into his cupboard, removed a ruffled-oval MacKenzie side dish, and placed it on the counter. Then he removed an egg from the fridge, cracked it on the marbleous counter-top, and dropped it into the dish. His face was shiny and red; steamed, fighting mad. "Now, this is yellow, damn it! I want y-e-l-l-o-w in here, not his namby-pamby beigey crappy color you've painted. Look at this egg—now this is yellow!" he said, pointing adamantly at the yolk.

"Okay. Let me get the color chip book and you can select the exact shade you want," I said. Taxes were due again. Searching through the yellows several times, he finally settled upon the shade that gave him the most joy, #127, electric school bus yellow. Definitely not your mellow yellow.

"Yellow is such a happy color for a kitchen, don't cha think?" Nikki chirped, already happier. He'd selected the shade he felt was closest to egg yolk and I did not disagree. I bought the hideous paint—and a pair of sunglasses. He departed to "run errands," the school-bus-accident yellow was painted over the boring beige walls, and we were nearly finished when he returned. From way outside you could see the room glowing like a high-intensity mercury parking lot light at midnight.

"Oh my!" he said, taking one look. "Oh dear, that is awfully bright, honey. I may have made a teensy little mistake. That is sooo yellow, I don't know if I like that, or not."

Not.

It took three full gallons of snow white, added to a half gallon of the remaining egg yolk, to create a color that he found happy enough to settle upon. Even after diluting it to his satisfaction, I still had to wear the sunglasses when applying it to the walls, because it was that bright. But I never had to say a word about the yell-ah, or the day's work lost in the process.

"Now, about the border, Nikki, I was thinking of using the tulip decoration from your enormous MacKenzie casserole/bathtub. I'll paint red tulips with green leaves, one pointing up, and one down, and then zigzag them around the room. Here, I have it drawn to scale," I said, showing him the sketch.

"Oh, I like that, honey, and how big is it going to be?"

"Ten inches; the headers above the doorways will establish your size limit. I can make it to fill that entire space and create a custom fit, so it will go around the room uninterrupted."

"Ten inches, and a custom fit, I like the sound of that, honey. Now, I want you to repaint this boring ceiling today, while I'm here, because I want to make sure you're doing exactly what I want. I don't want that pastel shit you painted. I want bold, dramatic. Remember, the customer's always right, and I'm the customer, so I'm always right! Right?"

But we managed to reach a satisfactory solution by compromising. I painted exactly what he wanted, wherever he wanted it. Fluffy white clouds had small patches of in-your-face dark blue poking out here and there, with scads of shockingly green trailing ivy flowing from that expensive chandelier. When I threw in a couple of bright orange monarch butterflies, gaily flittering around, to shut him up, it was completed to his satisfaction.

I tried convincing him that it probably wasn't a good idea to paint the wainscoting with a black-and-white checkerboard, because the pot hanger, steel security door, and kitchen floor were going to be painted with a check also, and for me that would be *waaaay* too much. Compromising again, we did almost what he wanted. By using the wall color for a background, and a lighter shade of yellow for the check, I made a yellow-on-yellow checkerboard, in the lovely new MacKenzie-Childs Courtly Check.

From that point on I pretty much prostituted myself, and renamed my business Art Whore. I painted whatever he wanted, wherever he wanted it, because it was futile to fight him. We'd crossed over the edge long ago. The massive Victorian woodwork was marbleized in a rusty peach color, with pearly white veins, and even the light switches and plug plates were painted with gaudy colors and busy patterns, in the MacKenzie-Childs fashion.

The big backboard that held up the massive cast-iron pot hanger {for the cookwear he never uses} was painted with yet another black-and-white check. And the security door was painted exactly as he'd envisioned it, with a gargantuan crusty urn, just oozing with garishly colored flowers, and yet another fucking black-and-white check for the background. It was Las Vegas on steroids, and he loved it, loved it, *loved* it. Like Mickey Mouse playing the wizard in *Fantasia*, he was creating his fantasy.

"Ya know, Murf, if I could paint the way you do, this place would be gaudy as hell," Nikki said.

"God help us."

After the painting was finished, he wanted to make some serious acquisitions. What he really needed was thermal windows, a new roof, and furnace, but nobody saw those boring things. Instead, he bought a sixty-inch-round MacKenzie glazed ceramic table, in their pretty Myrtle pattern, and four ridiculously expensive, hand-painted fish-back chairs. So it shall be said, so it shall be done.

He was just thrilled; it was all coming together so nicely.

The recently refinished wooden kitchen floor, which never met his critical approval, was faux painted in yet another fucking checker-board, and varnished. Now, remember, he wanted it rustic, but while drying the varnish bubbled, leaving tiny pockmarks, and that very much displeased him. We had more words, which I will spare you. The very next week Brad installed a brand-new twelve-by-twelve, black-and-white ceramic tile floor, over the one I was just paid to paint and distress.

When all was said and done, all parties were worn down, exhausted, deflated, and ready for the insanity to end. Everything that could possibly change was changed, and several times. Poor Chiquita was cleaning drywall dust from drawers, closets, and crannies for months, and the two inbred Persian pussies were relieved as well, because now they could come out of hiding and reclaim their palace.

And there it was—Nikki finally had the fabulous fucking kitchen of his dreams. So the first thing he did was put up red velvet rop-ing to seal it off, because it was mostly for display, and he went back to frying pork chops on the George Foreman countertop grill so he wouldn't dirty up his brand new kitchen. Once again, peace reigned in the queendom.

Chiquita was cleaning and performing all his other functions at the Château, plus working for Katie and Lucy, and selling stuff at the flea market all summer. But after Rob moved out he discovered he needed a few more bucks, so he took on a couple of new cleaning clients, both referred by Nikki.

But somehow Chiquita had just plain lost interest in life. When he couldn't afford health insurance any more, he stopped taking Ritalin, which helped focus his thoughts, and without it he was scattered as hell. He also started to slack off from his previous hyper-cleaning behaviors. After lazily throwing in a load of laundry, he'd run home to catch an episode of *Green Acres*, and be back in an hour *or so* to toss them into the dryer. Then he'd run home to catch *The Beverly Hillbillies*, return to the fold clothes, and put them away. Returning home for lunch, he'd watch the noon news and then slide into the afternoon with *Mr. Ed*. Between *Petticoat Junction* and *Leave It to Beaver*, he'd do a little light cleaning, go back home, and return to Nikki's after *I Love Lucy* to wash the multitude of mirrors and the inside windows. But that was only after checking the progress of his online auctions.

"Boy, the house certainly smells clean, Chiquita. What have you been using to make it smell so fabulous?" Nikki asked, when returning from work to find him folding towels.

"That there is elbow grease you smell burnin', Stella."

Why...that was the most peculiar thing, because when I asked him that exact same question, this was his reply: "There's a little trick I discovered, and if ya can keep a secret I'll share it with ya. Ya see, she don't think the place is clean unless it stinks a certain way. I tell ya, Stella, I can clean my ass off over here all day long and she won't notice a single thin'. So, now I just clean half a day, but I make sure it stinks good and plenty before I leave. Now, you and I both know that it don't have nothin' to do with how the place smells, you actually have to do some cleanin'."

Leaning in real close, he whispered, "First ya take some of these here Downy dryer sheets, the 'springtime fresh' ones, and ya place 'em over the furnace filter and the floor vents, so's every time the furnace comes on you get a brand-new whiff of springtime freshness. There's that little trick, and this one: I buy this Spring Meadows mortuary carpet cleanin' powder, in fifty-pound bags, and liberally spread the shit around. It smells like a funeral home full of flowers. He thinks he's died and went to heaven, and I've been over here cleanin' all day long."

"Why, Chiquita, that's absolutely wicked."

"*Wicked my ass!* You just try cleanin' over here, especially that disgusting bathroom of his, just once. I just hate cleanin' that filthy crapper; I practically have to wear a hazmat suit. Besides having all the ca-ca, there's that damn blond yak fur that's stuck all over everything and then glued down with the tacky Aqua Net hairspray he douses himself with. It's a wonder there's any hair left on those rugs of his at all the way the damn things shed! Shit, I work my ass off over here, and he's always accusin' me of just bein' over here all day watchin' porn and jackin' off, instead of workin'."

"Oh, yeah, I saw how hard you worked here today. By the way, what happened on *The Hillbillies* today?"

"It was so funny, Granny cooked up a batch-a her spring tonic, and Mrs. Drysdale got bombed on it and went traipsin' off, *happy as can be*. Now, you just keep that information to yourself, Judas."

"So you mean to tell me he has more than one wig?"

"Oh, heavens yes, Stella, where have you been? Look, he has a whole closet chock-full of yak fur. I tell ya, Stella, somewhere over in China there's a whole herd of neck-ed yaks roamin' around, scalped; given up their hides just to make him beautiful."

He pulled the gilded closet doors open and revealed several shelves with hair appliances in different shades of blond, with varying lengths, styles, and degrees of preparedness. All the spare hairs were mounted on white Styrofoam wig forms, with eerie felt-penned eyes that stared at us unnaturally.

There were also hundreds of other hair care products: tiny brown glass bottles of hair dye lined up like toy soldiers, which were used for coloring the itty-bitty bits of hair still left on his head, his eyebrows, sideburns, and the sometimes-worn mustache. A case of turquoise Aqua Net hairspray cans sat next to stacks of stained-up terry cloth towels, dye-discolored rubber gloves, a leopard beauty cape, and glass bowl and brush for application.

"Well, he certainly is unique. And it must make him feel prettier."

"Unique? For Christ's sake, when they made him they broke the mold and then they kicked the mold maker's ass."

— ~

Nikki was never pleased when he had to wait to be serviced. He'd already given up three of *his* Chiquita days to those two greedy girls, and as a result felt he was the last person to get his lawn cut, windows washed, and house cleaned. It was getting damn irritating, and he'd let Chiquita know it.

"Goddamn it, Jim, you were supposed to have this overgrown hay field mowed a week ago, and just look at it—it looks just like the trashy neighbors' lawns. Can you explain why *I* am *always* the *last* one to get my needs taken care of?"

"Well, for your information, *Nikki*, it has rained for three days in a row, and I was working the other four days. Do you mind if I take a day off? You take off three whole days a week, ya know."

"Well, I happen to work ten- and twelve-hour days; too, I'll have *you* know, *Missy*."

"Well, it's not going to happen today."

"Well, let's just forget about it altogether. I can get someone else to mow the grass. You just do what you have to, and I will do the same." Nikki turned and stormed away. Feelings were hurt, and they stayed that way for some time—you cannot take back angry words. But the final straw happened when Nikki came home early one afternoon and found him missing altogether. He'd usually be home around seven in the evening, but on that particular day the salon closed at eleven, because a drunken bitch had hit a power pole, causing a power outage, and you just can't make beautification without serious electrification.

Chiquita hadn't been there *at all*. He sniffed around and couldn't smell a thing, so he called him. When he didn't answer, it irritated him even more, and he left a nasty message.

"This is Nikki"—as if it could possibly be anyone else—"and just *where* the *hell* are you?" Click. Then he went on a manhunt to track the malingerer down. He suspected he was seeing another woman. Secretly snooping, he discovered he was at Katie's instead of *his* house and became even more irritated. "He was supposed to be working for me. I have needs, you know. Goddamn it, I'm calling his scrawny ass up and letting him know that he's put me off for the very last time."

"This is Nikki. Just where the hell are you and why aren't you over cleaning for me? This is *my* day, and you have put me off *yet again*?"

"Nikki, I told you I was helpin' Katie pack. She's leavin' for Africa to help the missionaries care for dyin' lepers," Chiquita said, most apologetically.

"I know you're at Katie's because I can see your ratty-assed van parked there right now. You did *not* tell me that, because I would have remembered that. You needn't bother coming anymore —ever. Return your keys, because your services are no longer *required* or *desired*."

Click.

　—　—

I was not immune from his wrath either. Now it was now my turn in the woodshed. It seemed Nikki was in the mood for a life change, so he called me. "Denial, I want change."

"You got a dollar? I'll bring you over four quarters."

"I am *not* amused. I want you to come over here and marbleize the woodwork in this living room. I want white marble with black veins— crisp, clean, and now."

"It's already marbleized. You had that painted just a couple years ago."

"It's been almost ten years. That stuff is old, tired, and yesterday. I want crisp, fresh, today, graphic, white marble with black veins. How soon can you get over here and get this done, anyway?"

"It's going to be about a month. I'm quite busy right now."

"*What?* Three weeks? You've got to be kidding. This displeases me immensely, *you know.* I hate waiting, you know."

"Believe me, I know."

"Well, put me down in the books. Just where the hell are you working, anyway?"

"I'm working at Joan's."

"*Her?* Oh hell, you can take care of her later. I need this done right away. Unlike some people I know, *she* likes me. I'll call her up and she will let me take cuts."

"Well..." she said, "I told him he could jest kiss my royal ala-bastard Scottish arse."

Four weeks later, I arrived on Monday morning to marbleize the woodwork, and nothing had been moved. None of the paintings had been taken off the walls, the Tara window treatments were still hanging at the windows, and nothing was done to facilitate painting. So the morning was wasted taking down the opulent window treatments, moving the massive furniture, and taking a museum's worth of paintings from the walls.

(This reminds me of a joke. What is the difference between a straight man and a gay man? Answer: curtains and window treatments.)

After exposing the woodwork, another hour was spent washing layers of greasy cat fuzz and plaster dust off them, and all because of Chiquita's housekeeping shortcomings. When arriving home from running all his errands, he was already peeved. "Denial, why haven't you done anything *yet*?"

"Are you serious? Do you actually think the furniture has moved itself, or those giant gone-with-the-window treatments just jumped down from up there? And do you have a picture of the type of marble you want? Because I asked you to find a picture."

"No, I don't have a picture. I want white marble with black veins. How hard can that possibly be? And how long is this going to take anyway? I don't want my house torn up forever."

"I'll probably get the woodwork cleaned, taped off, and primed today. I will marbleize it the next day or two, and varnish it the following day. There's a lot of woodwork, so about a week." He suddenly turned a lovely shade of scarlet, a color that was usually quite good on him, and stomped out of the room, most displeased. Forging on, I painted the woodwork with the gray primer.

"What the hell is that?" he said upon returning, "I wanted *white* woodwork, not *gray*."

"It's the primer, Nikki. I told you it was necessary to block out the old marble underneath. I'll build up the white as I do the veining. You'll need depth; you don't want it to look fake."

"Maybe not fake, but definitely *white!*"

He was not pleased, and it seemed there was just no pleasing him. He was mad, mean, and miserable, and I was not in the mood for another of his tantrums. I could feel one coming on, and figured Thursday would be the showdown.

"Are you done?"

"I thought so, yes. I'm going to varnish it today."

"Well, I don't like it. I don't like it one bit. This is not what I wanted at all. I clearly told you I wanted white marble with black veins, and you give me this busy gray bullshit."

"I can add more white, if you'd like."

"I don't like. Don't bother. You're done. Just pack up your belongings. What do I owe you?"

"Don't you want me to varnish the woodwork?"

"No. You've done quite enough already. Now, I'll ask you again, how much do I owe you?" We settled up, I went on my way, but I could tell he was really steamed. I wasn't thrilled either. As I was pulling out of the drive, he was calling another contractor to repaint the woodwork: *white* with *black* veins. How hard could that possibly be? When he was told that he'd have to wait five weeks to have it painted, and he would have to rehang the artwork, curtains, move the furniture back, and then go through this mess again in five weeks, well that just made him all the madder.

We did not speak for quite some time after this episode.

Bless his persnickety heart.

What Are Friends For?

Suddenly the dogs were going berserk, barking and howling, jolting him awake, and heading for the front door, the one he never used. Chiquita couldn't figure what the commotion was, and checked the visually impaired digital clock next to the bed. It was four twenty.

Fumbling around, he yelled, "Where the hell are them glasses?" He couldn't see shit without them. Flipping on the glaring overhead light, he gingerly tiptoed his way through the cluttered debris field of a bedroom to the front door, where the dogs were barking, and having conniption fits.

"Duke, shut up! Rotunda, shut up!" Straining his weak Mole Man eyes, he peered through the tiny peephole into total darkness, and didn't see a thing. But the dogs were still going insane. *Must be a coon, possum, or maybe a skunk*, he thought. "Duke, shut up! Rotunda, shut up! Shhhhh!" But he just couldn't silence them.

So he left the tiny peephole and walked into the courtin'-room, squinted out the window, and gasped! "Dear God!" he shrieked, because Nikki was lying prostrate on the porch. Flying to the foyer, he frantically unlocked all three dead bolts, and peeled open the swollen squealing door.

"Nikki, oh God, what's wrong, honey? Look at you—you're white as a sheet. Jesus help me."

Breathing in shallow labored pants, he was trying desperately to speak. "I c...c...can't ...b ...b...breath...h...he...hell...help...me."

Seeing it was only the neighbor lady, the dogs ceased their frantic howling and went back to their nests. Chiquita tried getting Nikki up from the dewy porch, but he was practically dead weight, livid, and struggling to breathe. His knees were bloodied and his bedclothes muddied.

"What happened to you, honey? Oh dear God! I better call a am-balance right away."

Nikki tried speaking, but was unable. "Craw," he breathlessly spat out.

"Craw? Crawl? You crawled all the way across the street? Oh dear God, you're awfull sickly, honey. We gotta get you to the hospitable right away. Now, you wait here and I'll go get the van."

Pulling the sin-bin onto the side lawn, he backed the van as close to the porch as he could, threw open the double back doors, rolled Nikki onto the burgundy braided rug, and dragged him into the van. He'd have to leave him lying on the filthy floor because there was no way could he lift him. Gray and ghastly, tiny specks of brick red porch paint were peppering his clammy skin. Scared shitless, Chiquita was driving like a madman escaping the asylum, because he could hear him gasping for breath.

Why am I so fucking stupid? I shoulda called a goddamned am-balance, he thought. Then he prayed that Nikki wouldn't die before they got there. Help me, Jesus. "We're almost there. Hang on, Stella. Don't die yet, we're almost there."

Screeching into the emergency bay, he slammed on the brakes, threw the van into Park, and flew out the door and went running in-side. "*Help! Help!* I need help now!"

Nikki was dragged out of the van—while still lying on the rug—and placed on a gurney. They quickly whisked him into the triage unit and strapped an oxygen mask on his pale, paint-peppered face, and Chiquita followed, praying hard as he could.

"Jesus, MaryJane, and Josephine, dominoes and biscuits. Ramen."

— ~

"What's happened to her?" the doctor asked Chiquita sternly.

"I don't know, Docker, he just showed up at my front door this way. He lives across the street from me and we haven't spoken in two years. I'm sorry I can't be more help-full."

"Does *he* have any medical conditions that you are aware of—epilepsy, heart trouble, diabetes, health insurance? Do you know what his name is?"

"Oh Jesus, yes, I'm sure he's insured. And his name is Nikki, Nikki Clark. I'm so sorry, Docker."Nikki Clark? Oh dear God, he does my wife's hair. Nurse, quickly, what are his vitals?"

"Heart rate and blood pressure way up, breathing labored. A fever of one hundred and four."

— ~

"Denny, I'm sorry to call you so early, it's Chiquita. It's about Nikki. He's awful sick, I took him to the hospital this mornin' and just got home. They think its ammonia. Seen it before, ya know."

"Oh my God, I haven't seen him since the marbleizing incident. Has he been sick long?"

"As you well know, since I quit we haven't spoken, and it's been almost two years."

"What happened?"

"Well...after Rob moved out I got myself more security, because this neighborhood is getting' just terry-bull. Ya know? Did you know that Flint was voted the most violent city in the country again? They're the titleholder third year runnin'."

"Go, Flint. It's nice to see us finally topping some important lists, we are overachieving in murder, robbery, assault, and unemployment."

"Anyway...as I was sayin'...I got myself these two big dogs now, and last night, about four in the mornin', the dogs just went berserk. Well, it was Nikki; he'd collapsed on my front porch. Seems he crawled all the way across the street on his hands and knees, through gravel and broken glass, and in his summer shorty pajamas no less. I tell you, he was just a bloody mess. You shoulda seen him."

"Did you put sanitary pads and purple rubber bands on him?"

"Oh, you're a twisted bitch." He burst out laughing till he had another coughing fit. "Oh! Thank you, I needed that, but seriously, he's real sick. I'm awful worried for him."

"I bet it scared the shit out of you, didn't it?"

"Sure as hell did. Honest to God, I thought he was gonna die in my van. I'm still shakin'. Had to administer myself a double dose-a vitamin-gin an' tonic for my frazzled nerves."

"Chiquita, cocktails at six o'clock in the morning!"

"Well, it's five o'clock somewhere just west of here."

"Why'd you drive him to the hospital? You should have called an ambulance."

"Well, I know that *now*. To tell you the truth, Stella, I had a few medicinal tonic waters last night, and wasn't thinkin' quite right. But you shoulda seen him, it was terra-fyin'; he was limp as a noodle, plastered to the porch, and peppered with paint pocks. I could barely drag him into the van. She weighs a ton, ya know."

"Don't I know."

He was held in the intensive care unit for five days as they stabilized his vitals and got his raging infection under control. On the sixth day of his hospitalization, he was moved to a private room where family was allowed to visit, so Chiquita and I went to see him.

"Denny, I've called up there ever' single day and they just give me the same old rig-a-marole—he's stable, responsive, but still in the critical care unit, and only family can visit. Like that'll ever happen. He's still really sick, ya know," Chiquita said.

"They tell me the very same thing."

We arrived at his room bearing a bouquet of gaudy flowers, but we found an unrecognizable withered old man lying in the bed, who was bald as a cue ball except for a monk's ring of unkempt hair surrounding his head, and tiny moustache.

"There's some bald old geezer in there. They musta moved him," Chiquita said, befuddled.

I squinted into the room and scrutinized the little old man lying in the sickbed, and I wasn't sure if it was him *either.* But the room was full of gushy flower arrangements, and that confirmed it *was* Nikki. Hearing us approach, he slowly opened his eyes.

"Oh dear God, it *is* him," Chiquita gasped, clutching his fist and biting his bony white knuckles. He saw us and fumbled with his oxygen mask, smiled weakly, and spoke haltingly.

"Hel...lo. Goo...good...to...see...you," Nikki breathily said, completely winded.

We had no idea it was this serious; he didn't look at all like the Nikki we knew. We never saw him without his hair on, and when scalped he looked like a tiny wayward monk, shrunken and waxy. Tubes and wires were running to and fro, monitors beeping away, and IVs dripping life-giving fluids into his fragile arms. Each of us took a chilled hand and he faintly smiled. Tears spilled from his eyes and rolled down his deathly white cheeks. We all had a moment. He was a very sick and unable to speak, so we kept him company until he fell asleep, kissed him on the cheek, and departed.

The nurses filled us in on his progress; it was ammonia. He wasn't circling the drain, but still a very sick man. Three days later we visited again and he was more alert, waving when he saw us.

— ~

"Stella, would you look at you," Chiquita quipped.

"Hello, Nikki," I added.

Pulling his oxygen mask down, he breathlessly uttered, "Okay, get it... over, go ahead, say...somethin'...nasty... have your fun with me."

"You look a lot better today, honey," I said.

"Oh, fuck you, too, you old bitch." He certainly had enough wind to say *that* without a problem.

"You look like Captain Kangaroo," Chiquita said. "Sorry, that just slipped out. The Tourette's."

"Come here, Chick-eat-ah, and let me give you a big ol' smack. Thank you... for helpin' me, hon-knee. I love you...bay-bee, you know that, don't you?"

"I'm sorry we haven't spoken for so long. I'm a stupid, stubborn fool."

"Come here," Nikki said, with arms opened wide. Embracing, they had a mushy moment.

But their mushy moment was quickly shattered. "Would you look at those two old lesbians making out in that hospital bed? Jesus, it looks like a fuckin' funeral home in here, there's so many fuckin' flowers. Well, you might as well have some more, ya dyin' old bitch. It's your wicked stepsisters and we brought you party favors: cheesecake, bourbon and coke, and coke. Whoo-hooo!"

It was the naughty boys from Salon Rich-Bitch, the gays he worked with every day, Barry, Timika, Sebastian, and little Ricky. A party quickly ensued, and the station nurses even joined in after being served a slice of Oliver T's heavenly cheesecake.

Nikki, being too weak to protest, was unable to fight them off, so they hugged him, gushed and fussed over him, and he just had to lay there and take it. And then, as if right on cue, Joany came swooping in like Auntie Mame (the Lucille Ball version).

"Oh my dear, *dear* friend, I came as soon as they told me the terrible news. Oh, just look at you, you *poor, poor* baby. Let Mum-ah fluff up those pillows, they look like soda crackers, all smooshed flat like that. Mum-ahs here now, so don't you worry 'bout a thing."

Then she snatched the pillows out from under his head, which flopped down and bounced on the bed, and set to fluffin' them something fierce. Jerking his head up, she shoved them back under and piled them up until his head was tilted at a most peculiar angle. Too weak to fight her off, he was tossed about like a rag doll in a cyclone and in between she prattled away to a captive hospitalized audience.

"Oh, Barry darling, how are you? Love that blouse you're wearing. Gucci, Gucci, *Gucci*. Saint Sebastian, look at you, you're so handsome it's a sin. And Little Dicky, give your Auntie Joanie a big huggsy."

"It's Ricky."

"And Denny, and Chiquita, too; my God, I guess the gang's all here. All we need now is some disco music and cocktails."

"Would you care for a wee thimble of courage, Joany?" Sebastian asked, winking at her.

"Oh, you're a naughty boy, sneaking hooch into a hospital. Certainly I want a nip, and what the hell has taken you so long to ask? Jesus, I'm-a 'bout-ta die-a therst."

It was rather peculiar seeing Nikki and Joany together again, because they hadn't spoken since the unfortunate Mrs. Mott incident a few years back. Depending on whom was telling "the story," it was either two incorrigible children vying for more attention and giving *wildly* different versions of the same incident, or an inconsiderate red-headed fat assed foreign bitch pushing her fat ass in where it didn't belong. (The Mrs. Mott story is located at the end of this chapter—enjoy.)

A week later Nikki was sent home to recuperate, and being weak as a newborn kitten, he could not possibly care for himself. Chiquita once again quietly stepped in and nursed him back to health, and it was a long-ass and ugly haul.

— ~

"I want you to know I really appreciate what a good friend you've been, Chiquita."

"*Oooh*, let's not get all mushy now."

"I mean it. I want you to know that I've made out my will, and left the house to you. So if anything should ever happen to me, it's yours."

"You don't have to do that, Stella, really."

"It's already done, so don't ever mention it again."

"Mention what?"

A month later Nikki returned to work, and on a very limited basis. He absolutely lived for his work, and truly loved his riches-bitches; his impressive stable of well-heeled blondes and a select few heavily high-lighted and cash-heavy brunettes. No one dared speak to him about the hospitalization, but most people did the math, and life went quiet-ly on with everyone ignoring the big pink elephant in the beauty shop.

— ～

Chiquita was primarily the interior domestic doing light houseclean-ing and washing towels, underwear, and socks, because his shirts and slacks went to the dry cleaners, and the fancy-schmancy linens were sent to the Vietnamese virgins in Minneapolis for purification, sani-tation, and meditation.

Brad stayed on as the household handyman, and the demi-estate grounds were maintained by the chief greens keeper for the We'rerich Country Club in Grand Blanc. He personally tended to the lush lawn and other yardly maintenance, except the pond, because another man did that. There was also an exterior window washer, snow-removal ser-vice, and irrigation company, and they were all hired to replace Chiquita when he quit, or was dismissed—depending on whom was telling the story.

Secretly he was satisfied knowing he was that invaluable, that it took at least six people to replace him and he was still needed. But their friendship was bruised, distant, and something had been irreversibly damaged.

It was around this time that Nikki began socializing with pretty high-toned people, top of the social order; at least the toniest Flint had to offer. He had purposefully created a better socialite lifestyle for himself that included viewing artsy openings at the art institute, enduring ballet performances at the music institute, having season tickets to attend the sym-phony, and became as cultured as buttermilk.

He'd also engaged a personal trainer, and leased a new Jaguar and Mercedes runabout, too. "You know, there's simply not enough room in the back of the Jag for the quantity of greenery that I require for the estate's grounds, and it's horrible to drive in the winter, so I place in storage during the offseason and only drive the runabout."

Around that same time Chiquita was cleaning for three clients, and then another one moved. It seemed everyone was moving, out Weekends would still find him selling stuff at area flea markets, and that gig worked well all summer. And on Fridays he'd hit the area yard sales, garage sales, estate sales, and junk stores, and purchase more "stuff" to store away and sell online during the winter.

A few years back Chiquita was selling his stuff in antiques malls and flea markets, but then everything quickly changed to e-commerce so he went there as well, and selling stuff online became his new compulsion, addiction; albeit a much more profitable one. But when he worked from home it was easier for him to drink; unobserved. Eventually his once-lovely home began to deteriorate, in direct proportion to his accelerated drinking. He claimed he felt bad about its condition and attempted to paint it one summer. So I chose him a sunny yellow - called Nacho Cheese, and when paired with warm off-white for the trim and the hunter green roof, it looked real nice.

During the summer he was completely solar charged and operating in his highest manic phase, so he scraped, primed, and painted most of the home's Second Street side. When fall descended and the light dwindled, he withered and stopped doing just about everything, and the house went unpainted for the next ten years. Just like clockwork, every summer he had these solar flares, followed by dark winter crashes, and he never noticed the pattern.

He did the same thing with the home's roof. He ripped off the old roof and reshingled the Second Street side with a new forest green colored shingle, and the rest of the house went undone; with the remainder of the shingles sitting in the driveway decomposing for a decade. From Second Street it looked lovely, with a new green roof, pretty yellow siding, and antique white trim. But from Nikki's vantage it was the same old rotting white trash hovel.

Then he began dismantling the gardens, too. "Hey, Murf, do you want some-a these hostas, ferns, or perennials? I'm gettin' ridda all-a these plants around here because the yard's too much upkeep. Why bother, the neighborhood's going to shit." I declined.

— —

Daylight dwindled, darkness increased, Chiquita's drinking escalated, and his outside interests, such as work, ceased. Eventually he was fired, or dismissed from the Château's staff, again, depending on who was telling the story. Nikki claimed he'd fired his ass after tolerating his shortcomings for as long as he could, and Chiquita claimed he'd stepped down to spend more time on the more profitable electronic commerce. That pretty much meant the friendship ended, too.

"You know it just irritates the hell out of me to look across the street at that composting shitpile of his. I wish he'd do something with that trashy place," Nikki said as we drove past Chiquita's house on the way to a movie. "You know, sometimes I think he does that on purpose, and just to irritate me."

"Sure he does, Nikki. Why else do you think he'd paint the Second Street side and not yours? I don't hear that much from him anymore either, especially since he took up with that kid, Jon."

"What the hell is that all about anyway, him livin' with that skinny-assed, pimple-faced kid?"

A month later, while meeting Nikki for lunch, I passed Chiquita's and instantly noticed someone had spray-painted the house and stockade fence with graffiti saying: "Die, faggot, die," and "This is a no-homo zone," plus, "Sissy boy bitches."

"Nikki, did you see that Chiquita's place has been tagged?"

"Jesus Christ, *yes* I saw it! How the hell could I miss *that*? I live right across the street, ya know. Do you know he actually accused *me* of doing that?"

"What?" I said, laughing.

"Yes he did! Marched right over here and banged on my window so damn hard that he damn near broke the damn glass, then he pounded on my front door, and yelled his damned fool head off. 'You did that, didn't you? You spray-painted my house, didn't you?'

"Well, I was dumbfounded, and I didn't know what to say. Someone spray-painted it all right, sure as hell wasn't me, probably some lowlife friends of that kid he's livin' with. I told him, 'You know damn well I go to bed at eight o'clock. What am I supposed to do, set my alarm to get up at midnight, put on my LaCroix camo, sneak over, paint the fence, and then go back to bed? I don't *think* so!'"

"Oh my God, Nikki."

"We're not speaking anymore. He won't be coming over here any more, at all. I'm completely through with him, done," he said, and rubbing his hands together in a dismissive gesture to prove it. But secretly he kept track of Chiquita through friends and clients, who gave him the dirt about his comings and goings. "He's dropped even more clients now, and down to two jobs a week."

Nikki and I still kept up, too, although less frequently. Most summers he would visit my cottage for the Charlevoix art fair, and many times he came with Chiquita; we all had great times. He'd let his hair down and relax, and mostly because there were few shopping experiences and no one to entertain; he did so love having an audience. Chiquita, being a nature boy at heart, loved to be in the woods, water, and wilds and we certainly missed his playful presence.

— —

I had always joked about people who lived in trailers, but really shouldn't have, because my mother lived in a trailer. But in her defense, it was a nice double-wide "modular home." Mine definitely was a trailer, a 1968 vintage model, on Kearsley Lake, just north of Flint. My single-wide was a time capsule with tall cathedral ceilings, large windows, and lots of natural light. The kitchen had a boomerang-shaped island with matching Coppertone appliances, and the bathroom was well appointed with a lavender tub, sink, and stool, and that's what clinched the deal.

Two nice-size bedrooms were located in the rear overlooking the lake, with the master bedroom having windows on three sides, and making it a light-filled and breezy room. It was a well-kept trailer in a nicely maintained park with mature trees, easy to care for, and cheap. I liked cheap, too.

Nikki's commented, "It's just a trailer with nice window treatments," and that much was true. Caramel-colored silk curtains dressed the large cathedral windows, framing the lovely lake views. The walls, doors, trim, and cupboards were all painted the same warm caramel color that coordinated with the wall-to-wall carpeting, making a golden cocoon.

Nikki's basement—sorry, his lower levels—cast-off forest green slip-covered couch became the centerpiece of the living room, and when paired with my antique English waxed pine pieces it made a comfy city home. There was even a small garden plot for a few tomato plants and some flowers.

To properly christen the place I threw a trailer-trash party featuring fifties foods, such as Jell-O, hot dogs, cheese-in-a-can served on a Ritz, Kool-Aid, baked beans, potato salad, Fritos and Twinkies. The gay boys from Flint were all invited, making a comfortable crowd of seven: Nikki, Mike, Chiquita, Sebastian, Barry, and Little Dicky. Linda, from Baker's Drugs thirty years ago, was my neighbor now and she was also invited, but politely declined because she didn't care to be around drinking since drying out a few years back.

That evening we had a gay old time, sharing stories of the good old gays, and all of us, except for Nikki, finished the evening at the Pink Poodle, with go-go boys and plenty of pitchers o' beer. Mike was far too gassed to drive home, so he stayed with me. Sometimes he drank so much it scared me, and that was a seven-pitcher night. The majority of the evening he kept right up with Chiquita, while go-go boys kept the rest of us entertained by shaking their barely covered junk in our faces for dollar bills, and we did not protest until we ran out of singles.

The Pink Poodle was doing everything it could to survive now, and go-go boys were the latest attempt to distract customers. I'm not sure if it was the addition of homones in the meat, or if it was fashionable to be a little queer now, but for some strange reason there were a lot more gays in Flint. And with five gay bars in town there was stiff competition for the queer dollar. In this post-*Will and Grace* world, we were well accepted, allowed out in public, and considered an absolute must to enliven boring straight cocktail parties.

The Poodle's interior hadn't changed in thirty years, except the elevated dance floor went the way of disco—out. Those same old café tables and chairs remained, but now ugly gray and industrial carpeting covered the sticky floor. Karaoke caught on with a vengeance, too, especially with several off-tune regulars, but it really didn't bring in any new customers, and it probably drove more away from having to listen to their drunken caterwauling.

Practically speaking, there weren't new customers because the clientele hadn't changed in the past twenty years, there were just a lot less of them, and they were aging in place. For the most part it was now a private drinking club for dried-up old fruits without any dates. A few younger and newer people appeared, too, but they were mostly drug-addicted male hustlers, crack whores, and low hanging fruit. And the old fruits who remained had been sitting with their drunken asses on the same stools for over forty years, and they were eventually memorialized in their names.

For the most part Flint's young and pretty queers were going to other trendy alternative clubs such as the Merry Inn, Pachyderm, Pink Triangle, and The Zoo. These new places were "metro-sexual bars," because there was an odd blurring of the boundaries between gay and straight happening with this next generation. But the trendiest people of all traveled to out-of-town clubs, because that was the preferred thing to do—get out of Flint.

Most of our contemporaries didn't go to the bars much anymore. Some grew tired of drinking and chasing around, and settled. Plus the penalties for drunk driving were very stiff, and it wasn't worth taking the risk of getting nailed just to go to a dingy bar full of aging fruits.

THE GAYS OF OUR LIVES

With Al Gore's invention, the Internet, dating was changed forever, because now you don't need to leave home to find a date, and that helped contribute to the demise of the gay bar. New websites such as Gay.com, Mandate, Manhandle, Craig's List, Dial-a-Man, and similar portals could provide you with door-to-door dates. Now you could now select from a tasty menu of men from your hometown, or just as easily shop anywhere around the world. Mates, dates, and sexual services could be procured twenty-four hours a day, seven days a week, and in any color, size, shape, or perversion you desired.

Whole new worlds opened up.

When we were young the queer bar was the perceived nucleus of the gay community and hub of most of our socialization, but it held much less significance in current gay society, and this one was just supplying drinks to aging addicts. The costs of associating drinking and socializing were very high, and many friends developed serious problems with alcohol...and other substances.

Linda, from the drugstore years ago, was living in Atlanta when her second marriage went up in flames, so she fled. She'd also left a high-stress job as a respiratory therapist, and became a babysitter. She always wanted a family, and had lots of love to give, so she started caring for other people's kids instead. While the kids were at school she quietly drank her problems away, and did so for years, but her problems caught up with her anyway.

A decade later she dried out, God bless her sober soul. When she learned her stepdaddy was dying of cancer, she came back to Flint because she was needed, but she was in pretty rough shape. That's also when she became Old Dyke Linda. I hadn't seen her in years, but they must've been difficult ones. Her eyes were ringed with dark allergic shiners, and her hair a sorry mix of gray and blonde, with the gray winning. Lacking sunlight, she was peaked and looked worn out, worried, and sleep deprived.

A few years back she had driven up to my cottage to lay her dog, Boomer, to rest, and that dog's death was just another heartache added to Linda's list of miseries. A few years before that she'd conducted a

323

similar service to place her stepdaddy's ashes into Lake Michigan, and
now she was doing it for her pet. The problem was she'd finished off
a fifth of Kessler's while driving to my place, and was working on her
second when it came time for the burial-at-sea ceremony, and really
gassed.

With her being way too smashed for an outing to Lake Michigan, I
suggested that we have the send-off at my lake instead. What lucky dog
wouldn't want to spend eternity at the lake? Reluctantly she agreed, so
we canoed out to the floating raft for the send-off. I was in the back
paddling, and Linda was in front weeping, smoking, and hiccupping.
Aligning her with the floating raft, I said, "Grab hold of the ladder,
pull the canoe closer, and then climb onto the raft."

"Okay, Bubba."

She grabbed the ladder, but instead of pulling herself closer she
immediately shot up like a lit bottle rocket, making the tipsy canoe
rock wildly. Then she tried to step across the ever-growing liquid
chasm and plopped one foot onto the floating raft, but the other foot
was still inside the canoe, which kept drifting farther away until she
was doing the splits. Without saying a word she disappeared into the
emerald depths, and I watched as she slowly vanished from sight until
nothing remained but scores of tiny carbonated bubbles racing to the
surface; smelling like Kools, Kessler's, and Coke.

Dear God, I thought, *"will I have to jump in there, drag her drunken dyke ass out,
and give her mouth-to-mouth resuscitation?* But then, she slowly floated to the
surface with her mouth gaping like a hungry goldfish, blowing out
eighty-proof air, and grinning like a kid on a hot summer day with
both halves of a strawberry Popsicle.

"I didn't make it, honey."

"You're all wet."

Once she was safely settled upon the raft, we conducted our solemn
doggy departure service. As I held tipsy Linda by the belt of her dripping pants, she emptied the ashes into the emerald depths and wept,
and we finished the service by reciting a doggone prayer. Later that
evening we held the wake, making the conversation turn serious.

"Bubba, I can't do it anymore. I've been drinking for over twenty years, and I'm numb. I can't feel anything anymore, and I'm scared to death that I'm gonna die if I don't quit. I want to get sober, but I'm afraid. Will you help me?"

"Certainly. We can get you some help."

"I'm scared to death, honey."

"I know. Don't worry—we'll get through this."

She was admitted into a substance abuse treatment facility where she was counseled, treated, dried out, and had been sober ever since, for ten years now. She also saw more sunlight, and seemed to have a better life. Moving to Flint was good for her because she grew much closer to her mother, and that was something she'd always wanted.

Her road to redemption began by drying out, and then she got a job, purchased a car, and then a mobile home, right next to mine. She also started a family and became the obsessive mother of five mangy cats, and herding cats became her new obsession.

Feeling she didn't have the wherewithal to reenter the high-stress field of respiratory therapy, she chose a less stressful, less demanding job instead, and one she could more easily handle. And even though she still suffered from seasonal affective disorder and depression, she was given medications that helped her better cope. She could handle stable, content, and comfortable, and was just that.

Her five kitties were her reasons to live now. The last mangy stray cat she took in she named Bruiser, because he was missing a chunk from an ear and had a rheumy eye and broken back leg that was never repaired, making him hobble and limp. He was also filthy, sneezed continuously, looked as if he'd been in a great many fights and hadn't won very many of them, and he carried every single scar.

"Who else would take in a cat like this? I had to do it," Linda explained. "I don't know where the other four came from."

"I do! I heard you opening the back door every night, dumping food in a bowl, and yelling 'here kitty, kitty, kitty' until they showed up—that's how."

"Well, we're a family now."

"That you are."

She could relate to animals better than people, and they were very lucky and relatable kitties.

— ~

Linda wasn't the only friend with "the problem." Substance abuse had become quite prevalent in the gay and lesbian community, because drinking and socializing often don't mix well. Mike, who was my ex, or my *why*, had his dalliances with substances, too. Some of his problems were caused by seasonal affective disorder, making him miserable all winter. But depression ran in his family, also, and he was clinically diagnosed as being bipolar, with a sprinkling of social anxiety disorder, too.

Somehow he went from being the most conservative guy I knew to one of the most troubled souls I knew. He had always been one to party hardy, and perhaps it was that unpredictability that made him exciting; you never knew what was coming. But there is a fine line between self-medicating and abuse, and some people never want the party to end.

But this was the 1990s, and the decade of excesses, and he was living excessively. He'd taken up with a messed-up hairdresser named Raun, was living in Detroit, and partying *waaay* too much. But also being quite democratic, Mike was an equal opportunity exploiter who abused alcohol, cocaine, and prescription drugs equally. Probably sex, too.

When we reconnected he'd already completed one twenty-eight-day treatment program, and twice after that I accompanied him as he checked himself in for another dose. Each time it would take another chunk out of him. But I gave him credit, because he kept trying. Eventually he surrendered to the flow and joined AA, where he received guidance, understanding, and support. And when he was attending meetings regularly, he was doing well with the program.

Depression ruled his life, self-medication complicated it, but in between he was bright, caring, generous, charming, charismatic, funny, warm, handsome, and very sexy.

A while back I discovered that many fucked up adults had fucked-up childhoods. Some times substance abuse has to do with unresolved issues from one's childhood, and past baggage. So, I thank God I had a boring upbringing and didn't care much for drinking; it wasn't my buzz of choice. A little puff now and then helped me get in touch with my maker, and dropped my shoulders a notch or two. I never cared for anything more exotic or mind altering than a puff of pot, or occasional drink.

People need reasons to live—and I had plenty of them. I liked what I did for a living. I'm an artist, for Christ's sake, and all we do is have fun all day; isn't that what most people think? And I have loving and supportive friends, and a family that I actually love and can relate to. God has been good to me. Bless my heart.

* You may now refer to the Mrs. Mott story...

Nikki and Joany Call Upon Mrs. Mott

For well over one hundred years the biggest name in these parts was Mott—and in particular, Charles Stuart Mott. He put the Mott in Mott's Applesauce—yes, that was him. The business and the name were sold many years ago, but that's where the money originally came from, applesauce. Several other minor factors contributed to his overall success as well, for instance, for sixty years he sat on the board of directors for a little start-up company called General Motors, and owned a controlling share of the company's stock. Mr. Moneybags Mott was so stinking rich that he even had his own bank and a several-story department store in downtown Flint, called Smith-Bridgman's. But those two little businesses just brought him a little chump change.

C.S's philanthropy and generosity are legendary in our community, and he greatly assisted in our city's growth and prosperity. He started many initiatives that helped Flint's citizens have a better quality of life, have more exposure to the arts, attain higher education, and gain access to recreational facilities. The Mott Foundation, which he initiated, funds many worthwhile projects both locally and nationally, including the Mott Children's Hospital in Ann Arbor and National Public Radio.

As a youngster I remember seeing old Mr. Mott speed-walking down Saginaw Street, our main drag. He didn't walk—he marched along, determined. But this lanky old man, who stood well over six feet tall, drove a cheap-ass Chevrolet Corvair. And this made no sense to me at all because he owned the damned company and could have any vehicle he wanted, and for free. Not him; he'd pull up to the curb in his sardine-can car, unfurl himself, and march into the store like any customer, only faster.

I also recalled seeing him wearing the same drab suit every day. His ancient suit was so pressed, and re-pressed, that it shined just like silk sharkskin. But the most prominent features upon his ancient narrow face were his big white cookie-duster mustache and a classical beak of a nose. He'd scurry about, all hunched over, head down, marching toward his destination, and determined.

It was widely rumored he was a real skinflint, too. You can bet he didn't accumulate all that money by spending it. He saved it. For Christ's sake, he owned the damn bank. When he died, at the tender age of ninety-eight, he left all the filthy money to his widow, Mrs. Ruth Rawlings Mott (of the Marjorie Kinnan Rawlings clan). He also left her their sprawling sixty-five-acre estate and placed her in charge of his foundation, which she skillfully ran for nearly thirty years until her death in 1999.

Reportedly they'd owned the largest house in town, and at that time, before McMansions, it may have been true. Theirs was an expansive and secluded parcel, sitting practically in the middle of the city of Flint. In the beginning this home was a self-sustaining and working farm complete with fruit orchards, chickens, and herds of cows, pigs, and sheep. The gurgling Gilkey Creek traversed through the middle of their pastoral property, and only added to its beauty.

It was also rumored he was so damn tightfisted that he wouldn't spend any money on the upkeep of the house or grounds, and the estate slowly slipped into decline. Most of the rooms still had the original paint, wallpaper, and window treatments from when it was built, in 1916. Consequently it was soot-covered, water-stained, ripped, and peeling from the crumbling walls.

But during the twenty-six years spanning between when Mr. Mott died and Ruth's passing, she had spent quite a few of his hard-earned dollars doing some major fixing up of the old joint. So much so that she eventually transformed it into one of the jewels of our community.

Part of their estate was bequeathed to the city of Flint to begin C.S. Mott Community College, a progressive and award-winning institution that was lovingly named in his honor. Their former home, now referred to as the Applewood Estate, is considered to be *the* crown jewel of Flint, and people come from miles around to tour the fully restored home and lovely gardens.

Beginning in 1977, the home and grounds were meticulously restored, beyond their former glory, and opened to the public for tours. This restoration made the estate into a museum of capitalist excess that was comparable with other robber baron estate homes, such as the Henry Ford Estate, the Pierce DuPont Estate, the Vanderbilt Estate, or the Dodge Estate, know as Meadowbrook.

Ruth Mott bequeathed the estate, home and grounds, to the city of Flint for the public to enjoy for perpetuity. Some of the Mott children and heirs to the family fortune escaped to far-off places such as Ann Arbor and New York City, and some stayed in the area to become our local royalty, married well, and built McMansions of their own.

Now, the little fairy tale that I am about to unfold takes place in the home of one of our local Mott heirs, and it involves our dear frenemies, the lovely Joany Meddler and our darling Nikki Clark. It's a lovely spring day, lilac time, and love is in the air.

— —

"You know, Joan, every time I run into that dear, sweet old Mrs. Mott, she asks me to stop over to her house for a visit," Nikki said. "She just adores me, you know. And why shouldn't she?"
"Oh, don't I know it to be true, Nikki. You know, she loves me, too. Why, each time I see her she practically begs me to visit, and says she thinks I'm a clever artist. She's just too kind, isn't she?"

"Too, too much. You know, Joan, *I've* known her for years now, and *I* always see her at the symphony and galas at the Art Institute, too. But you wouldn't know about that kind of culture because you don't attend those kinds of functions. You know, just like me, she's a big supporter of the arts."

"Oh yes, I agree with you wholeheartedly, you're *big* all right. I couldn't agree with you more. You know, every time she sees me in one of my handmade, hand-painted, hand-quilted, hand-decorated coats, she asks me about them, and comments on how handsome she thinks they are. She literally begs me to bring a few of my artsy things to her house to show her privately, an inmate showing, you know, because she just can't shop in town with all that notoriety, the paparazzi and all."

"Oh, don't I know it. And I can certainly feel her pain. She can't come into the salon for the exact same reasons—too rich and too visible. You know, it must be just awful having all that delicious money and not being able to go out and spend it."

"Can you just imagine?"

"Would love ta try. Well, now, Joan, why don't you just sit here a minute while I call her social secretary and set up something for Monday, on my day off. Why...just last week she was begging me, again, to stop over and see the fabulous new MacKenzie-Childs kitchen that she just had installed. Did I tell you, she had Richard and Victoria— *the MacKenzie-Childses*, the actual artists themselves—flown in from New York to do her kitchen? It took 'em two whole years to do it, too.

"I heard they created a scrumptious whimsical vision in sumptuous pastel prints, and hand-made and hand-painted every single solitary thing in that bitchin' kitchen; they hand made every tile for the back-splash, countertop, and the floor, too. They even made the kitchen sink. They made all the light fixtures, tables, chairs, dishes, door-knobs, curtain rods, rugs, and the paper-towel holder, too. It's just beyond words, and absolutely too, too, too fucking fabulous."

"Nikki, you know, she's been begging me to come over for a wee visit, too. I think I shall take pity on the poor old shut-in, too. We should go together, us two. Wouldn't that be great fun, the two of us going together?"

"Too, too."

— ~

Two Weeks Later

Nikki went to the drive-thru carwash extra-extra early to get his brand-new pewter colored Jag, with cocoa mohair carpet, cocoa butter leather seats, and Diana Ross Mahogany wooden interior extra shiny and still have plenty of time to blow dry before he was expected at Mrs. Mott's at high noon.

He'd dolled himself up extra special for the occasion, with brand-new clothes from head to toe, a new bigwig for the top of his head, and brand-new Prada pilgrim shoes for his Flintstone feet. He'd even adopted a more subtle hairstyle in a darker shade of blond, with caramel undertones. He also had a complete spa day that included a fresh coat of sprayed-on suntan, manicure, and pedicure, and a south-of-the-border waxing was in order, because sometimes it's the little things that make you feel prettier.

And speaking of looking prettier, he thought he was looking particularly ravishing, if he didn't say so himself, and he did. "You look simply ravishing today, lover boy, *muah*." It was barely eleven, and he wouldn't be due to arrive for an hour yet, but he wanted to cruise past the stately estate to get an early eyeful of the Mottly magnificence he would soon be experiencing.

"Ohhhhh my God, would you look at that *fabulous* fucking house. What magnificence! What beauty! *What the hell?* Is that Joan's fucking car?" he yelled, screeching to a halt in the middle of the brick-paved street. Joan's cheap-ass little Honda was parked in the drive. Turning several shades of red, underneath the sprayed-on orange suntan, he stewed and seethed; he was so steamed that he beamed.

"*So*, she says to me, 'I'll meet you there at noon.' *Noon my ass*, she's already there, and a goddamned hour early." Shoving the Jag into

Reverse, he stomped on the gas, backed past the house, and slammed on the brakes. Skidding, he threw it into Drive and swerved up the brick drive with the Jag still dripping wet. Parking next to Joan's shitty foreign car, he got out and gave it a good swift kick.

Ding-dong.

"Good morning, sir. And how may I be of help to you?" the starchy butler inquired.

"Yes, Mr. Butler, I'm Nikki Clark, and Mrs. Mott asked me to stop by for a meeting, at noon."

"Very good, Mr. Clark. Since it is barely eleven, and Mrs. Mott is with another appointment now, I will show you to the drawing room where you may wait. Please have a seat."

"S'cuse me, Rhett, but the meeting she's having right now, is it with a Joan Meddler?"

"Well, sir, 'tis a bit irregular, but yes, 'tis a Meddler."

"Oh, well then, I'm here with her."

As the butler opened the door, Joan was in the middle of her sales pitch, and her tangerine lips were feverishly flying, trying to get it all out, and it was all so important. The contents of her workshop had somehow been transported, and it completely covered the parquetry floor. How she managed to get all that shit, and her, into that little red Honda sedan was beyond me. She had quilted coats and quilted purses, quilted jackets, quilted potholders, quilted pins, and quilted Northern spread all over. And poor old Mrs. Mott was buried beneath a foot-deep pile of quilted coats, looking most bewildered.

"Now, these beautiful garments are entirely handmade, and we even make our own chenille. First we take lovely antique linens"—she forgot to mention they were the shitty soiled and rejected sheets from Saint Joseph Hospital's laundry—"and we sew several layers of them together, making them into a quilted batting. Then we cut through the bat in certain places to make designs, and then we shred the loose ends and make it into chenille. After that we hand-dye them, hand-print them, hand-paint them, and hand-decorate them. Aren't they hand-some? Here, let me give you a hand."

Joan wrestled with poor old Mrs. Mott, tossing her about as if she was a rag doll, and stuffed her into an enormous quilted coat that dragged the ground. The coat was overly adorned with vintage seed packets, gardening tools, and a multitude of multicolored flowers, which made her look like a frustrated midget gardener in a straitjacket.

When the door squeaked open, Joan was momentarily caught off guard, silenced for a magical millisecond, and as she paused to micro-breathe, he interjected, "Madam, a Mr. Clark to join you."

"Oh, Nikki love," Joany purred, "you're here a just teensy bit ear-lee. We will be through here in just a teensy minute, and then we can all have a nice wee chat. So why don't you just wait outside for a few minutes, until I'm finished here, because Ruthie wants to see all the lovely things I brought and made especially for her."

"Well!" Nikki spouted, and he marched right in and plopped right down directly opposite Joan. Then he commenced to sending saccharine-sweet smiles to Mrs. Mott from right side of his new face and shooting the stink-eye death wish to Joan from the left. Syrupy politeness prevailed in Mrs. Mott's presence, but seething tensions brewed between them during her mercenary manifesto. Joan was just as steamed at him and returned the ugly face as often as possible. But her sales pitch was tragically cut short, as well as their self-invitation-al home tour, when Mrs. Mott led them into the absolutely amazing MacKenzie-Childs kitchen, right on through it, and out the hand-painted back door.

Whoosh!

But let me tell you, those two minutes inside that kitchen were absolutely *orgasmical*. During their two-minute escort to the back door, Mrs. Mott described—in meticulous overwhelming detail—the de-lightful story of how the two artistics hand-painted every goddamned thing in the fucking place. To me it was like something from *Alice in*

Wonderland, while tripping on acid— it looked like the Mad Hatter's kitchen; pastel, whimsical, overkill.

"Why," Nikki gushed, "Victoria and Richard took fabulous and added a whole 'nother layer of fabulousness. That kitchen was so fucking fab-you-lisciously over the top there was just no coming back. Two snaps, three words: Oh! My! God! Almighty! Can you ever get enough MacKenzie-Childs? No. I don't think so either."

But somehow they found themselves standing back out in the drive before the stroke of noon, before either of them were even supposed to be there in the first place; prematurely ejaculated.

"Noon my ass. Just who the hell do you think you are *dismissing* me that way, Missy, like I'm your fucking servant? 'Just go away, Nikki, we're busy.' Jesus Christ, *woman*, I am not your servant! You cannot just *dismiss* me that way. And another thing, *woman*, she invited *me* here and you just pushed your fat foreign ass in."

"Now, Nikki, you know that's not entirely correct. She's begged *me* to come here, too; begged me a dozen times to show her my stuff."

"Not on my goddamned day, and not a fucking hour early, she didn't!"

"Let's not argue here, it's so low-class. Let's go down the street to Hooters where we can get us a wee cocktail and have a more civilized chat. It's much quieter there."

"Well, I watched her shove all that tacky quilted crap back into that shitty little foreign car of hers and drive off," Nikki related to me later. "Then I thought to myself, what the hell, why am I going over to Titty-City just to argue with her more? So, I just drove myself home."

*FYI: Mrs. Mott died just two weeks after their visit.

I'm just sayin'...

Chiquita Two

I have always been an early-to-bed and early-to-rise sort, and most people who know me would joke about my routine of being asleep by ten o'clock. So naturally I was long gone, deep in slumber when the 12:34 a.m. phone call arrived. Digital clocks don't lie. And most undoubtedly, any call arriving at that time of the night will not contain good news.

"Denny...I'm in trouble...I need help, bad."

It was Chiquita, and he sounded really loaded. I'd never heard him sound that way before, smashed, desperate, and scared; somewhere between bursting into tears and full-out panic.

"What's the matter?"

"I'm in trouble, it's all mucked up. It's all a mess. Don't know what to do, don't know who to call, got no one else ta turn ta. You gotta help me, I'm scared." Then he began to sob, a deep and gut-wrenching sob that came from somewhere in the depths of his soul. The kind of sob you don't like to hear, and definitely the kind you don't ever want to experience.

"I need to get outta here for a couple days an' get my head screwed on right. I'm in big trouble; everythin's all mucked up. They been robbin' me blonde. Got no money." Clearly these were the late-night ramblings of a drunk, but it was also a cry for help from a friend in trouble. I understood that much.

"What's wrong, Chiquita? Tell me what the matter is."

"Can…can me…me an' the dogs come out ta your place for a coupla days? It's so peaceful out there at the lake. I jus' need ta rest. Is that all right, won't be no bother?"

"What's going on, honey? What's wrong? You can tell me."

"I mucked up ever-thin'. It's all screw-dup."

"Screwed up what? What do you mean? Have you been robbed? Do you need the police? Are you sick? Do you need to go to the hospital? Should I call an ambulance?"

"No! No, nothin' like that! No! *No!* No am-balance, definitely not that. No police ether. I just need ta get some rest, ain't slept in three whole days. So tired…but I can't leaf the boys alone. They won't be no trouble, no trouble 'tall. They like it out the-air by the lake, with you."

"Chiquita, listen, can your friend Jon watch the dogs? Because my place is so small and they're so big. I don't know them that well, and to tell you the truth, they scare me."

"They're sa'posed to scare people, sill-e, that's what they arf-or, gar-dogs. 'Tween you an' me, they're just big bay-bees, ya know. But I, I, I, I don' know if he'll take-air of 'em or not."

"Can you call him and ask?"

"Not now, I'm on the phone with you."

"Is he the problem? Is that what's going on?"

"No, no, no, nothin' like that, Nancy Drool. I'll call ladder. Bye."

＊ ～ ～

"Denny…you the-air?" He sounded worse than the night before, much more scared.

"Yes, I'm here. You don't sound good."

"I'm not, it's all mucked up. I'm sick." Now he was sobbing.

"What's going on, Chiquita? What's the matter?"

"I just need to get some rest...I'm so tired...haven't slept in days. So tired."

"Maybe we should see about getting some help for you," I said, while trying to figuring out what to do. "Have you been drinking? Are you taking pills? What has brought this on? You've been sober for over three years now, and doing so well."

"Dunno, dunno. I'm worried about my dogs? They're all I got, and they need me."

"Did you call your friend Jon? Can he take care of them?"

"Dunno...yeah, yeah, yeah, called him, he ain't called back. Par-ta the problem, ya know."

"What do you mean; he's part of the problem? If he can watch the dogs that will definitely help."

"Yeah, yeah...'K...I'll call..." Click.

Not knowing what to do, I called my friend Bette, because she was a substance abuse therapist. She didn't answer, so I was leaving a message explaining the predicament, and was nearly finished when she picked up.

"Denny, is that you? What's going on?" She sounded as if she'd just crawled out of bed. "I heard your message recording but only got part of it. What's up?"

"It's Chiquita. And he's in trouble."

"Oh dear God. What is it? Has he been drinking? He's been so good for so long."

"Yes, he's been drinking and possibly taking drugs, too, but I can't tell for sure. He's definitely loaded, bawling, practically incoherent, asking for help, and I don't know what to do."

"He'll definitely have to go into treatment, and probably into detox. He can't do that by himself or he could die. Have you seen him? How bad is he?"

"No, I haven't seen him yet. I'm trying to figure out what to do before going over there."

"Give me a minute to think here. Jesus, help me. I just woke up. Let me find a cigarette."

The distinct sounds of a Zippo steel pocket lighter being flipped open, followed by the flint wheel being struck, and then the tinny lid being quickly snapped back down, was followed by an audible inhale. "Okay. Now, he probably doesn't have any health insurance, does he? So he'll have to go to Community Mental Health, and they will do an assessment. They'll probably check him into Hurley Hospital, to dry out."

"I'm sorry for waking you, but I didn't know who else to turn to. I'll get him there soon as I can. Thanks for your help."

"That's fine. You know I love Chiquita, always have, and I'm happy to help him. Even so, that little shit got away with everything I've owned that was worth anything while he was cleaning for me. But I'll add him to my prayer list just the same. Let me know what's happening, and good luck."

"Thanks, Bette, you're the best."

— —

By the time I arrived he was slumped into a rusty forest-green shell-backed lawn chair on the driveway, and he surely looked pitiful. Downright scrawny and gaunt, his wrinkled clothes hung loosely as if he was a scarecrow. It had been three weeks, or maybe a month since I'd last seen him, but he'd slipped very far, and very fast. When attempting to stand he wobbled, slumped back into the chair with a slow-motion plop, and then kept sliding right on out of it as if it had been greased.

Sitting in a puddle on the ground, and looking quite miffed, he was staring up at me as if I had something to do with him being there. But without his glasses he was squinting profusely and having an extremely hard time seeing me, couldn't bring me into focus, and his blurry bloodshot eyes were frantically moving back and forth like a Felix the Cat clock. I could smell the vodka oozing from him.

"What have you been doing, Chiquita?"

"Just sittin' here, waitin' fur you."

"Have you been drinking?"

"Lil bit. Yeah, lil."

"Anything else, taking any vitamins?" That's what he called phar-maceuticals now, *vit-a-mins*, like the proper English pronunciation.

"No. Jus' drinkin', jus' drinkin', that 'sall."

"How much have you been drinkin', Chiquita? Have you been drinking since last night?"

"Yes, sir, yes, sir. Did a good job, too, 'bout a half-a gall-on. Yes, sir, a whole half, ha, ha, ha."

"Vodka?"

"How'dja know?"

"Lucky guess. So did you reach Jon? Can he watch the dogs?"

I saw Jon's hulking Suburban in the drive, so I knew he was there. It was easily recognizable, a rusting tank painted in flat camouflage, with the rear window missing. For over five years, since he was nine-teen, he and Chiquita had an unusual arrangement; an Oedipus com-plex affair. We didn't ask.

"It 'sall good. All good. All taken air of. Where we g-in' 'gain?" he asked, trying to look directly at me, and still unable to make his eyes work in tandem.

"Bette says we should go to Community—" He cut me off midsentence.

"Oh! The old coot; how is dear old Bette? Ya know, I mist her."

"She's fine. She said for us to go to Community Mental Health, and they'll do an assessment."

"Men-tall-hell; wha' for? I'm drunk...not crazy!"

"I know. She said, because you don't have any health insurance you will have to be assessed and then referred, in order to get treatment."

"Oh...oooooooh. I don't feel so good, honey. I'm scared." Then he started crying. "Can you hep me stand? Can't even get my self up. What am I goin' to do? It's all mucked up."

"It'll be all right. Come on—let's get you some help."

He stood a little over six feet tall, but practically weighed a thing, and yet getting him up and in the truck was a real struggle. Moving super-slowly, he was attempting to fasten his seatbelt, which was both comical and painful to see, and after several failed attempts I could no longer stand it and buckled it.

"Say...I hate to be a pain in the ass, but can't help it. Call me a hemorrhoid. Can we stop an' get me some cigs, 'cause I haven't had any in days. Don't got no money, don't got no cigs. That okay? Can we jus' do that lil thing?"

"What kind do you want?" I asked, watching him unsuccessfully attempting to undo the belt. Slowly turning his head in my direction, and still unable to focus, he mumbled, "Marl-bro, men-tall, hun-nerd." I was surprised to find they were over six bucks a pack now, because when I'd smoked just a few years back they were only three and a quarter. Opening the pack, I handed them to Chiquita. "Here you go. I can't believe how expensive these things have gotten."

"Yes, sir, sss-pensive. Roll ma own now, much chipper, chipper. Say, you know what was s-s-spensive? Glass-nuts. When I got Duke fixed, they sent him home without no nuts in his ball-sack and he just didn't look right. So I had 'em put some fake nuts in there, you know—prostesticles—and then he looked lots better. Felt better, too. But talk 'bout s-s-spensive, whew, tree hun-nerd dollars for two glassy doggy dingle berries."

While laughing excessively at his remark, he continued to frisk himself looking for a lighter, like someone doing the Macarena in slow motion. I lit a cigarette and handed it to him, and he finally seemed happy to be smoking, but still went on searching himself. Sitting back in the seat, he finally smiled, with his tear stained face still shiny wet from the tears he'd cried minutes earlier. I cracked my window to allow the fumes to escape, and we drove to CMH in smoky satisfied silence.

Parking beneath the portico, I came around to help Chiquita, who was still fumbling with the seatbelt, incapable of focusing on it, and unable open it. "What the hell's wrong with this damn thin'?" he mumbled, clenching the shortening cigarette between his deteriorating teeth.

"All the old people have trouble with that," I said, helping him out and into a chair. "Why don't you sit here and finish your smoke, while I park the truck. Okay?"

"Yeah, yeah, 'sall good."

Dirty, badly lit, and vinyl coated, the waiting room looked more like a bus terminal than clinic. I helped Chiquita into a flimsy plastic lawn chair, because he could barely stand. A round brown woman sat across from us, clutching two little mixed-race children to her sides, and another couple sat together on the far wall staring blankly at a brawl unfolding on *Jerry Springer*. I waited outside of the bulletproof Plexiglass enclosure until a commercial came on and the supersized receptionist decided to glance in my direction. She was clearly irritated by the intrusion.

"Can I hep you?" she sputtered, all pissed off, and apparently irritated because she had to temporarily divert her attention from the Slimfast commercial.

"This is my friend, Jim, and Dr. Church, a substance abuse counselor, told us to come here so they can do an assessment. He's asking for help with alcohol addic..."

"Who tole you come here? Why day tell you come here? Dis 'ommunity men-all-hell. Dis ain't no sub-stance 'buse place. Unh-uh. Dis here for crazy people. You gotta go to Anon for abuse." And with that pronouncement, and a dismissive wave of her big brown hand, she turned her back on us and returned her attention to the television.

"Excuse me. What is Anon, and where is that located?"

"It ova on Flushin' Road," offered another woman behind the safety glass, wearing an ugly purple uniform. "They close for da-day, already. You have da make a point-men for 'morrow."

"He's asking for help right now, and he's not in very good shape."

"Maybe you should take him ova ta Hurley an' have him 'mitted."

"All right, thank you."

"Chiquita, they said we should go to Hurley Hospital."

"Oh no. No sir, I'm not goin' ta that wretched place. They threw me in-ta the loony bin there. You should never put a gay man in a strait-jacket."

"You're not in good shape, and you need help. What do you want to do?"

After a lengthy reflective pause, he said, "Take me to Gen-sis. Yeah, take me the-air. It's really nice out the-air, like a ho-tell."

Packing him back in the truck, we left the decaying inner city and headed to the gleaming new suburban hospital/ hotel. This sprawling complex was called a "health park," and it was comfortably situated on a large tract of meadowland, dotted with mature woods, with fields of wildflowers, and tranquil ponds. Their well-groomed grounds were traversed by paved walking paths, so you could mingle with nature and not get dirty while doing it. And it was definitely the highest-priced health care in the area.

While still smoking, Chiquita had fallen asleep, so I woke him to transfer him to a wheelchair. The well-lit waiting room was clean, comfortable, and decorated with a green and plum color scheme, sort of woodsy. Elevator Muzak played to a waiting room of mostly white and suburban patients. Jim was snoozing and slowly sliding out of the wheelchair by the time the matronly woman behind the intake window spoke. She was polite but curt, and there wasn't any obscuring bulletproof glass.

"What's the emergency? I'll need to see your driver's license and proof of insurance, please."

"This is my friend Jim, James Fagan, and he is not in very good shape. He has been drinking pretty heavily, and is asking for help. Jim, hand her your license."

"Mr. Fagan, do you live at the same address? Do you have any insurance?"

Jim awakened to glace in the direction where the voice came from, and tried to focus. "No."

"Is this the correct address, Mr. Fagan?"

Snapping back from a mini-nap, he responded, "Don't ya know where ya are, honey?"

"Yes, I do. What is *your* address, honey? Let me just put this armband on him," she said to me, and then wrapped the plastic hospital band around his wiry wrist. "Please take a seat, and someone will be with you shortly."

"Already got me a seat, in this we-all-chair," Chiquita said, smiling a decayed toothy grin, and winking in the direction of the voice. While awaiting his turn, Jim drifted in and out and slowly slid out of his wheelchair. I read a couple of outdated magazines. Apparently there was a triage process there, and a severed arm came before an indigent drunk, and we were probably at the very back of the line.

When they finally took us through the sacred stainless steel double doors and into the sterile and well-illuminated treatment space, Jim was placed upon the health care system's conveyor belt. First they took his vitals, blood pressure, temperature, pulse, and asked some basic questions.

"Mr. Fagan, do you know what day it is?"

Jim snapped back momentarily. "Don't cha know, honey? It's Twos-day." It was Thursday.

"Do you know why you're here, Mr. Fagan?"

"Well, yeah, I'm sick, this is a hospitable."

"Mr. Fagan, what seems to be the matter? Can you tell me what's wrong?"

Chiquita tried very hard to wake up, blinked in the general direction of the voice, and tried to focus. "Feels like broken glass inside-a me. Hurts real bad."

"What hurts, Mr. Fagan?"

Jim began making circular motions around his midsection with his bony hands. "Pain, sharp pains, like there's shards-a broken glass inside-a there."

"Have you been drinking, Mr. Fagan?"

"Not lately, no. But if ya got a lil somethin', sure Docker, sure. What th'hell."

"How much, Mr. Fagan?" the doctor said, taking another tack.

"Just a lil nip'll do."

"No, how much have you been drinking before you came here?"

"Oh, th-hat. 'Bout a fiff, I guest."

"Doctor," I interrupted, "he told me he'd finished a half gallon."

Jim opened his eyes wider and looked in my general direction, trying to give me the stink-eye, but couldn't make his face cooperate.

"Have you been here before?"

"Yessss, and it's nicer here. Isn't it?"

"Okay. Yes it is nicer here. Let me just check on a few things, and then I'll be right back."

"Yeah, yeah, it 'sall good—all goo...d."

When the attending nurse left, Jim looked up, asking, "How'd I dude?"

"Fine."

The emergency ward was bustling like a beehive; and busy with swarming people, too warm, white-noisy, and hypnotic. Jim nodded again off during the lengthy wait, and I had a difficult time staying awake. The privacy partition was once again pushed aside and a conservative young man entered carrying a stainless steel tray covered with a white cloth.

"Mr. Fagan?"

"Yessss," Jim said, waking and squinting in his general direction, while trying to focus.

"I'm the phlebotomist, and I'm here to take some samples. Is that okay?"

"Hep yer-self, Mr. Flea-Botanist, got plenty, and it 'sall good." Jim squinted at the attractive young man, somehow sensed he was cute, and smiled even more broadly. Thrusting out both bony arms, he said, "Hep yer-shelf."

With great efficiency the young man took the scrawny outstretched arm and extracted two tubes of dark red, eighty-proof blood, labeled them, placed a pink Hello Kitty bandage on Jim's bony arm, thanked us, and left. Twenty minutes later we were reawakened.

Next a pert pencil-pushing young woman with a precisely painted face peeled back the privacy partition. Clutching a clipboard tightly to her chest, she had a tightly wrapped bun atop her head with a well sharpened number two pencil shoved into it; clearly she was a number cruncher. Her buttoned-up white lab coat and sensible oxfords planted firmly on hospital ground. She looked like a disciplinarian librarian, or my sadistic alcoholic fifth-grade teacher, Mrs. Yuck, and scared the shit out of me.

"Hello," she said, in a clipped curt manner. Nodding in my direction, she approached Chiquita, who was lying on the ER table. When hearing her coming, he opened one eye, got a good look at her, and snapped it closed, pretending to be fast asleep.

"Mr. Fagan," she said. Jim did not respond. Then she said it much louder. *"Mr. Fagan!"*

Jim opened one bloodshot eye, and then quickly snapped it shut again.

"My name is Frieda Harassem, and I work for the hospital. They have asked me to speak with you about your outstanding balance with us." Momentarily glancing at her clipboard, she quickly snapped back. "Mr. Fagan, you have an outstanding balance of two hundred and seventy-three thousand, seven hundred and forty-two dollars, and five cents."

Jim laughed out loud and completely ruined his possum-pretending-to-be-asleep routine. "Miss Hard-ass, *yes* I am a ware. But I don't even have the five scents."

"Well, the hospital just wanted to know if you're aware of that outstanding balance. Are you still at the same address?"

"No, I'm here, at the hospitable."

"Where do you get your mail, Mr. Fagan?"

"You mean where can ya send the bills. Yeah, yeah, yeah. Same old dress."

"And are you currently employed, Mr. Fagan?"

Chiquita tried to pretend he was asleep again.

"Mr. Fagan," she demanded, even louder this time. *"Mr. Fagan!"*

"Yeah, yeah, yeah, I'm right here—I'm not deaf."

"Are you working now?"

"No, I'm sick now, have exterminatin' circumstances, an' I'm tryin' ta rest. Can't ya see that?"

"No. Mr. Fagan, do you have a job, are you employed?"

"No, honey, nothin' like that. I have allergies."

Clearly she was getting nowhere. It was obvious he was gassed, reeking of vodka, and having trouble speaking or even concentrating, and with each answer he became more incoherent. Finally she gave up. "Thank you."

Turning to exit, she squeaked out with her sensible shoes squealing against the shiny linoleum, and leaving us in her overly perfumed wake. Chiquita opened one bloodshot eye, winked at me, and said, "Got rid-a her bitchy ass, I did." Then he drifted off again. About twenty minutes later we reached the next stop on the conveyor belt, the privacy partition was moved aside again, and a young American doctor dressed in a white lab coat entered.

"Mr. Fagan?"

Jim blinked profusely, trying to adjust and focus on the person addressing him. "Yes, sir?"

"Mr. Fagan, my name is Dr. James. How are you doing today?"

"Na-sa good, Docker."

"What seems to be the problem? Where does it hurt?"

"Feels like I ate glass, and my insides is ripped all ta shreds. Hurts real bad."

"I see that you've been to this hospital before, and you were treated for pancreatitis; is that correct? Does it feel like that?"

"I don't know wha-tiz; I'm no docker, that's why I'm here. It just hurts real bad. Can I get somethin' for the pain?"

"Have you been drinking, Mr. Fagan? How much have you been drinking?"

"Ya, lil bit, just a little. Maybe 'bout a fifth, yeah."

"He told me he'd finished off a half gallon of vodka. And I don't think he's slept in days."

"Are you his friend?"

"Yes, I'm a friend."

"He's done this before, I see?"

"Yes, but he's been sober for over three years now."

"We'll have to wait for the lab results to come back, so we can tell what his blood-alcohol level is and the liver function tests reveal. Then we will decide what to do with him. He'll probably be admitted to detoxify. Meanwhile, I'll have the nurse give him something for pain and to help him rest. Okay?"

"Yes. Thank you, Doctor," I said.

"Nice meat-in you, Docker," Chiquita said, smiling broadly.

The looks of fear and panic were no longer on his tear-stained face, and he rested, knowing he'd be taken care of. He used to be so meticulous about his appearance, but now he had four days' of gray stubble peppering his flaky face, and his lifeless brush-cut gray hair was sticking out in every direction like a mental health patient after electric shock therapy, while other parts were pressed down flat as a pancake.

About half an hour later, while sound asleep, he was wheeled out of emergency and placed into a private room overlooking the western woodlands. Winter was fast approaching and yet the manicured lawn was still luxurious green velvet, and although completely leafless, the trees were illuminated by the golden gloaming glow of late afternoon sunshine. Chiquita was sleeping peacefully, bathed in the golden light as I departed. It was nearly dark by the time I finally reached home.

— —

The following afternoon I visited, and to cheer him up I stopped in the gift shop and bought a bouquet of overly priced orange alstromeria flowers. But when I got to his room the chubby nurse told me they didn't allow flowers on his entire floor, let alone in his room. Honestly now, they should post a sign in the gift shop: "Attention, hospital visitors—you may purchase these overly priced flowers for our guests. However, they are not allowed in any of the rooms. Thank you for your cash donations."

When they asked if I was a relative I simply replied yes, leaving it at that. His condition was considered quite serious, and they were trying to lower his blood pressure and get him stabilized. But meanwhile, he was completely zonked out and snoring like a bunkhouse full of drunken wranglers, with nasty breath that smelled as if he'd just eaten a rancid, week-old road-kill skunk.

When I visited the following day, they reported his blood pressure was slowly going down and his vitals were improving, but he was still coma-like, and seriously snoring. So I left him, leaving a couple of magazines, get well card, and a *huge* bag of breath mints.

Early in the morning on the fourth day of his institutionalzation I received a phone call. "Hey, Murf, where have you bin? You comin' up here, or what?"

"Or what. I've been there the last three days and all I did was watch you sleep. You didn't even know I was there. I left you a card, some magazines, and breath mints; thought you were in a coma."

"Magazines? Christ a-mighty, you left the damn *Advocate*, and *Out*. How queer is that? What time you gonna be here, anyway? I want you to brin' me some cigs."

"Those were the only magazines I had. Nikki thoughtfully gives me a subscription to those every Christmas. I brought you flowers, too, but they wouldn't let you have them. And you can't smoke up there—tobacco isn't allowed on the hospital grounds. No, I won't bring any cigarettes."

When I arrived he was sitting up in bed, and looking annoyed. "They won't let me have anythin' to eat, and I'm starvin' ta death. They have been pokin' me, proddin' me, pesterin' the hell out of me, but they won't feed me a thin'. I bin here since yesterday and they ain't fed me."

"You've been here for three days, Jim—actually, four now. This is Sunday."

"Really?"

"How are you feeling?"

"I just told you, I'm starvin'. When are they going to let me out of this loony bin, anyway?"

"Nice out, isn't it?" I said, trying to change the subject. "Thank God they got your blood pressure down; they were worried you'd have a stroke."

"Well, I hope it's a stroke-a genius."

"No, Jim, this was serious. I even called your dad to let him know you were in the hospital."

"Wad ya wanna do that for? Wad he say?"

"He asked if it was life-or-death, and I told him it was very serious."

Jim looked at me, appearing quite confused. "Is it really Sunday? What day-d I come here? You got my cell phone? What did my dad say?"

"You came here Thursday, and your dad said if it wasn't life-threatening he wasn't coming. You've been in trouble with this stuff before and it's your own damn fault; more or less."

"Figures."

"You said he was an alcoholic for years. Wouldn't you think he'd be understanding?"

"Alcoholic! He was a miserable fucking drunk, a mean son of a bitch, and then he found *Jesus*; as if that forgives sixty years of being an alcoholic abusive asshole."

"I called Nikki, too, thinking he should know. I know you two haven't spoken in a while."

"Wad you call him for? You didn't tell him I was in here dryin' out, did you?"

"No. I told him you were thrown into the loony bin, and only family can visit."

"Family, ha, you're the only one that ever visited."

"So, what are they telling you, anyway?"

"They don't tell me na-thin. Won't feed me na-thin ether. I had ta beg for a few measly chips-a ice to munch on to keep from starvin' ta death. You got more-a those pink mints? I already ate all them Canadian mints you left, those were *sooo* good. Ain't had no food 'tall. None 'tall."

"No, I don't have anything with me. Sorry."

His attending nurse was young and round, not wearing any make-up, retreating and nun-like. "Suzy, this is Denny. Denny, this is Suzy. She's bin taken real good care of me, except she's starvin' me to death, ha-ha, ha-ha, ha."

"Hello."

Suzy nodded in my direction, and I in hers. "Mr. Fagan, it looks like you're doing much better today. So, let's see if we can't get you some broth. Would you like that?"

"Well, *yeah*! Absolutely, and could ya put a couple-a chunks-a meat in there? Because they been a starvin' me ta death. Look how skinny I am."

"I can see you're being well cared for, so I'll call you later. By the way, I can't visit tomorrow because I'll be out of town all day."

The saddest look of abandonment was on his stubbly face as I was leaving, like a five-year-old who was being left on his first day of kindergarten, smiling bravely, but not convincingly, and trying to keep from crying.

When I returned to the hospital two days later, I found him sitting up in bed with his glasses on, face freshly shaved, dressed, and eating green Jell-O. "There ya are. I's wonderin' if I'd seed ya ta day. You ever had green Jell-O? Incredible stuff. Say, I'm getting sprung today. Can you stick around until they dislodge me, and give me a ride home?"

"Sure, I can do that, I'm off today. How are you feeling?"

"With ma fingers. I'm pretty sore, but glad to be gettin' outta here. No offense, Sister Suzy."

"They gave me five subscriptions that will need to be filled. So we'll have ta stop at the Wal-Mart's on the way home. You'll have ta borrow me the money. Don't have none 'tall."

"Sure."

An hour later we found our way in the glaring Wal-Mart Superstore's pharmacy, where he had two prescriptions filled costing around $30 each. Three others cost about $250 each; and having to pay cash, he chose to have the lesser-costing medication for blood pressure filled and get the rest later.

"This one tuba ointment for the flaky stuff on my face costs two hundred and fifty dollars, can you believe that? It's all a rip-off. Highway shrubbery."

"Have you spoken with Jon about getting back into the house? Did he leave you a key?" Before he could answer, a matronly woman in a sleeveless red-and-white pinafore walked in.

"Mr. Fagan? My name is Florence. I'm a social worker from the hospital, and I will need to ask you a few questions before we can discharge you. Is that all right?"

"Questions? What kinda questions?" Chiquita said, looking at her suspiciously.

"Well, *like*, are you still at the same address?"

"Yes, same old dress."

"Are you employed?"

"No."

"Do you have any hardships at home?"

"No, no, everything's fine."

"I'm sorry," I said, "I have to interrupt. His house doesn't have any water, electricity, or heat, and he's unemployed."

"Oh...you mean *that*. Yeah, what he said," Chiquita confirmed.

"Is there a history of substance abuse in your family, Mr. Fagan?"

"No, it's all good."

Again, I couldn't stand it. "Both his parents were alcoholics, and there was plenty of abuse."

"Oh...you mean *that*."

"Do you have a support system in place, for when you get home?"

"I'm pretty much self-supportin', Flo. But thanks for askin'."

"Would you like the number of some agencies that can help you; there's AA, Al-Anon, and Community Mental Health for counseling. I tell ya what, I'll just put all this information into your discharge packet, okay?"

"Yeah, yeah, it sall good. Thanks for comin', Stella. Bub-bye." After she left he turned to me. "You goof! What are you tellin' all that stuff to a incomplete stranger for? Jeez."

"*It's all good*? Is this the same man that called me last week cracking up? Didn't you hear her? There is help if you want it. You might be able to get your utilities turned back on."

"No, no, nope. Now, getting' back to my goin' home...I finally spoke with Jon, and he's left the keys in the Barbie-cue. Schmart, huh?" His bony tail was wagging, he was so happy to be going home.

— ⌐

Meanwhile, back at the ranch...

"Oh, thank you, Jesus! Home sweet home," Chiquita chimed, as we pulled into his crumbling drive. Well...it seemed that little Jon was no mental giant. He'd left the keys inside the grill all right, but it was locked inside the backyard, which had an eight-foot-tall, sharply pointed stockade fence surrounding it. And inside the house two giant man-eating dogs were barking ferociously, clawing at the doors and windows, snarling and trying to break out to eat me alive.

"Chiquita, the gate is padlocked. Is there some other way to get in there?"

"Christ a-mighty, Stella. The only way I know of is climbing over the fence on the Second Street side, by the steps to the second-floor 'part-mint."

After being just released from the hospital, he could barely stand on wobbly toothpick legs, let alone walk, but gingerly tottering he made it to the other side of the house, and plopped his bony butt down in the grass. Spying through a knothole in the weathered fence, I observed a junky yard where a shady oasis once existed, with manicured Japanese maples, lush ferns and velvety mosses, giant hostas, and carved stone statues of the Buddha. Now it was a trash-strewn mess, littered with dog shit. And the old house was molting and slowly sloughing off paint, suffering from years of neglect.

"First ya grab a hold-a the porch support post, right there, then ya stand on the fence stringer, and pull yourself up to the next stringer. Climb over the porch railin', and onto the second-floor deck. Then go down the stairs, open the grill, and get the keys."

For a fifty-six-year-old heart patient, it was a real workout. "I found the keys, Chiquita. They were inside the grill, just like he said. Do you want me to throw them over to you?"

"What for, silly? Open the back door."

"Are you kidding? Your dogs will kill me."

"Duke, shut up! Rotunda, shut up!" Chiquita yelled to the snarling animals. "They're fine, don't you worry 'bout them." But they just kept growling, snapping, and trying to eat the strange intruder: me. Duke, his big pit bull/boxer mix, weighed as much as I did, 150 pounds, and he could easily take my head off in one bite. I knew it. He knew it, too.

"I can't unlock this door. These dogs look awfully hungry, it doesn't look like he's been feeding them, and you've been away for five days."

"Jesus, Stella! Come over here an' help haul my ass over this pick-it fence."

"Chiquita, you were just discharged from the hospital; you really shouldn't be doing tha…"

It was too late. "Give me a hand here, will ya? Damn it," he said, already climbing the fence. Grabbing my hand, he slowly pulled himself up, and then delicately rolled over the railing and onto the deck. Completely winded from the climb, he sat down, lit up a cigarette, and panted out smoke.

When recovered, he tottered down the stairs and unlocked the door, and the giant man-eating dogs ceased their snarling and nearly wet themselves, wiggling, waggling with joy, and piddling all over the place. "Daddy's home. Have you kids been good? Oh. Oh dear. Oh dear God."

"Is it safe to come in? Are the dogs restrained? They won't eat me, will they?"

"Yeah, yeah. It's all good. Oh dear! Come in, but don't look at anythin'. It's really a mess."

Following a narrow path through the rubble-riddled lean-to porch, I entered the dingy, darkened debris field of a kitchen, and immediately noticed there had been an explosion of trash. Every single surface was completely covered with crap. The sink was heaped with dirty dishes and overflowing onto the filthy counter. Finely shredded pieces of yellow waxed paper littered the floor, and the place reeked of dog feces and urine. Ashtrays mounded with stale cigarette butts covered the coffee table, and piles of empty sports drink bottles littered the crap-covered carpet.

Stuff, stuff, stuff, and yet more stuff was piled everywhere. Paths traversed through the stuff and connected to other piles of stuff, and it was *way* beyond an ugly episode of *Hoarders*. The dank house was cold and cave-like, and the dead air smelled of old ashtrays and dog shit, with one stench dueling the other for dominance.

"Jon musta been feedin' 'em Mack Donald ham burgers for dinner. Look at all these shredded burger wrappers all over."

"Cheeseburgers."

"What?"

"Cheeseburgers. All that shredded paper is yellow, it was cheeseburgers."

"You'll have ta excused the mess, Denny."

"I understand."

"Duke, Rotunda, you gotta go potty?"

The giant dogs bolted for the door and knocked frail Chiquita over, and he fell back onto the crap-covered couch; once recovered he followed them out. So while they were out I examineed the place closer, and it was a complete disaster. The contamination had spread throughout the entire house; shit was everywhere. It was midafternoon and pitch-dark inside because every drape and blind was pulled tight. No fresh air to be found.

Needing to relieve myself of the morning's coffee, I went down the barricaded hall searching for the powder room. After climbing through a littered obstacle course of plastic room partitions and a tangled web of extension cords, I finally found the stool. Lifting the seat, I gasped, "Oh God," because a plastic shopping bag was taped over the side of the toilet, and it contained several days of excrement. Instantly dropping the lid, I backed out, hoping to find a sink to wash my contaminated hands. But that wasn't easily accomplished, because every sink in the house was heaped with dirty dishes. Then I remembered there wasn't any water anyway.

"Thanks for ever-thin'. I really appreciate it," Chiquita said. "I'll pay you back soon as I can."

"Chiquita, you don't have any power or water. How are you going to live here? It's November, for Christ's sake, you'll freeze to death. Last winter, when I was in Florida, I read about them finding a human Popsicle somewhere in Detroit. When the power company turned this poor guy's power off he froze to death, and afterward all they found was two stiff legs, with clean white socks, sticking straight out of a block of ice. I don't want that happening to you."

"I'd never wear white socks Stella—too hard to keep clean. Fiddle-de-de, I'll deal with that tomorrow. I'm tired now and need a place to fall down." Clearing a space on the sofa just large enough to sit his bony ass down, he slowly slumped onto it. Then Duke, his 150-pound dog, jumped on his lap and attempted to remove his face by licking.

"Duke, get off! They're afraid to leave my side." Then Rotunda, his big black blabradore, flopped down at Jim's feet, smiled with glee, and flashed us her big old belly and black boobies. She was so happy to see her favorite person.

"Daddy loves you, Rotunda. Thanks, Denny, I'll call ya tomorrow."

—◦—

"Mornin', Stella, it's tomorrow all ready. Ya up yet?"

"Yep, been up since five thirty. Did you get some rest?"

"Yup, I got me some good rest, but I nearly froze my ass off. I'm sure glad I had these big old dogs, because it was a two-dog night for sure. Now, I know that you've done a lot for me already, but I've got one more flavor to ask. Before I went in for the cure, every expense was spared, and that means I didn't pay the bills, so now I don't have any power. So here's the poop: I can get the juice turned back on if you can borrow me a hundred and fifty dollars. If I go down on the Consuming Power Company today, *right now*, and give them the cash money, they'll give me another thirty days' worth-a power. Maybe by then I'll have my feet back on."

"Can you be ready in about twenty minutes?"

"Make it a hour. Honk when you're here, no cameras." Jon had installed four security cameras on the house, one focused on the drive and garage, one surveyed the backyard and back door, one the front door and porch, and the last one viewed the front yard. Apparently Jon was an electronics geek and ammunitions expert, able to fix things and blow them up, and quite adept at vanishing, too.

"Okay, here's the poop," Jim said. "For years now I've been gettin' my power from the upstairs 'part-mint because it's still got power, but that bill is in Rob's name. That's the bill we're paying today. The bill for downstairs is so astrological it won't never be paid off; inta the thousands. So if I can keep the power on, and the cable for listing sales and Jon's porn, *if,* and *when* he comes home, then we're all good. I'll deal with the water situation later, or just keep gettin' it from you, like I done before. I tell ya, Stella, this house is made of toothpicks. It's all propped up with little, itty-bitty toothpicks."

The bill was paid, and the electric service restored. Then Chiquita began the process of powering his life back up as well. When I suggested he see a social worker for counseling, that didn't work for him, because AA was too structured. "That crap's for quitters." Instead he chose to jump back into e-commerce, get online, and get making money again. Photographing everything he had left of value, and listing it for sale on eBay, he began making money to redeem his ragged soul.

Unfortunately, while Chiquita was in the hospital recuperating, Jon had completely depleted their online account purchasing cheeseburgers for the dogs and booze, pot, and porn for him. So now he had to hustle double time. In two weeks he'd paid back the $150 he borrowed for the power bill, and was well on his way to paying off the loan for the prescriptions.

To rebuild inventory he was running to the thrift stores three times a day, and shopping as if his life depended upon it; because it did. He had an educated eye, and gleaned them for anything of value. Scrutinizing everything, and assessing its marketable worth, he would be especially delighted when he found any odd, unusual, and undervalued items. Running home, he'd look them up on the computer to learn where they came from, who made them, and exactly what they were worth. His plan was to resell the junk as collectible treasure, and net a tidy profit in the process.

Fridays during summer months were spent yard sale shopping for inventory, and when I had the time, I didn't mind riding along to pick up a few bargains. Rendezvousing at first light, we'd meet for breakfast and get down to work. Acting as copilot, I'd navigate, finding the best routes to take. A stop at McDonald's for Mcfood or a gas station to pee were the only breaks. It was serious work.

"Shoppers, make your selections because the bus is leaving. Push along, Stella. Either you want it or you don't."

Walking into a sale, he'd pleasantly greet the merchant, and then get right down to business. Scanning the room for quality, with search beam set on high, it took only a few seconds to find what he wanted. If he thought the price was right he'd snatch it right up, and if too high, he'd shamelessly try to get it down to where he thought he could make a profit reselling it. Gyp, screw, Jew, finagle, call it what you will, he haggled and wrangled, usually with humor, and almost always got what he wanted.

All winter Chiquita would sell the yard sale booty he'd pillaged from the countryside during summer, because selling *stuff* paid the bills. Progress was steadily made, and within a month of leaving the hospitality he'd caught up with most of his delinquent bills, except the power for his apartment and the hospital bills, which he'll probably never have enough money to repay. Oh, and then there was the water bill. Don't even ask.

Every few days he would drive over to my house to fill several giant plastic jugs with water. Most coincidentally, that usually happened at dinnertime. But Chiquita really didn't need very much water because he'd worked out a system. He used the Wishy-Washy Laundramat and psychic center, around the corner, for clothes cleaning and celestial consultation, and the neighborhood YMCA for showering and personal hygiene, since it was only two blocks away. The "borrowed" water was used for making coffee, tooth brushing, and light cooking. He collected rainwater in a recycled plastic fifty-gallon toxic waste barrel,

THE GAYS OF OUR LIVES

added bleach, and used it for washing dishes and nominal cleaning, and from the looks of it, he'd developed a serious allergy to house-keeping quite a while back.

Now, this part of the story confuses even me, and I'm the one tell-ing it, so bear with me. He *claimed* the power company turned off the electricity to his apartment ages ago, but the gas just kept flowing. His historic old house—which was from the turn of the century— had an ancient gas meter located in the basement and not outside like all the others. So when the electricity was terminated at the line the gas kept right on flowing because he'd never let them in to shut it off. And it had been flowing freely for over five years. (In Flint the natural gas and electricity come from the same monopoly.)

When I asked how that was even possible, he replied, "I was un-available to let them in durin' that entire five-year period. So the me-ter whirred away, and they just kept sendin' me guestimated bills. We had them security cameras installed just for that reason, so whenever we'd see 'em comin' ta turn it off, we would never answer the door." So he used their free gas to heat his home and water, when he had it, and his power was supplied by extension cords running from upstairs; and all this made perfectly good sense to him.

Around Thanksgiving the furnace went "kaflooey"—and that's a quote. Chiquita was usually able to fix things, so he investigated the problem, diagnosed the disorder, ordered the part, and installed it, but the furnace still didn't work. He tried everything short of calling a repairman, and the furnace still didn't work. So he moved to plan B.

Plan B. He had a perfectly good stove sitting in his kitchen go-ing unused most of the time, and he'd use that to heat the house. At first, in late November, he'd turn the oven on intermittently to kill the chill. As the mercury dropped, the lunacy ratcheted up. To maxi-mize the heating capacity, he built two-and three-foot-tall red-clay brick chimneys over the burners, and topped them with a pizza stone.

"If ya happen ta see any of these here Pampered Chef pizza stones while you're out junkin', pick 'em up for me, 'cause they come in real handy for toastin' things and warmin' leftovers. They'll radiate heat for hours after you've turned the burners off," he announced, in case you needed to know that sort of thing. "They absorb and radiate the heat most efficiently. Indubitably."

I believe this kind of living on the edge is what kept the pilot light burning under his bony butt. He certainly had enough money to fix his fucked-up furnace, but he wouldn't spend it. He went without water because he could mooch it from me instead of paying his bill and restoring service, and chose to asphyxiate himself using a cookstove for a free heat source, rather than repairing his furnace, and this made perfectly good sense to him. Was he resourceful, frugal, cheap, or just plain crazy?

Each morning he would call to indirectly let me know he'd made it through another night. "*Well*...last night was another three-burner night," and that meant it was very cold, but not completely freezing, because he needed only three faulty towers flaming. Most days he had two burners blazing, and that generally generated enough warmth for his kitchen and the *other room*. But if it was fucking freezing it was an oven-burning, four-burners-blazing, two-dog night, and the containers of "borrowed water" on the lean-to porch would freeze solid. During that wicked winter it happened quite often.

A wobbly, jerking, antique black wire-cage oscillating fan was used for the furnace's blower. Slowly yanking back and forth, it blew warmed oily air across the brick radiator chimneys, out of the kitchen, and into the shabby *other room* adjoining the kitchen. A ratty old mattress was flopped onto the cluttered living room floor, and that's where he and the dogs nested for the duration of that winter.

Frost, or something resembling it, coated the windows with an oily obscuring film. Blinds and heavy insulated drapes were drawn tightly, making it feel cave-like, and temporary partitions fashioned from blankets and plastic sheets were strung on clothesline and used to both insulate and separate the shabby living room from the parlor, bedrooms, and powder room. Depending on the temperature and their distance from the heat, they were used either as the auxiliary refrigerator or walk-in deep-freeze.

His living conditions reminded me of *Dr. Zhivago*, the part after the revolution happened. His was a *Mad Max*, survivalist, post-apocalyptic existence, and his days of rigorous housekeeping and anal-retentive order had ended. His home in no way resembled the clean—albeit overly decorated—and orderly life he had before. This was minimalist living, and his new decorating theme was "chaos."

And yet...his completely dysfunctional, disorganized business was buying old stuff from thrift stores and yard sales, and reselling the stuff in online auctions to unsuspecting purchasers locally and internationally. He was running a successful e-commerce company out of his crumbling chaotic house, and his "business"—and I use the term quite loosely here—was shipping items around the world daily, to such places as the Czech Republic, Japan, and China.

Rising at the crack of dawn, he'd stoke up on strong black truck driver coffee and hand-rolled, horse-turd generic cigarettes to commence his day. First he'd feed the dogs and let them out. Then he'd check the status of his online auctions and take care of those. Afterward he would photograph the new items to be listed for the day's sales and write a brief description extolling their many attributes. He called this process "product enhancement" or "adding yeast." Instead of the old stuff being posted as a cracked pot he had snatched from the curb, it was listed as: "Ladies and gentlemen, today we have for your approval a most unusual turn-of-the-century jardinière, complete with the original patinaed finish."

Early each morning, before most people were even awake, he'd head to the area strip malls to begin Dumpster diving. After scrounging up reusable refuse to use as packing materials, he'd take the stuff home, pack up the recently sold used stuff, and ship it worldwide via UPS, FedEx, and US Postal Service. He ran a very green company and had a well-oiled machine.

Two or three times a day he'd leave home to make his daily appointed rounds. After dropping the previous day's sales off for shipping, he'd recheck the Dumpsters for packing materials, and then go pluck the thrift stores. Beginning with the Saint Vincent DePaul, he shopped them all: the Salvation Army, AMVETS, Goodwill, and Habitat for Humanity were his usual haunts. Often he would visit them two or three times a day, so most clerks knew him by name, and some even liked him. He'd schmooze with the friendlier little old ladies, and they'd hold back items he'd like. He was shameless.

Chiquita made his living by buying and selling stuff and he was good at it, and like many other businessmen he greased the wheels of commerce. Some days he'd show up with freshly baked welfare peanut butter cookies, a dozen gooey Donna's doughnuts, or maybe a piping-hot pizza. "Say, girls, I just happen ta have this extra pizza-pizza here. Can I interest ya in a little sump-thin'?" Worked every time. He was raised to be resourceful, and he'd perfected the art to ridiculousness.

During the summer he'd check the Dumpsters, pick up the doughnuts, hit the yard sales, and be outside the thrift store impatiently tapping his foot and waiting for them to open at nine. "The early bird gets the worm," he'd say, and if that were really true, he could've opened a bait shop long ago.

Another old junker from Saginaw, weird Uncle Wayne, taught Chiquita the doughnut trick. "What you do is this, kid—first ya check the newspapers for yard sales and ya pick out the best ones. Plan your routes carefully, and make sure ya get there extra early; the earlier the better. If they open at eight you show up at seven thirty with a thermos of hot coffee and a dozen doughnuts. You just show up at the door and innocently say, 'Early, really? Well, my watch is busted, and I'm shopping for a new one. Oh, by the way, I just happen to have all these yummy doughnuts here, and I couldn't possibly eat all of them myself. Would you like one, maybe you'd like some coffee to go with that cruller? Cream, anybody?'" he'd ask, while pulling a pile of pillaged carry-out creamers from his pant pockets.

While chatting up the seller over doughnuts, coffee, and usually cigarettes, too, Chiquita would eventually wriggle his way toward the garage. "You got a watch in there? I know the sale don't start till eight, but if you don't mind, can I take just a little look-see, while I'm waitin' for ya ta open?" He'd walk away with treasures before the garage door was ever swung open. And because he brought the doughnuts, they usually gave him a break on the price, too. "Works every time."

Within a year of Chiquita's crack-up/breakthrough, he was up and running again—prospering. Jon finally returned home and all was forgiven, such as slovenliness and thievery, and together they'd forged a strange Oedipus complex/incorporation. Whereas Jon was at one time kept in the shadows, he was now visible and accompanying Jim while he was buying and selling, and a protégé to Mr. Fagan, the Artful Dodger.

"Chiquita, what do people at the flea markets think? Do they assume that he's your son?"

"Yeah, that's what they think, I just refer to him as Junior, but no one has ever come right out and asked me if I was schtuppin' him. He's your typical kid, likes guns, chain saws, and grenades; makes bombs in his spare time. And he's double jointed, too. Wink, wink."

Before long he was busier than a one legged man in an ass kicking contest, and they were making so much undocumented underground income that Chiquita was trying to find ways of hiding it, to avoid paying taxes. He even went so far as to ask me to go into cahoots with him.

"Hey, Murf, you're not making no money right now that I know of. So why don't you open a incognito online account in your name, and sell some stuff for me so's I can hide some-a my profits? I already made too much money this year, and they want ta tax me on it."

"The nerve of them heartless bastards. Chiquita, if you want to be in the game, put up the ante. That's how it works. And just how is this supposed to help me, anyway?"

"They're going to tax me to death, the heartless bastards."

Now...he *claimed* he'd already made over $35,000 that year, and the third quarter was not closed yet. But he probably wasn't telling the truth anyway. And after years of neglect he was making plans to repaint his deteriorating house, all one color—white. How very imaginative. He also planned on repairing his rotting teeth, and getting his lifeless gray hair dyed and even highlighted once again, as he did in the old days. It was full-blown summer and he was flying high, making money, and it was all good. Again.

It'd been a long slow crawl back, from not having enough money for a pack of cigs and living without water, power, or heat to becoming a successful third-wave capitalist making so much money he had to find ways to hide it. But by the grace of God, and his own determination, within a year's time he was back up and running, and even prospering in a terrible economy, where many others were failing.

Bless his eccentric heart.

Chairman

Mid-March in Michigan meant muddy mush was every-where. The rock-hard frozen ground began to thaw, ever so slightly soften, turning the melting snow into mud-colored Slurpee slush. The fuzzy little groundhog, holed up inside his snuggly underground chamber, sensed the subtle shift away from subzero temperatures, or maybe he felt the returning retrograde sun. Whatever the impulse was, for the first time all winter the prognosticating rodent poked his fat fuzzy head out to take a look-see.

It was a Thursday afternoon, Groundhog Day, and not much was happening on the home front. I was caught up with work, and had left-overs were in the fridge for dinner. The phone rang.

—◦—

"Murf, hey, whatcha doin'?"

"Not too much, just writing stuff down on my comp-you-tater. Why?"

"Why don't you run over to the Davison Salvation Army with me, and take a look see? I ain't been shoppin' there in quite a spell. And another thin', you should get out more often. It's good for old people ta get out."

"All right, come get me, smart-ass."

"See ya in fifteen, Stella."

He called everyone Stella. I don't know if he had trouble remembering names, or what. Next thing I knew we were inside the bustling brightly lit suburban strip mall Salvation Army, and sifting through aisles of used housewares and clothing. Aisle after aisle was stuffed with stuff. There was so much excess stuff out there, stuff, stuff, stuff, and yet more stuff, and this was the afterlife for stuff. I sorted through their used stuff as if I needed more stuff, even though I didn't. So naturally I found more stuff I didn't need: a Wedgwood blue cashmere cardigan with the teensiest hole in the sleeve for three dollars, and a 1980s-vintage Pee-Wee Herman doll, with a cockeyed pull string. And can you believe they were asking only three dollars? Handing it to Chiquita, I said, "Here you go, I already have one. Joany gave it to me."

"Say there, Stella, now that may really be worth somethin'—maybe a hundred dollars. Good eye there, thanks. That'll pay my cable bill for the month."

"How are you making out, anyway?"

"Good, good, the bills are paid; I got Gatorade, Cheerios, SpaghettiOs, cigarettes, and food for the pets. It's all good." Two more thrift stores were visited and their few worthwhile items plucked up before our last stop, in Grand Blank (the big nothing). We entered the Habitat for Humanity Re-Store and Chiquita went straight for the housewares. I went into the outbuilding where they stored old furniture, and immediately saw seven midcentury-modern chairs sitting up front. Recognizing them as classic pieces, I flipped one over to inspect the bottom, and found a wood-burned insignia from the maker, Hans Jorgensen Wegner. But what was even more significant, they were numbered, too.

"Hey, Chiquita, I found some chairs that really you need to take a look at."

"What? That fifties junk? You're the only one who likes modern crap. Everyone else hates it."

"It's sixties, and it's not crap. Look, there is a wood-burned stamp on the bottom of these chairs, and they're numbered individually; this one is number one twelve. They have the original upholstery and they're in excellent condition, practically mint."

"Mint, splint, they came from Flint and look like they belonged to a Protestant. Plus they want fifteen dollars apiece for them damn ugly things; that's more-n a hundred dollars, and I don't even have 'nough money left fur a pack-a cigs. Besides, I don't have no luck sellin' old furniture; it's just not worth my bother. I do better sellin' dishes, jewelry, and small shippable stuff. If I was ta sell them they'd be a pain to ship. I'd have to make a crate for each one, and it would cost a fortune."

"I'm telling you, they're worth it."

"Ya think? Because they don't look like nothin', nothin' 'tall. Do you have the money fur 'em? 'Cause I sure don't. I'll tell ya what—we could go halves; you 'n' me can be pardoners if you would lend me the money. What do ya think, Murf? Maybe you and me'll get us brand new computers outta this deal. What the hell, give me that hundred-dollar bill you been savin' for your retirement, Stella."

Later...

"Stella, are ya sittin' down? Well, find yerself a chair and sit yerself down. Ya know them ugly Hans-Jorgen-Wegner Scandinavian chairs we just bought? Well, them damn dumb thin's is worth a fortune. You won't believe this, but some guy in Germ-many has a set of ten of 'em listed for sale on eBay right now for thirty thousand dollars! Whew. I need a drink.

"Seriously, Stella, accordin' to my eBay findin's, them chairs is called 'The President's Chair,' because Presidents John F. Kennedy and Richard Male-hose Nixon both had their pitchers took in that very chair. Can you believe them chairs was in the White House? They come in ash, maple, and walnut, from what I can see, but these here are white oak, and I don't see a thing 'bout that. Now...this can be a good thing, could be bad, dunno. They've sold for eight hundred apiece and up, and these here are practically spearmint. Who'da thunk it, Stella? You was right all 'long. Never sold anythin' for that much money before, ever. Mostly nickel-an'-dime shit."

"I told you they were the real thing. I didn't just fall off the turnip truck, ya know."

"Yada, yada, yada. Now, I'll have ta figure out the best way to list these thin's. Do we list them separately, or as a set of seven? But that's an odd number. How about listin' one singly and then three sets of two? I'm goin' to have to get back ta you on this one; this will require some fineness."

Each day for the next several days I received more frenetic up-dates. "Murf, there's plenty a people lookin' at them chairs, like crazy, they're gettin' hundreds of hits, but no one is biddin' a thin' and it's freakin' me out. It's been four days and the online auction is 'bout ta run out, and if they don't sell soon I don't know what I'll do. I'll have ta take 'em ta the flea market, or somethin'.'"

"I have a fireplace, Chiquita, if that will help."

"*Well...*you're no help, Stella."

"Hang in there, the fat lady ain't done singin' yet."

—◆ ◆

The next day he called again. "You home?"

"Yep, what's up?"

"Got sump-thin' for ya; just thought I'd stop by and drop it off."

"Sure, come on over and I'll put on the coffee."

As I passed a piping mug to Chiquita, he took it and thorough-ly saturated it with the sickeningly sweet hazelnut-flavored creamer that he loved, and then added a little coffee to give it color. Digging deep into the pocket of his ratty bomber jacket, he pulled out a wad of crumpled small-denomination bills and threw them onto my table as if they had cooties.

"What's this?"

"It's the money for them chairs."

"Money for them chairs? I thought we were partners on them chairs. Won't there be expenses for crating and shipping them chairs?"

"Well, Stella, just how did you think this deal was goin' ta work, anyway?"

Reflecting on how he operated, I put the ball back into his court. "How do *you* think this deal should work, *partner*?"

"Well, it's like I said all along, Stella, why don't you let me give you your money back for them rickety old chairs, and you and me'll both get brand-new computers when they sell. That thing you're workin' on now is an antique, a damn dinosaur, and I don't know how you've made it last this long. Yes, let's just do it this way, and when this is over we'll both have new computers."

"OK, *partner*, if that's the way you want it," I said, fully aware that I was trading my fattened cow for some used magic beans. For the next several days I didn't hear a word from Chiquita, which was most unusual, because I had every day since his crack-up, sorry, his breakthrough way last fall. So I took the opportunity to badmouth him every chance I could. First I called Nikki.

"That bad Chiquita, shame on him," he said.

"Indian giver," I replied.

— ❧ —

A few days later he called to give me another update. "This chair sale's turnin' inta a nightmire. The last chair I sold cost me fifty dollars to ship, so I put a fifty-dollar guesstimate ta cover the costs. Now I find it'll cost me two hundred and fifty dollars ta crate a chair that sold for eight hu..."

Stopping in midsentence, he caught himself just short of admitting the chair sold for eight hundred dollars. The next few days he'd call giving further updates, and surprisingly mooched his water from someone else. (Did you notice your water bill being markedly higher in March, Nikki?)

"It now appears there's been some sorta glitch sendin' the funds from Japan. Apparently the chair was purchased by some big Jap-a-knees con-glom-irate, so the refunds have ta be sent from Jap-land ta the US, via Seattle, and then deposited inta my account. So, now they want me ta crate this chair up and ship it ta Seattle. They'll probably sneak it across the border inta Canada at midnight, and then ta Japan; saves on taxes, or somethin'."

Two days later I get another call. "Murf, I got more bad news. I Googled that gook company and it seems they may be a bit shady. The funds still aren't showin' up in my account and I'm worried this deal may not happen at all. I *have got* to pay the taxes on my house or they're goin' ta sell it out from under me at a tax sale. I'm three years in the rears."

"I'm sorry to hear that," I said, laughing.

"*You* are laughin' entirely *too* much about this whole fresco, Stella."

Two days later he called again. "Murf, I'm watchin' the security cameras an' there is two guys outside wearin' orange security vests an' carryin'orange glow-in-the-dark paint. They're pokin' 'round my drive and yard, and markin' stuff off. They're ether from the city accessorizer office or the power company. And I think they're goin' ta turn off my utilities."

"Utilities? What utilities? I thought they were all shut off ages ago."

"You're somewhat correct, Stella, there's no electristicals downstairs, but the gas has been runnin' for years; you've seen my combination cookstove, and home-heatin' appliance. But it now appears they're goin' ta cut me off, and then I'll really be cooked."

"What you going to do?"

"Can I borrow your spacious heater?"

"Well, if you don't have any power it won't do you much good."

"Stella, you still doesn't get it, do ya? I still have electristicals"—a reference to Lisa Douglas from *Green Acres*, season one, episode number twenty-five—"coming from the upstairs apartment, just like I always did. I just wan' ta cover all the bases, ya know. I hope to God my PayPal 'count shows the credit for this chair sale soon, 'cause I really need ta get some money, and bad."

"If I know you, you've got some money stashed. I swear, you'd do anything to save a nickel."

"Well, *yeah*, a nickels a snickel!"

"Chiquita, you are so cheap, I remember when you hauled your dead mother to the crematorium in a cardboard box, on a borrowed snowmobile trailer, just to save a couple bucks."

"Coupla bucks my ass, try a couple-a hundred."

"That's why I don't understand you at all. You'll haul your dead mom to the gas chamber to save a couple hundred, and then you'll turn around and spend three hundred dollars to have prosthetic testicles put into your neutered dog's nut sack."

"Well, he just didn't look right without those crystal balls."

The very next morning, that cute little Matt Lauer reported that the largest earthquake ever recorded, registering 10.0 on the Richter scale, had just hit Japan. A massive tsunami had inundated the entire northeastern coast of Japan, which was terrible news for Japan, but even worse news for Jim. The chair deal looked in peril; there hadn't been a word from Seattle about the money transfer, and he was sweating bullets, chain smoking like a waiting room full of expectant fathers, pacing and drinking enough black coffee to run a truck stop for a month. For three weeks he was this way, crazed.

"Stella, you know them guys that was out there in them orange vests? Well, they come back with a backhoe and shut my gas off. The bastards dug a big hole in my front yard an' shut the shit off."

"Those heartless bastards, after giving you free gas for five years. How dare they?"

"Don't know what I'm goin' ta do now. Last night I made burgers in the 'lectric perk-ya-later; not bad ether. 'Bout halfway you gotta pull the core out, flip 'em over, and then perk the other side."

"Chiquita, here is another home appliance cooking tip: you can make a real nice grilled cheese sandwich using an iron. David says to set it on Cotton; works just great, and nonstick, too."

"Thanks for the tip, Stella. Oh, I know I can make this work. But I gotta be real careful with what all I plug in around here, 'cause we keep blowin' electristicals."

"Say, Chiquita, just how big was your unpaid gas bill anyway?"

"Don't rightly know for sure. They been guess-ta-mate-in' for five years now, but they guessed I owed somewheres in the neighborhoods of ten thousand dollars, but they were just guessin', ya understand. They haven't actually read the meter in six years."

"Your whole house isn't worth that much."

"You think I don't I know that, Stella? I argued with City Hall on that there very point, and tried to get my improperly taxes lowered. The last notice they sent said my house is worth six thousand, and that was grossly infatuated."

"What do you figure it'll take to have the water turned back on?"

"Water, phffft. Last time I checked it was about twelve hundred dollars. I've been livin' for well over a year without any water now. Maybe I should go down there tomorrow and see just what it would take to have it turned back on."

"Good idea, then you can quit 'borrowing' it from me."

"Stella, be seriously. I don't know what I'm going ta do if this chair deal don't go through; I'm practically out of cookies, no money left 'tall. An' I'm only sellin' nickel-and-dime stuff."

"Chiquita, just like Bill Clinton, I feel your pain."

∼ ⌣

"Hey, Murf, guess what? I went down to City Hall yesterday and talked to the nicest woman you would ever want ta meet; works in the water department."

"Really? That's peculiar, because I've heard nothing but horror stories about Flint's water department. The water is poisoned with lead and Legionnaires' disease, it's toxic and caustic, and the water department is inept and mismanaged. It's probably saved your life not having water."

"Not true 'tall—lovely people. We had ourselves the nicest chat, and come ta find out she knew my neighbor Sister Wilma, ya know—the one who just passed into glory. They went ta the same church, Mount Pisgah Baptist Holy Temple Church of God in Christ."

"Amen."

"Yes she did. Now, she said there was an outstandin' balance of eighteen hundred and forty-six dollars and thirty-seven cents for water supplied to this address. 'In what name?' I asked Beatrice."

"Beatrice, was it?"

"Yes, Beatrice Brown, a lovely woman, Christian woman—pillar of her church. She said a Mr. Bill Hopsack was listed as the homeowner. 'Well,' I said, 'Beatrice, he was my second husband and he's been dead for over ten years.' Well, come to find out, she was a widow, too. We had us the nicest little chat about gardenin', antiques, recipes, all kinds of maladies, and it was right 'bout then that she decided I could get service to the house in *my* name, and they'd just forget about that nasty-old Bill-bill. An' for a mere hundred dollar deposit I could get new water. Wasn't she was just too kind?"

"Too, too, you lucky bastard."

"So, Stella, can you borrow me a hundred dollars?"

Another four tortured weeks passed before the "chair deal" was finally consummated, paid for, shipped to Seattle, and smuggled across the border on the underground chair-rail-road into Canada.

"Now we have precedence on the presidents' chairs, authentication, and that proves they're worth just what those Japs paid for it. That'll make sellin' the other six a cinch. I'm listing another one today. Daddy needs to pay his new water bill."

"Daddy needs to pay Denny."

A week later, I receive another phone call. "Guess what, Murf. Some guy in Jap-land wants ta buy the next chair. And because I sold the last one for eight hundred, and lost money, he'll pay the shippin'. I tell ya, Stella—those Japs are nutso for this retro stuff. The gook who bought the last chair has a shop in Tokyo, where he resells this stupid old stuff. Do ya know, he'll charge five thousand dollars apiece for those chairs we paid fifteen dollars for? I'm gonna see if he wants ta buy all six of 'em; what the hell, it's worth a shot. Keep ya posted."

Now, mind you, throughout the entire winter he'd been coming over for free water, and usually a home-cooked meal, too—except during the chair sale estrangement—and all the while keeping me posted of the progress of the chair sales, and I just wrote it all down.

~ ~

"Murf, Chiquita. Ya busy?"

"Not too. Why, what's up?"

"Got a brand-new comp-u-tater here with your name on it. Would ya like to meet it?"

"What a surprise, absolutely. I'm just about finished with work. How about in an hour?"

"See ya in ten minutes."

~ ~

"Now, this here mouse is completely wireless, and the new keyboard is wireless, too. They're lots different from the one you've used, because there's no annoyin' cord. You'll love it. It's a hundred times faster, too, with much more remembery. Now, Jon'll take your old computer 'part, and transform the data onto your new computer. You won't have to worry about a thin'."

"Can you tell me what you're using this computer for, Den?" Jon timidly inquired.

"Basically word processing and I'm currently working on two novels and several short stories. I also store photographs, and I use it for emailing and business."

"Okay, let me transfer the hard drive's information now, and we'll transfer your memory later." My computer was completely disassembled, part by part taken apart; spread all over the floor in a hundred pieces, and lying right where everyone had to walk. On the fourth day he took my hard drive home to manually transfer the files, saying, "It's taking much longer than I anticipated." Apparently my old computer's software was not compatible with the new format. On the seventh day I was back up and running, with a new tower, wireless mouse, and keyboard. But knowing Chiquita, those parts were probably salvaged from a retired Soviet Sputnik he got a good deal on.

"Okay, Stella, yer up an' runnin' again. You'll have ta wait a bit for the flat-screen moniker. I'll have ta sell another chair."

On the summer solstice, June 21, a sleek black flat-screen monitor arrived. Chiquita connected it, using my old speakers and printer, which gave me a "practically" new operating system. But then…less than one year later, my new computer started repeatedly sending me "low memory" messages. When I took it to the local computer repair shop, the nerdly young man said the tower was over ten years old, and he showed me a sticker on the back dating from seven years earlier—officially making it older than the one I replaced.

So…from our 50/50 partnership I received a computer tower that was *older than the one I had* {which Jon kindly removed for me—free of charge}, a new flat-screen monitor, and a wireless mouse. Chiquita, on the other hand, made only a few measly thousands on the sale of seven chairs that I found and paid for. Bless his shifty heart.

Just when Flint hoped it had hit the bottom, the bottom was lowered. Things worsened, and we didn't think that was even possible; more factories closed, more jobs were cut, and the screw was turned once again.

This was the summer of the sales: yard sales, rummage sales, garage sales, and moving sales, because the next wave of people were losing their homes and selling off everything they'd accumulated during a lifetime.

These home default sales were easily recognizable because of their children's items, Christmas trims, lawn care tools, and things they wouldn't need in their next life—living in their car. These defeated people were quietly selling everything and leaving in shame. And it didn't matter if they were being evicted because of a short sale or mortgage default, because the end result was the same—they were going down.

Pale-faced and zombie-like, these poor people stood paralyzed while witnessing their slow-motion descent into financial quicksand, sinking further into the economic abyss daily, and going deeper than they'd ever dreamed possible. Some of these defaults started with a job loss, a medical emergency, or an adjustable-rate mortgage skyrocketing, and sometimes shit just happened. No matter the cause, they had a hefty mortgage they could no longer afford and they were going down.

The heartless bastards at the banks, which I remind you were recently propped up using *taxpayer money*, would not negotiate with the homeowner—and they still won't. Consequently a third of the homes in the Flint area were in financial trouble and either delinquent with their payments, listed for sale, going through a negotiated short sale, in the foreclosure process, or already abandoned. And selling a home in Flint was nearly impossible, because the supply far exceeded the demand.

When the housing bubble burst in 2006 the hyperinflated stock market popped as well, and the global economic turndown resulted. Consequently, the value of *creative securities*, which were *tied to those real estate values*, plummeted. This financial collapse happened partially because of the recent easing of banking regulations, which made access to money easy for just about everyone. Risky loans were written to unqualified borrowers, and then Wall Street created complicated fabricated derivatives with those newly minted and worthless mortgages, bundled them as secure investments, and sold them to an unsuspecting public.

The greedy bankers made big money approving every worth-less fraud-you-lent mortgage they wrote to people who couldn't afford them. Then they bought mortgage insurance to cover those shaky loans if they defaulted, and when the loans failed they were compensated, and either way they profited. In essence, they were gambling in a game they had fixed, and their losses were repaid with taxpayer money. But the worst thing about it is, to this day the game continues unchanged. Privatize the gains, and socialize the losses.

～ ～

Chiquita took full advantage of these sales. At times he could be downright shameless, especially when he was driving for a bargain. After all, to him the difference between what they'd ask for something and what they'd take was more profit for him. So if they're asking fifty dollars, there was no harm in offering thirty, because they wanted to get rid of the stuff anyway. Right?

It was a Friday fall afternoon, early bird day, and the first day for weekend yard sales. While most people were still at work, Chiquita was driving through flat farm country west of town when he and Jon-boi spied another sale. He pulled into the unkempt farmyard, where he saw an old farmer in patched overalls limping out of a lean-to shed attached to a peeling red barn. Rusty farm implements were sitting under smelly oiled tarpaulins to shelter them from inclement weather, and the used-up items were spread on plywood sheets straddling two-by-four wooden sawhorses.

"Afternoon," the ancient farmer said.

"Afternoon, young man," Chiquita replied. "Givin' up farmin', are ya?"

"Well, no sir, not 'xactly; least not ba choice."

"You got any old dishes?"

"Well, yeah sir, the wife has a few boxes a her good stuff packed-up over yonder. There's newspaper betwixt 'em, but you're welcome ta look."

Jim began examining the crappy contents but found nothing of resale value, mostly chipped-up old dime-store china wrapped in yellowed newspaper that reeked of stale cigarette smoke. Meanwhile Jon-boi was perusing the men's section where tools, guns, and things with motors were located. Chiquita always said that Jon was good with his hands.

"Can I take a look at them old chain saws you got there, Mister?" Jon politely inquired.

"Hep yerself, son."

"Hey, Jimmy, I want you to buy them chain saws."

"What the hell do you want them rusty old things for? You got so much crap lyin' 'round that backyard now that you can't even walk through there. Nope."

"No, Jimmy, you don't understand, we *need* these," Jon replied, most emphatically.

"Okay, young feller, whaddya want for the whole lot-a them rusty old saws, anyway?" Chiquita inquired, sounding most irritated.

"*Why*...them aren't rusty, Mister. Don't rightly know...was wantin' ta sell 'em separate," the farmer said, taking off his green John Deere cap and scratching his spotted head.

"Tell ya what; I'll give ya a hundred an' fifty for the whole lot."

"Well, now, don't rightly know 'bout that. Give more 'n that fur ever' one-a them."

"Okay, tell ya watt, I'll give ya two hundred cash right now, and you'll be ridda the rusty junk."

"Don't know 'bout that...Well...well..."

Jim stood there holding two hundred-dollar bills in his scrawny outstretched arm, not blinkin'.

That very same weekend he sold every one of the saws at the flea market for what he paid for five of them, and made a tidy profit. "I didn't know about chain saws but Jon did. I tell ya, Stella, you'd be surprised, there's a collector of just about every damn thin' there is. I swear."

Jon hauled the chain saws to the van. Walking back to the farmer, he inquired further, "You got any guns, grenades, knives; fun stuff like that?"

"Wait here a mint, son," the farmer said, as he limped away. A few minutes later he returned with a dusty box containing what looked to be ancient war relics.

Spying a pair of old binoculars in the crate that probably measured close to three feet long, Jon said, "Lemme see them binoculars, will ya please, Mister?" He'd never seen anything like them.

"Brought these here spyglasses back from the war, got 'em off a Jap destroyer we took in the South Pacific. We all wanted souvenirs, see, so when we boarded the ship, I headed straight for the captain's quarters, and that's where I spied them glasses. Had 'em put away for over sixty years now; guess we won't be needin' 'em where we're headed."

"I want these, too, Jimmy."

"Now, what the hell do you want them musty old relics for? You got enough shit already."

"But Jimmy!"

"Just what do ya want for those moldy old thin's anyway?" Chiquita asked, rather indignantly.

"Well, now, them ain't moldy, Mister, mebbe a trifle dusty…"

"How much?"

"Well…gotta get mebbe a hundred dollars or better?"

"No way, José. Put 'em away, they're way too much. Forget it. Ya can't have 'em so just forget about it. It's just more crap ya don't need."

"But you don't understand, Jim. I *really* want them. They're neat."

"Neat, schmeet, pick up your feet, and get your butt back in the seat. Let's go."

"Tell ya what, Mister, you just take a look through them field glasses, an' you'll see. You can spot a horsefly on a outhouse two miles down the road. You just try 'em," the farmer demanded, and he practically forced the glasses upon Jim.

Chiquita accepted the weighty binoculars and attempted to look through them. "Jeez, them are heavy. Junior, come here and help me hold these up." Jon obediently stepped over and balanced the spyglasses on his shoulder. Taking off his Coke-bottle glasses, Jim squinted and peered into them.

"Wow! They really do magnify stuff. And yes, I can see the fly. And no, you're not getting 'em, not for a hundred, not for fifty. I'm tellin' ya that right now."

"Would you take thirty dollars for them glasses, Mister?" Jon politely asked the old farmer.

Now, I suspected that Jon and Chiquita had worked themselves out a little routine, and they were running it on the old dirt farmer.

"Well...I don't rightly know as I should be sellin' those 'tall," the farmer said, hobbling away.

"Okay. I tell ya watt. I'll give ya twenty-five dollars cash—right now—and you'll be rid of one more old piece of crap," Jim said, holding the money in his outstretched hand.

That same afternoon, my phone rang. "Murf, find yerself a chair 'cause I got another story for yer book. Guess what we me an' Jon-boi found out in Mount-Rose ta-day?"

"What's that, Chiquita?"

"Emperor Hero-he-toe's field glasses, that's right. This old farmer was sellin' a bunch of busted old junk, mostly rubbish, but he also had these ancient spyglasses that was darn near three feet long, too, with six-inch lenses, and heavier 'n crap. So, I gets home, does my online research, and discovers that these things was rare as hell. Was only one pair-a these was made for each ship in the Jap-knees fleet and they're all accounted for except for four. Hot damn! The last pair sold ta a museum in Germ-many for four thousand. Can ya believe it, Stella?"

"Unbelievable."

"Gotta go because I'm listin' this priceless hysterical arty-fact online ta see how much cashola I can get fur it. See ya, Stella."

"Murf, grab yerself another chair, 'cause you are not going ta believe what's happenin'. Them spyglasses haven't even been listed for an hour yet an' the auction is goin' absolutely berserk; lit up the switchboard like the Rocket-feller Christmas tree. I'm gettin' sideburn offers from Germany, Israel, and Jap-land, and museums are sendin' me emails like crazy. What should I do?"

"How many days will the auction be running?"

"Three."

"Respond politely to the emails, and let the clock run. Be patient and just see what happens."

"Holy shit, I can't stand it. I'm runnin' outta toilet paper."

— —

The next day Chiquita called four times. "Murf, some museum in Germany wants them glasses real bad, and they're makin' me a four-thousand-dollar sideburn offer."

"Let it ride. If they want them that badly they'll pay that much at the auction. It will just drive the price higher, have faith."

"Jesus Jiminy, you're no help."

— —

"Murf, now the IRS wants in on the auction action, and I'll have to pay taxes on this sale.""You're a big boy now. Pay the taxes, ante up, and get in the game."

"Well, no, I don't like that kinda talk. I have principles, you know."

"Yes, I know, I have seen your principles, and they are set very low."

"You don't have any income this year that I know of. Would you care to open up an incognito online account in your name where I could bury some-a my recently earned prof-its?"

"And just how is that supposed to help me? No, but thanks for the generous offer."

"What the hell am I goin' to do, Stella?"

"Well...the Jewish people have a saying for times such as this. 'Such problems I should have.' Having too much money is not a problem. Would you please try remembering that just a year ago you had big problems and no money? This, my friend, is not a problem.

Mazel tov!"

Somersault

(Definition: a complete overturn or reversal—the body
turning end over end)

A miserably, sultry, steamy day of steady rain turned into a
blackened starless evening, as the last of summer's fever was
sweating itself out. Late August, still eighty-two sticky degrees on a muggy Saturday evening, not a bit of breeze, and the only
relief from the heat was the old turquoise oscillating fan. Slowly rotating back and forth, it contributed its syncopated din to the wallpaper
of hypnotic white noises: cricket choruses, tree frog songs, and katydid
calls, all keeping time with the wall clock.

Finding the bedroom stuffy and stifling, I moved to the back room,
where the patio doors and windows were all open, hoping to catch an
errant breeze strayed from the lake and some cooling relief, but there
was none to be found. Sweating it out in front of the flip-flopping fan,
I finally fell asleep somewhere around midnight.

Suddenly I was jolted awake by the cell phone as it chimed its annoying electronic tones, lit up, and danced upon the coffee table.
Glancing at the display, I saw it was Chiquita and said a prayer, hoping
someone hadn't died.

"Hey, Murf, whatcha doin'?"

"What?"

"Ha-tout, ain' tit?"

"It's two thirty, Chiquita. Has Nikki died?"

"Oh my God. Nick-e died? Real-lee? Wha' happen'?"

"What?"

"Ahhh, nobody's dead overt the-air, I'd-a seen the am-balance. Say, did-in we have us some fun lass summer yard-sale-in?"

"Chiquita, if you called just to chitchat I'm hanging up."

"Wad I say?"

He'd definitely been drinking, was slurring words, and I'd decided I wouldn't talk with him anymore when he was like that. What a shame, he had been sober for well over a year this time. But autumn was again descending upon us, daylight was dwindling daily, and we were heading back into the darkened tunnel of winter. And just like clockwork, poor light-deprived Jim was once again crashing. For the next few weeks we had very little contact, just a few emails.

Then, quite suddenly, and most unexpectedly, Duke—Chiquita's giant pit bull/boxer/moose—dog, became very ill and died. Poor Chiquita took his death very hard, and sank deeper into an already darkening depression.

"Denny, it was terrible, I tell ya. Poor Duke come in from the backyard an' ran right smack inta the wall. Bammm! He just stood there lookin' up at the ceilin', all confused, an' bleedin' from the eyes. *Snap*, went blind, just like that! We took him to the vet's, but they could'nt hep 'em. Said, 'Take 'em to Michigan State Vet-nary Hospitable, in Lance-in.'

"So Jon an' me drove him overt the-air. And for a coupl-a days it seemed like he was gettin' better, but then he got lots worse an' died. Now poor Rotunda just wanders around this big old house lookin' for him, and howlin'. Won't shut up, or sit down. To top it off, the mess cost us fifteen hundred dollars, an' all I got was another dead dog to bury.

"Thank God it's not January with the ground frozen."

I am not sure exactly what he was using this time. Alcohol and morphine derivatives were his past favorites, but after a year of sobriety he was definitely using something again.

— —

The weather was turning ugly, again, but luckily I was leaving town and for the next three weeks I'd be working in sunny Southern California, and the time passed all too quickly. When back in Flint I sent an email to Chiquita asking how things were going. This was his reply:

"Things is bad over at Twelve Oaks. Aunt Pity-Pat is not doin' so good, not good 'tall."

Apparently he'd been quite troubled in my absence, and sought counsel. First he consulted with his former cleaning client, and trusted street therapist, Dr. Church. After taking one look at him, she knew he'd been drinking again—and a lot. Being a crackerjack substance therapist for years, she knew the telltale symptoms.

"As soon as he came in I knew he'd been drinking heavily. When people drink excessively their liver and pancreas cannot metabolize any more alcohol, and they begin to exhale it through their lungs. I made him sit down, take off his glasses, and stare me straight in the eyes. His eyes were all bloodshot, with lots of little broken blood vessels. I told him I knew he was using again, and he broke down and bawled. He took that dog's death awfully hard. He was very close to him."

"I know. I really feel sorry for the poor guy. It's like having Nikki pet-sit for you."

"Oh no, you didn't just say that. Bad Den! But seriously, I told him I was onto him."

Chiquita, figuring he was already fingered, voluntarily readmitted himself. On the third day he rose from the bed and called, asking me to visit. On a gloomy fall afternoon I arrived at his private room. The bed was monitored with an alarm so he couldn't leave, and a twenty-four-hour suicide watch nurse was stationed with him to make sure. When approaching his room I could already hear him squawking.

"Nurse, I'm tellin' ya, there's somethin's wrong with this here tell-vision. It's busted, there's a big purple blob on ever' single channel."

"Put your glasses on. Don't you know, that's Barney, honey?"

"Well, Barn-e Hon-ey muss be real poplar, 'cause he's on ever' sin-gull channel."

"Let me see that, honey," the annoyed nurse said, taking the remote as I entered the room.

"Hey, Murf, somethin's wrong with this tell-vision. All its gets is a big purple blob."

"Why, there's something wrong with this remote control. I'll have to find you a new one. Can your father stay with you while I get you another?" she asked, looking directly at me.

"Yes, I can babysit him," I said, and on that reply she gladly fled. "I'm only seven years older than you. Why does everybody think I'm your father?"

"'Cause I got hair. Ha-ha," Jim said, laughing till he coughed his deep rattling smoker's cough.

"It wasn't that funny, Chiquita. Speaking of hair, what the hell's happened to yours?"

"D'ya like it? It's called 'Light Golden Fawn.' Nikki died it; went to the salon an ever-thin'. Paid cash money just like a reg-a-lar customer, but I couldn't 'ford ta get the headlights."

"Kinda looks like you stole Ronald Reagan's hair."

"Gee, thanks, Dad."

We had a brief visit, mostly because he was still gassed on something and drifting in and out of consciousness. The following morning he awoke, sober and pissed, and checked himself out of the hospital *against* their advice.

Three days later...

At four thirty in the morning my phone rings, jolting me out of a very sound sleep. Scrambling for my glasses, I noticed it was Generous Hospital, and probably Chiquita, so I didn't answer. After finishing work I called the hospital and inquired if he was a patient, and instead of answering my query they automatically connected me to his room.

"Hullo," Chiquita answered, flatly.

"Chiquita, what's happened?"

"Had me a teensy slipup."

"What do you mean?"

"Well...you 'member the lass time I was here, lass week? Well, they wanted me to stay for the whole treatment, but I checked ma-self out early, 'cause I wanted ta get back ta work."

"I know, I drove you home, remember?"

"Oh, yeah. Well, for the first couple days ever-thin' went good. Then Jon comes home, an' we had a coupla beers, some vit-a-mins, and one thin' sorta led to 'nother; had me a teensy slipup. *But in my defense*, the very next mornin' I got myself right back in here for the cure."

"Glad to hear it."

"Could you come visit me? Don't have nobody ta visit. I haven't heard a single word from Jon since he dropped me off three days ago. You know what he says to me? He says, 'You good now?' Then he boots me *outta my own van*, and leaves me standing at the curb, and drives off."

"I just got home from work, Chiquita. I'll see you in the morning."

"He took my wallet, an' the house keys, too. He left me the phone, but the battery's dead so it's useless. So bring me a phone charger an' two cigs when you come."

"You know that is a smoke-free campus, and you can't smoke any-where on hospital grounds.""Yesssss, I know that. But it'd make me feel so much more come-for-table if I had a couple just in case the world en-did while I was in here. Would you please indulge an old coot, Nurse Ratched?"

"No, see you in the morning, McMurphy."

The next day I received a call from Chiquita. "Stella, they're going ta spring me ta-day. Can ya come an' get me? If not they'll give me a bus pass to downtown, and I'll have to hoof it home through the snow. Call me, Room 3166—an' hurry. They've been real mean to me."

Standing at the curb, he was holding a pink vinyl Hello Kitty suitcase in one hand and white drawstring hospital release bag in the other. Not wearing any glasses, he was blinking profusely but smiling as if he'd just won the lottery, apparently still quite pleasantly buzzed. He wore an old bomber jacket with a ratty-fur collar and oversize knee-length ghetto-style orange plaid shorts, and his bony blanched legs were shoved into dirty white tennis shoes without any socks.

"What took ya so long, Stella? Get me the hell outta this stinkin' fresh air. I need some smoke."

"I left as soon as you called; it takes half an hour to drive out here. I'm not a taxi, you know."

"Don't I know it, *they are* on time. Punch it, Stella, an' get me the hell outta this fruit dehydrator," he said, while stuffing his crap into the cab and slamming the door shut. As we drove through the well-manicured grounds, he happily prattled away about his latest incarceration, while still being pleasantly buzzed. Then suddenly he started shouting as if his bony ass was set afire.

"Haaaaa! There's a inconvenience store. Pull in quick. I need some cigs, bad. Don't have no money, so you'll have ta buy. Pull in now. Hey, hey—*hey*! You just passed it, why didn't you stop? That's okay, there's another on the other side-a the freeway, an' you can stop there."

"Believe it or not, I had plans tonight, and I'd like to get right home."

"Hey, pull in, *quick*! Hey, hey, *HEY*! You missed it *again*. What da-hellsa matta, Stella? Why didn't you stop ta get me some cigs? I am dyin' for a fag, an' you didn't stop, *again*. I've bin smokeless for *three whole days*."

"Jim, I have company coming for dinner, and I'm supposed to be cooking now."

"Well! 'Scuse me for in-ter-up-tin yer dine-in' plans, Julia's Child, I didn't real-eyes you had such pressin' social ovulations."

"Chiquita, do you have anyone left that you can call when you're in need? Where is Jon? Can you call him to pick you up, or depend on him for anything?"

"Oh, he's talented, I tell you. Double jointed, you know—nimble."

"And apparently he's quite good at disappearing, too. Just where is he now? And where is your van? Don't you remember? The last time you went in for the cure he robbed you blind, hijacked your van, and you didn't see him for thirty days."

"Oh, that, yeah."

As I was dropping him off in his driveway I noticed his lazy neighbor, Paula, sticking her dyed-black Brillo Pad head out the second-floor window, and then throwing down a dirty white sock heavy with keys to his house; pack of cigarettes, and a lighter. She was too damn lazy to walk them down. Through the rearview mirror I could see him sitting on his Hello Kitty suitcase, puffing away on his precious cigarette and smiling like a boy who'd just been given a pony.

Two days later, at five o'clock on Sunday morning, the phone rang, and it was Chiquita. He was well toasted. "Stella, I just got your e-males. All's finer here; 'sall good."

"Well, thank God, because I haven't heard from you since I brought you home from the hospital, and I was worried that you were frozen."

"We're good here. Well...sorta. I fell down the steps last night, but other than that I'm okay.""Fell down what steps? You live on the ground floor."

"Yeah, I do. But it got mighty cold in here last night without no heat, so I went upstairs, 'cause heat rises, ya know. Well, the steps musta froze over overnight, 'cause I got 'bout half the way up and whoosh, I went tumblin' back down, backward, an' bumped my head. It was bleedin' pretty bad so I calls up Paula and asked her for help. She told me ta wrap my head in a dishrag an duck-tape it up, cause *she* wasn't takin' me ta the hospitable. So I did. It's-all good."

"You're okay, though? Do you mean to tell me that with all that money you made last summer, you never got your furnace fixed?"

"Don't you 'member, Stella? It was hotter 'n hell last summer, didn't need no heat."

"Chiquita!"

"But wait, there s'mores. While I was in the hospitable, Jon totally cleaned me out. I mean locks, stocks, an' barrels. Took the computer 'n' printer, television, and ever-thin' you could plug in. Then he took all the merchandise we had listed for sale on eBay, drained the PayPal 'count, checkin' 'count, and savin' 'count, too. Then he took my wallet an' keys, an' I hain't seen that no-count since."

"Please tell me again what you saw in him."

"Did I mention he was double jointed?"

"You did, and it must bring you a great deal of comfort right now."

"Oh, it 'sall good, 'cause I found me a credit card in Target's parkin' lot today, an' I got me a brand-new computer. So I'm up and runnin' again an' it 'sall good. I use MagicJack for phone now, an' I didn't have no computer, so I couldn't return your calls."

"You 'found' a credit card? I don't want to know any more. Goodbye."

"Stella, wait a mint. We're smoke-free over here. You wouldn't wanna bring me some?"

"You're correct, I wouldn't wanna. Goodbye."

— ✦ —

Sunday afternoon was cool but crisp, with an unusually deep blue sky, which contrasted sharply with the red and amber leaves of autumn. And after the first hard frost of fall, the leaves were dropping like crazy. I was uselessly raking them when I looked up to see Chiquita's van pulling into my drive. Maneuvering in superslow motion, he slid out of the van, and sleep walked over.

"Mornin', Stella."

"What the hell happened to you? You look like someone beat the shit out of you."

"You 'member, I tole dew I fell down the steps."

"Chiquita! You don't get those kinds of scratches from falling down steps. Those are fingernail gouges. Look how evenly they're spaced."

"Yada, yada, yada. Hey! I think I fur-got sum subscriptions in your truck, when I come home from the hospitable the other day."

"No, you didn't leave anything in there. You got out holding the same things you got in with—a white plastic drawstring bag from the hospitable, and your pink Hello Kitty suitcase."

"Can I just look? 'Cause I need them subscriptions filled. I'm all outta ma meds."

"Out already? Let me get my keys."

"Can't imagine where them went."

"See, they're not in there, probably in the white plastic bag the hospital sent you home with."

"It's the damndest thin', can't find 'em anywheres. Hey, Murf, you 'member my neighbor, Paula?"

I suddenly noticed her sitting in the passenger seat. "Hello, Paula. Sorry, I didn't mean to ignore you, didn't even see you sitting there."

"How you doin'?"

"I'm fine, just stupidly trying to rake up these leaves before winter comes."

"We're goin' to get me some kera-scene for my spacious heater, 'cause it's gettin' pretty nippy out, an' I don't have no electristicals no more. Can you believe those in-con-sitter-ant bass-turds went an' shut the power off, just 'cause I didn't get the bill paid on time? An' while I was in the hospitable!"

"Nothing's in here, Jim."

"Thanks for lookin', Stella. It's th' damnedest thin'."

Three hours later I received an email from Chiquita, via Paula. "You was right, Stella. Them 'scripts was in hospitality bag all long. All is well in Bug-tussle. Love, Clara." The following day there were a couple of more calls, which went unanswered because I was working out of town. On the way home I phoned to find out what was up.

"Murf, I me got 'nother teensy problem over here. Since Jon cleaned me out I decided it was prob-a-lee a good time to do some cleanin'. *Well...*I had this be-you-tea-full paintin', an' it was ma favorite. Well, it was purdy dirty from cigarette smoke an' burner soot, so I sided ta clean it. So I asks my PhD art degree neighbor, Paula, what ta clean it with. 'Stella,' I say, 'should I use bleach, or pneumonia?'"

"Silly boy," she says, "don't use neither-a those, use rubbin' alcohol.' So I takes me a rag, soaks it real good, and starts cleanin' the paintin'. Well...the whole darn thin' comes off, and sticks itself to the stupid rag. Like the Shroud of Turn-in. Can you maybe touch it up a lil bit? I got the pains."

"Chiquita, I know how this works. The pope says to Michelangelo, 'Hey, Micky, I want you to paint this little-bitty church for me, it's just a tiny chapel—pffft, piece of cake—and all you have to do is the ceilin'. Some other guy is doin' da walls.' How about if I stop on my way home and take a look?"

"No, that's prob-lee not a good idea, 'cause the place is a disaster. I'm cleanin' house ta prepare for my upcomin' *Architectural Digest* shoot, you know. They been beggin' me ta do a spread."

"Okay, suit yourself."

"What the hell, you saw it lass year when it was way worser, with shredded hamburg wrappers all over. Okay. Call when you're here, 'cause ever-thins locked up tight since Jon robbed me blonde."

"Cheeseburgers."

He looked like shit with his head wrapped in a yellow dish towel, with his hair dyed undertaker brown, matted with dried blood in some places, and sticking out in others. Not wearing any glasses, he was squinting like a mole suddenly thrust into the noonday sun, and blinking profusely. A goose egg – size black-and-blue bump bulged from the middle of his forehead; bruises, scratches, and scabs dotted both bony forearms, and he was moving like a tranquilized tree sloth.

"Come on in, but be careful where ya step. You know the drill. That Jon cleaned me out good this time, took the TVs, stereo, computers, and all the merchandise. He didn't even leave me enough money for a pack-a cigs. An' you wood-dent get me none, neither. What was that 'bout, anyway?"

"Chiquita, this place looks like the Saint Vincent de Paul after a tornado went through it."

"Wha'?"

Now he was tearful. "As you well know, I had just got outta the hospitable and I had no money, 'tall, so I prostated ma-self, I swallowed my pride...an' asked Nikki for alone. 'Can you please borrow me some money, maybe just a hundred till I can get back on my feet?' An' you know what that mad old cow said to me? She says, 'Sorry, honey, I don't have a penny in the house.' Bull-shirt, she's got that safe in there just stuffed fulla money, an' I know the comb-nation. Lyin' bitch."

"You must have found some money somewhere, because you've got a bag of tobacco the size of a bed pillow sitting there."

"Yeah, it 'sall good. So you can fix the paintin', or what?"

"Or what."

"*What*, what? I thought you did that rest-a-ray-shun stuff."

"Yes, I can fix it, I do know how. But I think you should leave it that way, so every time you look at it you'll be reminded of the stupid shit you do when you're fucked up. Frame the cleaning rag, because that's where most of the painting is now."

"You sure are one twisted sister."

If *I* was twisted he'd be a corkscrew. He was a mess, and the house a disaster, only with a lot less stuff. The painting was fucked up, and so was he. Maybe he wasn't drinking, but he was definitely screwed up on something, most likely painkillers from his latest incarceration.

"Murf, this is Nikki. I *saw* your truck at Chiquita's today? What the hell's going on with him?"

"Yes, I was over there, and I don't know what's going on. He's fallen off the wagon again, and big-time. He's really a mess right now, and not in good shape."

"Why, just a few weeks ago he was in the salon getting his hair dyed, and doing real good. Then the other night he comes over here looking like shit, and begging for money. *Well*...I told him I didn't have any and he left. Then I watched him go over to that mess Paula's, and she let him in."

"They came over here last Sunday looking for some prescriptions he was just *certain* he'd left in my truck. She sure is a snaggletoothed thing, isn't she?"

"She's a fucking mess. That snatch-headed old whore has been his goddamned drug dealer for thirty years. Just trash."

"I told him there weren't any prescriptions in there, but he insisted on looking anyway. Addicts have a one-track mind, you know: *get more*."

"Well, he was a blubbering mess, had been drinking. You could smell it all over him."

"He's been on quite a roll lately. He's been in the hospital twice in the last few weeks."

"*Twice?* My God, I had no idea."

"As you know, you can't talk sense to someone when they are drunk."

"*Well*, I'm certainly not giving him any money to drink up; the nerve of him, coming over here and asking *me* for money."

"You might want to say a few prayers for him. I'm afraid he'll end up in the morgue, or prison."

"Well, I'm through with him."

— ~

Four days later Chiquita came down, somewhere near earth's orbit, and began to mend fences.

"Murf, I went to the bank ta-day to open up some new 'counts, because Jon Madeoff with all the money. He closed up the bank 'count, checkin' 'count, drained the PayPal 'count, and had the cable turned off ta boot. Then he hijacked my businesses, stole the stuff we'd already sold online, and took the money they paid for the stuff. Now I'm lie-able for those sales, but I don't have the stuff to ship or the cash to refund them, and can't make more money till I get this mess straightened out."

"Mendacity, lies, and deception. He really is a little shit, isn't he?"

"Oh, that's not the wurst of it. This is nothin', nothin' like the time he broke my arm. I'm glad to be rid of him."

"Chiquita, Chiquita, Chiquita."

"I probably shouldn't be tellin' ya this neither, but the next time ya come over you'll see it, or smell it. Now remember, this happened while I was still reoverin' from the last trip to the cure. *Well...*'bout a couple-a days ago...I run outta gas for the spacious heater, an' it was gettin' pretty nippy in here. So I fired up the little green enamel Coleman camp stove an' put a basin-a water on top ta make steam.

Well... the stove was sittin' on the counter, just a *teensy* bit under the upper cupboards, and they musta sorta gotta little bit scorched. Oh *hell*, they was smokin' somethin' fierce, damned near caught afire and nearly burnt the house down again. You shoulda seen it, Stella, everthin' inside-a there was blacker 'n coal. Now I got another whoppin' mess ta clean up."

"My God, Chiquita."

"Oh, it's okay, Stella, we can fix this. The kitchen needed paintin', anyway."

"I'm sorry, but I just have to ask—you said burned down *again*. Wha' happened?"

"You mean the other time I nearly burnt the house down? Well, I am usin' land-turds for light now, because I don't have no electristicals. *Well...* the land-turd was hung on the top cupboard, because way up high it can eliminate the room better. *Well...*I sorta fur-got about it bein' up there, swung the door open kinda fast, an' it went flingin' across the room; fell onta the floor, an' burst inta flames. Had ta waste damn near a whole bag a flour puttin' the fire out. What a waste a wheat."

"Chiquita, Chiquita."

"Hey, Murf, you want to meet me for breakfast? I got some empty coffee cans for ya."

"Sure. Grandma's Restaurant, at eight?"

"Nope, I'll stop over ta your house with them coffee cans before."

The next morning Chiquita arrived, wearing that too-small leather bomber jacket with the ratty fur collar. Draped around his scrawny neck were several gold necklaces. Bracelets were banging round his bony wrists, and he looked like an aged-out male hooker. It was thirty degrees, and he was wearing oversize orange plaid summer shorts with a camo midriff top, revealing his taut belly button. When he noticed me staring at his attire, he responded, "Couldn't find anythin' clean ta wear—sorry. *Oh, shit*, I forgot them damn coffee cans, too."

"What's with all the bangles, Chiquita? You look like Mr. T's queer brother."

"I bin goin' through all the jewelry and sortin' out the real gold an' silver from the crap, 'cause I'm outta money again. Last night I recollected all the trinkets I had an' put 'em on for the last time. You're goin' to have ta buy breakfast, Stella. Got no money."

"Figured."

"But first I have one more teensy flavor ta ask. Can you borrow me your wireless mouse today? 'Cause Jon stole mine when he took the computers, and I need it to get online ta make some money."

"Can you have it back by five?"

"Sure, it 'sall good. Stella, you 'member last summer, when I was up and runnin' at a hundred 'cent and at the top of my game? You and me was yard salin' ever' weekend, an' I was sellin stuff at the flea market an' publishin' them eBay listin's right to left. Wasn't that sum-thin'?"

"Hello! Newsflash: you have not been a hundred 'cent for quite a while, honey. You're lucky to call it seventy percent. Normal people have power, heat, water, toilets, and a shower. You have a house of toothpicks even when you're doing well."

"Now just wait a mint! I was doin' real good there last summer."

"Maybe you were, but you didn't fix your furnace, or get your power turned back on."

"Oh, you mean *that*. *Well*...who needs heat durin' the summer? Was hotter n' hell. Oh, an' that 'minds me, there's one more little thing. You 'member when you let me use your credit card, before I went in the dehydrator the lass time, when it was a emergency? Well, Jon musta found the number an' used it to pay for stuff online, 'cause I just got confirmation the card was used to pay for munitions, for two hundred and forty-nine dollars. Don't recall the chage."

"Just so we're clear now, please don't ask to use that credit card again, because the answer is no. And don't ask for money either, because the answer to that is no as well. You're fifty years old now, and it's time for you to become responsible and clean up your own messes. I will still be your friend, but I won't enable you in any way. Okay?"

"Yeah, yeah, it 'sall good."

Five thirty that afternoon, the phone rang. "Hey, Stella, you won't believe it but I got more 'n eighteen hundred dollars for all them crappy trinkets. So now I got the money you borrowed me, and your computer mice. You gonna be home? I'll bring 'em over."

⟨ ⟩

Early November's weather had turned gray and chilly, ice began to form on the lakes, and the sun went away to a warmer place for several months' vacation. A cold war, of sorts, had developed between Chiquita and me as well, and I didn't hear from him for quite some time after taking my new, tough-love approach to his plethora of problems. A few emails were sent, but no replies received.

Email to Chiquita: "Are things all right at Twelve Oaks? I can't reach you by phone."

Email response four days later: "Dropped the phone into the toilet. Not currently working—all wet; being dried out in a bag of rice. That was the only remedy, as to wetness abatement, that Wal-Mart could offer. It's starting to work, but needs more time in the rice bag."

Chiquita had not been in the Saint Vincent De Paul thrift store for so long that the counter girls were looking emaciated and gaunt from not eating his edible bribery; they were practically skin and bones. Word was, they saw him once, wearing dark-tinted movie-star sunglasses {very much like the Gucci ones Nikki had *once* owned} and acting most aloof and mysteriously. They also said he didn't have much to say, which was most unusual, just bought a bunch of old Christmas stuff and left.

— ~

Wednesday afternoon, the day before Thanksgiving, the phone rang, and it was Chiquita. "Murf, ya still speakin' ta me?" He'd obviously been drinkin'.

"A happy Thanksgiving to you, too, Chiquita. Let's just say I am disappointed."

"Well, sit down an' get your note pad out, 'cause I got a whole 'no-ther chapter fur yer book, an' you won't belief this one. *Well*, there I was in Southfield, followin' Rhonda in my van, 'cause I've got no idea where the hell I'm at."

"Wait a minute, back up, who is Rhonda, and why were you in Southfield?"

"A friend, and we's doin' a flea market ta-gather. Ya caught up now? Okay. Ya see, she made it through the light just fine, but I didn't quite make it. Then these two stupid cars just run right through the green light and smacked right into my van, an' broadsided dit for no good reason. The airbags blew up an' white powder was flyin' ever-where. Next thin' you know red lights are flashin', an' a coupla am-balances show up, coupla wreckers, an' three damned cars fulla po-lease."

"Chiquita, Chiquita."

"Oh, there's-more, so don't put yer pad away yet. Then the po-lease took my lie-sense an' resignation an' asked if I'd been drinkin' or takin' drugs. 'Why, core-snot, Ossifer,' I said. Well, they searched the van anyway, lookin' for booze, pot, pills, or somethin', and didn't find any thin'. Thank God it was all back at the no-tell. They wrote me a ticket for causin' the ax-dent, an' another because the plates on the van was from Jon's old Suburban, an' they'd 'spired. He'd switched 'em on me; so there's another fine mess I can thank him for. So now the van is in the Southfield compound, and it'll cost me eight hundred dollars, cash money, ta get it out. And with them chargin' incest daily, the bill gets bigger ever' single second. What a mess. What a mess."

"But you're all right? Did you go to the hospitable?"

"Yeah, yeah, fine, fine. Not a scratch—nobody hurt."

"Well, I'm glad to hear that. I filed a report with Visa about those charges Jon made using my credit card. They're initiating an investigation."

"He's the reason why my van was compounded. I mean, I could drive the damn thing, wasn't even a scratch on it, but you shoulda seen those other cars. They was scrunched."

"And you're all right?"

"Yeah. I got another black eye from slippin' in the backyard and fallin' last night, but I didn't get hurt in the car accident...if that's what you mean."

"Yes."

"And now Jon has completely taken over the company—that I built. He just stole it, locks, stocks, 'n' barrels, but that's okay, because he's screwin' up and gettin' lotsa negatory feedbacks from customers."

"He couldn't have taken anything from you so easily if you weren't fucked up; he took advantage of that. Let it go, give it to Jesus, and move on. You can easily start another company."

"You've been so damn icy lately, I didn't know if I should even call you."

"I just wanted you to know that I will no longer be enabling you."

"I know that. I'm not askin' you to be labeling me. You're about the only one left who even speaks ta me, 'cept for Paula, and she's my damn drug dealer. I need help, not money or help cleanin' up my mess. I need help 'cause I'm losin' it. I can't continue this way." And then he began to sob.

"There's help for you, you just have to reach out and accept it. There's a gay AA group that meets twice a week. They really helped Mike cope. And aren't you lucky—they meet at seven thirty at Woodside Church, on Sundays and Wednesdays, and that's tonight? You can easily walk there; it's just a couple blocks away."

"I'm scared. Will ya go with me?"

"This one is yours alone, Jim. There is a reason it's called anonymous. You will have to do this on your own."

"I'm so scared, honey, it's all fucked up."

"I know."

— —

Eleven days went by before he called again, and when he did he was snotty drunk. We spoke again, and had another conversation he probably wouldn't remember. I told him to call back when he was sober, thinking I might never hear from him again.

— —

Another month passed, and the temperatures plummeted into the single digits, and if you were living without heat that was a bad thing. Chiquita called to inform me that he was calling an ambulance to check himself into the hospital.

"I spoke with your friend Gigi last night. She's real nice, a real peach; sounds real educated. She told me to call a am-balance, an' made range-mints for me ta get checked inta Hurley."

"Good. Please try and remember this: you have proved you can successfully quit drinking; in fact, you have done it several times. The problem you have is maintaining your sobriety. You'll need to learn when to ask for help. Instead of asking for permission, you're asking for forgiveness after you've fucked up. The time to ask for help is *before* you start using, not after you've finished a bender. It's too hard on you, and you're killing yourself. You're also exhausting everyone who loves you. Eventually you will run out of chances. Chiquita, you wear people out, and they give up on you."

"Don't give up on me, Stella."

"I'm still here."

— —

Four days later he was discharged from the hospital. "You won't believe the mess I come home ta find. An' I mean a really big stinkin' mess. Paula 'greed to feed Rotunda, and that's about all she did; didn't let her out near enough. Poor old Rotunda was left all alone in this big old house an' she howled somethin' terrible, an' she must-a worked up a real bad case-a the diarrhea, cause she shit all over. Talk about a stinkin' mess, woof! I had to heat water on that old camp stove to clean it up."

"Good thing she was able to feed her, because you certainly don't want Nikki pet-sitting."

"*Oh God no*. And thank God it didn't freeze up while I's gone."

"Chiquita, Chiquita, Chiquita."

"Say. I spoke with your friend Gigi, and I'm goin' to my first meetin' tonight."

"I'm glad to hear that. They'll just love you in AA, you'll be their darling. You'll keep them entertained with your stories; you're so good at telling them. Bette says that the nicest people on the planet are addicts."

"I'm not very good right now, all shaky, and weak as a mitten. Don't know if I can go tonight."

"There will be a meeting when you are ready. Every night there's a meeting somewhere. So don't worry if you don't make it tonight. Rest up and go tomorrow. I'm glad you are asking for help, because it's there for you. Take it."

As I hung up, I prayed, *God, please bless his troubled heart, and look after him.*

Nikki Takes a Trainer

For just years, and years, and years, and years, (he was *reallllly* old now), Nikki ate anything and everything he pleased. Life was just one big old smorgasbord. I believed part of this gluttonous behavior stemmed from not having enough to eat while growing up. Never knowing when the next meal would arrive, he'd learned to eat everything he could, as fast as he could, because there were five hungry boys chirping to be fed from the same skinny worm.

Nikki stood five ten as a svelte young man, and had a twenty-eight-inch waist. But that was when we all were young; well, I was young, and he was always old er. When he started working and eating better he began to fill in, and didn't like it. But then he discovered those lovely black beauties, the fabulous go-go pills his doctor supplied, and found he could more easily keep his slim girlish physique with the extra pep supplied by mother's marvelous little helpers.

The problem was, once he got hitched and left the party life behind, and became domesticated; he began practicing his latent homemaking skills. Being hillbilly by birth, he naturally fried everything, and loved pan-fried pork chops served with greasy onion gravy; bacon-laden German potato salad served with dripplin' dressin,' and crispy deep-fried chicken served with milk gravy and mashed potatoes. He also loved to bake decadently delicious desserts for his handsome hunky husband, and like many other married men he began to fill in, blossomed, and grew some serious curvature.

Later in his life he started making buckets of money when he became the local hairdresser to the stars. He did Bill Clinton when he came to town, Paul Lynde when he appeared at Star Theater, and the men of the Ice Capades each winter when they were here to escapade. He was a well-heeled man of the world, who'd developed a taste for haute cuisine, and he insisted on eating at the best restaurants in town, the country, and the world. But I happened to know he loved his greasy ol' down-home cookin' just as much, and maybe even more; with Paula Deen bein' his patron saint.

When a group of us went out to eat, he was still quizzing the table. "So what are you ordering, Denny? And you, Chiquita? The fish you say? I don't do fish, unless it's that pecan-encrusted trout that's fried in butter at the Red Rooster; but then I'll only eat the nutty crust. That's about the only fish I can tolerate. Well, there was that time when you made grilled salmon at your cottage, Denny. That was pretty good. I probably could have eaten it, if I *had* to eat fish."

"Yeah, but you had to have two big old greasy kielbasas instead."

"Oh yeah, that was simply scrumptious, wasn't it? Those big old greasy sausages cooked over a campfire, and just like I like 'em, long, black, and greasy; yum, yum, num."

"Stupid me, I go out and catch a beautiful salmon, filet it, marinate it in citrus juice, dill, salt, and sugar for two days. Then I baste it with a mustard and maple syrup glaze, slow roast it over applewood coals on a soaked cedar plank until it falls apart, and you want sausage."

"Yeah, like I said, that greasy garlic kielbasa was really delicious. Now, don't get me wrong, hon, that fish was tasty, 'cause I had a little nibble, remember? I just don't do fish."

Most of his meals were eaten at a Coney Island or hamburger joint. "Make mine deluxe, bring me a double-meat and double-cheeseburger, with extra bacon, and give me a vat of mayo on the side. You can just keep that lettuce and tomato crap. Then you can give me a large order of chili cheese fries, and don't be stingy with the cheese either. Then you can give me a double chocolate milkshake, with extra whip cream, and a cherry on top. Num, num, numm. You want one, Murf? They're *awful* good."

"No! But thanks for offering."

He'd often urge you to indulge in his decadent food-a-holic treats, to lessen his consumptive guilt, as if there really was any.

"Waitress, what kinds of pies do you have today?"

"Well, hon, we have Dutch apple, sour cherry, very-berry, peach, pun-kin, and pee-can pies."

"Bring me a piece of pecan pie, warmed in the microwave, and put a big plop of ice cream on top. And bring me my pie before my dinner, because I want to make sure I'll have room for it."

"Certainly, sir."

After having dessert he would start on his meal. "Oh my God, these chili cheese fries are simply heavenly. Have some, Murf. Chiquita, you wanna try some?"

"Dear God no. It looks like a car wreck served on a dinner plate. Are you kiddin'? Those bloody grease-drenched fries look like they're hemorrhagin' ta death."

"I know, they are simply scrump-dilly-ish-such."

I could not share his foodie enthusiasm either. Those deep-fried potatoes were sopping wet and totally obscured with red-orange grease.

After taking a poll of what everyone was ordering to eat, he ordered an item from the menu "for the table," something that sounded just too good to pass up, so we could all have a little nibble. He only thought of others."Oh, waiter, what's that you're serving there? Fried what? It looks absolutely divine. I'd love to try a little nibble a that. Maybe we should order some of that for the table, too."

An undesired repercussion of all this conspicuous consumption meant that quite often he was suffering through some radically restrictive weight reduction. Over the years he'd gained and lost hundreds of pounds of ugly fat on countless diets. There were many strange diets, such as the Pritikin, Atkins, and Scarsdale plans. Then there was the never-eat-white-foods diet, which was followed by the eat-only-white-foods plan. He tried the eat-as-much-watermelon-as-you-want diet, and the eat-only-grapefruit plan. On the carnivore diet he consumed only charred flesh, and that plan was followed by the Nazi vegan diet where you couldn't eat anything that ever lived.

One convenient diet even shipped flash-frozen healthy meals with sensible portions right to his front door. He hated sensible. And sometimes the diet wasn't a meal at all; his sustenance was nothing more than a thick, chalky, and nasty diet shake. He would be diligent and eat the taste-free mush, but always felt as if he was being deprived. Forever yo-yo dieting, he'd tell us he'd just lost twenty pounds, and yet each time we'd see him he was just as big or even larger. Many of these crazy fad diets also included "days off," and on those glorious days he could have *anything* and *everything* he desired. And he was very desirous. Coincidentally, that diet did not work very well either.

Losing weight slowly bored him. And like Tina Turner, he never, *ever* liked doing anything nice and slow. Most of all he hated being *deprived*, and not being able to indulge in those decadent rewards and tasty treats that made him happy and life worth living. Sweet rewards such as the shockingly pink marshmallow and coconut plastic-foam-covered Little Debbie Snowballs; he simply adored those toxic things. "Is there anything more scrumptious on the planet? No, I don't think so either."

Things eventually became so bad he even tried exercizing. But that bored him, too. Sweating, forget that shit, it stinks. Eventually he quit it all, quit going to the gym, quit dieting, and ate whatever the hell he pleased, whenever he pleased, and purchased bigger clothes each month. Guilt and shame motivate many people to diet, but not Nikki; big, blond, and brassy suited him.

His life was a constant battle between deprivation and reward, feast and famine. When he finally reached his target weight, and the diet was ended, the pounds he tried so diligently to lose were slowly gained back, along with a few extra each time. Because when the diet ended he'd go right back to his bad eating habits, and never, ever exercised.

At his top weight I would guess he was hovering somewhere around the 275-to-300-pound range.

Some people didn't know it, but eating was one of Nikki's favorite indulgences. And ever since he was a youngster his favorite meal was breakfast. Tony's was his favorite breakfast spot, because you were served a pound of bacon with a breakfast. Yes, you heard me right, a whole pound of bacon, along with a heaping pile of fried potatoes, up to a dozen eggs, and the toast of your choice. That burgeoning belly-buster was piled so high it spilled off the platter and onto the table. And that enormous single-serving breakfast would've been enough food for our entire family of six when I was growing up. There was enough bacon left over from a breakfast to have a week's worth of BLTs.

"Evenin', the name is Shirley, and I'll be taking your orders to-night," the smiling waitress said.

"Morning," Nikki retorted, quickly correcting her. "Now, I was thinking I'd like to have the blueberry pancakes. Now tell me the truth, now, Shirley, do they taste any good?"

"Oh, yes, sir. I love 'em. Eat 'em for breakfast myself."

"Okay. Now, do they put those blueberries inside the pancakes, like they're supposed to, or do they put a plop of that crappy purple pÿudding' pie glop on top?"

"Oh, no, sir, they're real blueberries, and they're inside, just like they're supposed to be."

"Are they big?"

"Why...*yes*, they're floppin'-over-the-plate big. And an order comes with three, but I order only two, 'cause I can't finish that many and I'm a pretty big girl." She was big all right, but she was no girl, at least sixty, and Nikki's size and shape: pear.

"Okay. I'll have those, and an order of bacon fried good and crispy. So don't you be bringing me any of that limp-assed white wilted crap."

"Very good. And to drink, sir?"

"Coffee, *black coffee*."

"Certainly, sir."

As she took his order, I studied her. Short salt-and-pepper hair was cut into a soft brush-cut style, and her friendly round face was nicely framed by stylishly updated cat-eye glasses. She definitely had a fashionable flair, with great big artsy earrings and loose-fitting knit, cotton comfort clothes from head to toe. Even though she walked with a noticeable limp, she was quick and efficient.

"You know, one thing I absolutely *detest* is when I order *black* coffee and the waitress asks, 'Do you want cream with that?' For Christ's sake, *black* means *black*, no cream! What part of that don't you understand?" Nikki had finished announcing, just as she arrived.

"Oh, hello, Shirley, and thank you," Nikki said, suddenly all syrupy sweet.

"You're very welcome, sir. There you go, just what you asked for, hot, *black* coffee."

"Ya know, Shirley, I like my coffee like I like my men, *hot, strong,* and *black*. Now, as I was saying, I think I'd like a glass of orange juice, too. Now, tell me, is that juice fresh squeezed?"

"Why, certainly, sir."

"Okay, you may bring me a glass."

I'm not sure why, but we all watched as she hobbled over to a large square fountain drink machine that dispensed an orange-colored juice drink in a flashy fountain-like fashion and placed a red plastic tumbler under the spigot. Pulling down the chromed lever, she withdrew a single serving. Quietly hobbling back to our table, she placed the glass of orange/juice/pop in front of Nikki.

"*Now, wait just a minute here!* You just told me this juice was fresh squeezed, and I just watched you go over there and get it out of that pop machine."

"Well, then, sir, didn't you see me *squeeze* that handle and make that juice come out?"Touché. She got him right back, and we all howled, including Nikki.

"Now, waitress, while you're here, do you have any more butter somewhere? Because peeling these teensy little foil packets open will just never do for me. It's crippling my delicate hands."

"Certainly, sir, let me find you more butter." Shirley wobbled away and came back with a clear glass bowl filled with about a cup of melted, yellow-orange butter-like substance and placed it in front of him. He looked up and beamed.

"Will that be enough for you, sir? Because if not, I can get you more."

"Oh, no, this is perfection, thank you so very much. You're much too kind."

Boy, did she have his number, and he was becoming a happy customer.

"You know, I don't know why it is, but ever since I was a little girl I just loved the taste of..."

"BUTTER!"

All three of us yelled before he could finish the sentence. "We know, Stella, the whole world knows now," Chiquita chimed. "Speakin' a butter, ya know what I heard the other day? The Kansas State Fair's best seller this year was deep-fried butter kabobs. Heard it was a real big hit, too."

"Oh, just imagine how scrumptious those must be. They must have-ta freeze the butter first, like when making fried ice cream. Oh, I wonder if they roll it in nuts or breading first. Yum, yum, yummy."

Our breakfast arrived in a flash, and Nikki immediately took the butter substitute and doused the Paul Bunyan–sized stack of pancakes. Carefully lifting each one, he poured the butter under, in between, and on top. Then he repeated the process with a half bottle of Uncle Tom's Cabin imitation maple-flavored syrup. The gooey mound was a three-layer cake, dripping with amber ooze, and the sticky, steaming stack seemed to be mysteriously absorbing the amber fluids as if it was alive. He quickly carved off a chunk and shoveled it into his eagerly awaiting mouth.

His baby blues rolled back into his head as if he was having an epileptic fit, or was in the throes of orgasmic ecstasy. "Num, num, num. My God, this is simply heavenly, absolutely perfection. Anyone want a taste?" he asked, speaking with his mouth crammed with partially chewed cake. We all tried not to look, but it was like the accident on the highway with the severed head—you just had to. After finishing the entire plate, as well as an extra-large side of extra *crispy* bacon, he swabbed the platter clean with his index finger until it was squeaking.

"That was simply scrumptious," he said, and smacked his sticky lips together to demonstrate his delight. "I just love this restaurant."

Pulling out a huge wad of rolled-up bills from the pocket of his wrinkled-up, syrup-stained shorts, he paid for the entire breakfast, and left an obscenely large tip for quick-witted old Shirley. She'd had his number all along. The baby blue summery shirt covering his big bloated belly was stippled with sticky greasy splotches, and he was simply beaming.

"My God, Nikki, your cholesterol must be through the roof, the way you eat," I said. "I don't understand it at all. Even though I eat a sensible diet of fruits, vegetables, grains, and exercise, my cholesterol is still too high and I have to take cholesterol-lowering medication. Yours probably isn't even measurable."

"Oh, I've never had a problem with that cholesterol stuff, never have. I've never paid any attention to that shit; I eat just whatever I want, and whenever I want it. I've never exercised a day in my life except for high school gym, and only then because they made me do it. And just look at me, I have this fucking fabulous flawless body. Guess I am just blessed."

"Amazing, and only further proof that all men are not created equal."

"Ain't that the truth, honey, ain't that the truth."

—⁓ ⁓—

For many, many years Nikki lived this self-indulgent way, eating his way around the city, state, country, and the world, consuming only the best that life had to offer. Oh, yes he was a capable enough cook, but preferred to eat out and be "serviced" instead. That way he didn't have to cook or clean the mess. He liked being waited on, expected good service, and was a very demanding customer.

A hurried lunch at work was usually fast-food takeout. And after spending all day battling ugly in the beauty trenches, he was exhausted by night, so dinners were mostly takeout or a restaurant and cooking was relegated to weekends and holidays. He wasn't adventurous in his eating either, because when we were in Istanbul, Chiquita and I tried the exotic street foods and loved them. Nikki loathed them. Looking at us most horrified, he said, "Dear God, you two *did not eat* any of that food off from the sidewalk did you? You're gonna die of ptomaine poisoning! The guide books advise you to never, *ever* eat off the street in a foreign country. They say to always eat at a reputable American place or a European restaurant with a minimum of four stars, or at the least a McDonald's, like Aunt Ronnie."

When in Greece and completely surrounded with seafood, he ordered lamb or greasy Greek sausage. Occasionally, he'd have a nibble of calamari that he purchased "for the table," as long as it was deep-fried and smothered in cheese, garlic, and tomato sauce so you couldn't tell what you were eating. Occasionally he'd eat shrimp, if they were carefully hidden amongst pasta, covered with extra cheese, and smothered in creamy Alfredo sauce, but never fish alone. He just wasn't that kind of a cat.

But things do change, if we like it or not. *Not.* And if we are lucky, old age eventually catches up with all of us, Nikki. Even if you don't look your age, you are, Nikki. Sometimes she will politely tap on your door, sometimes she will knock loudly, and sometimes she will kick the whole fucking door in. Having a mild heart attack at fifty-one, my experience was more of a polite kicking in of the door. Nikki's little awakening was more of a polite tapping on his door, a teensy little scare, if you will.

Heart palpitations that did not involve decadent food, extravagant purchases, or an attractive black man began troubling Nikki. At first, as most men do, he thought they'd go away if he ignored them long enough, but they didn't. Finally they got so bad he had to visit his doctor. He was diagnosed as having trouble with the old ticker and referred to a cardiologist.

"Mr. Clark, I have looked at your insurance and see you have a very good plan, and that's a very good thing. It's also a very good thing you came to see me when you did, because *you* are a very sick man. My extensive and expensive testing indicates that you have developed some serious narrowing to the veins supplying your heart. Those valuable vessels have become severely constricted, and there are several areas that could potentially become blockages. You're a veritable ticking time bomb. Surgical intervention may be needed immediately, at any moment—if not sooner; angioplasty, catheterizations, stents, major capital extraction, or possibly even open-heart surgery."

"Oh dear God," Nikki gasped, clutching his lovely chest. "Is it that bad?"

"It's worse than that. Get your affairs in order, Mr. Clark. I suggest that we immediately start you on cholesterol-lowering medications, blood thinners, and heart rhythm regulators until we can figure out the best course of action to take."

As you can well understand, Nikki was shocked by the devastating heartbroken news. He returned home and found his two overfed, hairball-hacking Persian pussies, crawled into bed, rolled into the fetal position, and bawled for the rest of the day. Salty tears fell on his lovely new Needless Markup eight-hundred-thread-count Egyptian cotton summer bedding ensemble that had just arrived, in the exquisite Angelique pattern he so dearly loved.

"Have you received a second opinion, Nikki?" I asked.

"Well, *no*, they did all those tests and everything. It's pretty much official."

"Not necessarily, Nikki. Tests can be interpreted differently. The greedy bastard who did my hernia surgery told me I had two of them, one on each side, and wanted to perform two surgeries. After going for a second opinion I learned I only had one hernia, and they almost always do both repairs at the same time; the sadistic money-grubbing bastard."

"Well, maybe I should do just that, get myself a second opinion."

"You probably already know every cardiologist in town. Would you like my doctor's number?"

"No, but thanks for offering, honey. I will definitely get a second opinion, now that you've mentioned it."

"Bless your heart."

Two weeks later

"Nick, I want to thank you for coming to see me."

"Oh no, thank you, Dr. Erich. Thank you for seeing me; I trust no one's opinion more."

"Thank you for saying that, Nick. Okay, here's how it looks. I've examined the results from your stress tests, the electrocardiogram, echocardiogram, and your MoneyGram, and I don't think you will need to have surgery now. Definitely not. The problem has to do with your heart's rhythm, and we can fix that with medication. I'd hate to crack open that lovely chest of yours, it would be a shame."

"Oh, what a relief," Nikki said, blubbering up.

"Now, you will have to make some serious lifestyle changes, you understand. First you should start adhering to a low-fat diet, get regular exercise, and start taking heart regulating medications to alleviate those annoying palpitations. Okay?"

"What was that second thing again?"

"Exercise."

"You mean like sweating? Uh-uh."

"We'll talk about that later. Let's just get you well now."

Nikki never admitted his age, to anyone, but those of us who could still add knew he was sixty-five. Even though the face-lift made him look and feel younger, he was in reality getting *really* old. We never thought any of us would make it this far, but there he was making lifestyle changes and planning for a future, albeit one with severe butter consumption restrictions. You can say bye-bye to Paula Deen, Nikki.

Before long he was feeling good as new and up to his old tricks of eating junky food and never getting exercise. How quickly they forget. It was well over a year later when he had another knock on his door, and this time it was much louder, like Mike Tyson showing up when you owed him money, and it was really scary. And when he took the whole diet and exercise and health consciousness thing seriously, he took it to the next level just as he did with hair-doing, interior decorating, gardening, shopping, and everything.

Over the years he'd joined gyms, such as Planet Fitness, Universal, Gold's, or Vic Tranny {a gay/alternative health club}. Having the best of intentions, he tried to exorcise his fatty demons away. But gyms were not a good fit for him, and even though he liked looking at pumped-up hot men, he did not like the constant comparison. He never fit into the whole male competition thing, and absolutely hated the public shower with all those naked men...and him.

Now, he knew that a couple of his rich-bitch clients had themselves a personal trainer; these spandex-clad people who came to their house a couple of times a week and made them sweat their fat asses off. He fancied it would be something like an episode of *Hung*, where this unbelievably hunky brown man would show up at his door—with big bulging biceps and a bulging personality (wink, wink)—to make him sweat off a few, teensy-weensy unwanted pounds.

"All I need to do is take off a few *teensy-weensy* pounds of baby fat and then I'll be absolutely flawless." But the truth was nothing like his fantasy, it was ugly. He needed to shed at least seventy-five pounds, and the trainer was probably a hateful Eastern European woman with a thicker mustache than his, chapped hands, nasty breath, and a rotten disposition; who would be constantly insulting and humiliating him, calling him a "pudgy marshmallowy girlie boy." He decided to discreetly inquire around the salon about these personal trainer thingies.

One of the recent inductees to the salon hierarchy, an exotic mixed-race boy named Timika, explained it to Nikki. "My lover, Spruce, and I have this guy named Rudolpho who comes three times a week, for an hour each time, and he works us out real good. *Really* quite affordable, and seriously, he's like *really* good. He stretches us—butt good—does some downward dog and stuff like that, with little resistance. Cardio, you know—stuff like that. There's no gym full of sweaty and stinky old women, or fat old men. It's *really* made a big difference. Like, *really*."

As if you really needed to hear that sort of thing from a skinny, twenty-seven-year-old twink with a flawless body. Nikki discreetly asked for Rudolpho's number.

"Is he cute?" he asked, thinking of chorizo and Spanish food.

"No, not really, but he has a really nice body."

— —

So the die was cast, and Nikki made the appointment to have his exorcism. "Be gone ugly fat, I command you out." And Rudolpho was exactly what Timika had said, an all-business trainer with an amazing body and a face meant for radio. They would meet three times a week for an hour each time, on Sunday morning at seven, and Monday and Thursday mornings at five thirty.

You better believe Rude made him sweat his fat ass off. Gradually he pushed Nikki further each week, bending, stretching, reaching, firming, tightening, toning, slowly and steadily strengthening each time, and miraculously he began to lose the excess weight. Surprisingly the pounds began to melt away, and he didn't look like a shar-pei in the process. Within weeks he was getting compliments from people noticing his weight loss, and commenting on how healthy he looked.

And after returning from Florida for the season, I immediately noticed he'd lost an amazing amount of weight. "My God, just look at you, you're literally melting away." And it was true; over a year's time he'd lost nearly sixty pounds, and looked and felt just great; everyone said so, *really*!

"Believe it or not, I'm actually eating sensibly now. I actually like yogurt and kale. But I still haven't reached my target weight yet, because I want to lose twelve more pounds so I can fit in those size-thirty European jeans. You know, you can never be too blonde, too rich, or too skinny."

— —

Later that year he reached his target weight. Then the new "Nikki Lite" thoughtfully took his old fat clothes to the homeless shelter, because he figured he'd never need them again, and while purging his excesses he took those nasty old—and unbelievably expensive—Frette linens—to the shelter, too. Oh, he'd dearly loved them *once*, but then he found something even more extravagant to replace them: Pratesi linens, bedsheets made of freshly minted money. I'm sure the men at the shelter appreciated the lovely luxury linens, and the classy fat-ass clothes, too.

Several weeks later, during a late afternoon luncheon at his formerly favorite greasy restaurant, he made the announcement that he'd officially reached his target weight. But it was difficult to believe he was ever going to stay that way, because I saw the way he coveted the luncheon plate being served to the woman seated at the next table over.

Shirley came hobbling over. "Afternoon, gentlemen, and what can I get for you?"

"It's still morning for ten more minutes, Shirley. Tell me, what is it that she's having over there? It looks simply divine."

"Why, that's the blue plate special, Nikki, a double-bacon double-cheeseburger with all the fixings, coleslaw, and an order of curly-cut fries."

"Well, give me one of those, and bring me a Diet Coke."

Who says you can't teach an old dog a new trick?

Bless his skinny heart.

Strike Three

When Chiquita came home from the hospital for withdrawal *this time* it was not like the last time, the time a year ago, or the times before that. He was definitely in worse shape physically, bruised, and blackened, moving super slowly, and returning to a powerless home without any heat. Even though he was penniless and starting back at square one, he was not broken or defeated. He felt that something had shifted in him this time. He'd been given another chance, and he had the gumption to make it.

Remaining in contact daily, I was what you might call supportive from a distance, because it is difficult to help someone by not helping them, or enabling them.

⚊ ⚊

"Mornin', Chiquita. You up?"

"Almost, we're just waitin' for the sun ta rise over here. Saves on land-turd fuel, ya know."

"I swear, you're just itching to burn that old house of yours down yet."

"No, don't wanna do that, but awanna be warm. An' speakin' a warmth, ya know what I discovered the other day? That I can burn reg-a-lar old gas in them land-turds, and I won't have ta spent twelve dollars a gallon for that darned land-turd fuel anymore."

"When you say gas, do you mean gasoline like you'd put in a car?"

"Yup, reg-a-lar old un-lead-did gas-a-lean. I get enough lead from my water. But ya gotta be awful careful with gas, 'cause one teensy little mistake, and *poof*! Lost my darned funnel somewhere's around here the other day, an' it's kinda hard pourin' that stinkin' stuff in-ta that itty-bitty hole without it. I'm all shaky now. Jon was lots better at doin' that kinda stuff. Sometimes I still miss him."

"You really are nutso, aren't you, and you have amnesia, too? Have you forgotten how he went *way* out of his way to fuck you over—big-time—robbed you blind, beat you up, broke your arm, took all your money, and hijacked your company?"

"Oh, you mean *that*."

"Chiquita, Chiquita. Speaking of warmth, just what is wrong with your furnace, anyway? I know it hasn't worked in over two years."

"Oh, it's just missin' some small reg-a-later thin'."

"Is that all?"

"Ya, ya, yada, yada, yada, push along, Stella. Say, did I tell ya that Paula took me around yesterday? Well she did, first we stopped at the gas station ta get gas for the land-turds, kera-scene for the spacious heater, and two tanks-a profane gas for the bar-be-que, too; 'cause I'm cookin' on that now. I tell ya, Stella, her van was nothin' but a rollin' tank bomb, we was haulin' gas-a-lean, kerra-scene, and two tanks-a profane gas."

"Yeah, and the two of you were probably sittin' up front, and smoking like fools."

"Well, *yeah*. You say that like smokin's bad for your health, or sump-thin; sheesh, there's nothin' worse'n a reformer smoker. That was the other thing, she took me ta the ta-back-a store; too, because my rollin' machine busted. The darn thing just went kaf-looey! But she didn't take me to everywhere I needed to go though, 'cause she's only good for a few hours each day now. Got the cancer, ya know."

"No. I didn't know."

"Yeah. She's lived next ta me for over twenty-five years, and been a good friend."

"Really? I thought she was just your drug dealer."

"Well, *yeah*, that, but she's been my friend, too. Now, I understand that you're not goin' ta lend me any money, or help me, *labelin' me* as you put it. But I was wonderin' if I could use your computer ta publish some eBay listings, so I can make a little money? The lie-berry's closed today and d'marrow, and since I don't have power I'm working out of there now. I wouldn't ask if it wasn't important. Did I tell ya they're auctionin' off my van next week if I don't pay them two thousand dollars?"

"Yes, and I'm sorry to hear that. Ain't it always somethin'? Yes, you can use the computer."

"Can you pick me up?"

"In about an hour."

"Now works better for me."

"My God, Chiquita, you smell like an oil refinery."

"It's that damn kera-scene. That spacious heater makes the whole house stink, an' ever-thin' that sin it. Can we maybe swing by the post office a minute, so I can ship out a couple-a thin's?"

"Get in."

"I found a whole stack of 1963 *Field and Stream* magazines under that yellow couch Nikki gave me when I was cleanin', and I'm goin' ta publish 'em today; should get three dollars apiece."

"Chiquita, I swear, you're still trying to empty the ocean with a teaspoon. You need to get hooked up with the people from AA; they will help you get your life straightened out."

"But I don't wanna be straight, Stella."

"*Clara*, you could get your power turned back on and still be gay, and you can get your furnace fixed and still be queer. You need a support system. You can't be running around without a babysitter."

"Yada, yada, yada, I'll take-air of that later, right now I need ta get some money comin' in."

"You could probably get food stamps, utility assistance, and a disability."

"Yada, yada, yada, I know all that."

"Have you ever seen that movie *Groundhog Day*?"

"Oh *yeah*, I just loved that furry little groundhog, he was so cute and cuddly."

"I was referring to you living the same day over and over, with nothing changing. Look at you, your eyes are blackened, you're scabbed, bruised, limping, and hunched over. I bet Community Mental Health could help you qualify for a disability. I would be happy to write a letter on your behalf: 'Please give my friend Chiquita a disability; I can certainly certify, he is critically cracked.'"

"Yeah, yeah, yeah that's all good, Stella. Can we just go ta the post office, or what?"

"Or what. Jimmy, it's difficult for me to care about you when you don't seem to care."

"Push along, Stella. Push along. That's what I do."

Three weeks passed and nothing much changed. He wouldn't call me very often because I pestered him. Even though he was sober now, his life was more difficult than he'd ever imagined. Eventually his van went to auction, because he didn't have the funds to redeem it. So he bought a bicycle and looked up the bus schedule.

"What the hell, Stell', I can buy me a better used vehicle for lessen they want ta redeem that old tin-can. As of now, the bill for totin' and steerage, with compound incest and fleas, is aproachin' two thousand dollars, and those usury bass-turds will want more blood every single second."

Not having a vehicle was a pain in the ass in many ways, because he'd lost his independence. Living without electricity precipitated many changes, too, because now he had to use the library to run his business and stay warm. That meant hiking there in the dead of winter and schlepping everything he needed to run a business, so he did. He would industriously rise before the crack of dawn to be the first person at the door when they opened at eight, and stayed until they closed at six. Before dark he'd head home to light the lanterns to chase away the dark, and ignite the kerosene heater to keep the cold at bay. And you'd better believe, he made damn sure to keep his precious pipes from freezing, and he thanked God each day that he had water, even if it was only cold and leaded.

Each day he'd take along his ÿrecious cell phone, in hopes of finding a neglected out-of-the-way outlet to charge it. At least while there he'd be warm and have bathrooms, but it was extremely inconvenient. Those inconsiderate smart-asses at the library wouldn't let him smoke in there, and once your computer station was assigned you'd better not go outside to have one, because there were four hungry people in similar circumstances waiting in line to use it soon as you left.

Throughout that winter Chiquita remained unusually optimistic and forged on. This newfound optimism partially stemmed from having a much milder, El Nino winter. During his last trip to the dehydrator he was also given antidepressants, and Ritalin, which helped him cope and focus. And he also started to to generate income from selling small items online, which helped everything else.

That was also the winter his neighbor Paula began undergoing chemotherapy, and it must've affected her heart, too. Just like the Grinch's, hers musta grown a coupla sizes. Now, she had been a professional student all of her life, and was smart enough to realize that as long as she was going to classes she wouldn't have to repay the student loans. So she attended college classes for over forty years and eventually learned a lot of BS, earned an MBA, and received a PhD in A-R-T. Now, you all know what BS is. Well, a PhD just means that the bullshit is piled higher and deeper. And you don't need a PhD to know that a useless *art degree* was never going to get her a *real job*, especially in Flint.

But while Paula was attending the university and getting all her "higher learning," she had also figured out how to navigate "the system." Other than her little "recreational pharmacology" business, she'd never worked a day in her life, and she was practically old enough to collect Social Security. So she took Jim on as her charge, and shuttled him around to the churches that provided food pantries and offered emergency financial assistance. Thank God these faith-based organizations stepped in when the government slashed and burned the social safety net, because without their humanitarian assistance many people would have had nowhere else to turn. So Chiquita began to get the help he needed.

When Paula's condition worsened and she was no longer able to drive she sold the rusted remains of her van to Chiquita for $600 {on installments, no less}. Now that he had wheels again, and independence, *he* could drive *her* to *her* appointments. But he could also shop for merchandise, sell stuff at flea markets, and generate more undocumented underground income.

Then Paula Smart used her MBA degree to give Chiquita a brilliant cash-generating business plan. "Jimmy, you've got yourself a real cash cow just sitting here unused, this big old historical house with two big old apartments, and just two short blocks from the university. Now, the college will pay you twenty dollars a day to put up their students, so you'll put two into the luxury penthouse apartment and three in the downstairs townhouse. They will pay for all the utilities, and you will make a hundred dollars each day, and clear three thousand each month. Then you can rent the apartment below me for five hundred a month, still use your garage and yard for the business, and come out way ahead."

Finally his needs were being met, and his life was beginning to change for the better. Jim was grateful for Paula and her intercession and with God's intervention somehow his enormous power bill was paid and the gas and electric services were restored, and his furnace was fixed, too. So for the first time in many years he had power, heat, leaded water, and even pirated cable {unbeknownst to Paula}. But wait, there's more. Chiquita claimed those services were not merely restored; somehow he received a credit for $2,300, because of a computer glitch. Can you imagine that? After getting free gas for five years they owed *him* money; but really now, I knew Chiquita musta putta lotta yeast into that story. Nonetheless, his life was slowly getting back on track.

Because the hospital wanted to be reimbursed for his many hospitalizations/recuperations/ vacations while there repeatedly dehydrating, he was finally considered to be disabled, and placed on Medicaid. Thus he began to receive health services, including a physician and prescriptions, dental services and dentures, an eye doctor and eyeglasses, a free government cell phone and minutes, food stamps, and a psychiatrist for prescribing mind-altering legal drugs.

His new head shrinker prescribed Ritalin, and that helped to focus his thoughts. He was also given a serotonin uptake inhibitor, which helped raise his serotonin level and improve his overall mood, and that helped him better cope with the stresses of his life. Because he was also dignosed as being slightly cracked, some powerful psychotropic medications were administered. There were complications.

The one medication, Brainsick 2.5 mg, caused extreme insomnia, which kept him awake for four full days. On the fifth day he started hallucinating and imagining that Kelly Ripa and Sherry from *The View* were over for coffee and chitchat. Now, you and I both know that nobody in their right mind would *ever* want *that* happening. He even accused that so-and-so Kelly of stealing his Gucci glasses, which mysteriously went missing at the same time she was supposedly there.

I'm just sayin'…

So they took him off that medication and tweaked his other meds a bit further, until they got him fairly stabilized, and as close to normal as he'd been in years. Those medications also slowed him down a bit, which wasn't all bad. And thankfully all of those things helped him to make sense of his oddball life and errant behavior, and got him thinking *right* again. {But definitely not straight.}

When all was said and done, he was doing quite well and his life had improved. But he will still continue to do his little dance on the razor blade's edge, because that is who he is.

Bless him Lord, and watch over him. He'll be needing it.

Bless His Heart

A perfect spring morning in May, the kind of day you've dreamed of all winter.

The shockingly fuchsia redbuds had finished with their flashy blooming and it was now the apple trees' turn to show off their snowy blossoms, and they were out in full force. Big beds of spring bulbs were bursting into bloom, with red ruffled tulips, sunny yellow daffodils, pale velum jonquils, and heavenly scented hyacinths thrusting toward a royal blue cloudless sky.

Springtime's air is the freshest we ever experience in this former factory town, and one could almost call it sweet smelling. And Flint looks its absolute best when the Asian pear trees lining its red-brick paved downtown streets are erupting into fragrant masses of delicate white blooms.

But I must admit I was feeling rather peculiar on that particular morning and thought I might be coming down with something or had a touch of the flu. The morning coffee did not agree with me. I didn't have an appetite and even had a little indigestion, which was rather odd, considering I hadn't eaten a thing.

On this picture-perfect morning the sun had risen nicely as I was driving to work, renovating a stately home in the Miller Road estates, arguably the city's nicest neighborhood. After changing into my work clothes, I pried open a can of paint, and the fumes instantly made me feel more nauseous. I felt clammy, things began moving in a slower motion, and walking was an extreme effort, like wading up a stream against a swiftly moving current. Something was definitely happening with me, and I knew I should probably get to a hospital.

Walking from the truck to the emergency entrance I had to stop three times. I would start and take a few labored steps, and then stop and rest, catch my breath, and start again. After taking one look at me they immediately whisked me into the critical care unit to begin treatment.

Test results confirmed the presence of troponin enzymes in my blood gasses, which indicated that a myocardial infarction had indeed occurred, a heart attack. An echocardiogram spotted the vein block-age, and blood thinners were administered to dissipate the clot. Their heartfelt intervention also included a balloon angioplasty procedure to open the blocked vessel further, and a medicated stent was surgically implanted to {hopefully} keep it open.

On the fourth day I was doing well enough to be moved from the critical care unit into a semi-private room on the twelfth floor. My bed, being closest to the window, offered a panoramic view of Flint, and it looked pretty damn good.

"Ya know what I heard somewhere? Most heart attacks happen on a Mundaneÿ, because nobody wants-ta face-a 'nother week-a work. And another thin' I heard, sixty percent-a them people don't survive their first aÿttack," Chiquita said, while wildly chomping on Nicorette gum.

"Shush! Now, that's a terrible thing to be saying. We're supposed to be here cheering him up, not delivering a death sentence," Nikki said, reprimanding him.

"Well, he did survive. Didn't he? That's all I'm sayin'...I'm not cas-tin' no nasturtiums."

Even a deaf man could have heard the two of them approaching.

"Dear God," Nikki gasped. "Just look at him—he looks just ter-rible, like an eighty-year-old man." Then he began tearing up, as he squinted at the comatose old geezer lying in the bed next to mine.

"*He* is in a coma, and *that* isn't *him*. You goof, he's in the other bed by the winda," Chiquita said. "Jesus, Stella, I wish you'd wear yer glasses. You're blinder 'n a bat, and vainer 'n a weathervane."

"Oh...how are you, honey?" Chiquita asked, suddenly becoming misty-eyed.

"My God, we couldn't believe it when we heard the terrible news. Now, don't you try to talk, because that blabbermouth Joanie already told us all about it," Nikki whispered, misty-eyed, too.

"Stella, I tell ya, you got more wires runnin' inta you than my home enter-tain-ment center do. Sorry, the Tourette's," Chiquita added. "How are ya feelin', honey?"

"With my fingers," I breathlessly replied.

"Oh, you're still a twisted sister," Chiquita said, smiling his crooked but newly dentured grin.

— ‿

At first it was difficult breathing. Getting enough wind to even speak was an effort, and about all I could manage were short breathless segments.

When people visited their faces revealed what they dared not speak, and they registered worry, fear, and pity. Old dyke Linda's lower lip was quivering something terrible when she came to visit. She was certain it was curtains for me, and already had me dead and buried. I was the one lying in the hospital bed, but she was in worse shape.

She survived.

I made it, too, but it was a long road back. Luckily, all the significant people in my life were there to help me through this difficult passage. My wonderful immediate family, and my dear friends, too—old dyke Linda, Nikki, Chiquita, Bette, Katie, Joany, and Gigi. Bless your hearts, one and all.

And Dear God, please bless my recently repaired heart, too.

— ‿

The song "One More Walk around the Garden," from the musical *Carmelina*, is meant to play as performed by the three tenors from the 1979 cast album.

— ‿

As you've read, the last few years have gotten tougher; for me, for Chiquita, and for many others as well. My long time pal, old dyke Linda, had her share of problems, and so did my former paramour, Mike. My dear friend Nikki had more than his share of shit lately, too.

Nikki's sweet baby brother, Kenny, was probably about the only person in the world he truly loved unconditionally, and when he was diagnosed with lung cancer, the devastating news nearly broke Nikki's heart. Kenny never complained about having to endure the tortuous treatments and underwent repeated rounds of toxic chemotherapy and deadly doses of radiation. But all of their interventions proved useless as the ravaging cancer raged on. In the end there was nothing anyone could do to save him, so Nikki insisted that they make him as comfortable as possible, because it pained him something terrible to see his beloved baby brother suffer. And it nearly tore his heart in two to think of losing the gentlest loving soul he ever knew.

Now, you remember Ned, Nikki's twinkle-toed younger brother? Well, a few years back he was diagnosed with advanced emphysema, and eventually became disabled. When he unable to work he moved in with Kenny and Lois, and they all shared a modest modular home that Nikki quietly paid for. But as Ned continued to deteriorate he eventually became so diminished he was not able to do anything. The debilitating disease left him exhausted, making everything an effort and him ancient way before his time. Toward the end he was content to stay in his air-conditioned room watching cable TV, and smoking with the oxygen mask on.

Nikki had been trying to prepare for the inevitable, because he realized that sometime soon Kenny would be leaving. After all, he was the one taking him to his treatments and receiving regular updates from his doctors. But then, quite unexpectedly, his brother Ned came down with another lung infection and this one really knocked him down, so low that he was gone in less than a week. Nikki was totally devastated, unprepared for his untimely death, and taken out at the knees.

In the depths of his grief, Nikki was left to arrange and pay for a small service and cremation, so the dysfunctional Clark family could have their little hillbilly send-off. Afterwards Nikki took Ned's cremains home, because he wanted to scatter his ashes in the beautiful woodland garden.

"Ned's gone now, you know, Kenny, and he won't be coming home anymore. These are his remains, here in this pretty MacKenzie jar. I'm going to scatter them here in my pretty garden, so Neddy will be with me forever and I can visit him whenever I want to, and think pretty thoughts."

"I wanna be here whiff you guys, too, like we used to be in Grandma Effie's god-den. You 'member Nikki?"

"Yes, I 'member, Kenny, and I would like that very much."

"You're the bess butter ever, Nikki."

"No, *you* are the best butter ever, Kenny. You."

⌁ ⌁

Of course, Nikki, being Nikki, felt the need for some sort of embellishment to symbolize the significance of this sacred spot, so he seriously shopped until he finally found a fabulous flower-like piece of hand-blown glass. In fact, he liked it so much that he bought three of them, to act as artsy memorial markers for the three beloved Clark brothers, sons of Flint, when returned to its gritty soil.

A sturdy metal shaft was shoved into the ashy ground to support them, with one being red, one green, and the last one yellow. Nikki grinned at me and said, "Naturally, Ned is the cocksucker red, and Kenny will have the dappled green one when he goes. Mine is the sunny yellow one, because it's the prettiest, don't cha think? When I'm gone I want to be here in the garden with them. Would you see to that for me, Denny?"

"Consider it done."

⌁ ⌁

Less than a month after Ned's passing Kenny came to join him in the spectacular shady garden where he will be spending eternity, in the loveliest woodland garden ever constructed, along the south side of the fabulous Château Ghetto.

⌁ ⌁

"I was so sorry to hear about Kenny's passing, Nikki. You certainly have been through a lot lately. And I just want you to know that I'm here for you, and I love you," I said.

"Thank you, and I know you do, honey. And God knows you've been through more than your share of shit lately, too. I love you, too."

Embracing, we held each other for quite some time, having a moment.

"Thankfully, the end wasn't too hard on poor Kenny. You know, he never complained. But that nasty fucking cancer got the best of him pretty quickly. In the end, he just went to sleep and never woke up. And you know, he had the sweetest smile on his face when he went. The poor guy...never hurt a fly..."

"I'm so sorry for your loss, Nikki."

"Thank you, honey. Ya know, this all has hit Lois pretty hard, too. For the first time in her life she's all alone. You see the pretty purple glass flower in the back of the potting shed? That one is for her. We had tried to prepare ourselves for Kenny's leaving, but Ned...that one bowled us both over. I just wasn't prepared for that. I don't know how... I'm going..."

He began to silently weep, and I held him. It had been a difficult few years for us all.

"You know, Nikki, when my mom died it was about the worst time in my life. And I really appreciate your being there."

"I am glad I could be there for you. I know how terrible that was for you."

"But when Mike died, just a year after that, that one really took me out."

"I love you, Murf."

"I love you, too, buddy."

— —

Now, this is the honest-to-God truth, and I will I swear to it on the Bible. I have never seen such tall, sturdy, and beautifully blooming lilies in my entire life. The lilies that populated the spot where Nikki scattered Ned's ashes, and then Kenny's, and eventually Lois's, too, grew to be over eight feet tall and were absolutely loaded with sickeningly sweet blossoms. Towering above all the other lilies by at least three feet, they definitely *waaay* outshined them.

"Sparkle, Zena, sparkle," Nikki chirped to the spectacularly showoffy lilies while watering them. He used to say that to Ned for good luck when they entered the gay bar looking for a mandate, or while trying to outperform each other on the dance floor. "Just smell those lilies, will you, Murf—that perfume will knock you on your ass. I always said that Ned wore too much perfume."

"They are awfully heady."

"So was Neddy. I always told him he was full of shit, too, all fertilizer, and this just proves it. Just look at the size of those fucking lilies, would you? They're fucking fabulous! This garden has never looked, or *smelled* so good. Can you just imagine how fabulous this garden will look when they throw my fat-ash in there?" Nikki said, grinning from ear to ear with a tear-stained face.

"Well...You certainly have given this gardening your everything."

"You know, I never imagined I would actually *want* to be spending eternity here, in Flint. I always thought the Amalfi Coast would be a much nicer place to do the time. Way back when I was a younger girl, I'd often imagined my funeral, and thought it should be something like Elizabeth Taylor's entrance into Rome, from the movie *Cleopatra*. I would have me *six, big, strapping*, muscular, and oiled black men wearing little white linen loincloths the size of postage stamps, carrying me down Saginaw Street on a golden glittering platform. All of my clients will be lined up at the curb bawling their eyes out, and looking like the nasty old hags they really are."

"You have such an imagination, Stella."

"It's gotten me this far, honey, it's gotten me this far."

The Times Are a Changin'

During ancient times homosexual people were regarded quite differently than they are today. Queers were often enlightened individuals holding prestigious positions in society such as priests and priestesses, shamans and visionaries, artists, caregivers, musicians, healers, and were the keepers of culture. Embodying both male and female sensibilities, they were thought to inhabit both worlds.

But in modern times gays were not thought of that well, they were often ostracized and killed. Even during the 1960s and 1970s, when I was maturing, people were still being institutionalized for having same-sex inclinations. Homosexuality was considered to be a mental defect, as recognized by the AMA's *Diagnostic Statistical Manual*, and thought to be incurable. The truth was, during those darker decades there wasn't much evidence of gay life existing in America at all, except for a few "fringe" groups in some major cities. Then Stonewall happened in 1969, and things slowly began to change.

In the 1970's there was slow and steady progress made toward gay rights, and people "came out" of their closets like never before. In 1977 Harvey Milk, an openly gay man, was elected to the Board of Supervisors in San Francisco, but he was aslo assisinated just two years later.

During the 1980s the Supreme Court upheld the "rights of states," which allowed the states to continue *criminalizing* those found engaging in *consensual* homosexual, gay, or lesbian sex (Georgia). When the terrible AIDS epidemic appeared in the 1980s it first was labeled as the "Gay Plague," and for years afterward gays were linked with the dreadful disease that mostly killed heterosexuals.

In the 1990s President William Jefferson Clinton {Bill} enacted DOMA, the Defense Of Marriage Act, which instructed the federal government to deny spousal benefits to couples of the same-gender. He also signed DADT, or "Don't Ask Don't Tell," into effect, which kept openly gay, lesbian, and transgender persons out of the military.

At the beginning of the new century, 2000, gay marriage was still a lighting-rod topic that was opposed by every single state of the union. The Republicans used our nation's hatred of homsexuals to win elections, and during the 2004 and 2008 election cycles even the liberal Democrats rejected us, when both parties' openly opposed same-sex marriage.

In fact, the first time an American president ever addressed the "Gay Agenda" at all was on June 30, 2011, when President Barack Obama was questioned about the topic during an afternoon news conference. This was his reply. And I quote:

"Let me just start out by saying that this administration, under my direction, has consistently said we cannot discriminate as a country against people on the basis of sexual orientation. And we have done in the last two and a half years, that I have been here, more than the previous forty-three sitting presidents to uphold that principle, whether it is ending 'don't ask don't tell,' making sure that gay and lesbian partners can visit each other in hospitals, or making sure that federal benefits can be provided to same-sex couples. Across the board, hate crimes, we have made sure that it is a central principle of this administration, because I think it's a central principle of America.

"Now, what we have also done is we've said that DOMA, the 'Defense of Marriage Act,' is unconstitutional. And so we've said we cannot defend the federal government poking its nose into what states are doing and putting their thumb on the scale against same-sex couples.

"What I've seen happen over the last several years, and what happened in New York State last week, I think was a good thing, because what you saw was the people of New York having a debate and talking through these issues. It was contentious, it was emotional, but ultimately they made a decision to recognize civil marriage. And I think that's exactly how it should work.

"I think what you're seeing is a profound recognition on the part of the American people that gays, lesbians, and transgender persons are our brothers, sisters, our children, our cousins, our friends, our coworkers, and that they've got to be treated like every other American. And I think that principle will win out. It's not going to be perfectly smooth, and it turns out, that as president, I have discovered since I've been in office, I can't dictate precisely how the process moves. But I think we're moving in a direction of greater equality, and I think that's a good thing."

Those powerful words were delivered during a press conference, when President Obama responded to a three-part question posed by NBC's reporter Chuck Todd, and they were the most significant words ever spoken by a standing president concerning gays, lesbians, transgender peoples, and their rights. We'd come a long way in the forty years since Stonewall, but we were not there yet.

The bill to repeal DOMA was enacted in December of 2010. On September 20, 2011, the US governmental policy on homosexuals serving in the military, known as "Don't Ask Don't Tell," quietly slipped away. From that day forth the US military and the federal government were opened to homosexual peoples, and the Pentagon was changed into a triangle, a pink one.

On May 9, 2012, President Obama held a midafternoon press conference, and therein stated his endorsement of gay marriage, which was, by any measure, a monumental moment for all homosexual people. That was also the first time a sitting American president took sides on what many consider one of the most contentious civil rights issues of our times.

And on that very same day the voters of North Carolina passed a statewide constitutional amendment banning same-sex unions, and thus became the thirty-first state to pass such an amendment. So the pendulum continued to swing both ways.

Recent scientific findings have shown that being gay is not a choice at all—it is genetically displayed the same as blue eyes and red necks. Scientists have studied the brains of "gay" males and compared them with the brains of just "straight" males, and noted several significant physiological, neurological, and anatomical differences. Not surprisingly, their brains are more closely aligned with those of women, and lesbians more similar to straight men.

But if you were not born "that way" you might not understand the many ramifications of being created so differently. So, if you would, do *try to think about it*. Why would a person *choose* to expeience a lifetime of hatred and rejection, alienation, institutionalization, marginalization, and incarceration just for being born who you are, and as God made you?

When I was young there was not a template for being gay. In fact, there weren't many openly gay people at all, but we still knew "it" when we saw it. When that flamboyant Liberace performed, good folks wanted to believe he was straight but still suffering from the nasty breakup he had with that emasculating foreign figure skater Sonja Henie, some forty years ago, and then they could feel better about enjoying his showmanship. Puh-leaze, Louise. Didn't we laugh at silly Uncle Milty when he pranced around wearing a curly wig and slinky dress, while camping it up? Wasn't that quirky Paul Lynde a laugh riot? And didn't we just love that outrageous lisping Charles Nelson Riley? Gay, gay, gay, gay, gay. We certainly knew "it" when we saw "it."

But within the last few years many people's attitudes about "it" have changed, and there has been a greater acceptance of gays, lesbians, and transgender people. Some of the shifting of attitudes has occurred because we are more visible, appearing on television, in politics, and even in professional sports. There is even a gay television network now, called Logo. And now there are many celebrities who are "out", such as Ellen DeGeneres, Rosie O'Donnell, Rachel Maddow, Robin Roberts, Anderson Cooper, and Neil Patrick Harris, just to name a few.

Increased visibility has helped gays, lesbians, and transgender people to become mainstreamed. Now there are gay characters appearing on sitcoms, in soap operas, and even in politics, with Barney Frank. When Olympic gold medal winner Bruce Jenner recently transgendered and become a woman known as Caitlyn, his/her transformation captured the nation's interest and focused new awareness on the fluidity of sexuality. Professional sports have come a long way, too, because there is an "outed" football player named Michael Sam, who recently declared his *homo*-sexuality, and was shortly afterward drafted by the Rams; how apropos.

Ultimately, the simple act of making ourselves visible has greatly assisted our acceptance and assimilation. The truth is, we have always existed, and we were always there, living covertly, usually undercover, underground, and maybe even under your roof.

There may even be a glimmer of hope for the Catholic Church in the future as well, because when the new pope, Francis, was quizzed on his stance on gays in the priesthood, he responded, "If someone is gay and he seeks the Lord, and has goodwill, who am I to judge?" And thank God he is finally shining a light into the Church's dirty closets and dealing with the long-neglected pedophile priest problem.

In 2012, during his second inaugural address, President Barack Obama stated: "Our journey is not complete until our gay brothers and sisters are treated like anyone else under the law." This queer-affirming quote was probably the most far-reaching to date acknowledging the movement toward equality for homosexual people.

A significant decisions concerning same-sex matters occurred on June 27, 2013, when the Supreme Court ruled that same-sex couples were entitled to receive federal spousal benefits. The High Court also declined to render a ruling on a California case, and that very deliberate inaction allowed the same-sex marriage licenses that were already issued to be recognized, which cleared the way for them to have equal rights and benefits with heterosexual unions.

Then on October 6, 2014, without any explanation, the Supreme Court released a series of short briefs that effectively let the decisions of three federal appeals courts' stand, which thereby allowed the same-sex unions that were already sanctioned in those states to be recognized. That decision may have been the precursor to having same-gender marriages recognized nationally, and it increased the number of states that acknowledged those unions to twenty-four.

By May of 2015 thirty-seven states had acknowledged same-sex unions. Then on June 26, 2015, quite surprisingly, and by a close vote of five to four, the US Supreme Court ruled that denying same-sex couples the right to marry was a violation of their due process and equal protection under the law, as it is guaranteed by the Fourteenth Amendment. So, from that day forward same-sex marriages would be recognized by all fifty of the states, the District of Columbia, and eight Native American Indian tribes. In acknowledgement of that historic achievement that evening The White House was illuminated by a rainbow of multicolored lights.

Gay rights have not been an exclusively American agenda either. In 2013 the United Kingdom approved same-sex marriage. In May 2015, Ireland, a majority Catholic country, came out and heartily approved gay marriage with a resounding popular vote of nearly two-to-one. And as of now, nineteen nations have approved same-sex marriages, but definitely not Iran, because they have no gays at all.

To paraphrase President Obama, "Social progress sometimes comes in small increments, and then there are days when that slow and steady effort is paid off with swift justice that arrives like a thunderbolt." The people have spoken, and the government has listened.

President Obama also stated: "America is a place where you can write your own destiny."

Gay people have been writing their own destinies for decades. I have known gay couples who have been monogamously coupled for over forty years, and others who have raised families, saw them graduate, and get married. Now, like sanctioned heterosexual couples, they will also have the benefits of being married, and if lucky grow old together.

For if we truly profess to be a nation of equal rights for *all the people* we cannot withhold them from anyone, no matter their creed, color, faith, sex, political beliefs, or sexual orientation. Because sexuality it is not preference at all, it is a gift.

Bless your heart.

The End

Amen

www.ingramcontent.com/pod-product-compliance
Lightning Source LLC
Chambersburg PA
CBHW031123090426
42738CB00008B/958